THE FOWL AND THE PUSSYCAT

Victorian Literature and Culture Series

Jerome J. McGann and Herbert F. Tucker, *Editors*

THE FOWL AND THE PUSSYCAT

Love Letters of Michael Field, 1876–1909

Edited by
Sharon Bickle

University of Virginia Press
Charlottesville and London

University of Virginia Press

Printed in the United States of America on acid-free paper

First published 2008
9 8 7 6 5 4 3 2 1

Library of Congress Cataloging-in-Publication Data

Field, Michael.
The fowl and the pussycat : love letters of Michael Field, 1876–1909 / edited by Sharon Bickle.
p. cm. — (Victorian literature and culture series)
Includes bibliographical references and index.
ISBN 978-0-8139-2751-0 (cloth : acid-free paper)
1. Bradley, Katharine Harris, 1846–1914—Correspondence. 2. Cooper, Edith Emma, 1862–1913—Correspondence. 3. Authors, English—19th century—Correspondence. 4. Women authors, English—Correspondence. 5. Lesbians—Great Britain—Correspondence. I. Bickle, Sharon, 1966– II. Title.
PR4699.F5Z48 2008
821′.8—dc22
[B] 2008024052

Frontispiece: Michael Field (Katharine Bradley and Edith Cooper), photograph, silver gelatin carte-de-visite (likely a copy of a plainotype), 1884–89, by Bromhead, Clifton. (Mark Samuels Lasner Collection, on loan to the University of Delaware Library)

To Michael and Giles

Contents

Acknowledgments

This edition could not have been completed without the aid of several extraordinary people. Foremost among these are Associate Professor Maryanne Dever of the Centre for Women's Studies and Gender Research at Monash University; the late Professor Harold Love of Monash University; and Professor Holly Laird of the University of Tulsa. I am deeply grateful to Maryanne for her supervision and support, as well as for the many hours of her time she has devoted to this project, and for the benefit of her considerable expertise in feminist archival studies. I am indebted to Harold, who taught me so much about editorial and annotative practices, who reviewed my transcripts, and whose encyclopedic knowledge of English literature and history enriches this edition. Throughout the preparation for publication, Holly has been extremely generous with her limited time, and has provided insightful and invaluable advice for improving the manuscript.

This edition has profited considerably from enthusiastic readers. Professor Margaret Stetz of the University of Delaware has been a passionate supporter of this edition. Margaret and her partner, Dr. Mark Samuels Lasner, have shared their wealth of knowledge on the 1890s, granted me access to the Lasner collection, and have been incomparable hosts on my forays to the United States in search of Michael Field. I would also like to thank Professor Yopie Prins of the University of Michigan and Professor Virginia Blain of Macquarie University for their encouraging examination reports and for recommending publication of the original thesis.

At the University of Virginia Press, I would particularly like to thank Cathie Brettschneider and Angie Hogan for their patience during preparation of the edition. I am grateful to Ellen Satrom and Colleen Romick Clark for lending their considerable copyediting skills to this project.

I thank Michael Field's literary executor, Leonie Sturge-Moore, for permission to use the letters, and for providing me with additional material about their history during the long period in which they were in the safe care of her family.

The assistance of reference librarians in several major libraries has been of vital importance to the production of this edition: Richard Overell and his staff at Rare Books in Monash University's Matheson Library; Colin Harris and his staff at the Bodleian Library; and the librarians of the British Library's Manuscript section, the Houghton Library at Harvard University, the Women's Library at London Metropolitan University, and the Pierpont Morgan Library in New York. I would also like to thank the curators of the Fitzwilliam Museum in Cambridge who let me see—and hold—the Pegasus pendant.

I wish to thank Mark Samuels Lasner for permission to publish the joint photograph of Bradley and Cooper; and the Trustees of the Bodleian Library for permission to publish images from the letters. In addition, I am grateful to the following people and institutions for permission to reproduce images from their collections: Special Collections at Bristol University; the Ruskin Library at Lancaster University; the Women's Library; the National Portrait Gallery; the Berenson Archive at the Harvard Centre for Studies in the Italian Renaissance, I Tatti, Florence; the Pierpont Morgan Library; and Peter and Roger Sturge.

I would like to thank Dr. Judy Mackenzie, who first conceived the idea for an edition of the Bradley-Cooper letters. I hope my endeavors have done justice to her vision. Finally, thanks are due to Dr. Erica Hateley and Dunya Lindsey for their generous assistance in reading drafts, and for providing welcome distraction while selflessly consuming heroic amounts of coffee at "The Den."

The publication of this volume was supported by a Monash Publications Grant from Monash University.

The letters are reproduced by kind permission of Leonie Sturge-Moore and Charmian O'Neil.

Introduction

Michael Field was the name adopted by Katharine Harris Bradley (1846–1914) and Edith Emma Cooper (1862–1913), the collaborative authors of nine volumes of lyric poetry and twenty-five historical verse dramas.[1] Michael Field initially effaced Bradley and Cooper before the public eye, and the ordinary English maleness of the name declared their vocation: "to give the English people plays—full of poetry and religion, and humour, and thought" (letter 99). Field's usefulness as a disguise was short-lived, but Bradley and Cooper continued to publish as Michael Field, not only because Field functioned as a recognized name under which to circulate their texts but also because the identities produced around Michael Field soon expanded into their private lives, becoming an integral part of their unique marriage. Indeed, in comparing their relationship to that of the Brownings, Katharine Bradley wrote: "Those two poets, man and wife, wrote alone; each wrote, but did not bless or quicken one another at their work; *we are closer married*" (original emphasis).[2] As the lovers Michael and Field, Bradley and Cooper created for themselves a space in which to craft a relationship more perfect than that of the Brownings, and in which they could realize the aesthetic project of experiencing life as art.

Yet Michael Field was not the first identity to emerge from the fertile imaginations of Bradley and Cooper. As the letters in this volume demonstrate, Bradley and Cooper played with identity in the form of humorous pet names long before they began to shape their authorial subjectivity. The earliest of these pet names were "the Simiorg" or "All-Wise-Fowl" (Bradley), a name derived from pseudo-Arabic tales of an all-knowing bird (see letter 1 n. 1), and "the Persian Puss" (Cooper), a name that may acknowledge the often-discussed family perception of Cooper as having a nervous disposition. Holly Laird has noted the complex wordplays that link the earlier Bradley-Cooper pseudonyms, Arran and Isla Leigh, with the later Michael Field.[3] These letters endorse and extend Laird's argument about the importance of wordplay in the Bradley-Cooper pseudonyms.

What impresses the reader of the letters collected here is the centrality of wordplay and puns, wit and nonsense, not only in pet names but also in Bradley and Cooper's view of late-Victorian culture and society. Here are the origins of that rich imaginative life later revealed in "Works and Days," the joint journals populated by some of the most significant figures of fin-de-siècle London under such fanciful names as "Fairyman," "Basilisk," and "Doctrine."[4] The skills for writing keen, sometimes cutting, commentary on the foibles of late-Victorian lions were practiced here in observations of family life. More than that, the shared sense of humor and absurdity apparent here are key foundations for the intimate inner life of Bradley and Cooper, part of what bound them together as poets and lovers within "a home darkened by religious observance of a sombre kind."[5]

The letters reproduced in this edition not only provide insight into the lives of Bradley and Cooper but also will prove invaluable to scholars interested in the works of Michael Field. They represent a treasure trove of almost untouched manuscript material from the critical early years of the collaboration. The letters contain both published and unpublished poems, which circulated between Bradley and Cooper often as billets-doux. While Michael Field are presently drawing critical attention primarily for their lyric love poetry, the letters are most revealing about their intriguing dramas. Here we see the negotiations that surround the production of dramas such as *The Father's Tragedy* (1885), *Loyalty or Love?* (1885), *Brutus Ultor* (1886), *Canute the Great* (1887), and *The Cup of Water* (1887). In addition, there are significant new perspectives on the various pseudonyms: Arran Leigh (Bradley), and its subsequent extension into Arran and Isla Leigh to include Cooper; John Cooley; and Michael Field.

As well as bringing Bradley and Cooper, and the works of Michael Field, to life, these letters illustrate the exciting cultural milieu of late-Victorian Britain from the point of view of two aspiring young aesthetes. Bradley and Cooper shop for Morris fabrics and blue china; they critique Irving as Shylock and Ristori as Lady Macbeth; they visit the Grosvenor Gallery to comment on the newest paintings and to people-watch. The experiences of these female urban flâneurs contain much that will contribute to our knowledge of late-Victorian aestheticism and aesthetic commodification, performance and theater history (particularly High Victorian impressions of Shakespeare), and art history, as well as understandings of Victorian women's use of public space. Many of the early letters in this volume are devoted to Bradley as a woman traveler in Italy, and provide a remarkable insight into the Victorian tourist gaze. Subsequent letters from the early 1880s grant the reader a rare insider's view of the early women's rights movement in Britain and Europe, and throughout these letters there are fascinating glimpses of what academic life was like for this first generation of university women. Later letters from the 1890s and early 1900s show the poets moving away from a provincial life surrounded by family and friends to a wider literary circle, including such figures as Robert Browning and John Miller Gray.

The Love Letters of Michael Field

This edition brings together for the first time a personal correspondence once thought lost by critics. It is the first modern scholarly edition of any of Michael Field's writings. Most of the 168 letters included in this volume are from the Bodleian Library at the University of Oxford. These are supplemented by a small number of letters from the British Library, and from uncatalogued Bradley-Cooper letters held by the Pierpont Morgan Library in New York. The Pierpont Morgan letters are included here because they provide a missing link between the Bodleian letters and the later joint journals. They were written after the death of Cooper's mother, when Bradley and Cooper were setting up house independent of family. Their short and often perfunctory nature maps the move away from letters toward journal writing as the primary mode for documenting their shared life.

Family and Social Life

Katharine Harris Bradley was born in Birmingham, England, on 26 October 1846. She was the second daughter of Emma Harris and Charles Bradley Jr., a northern tobacco merchant who died in 1848, when Katharine was only two years old. In spite of the eleven-year gap between Katharine and her sister, Emma, they seem to have got on well, spending much of their childhood with their Holinsworth cousins Frances (Fanny), who married John Brooks, and Ellen (Nellie), who married an Anglican clergyman, David Reith.

Katharine's sister, Emma, married James Robert Cooper in October 1860. Emma also had two daughters, Edith Emma (born 12 January 1862) and Amy Katharine (born 5 March 1865). In July 1867 Katharine and her widowed mother

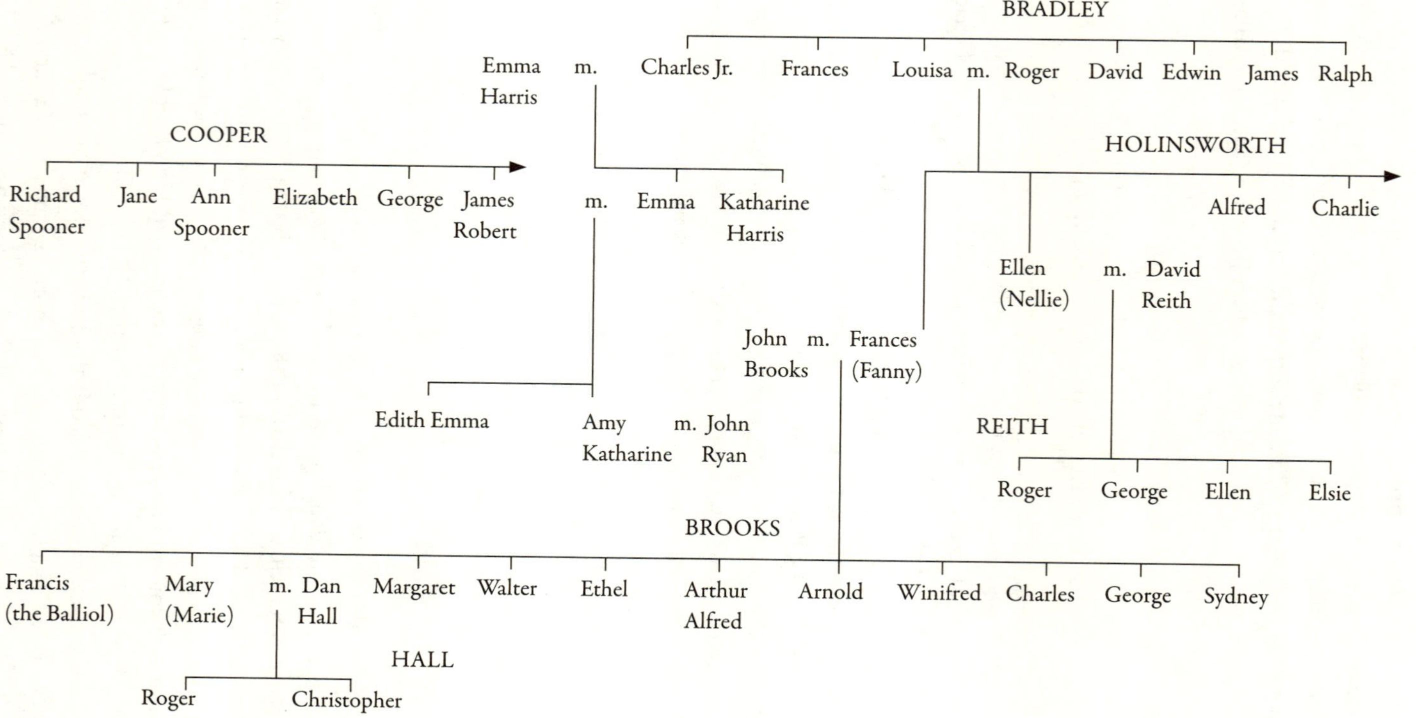

Bradley-Cooper family tree. (Compiled using the *1881 Census,* Ursula Bridge's unpublished "Diary of Michael Field: A Biographical Study of a Forgotten Poet" [MS. Eng. misc. d. 983. BOD], and Ivor Treby's *Binary Star*)

joined them to create an extended Cooper-Bradley household in Kenilworth.[6] Emma Cooper became an invalid after the birth of Amy, leaving Katharine with the responsibility of running the house and caring for her nieces.[7] Katharine's mother died of cancer in 1868, and shortly after the family left the north of England forever. During the 1860s and '70s, the Coopers moved about: they lived in Newton Leys, in Solihull, and in Freshford, near Bath. In 1879 the family finally settled in Stoke Bishop near Bristol: father, invalid mother, two half-grown nieces, and aunt.

Katharine Bradley seems far from the preconceived model of the Victorian spinster aunt. During the years in which her nieces were growing up, Katharine studied: she attended classes at the Birmingham and Midland Institute between 1863 and 1867 (letter 2 n. 2); the Collège de France in 1868; and Newnham College, Cambridge in 1875.[8] As one of twenty female students at Newnham College, she met the first female lecturer in economics at Cambridge, Mary Paley Marshall. Marshall called Bradley "the Newnham Poet,"[9] possibly because of *The New Minnesinger and Other Poems* (1875), the (single-authored) book of verse published under the pseudonym Arran Leigh.

It is in 1876 that the correspondence collected in this volume begins, with a Christmas poem from Bradley to her young niece Edith Cooper. Cooper was then only fourteen years of age, but she had already written her first works, "The Iwl-Dû" and "Atys and Adrastos" (both unpublished, currently held in the Bodleian Library). Bradley's pride in the achievement is evident in her celebration of the young writer as the "Voice-to-be" (letter 1).

In the earliest letters, the enthusiasm of Cooper's hero-worship for Bradley is touching. In August 1880 she wrote, "But all the time I have constantly thought of you, watched you from my common-place bit of England—you who are miles upon miles away from my love in blue Italy—with the golden exclusiveness of the sunflower for her distant sun. It is such a pleasure to me to do any thing for you—Even to dust your mantel-board" (letter 11). Cooper's description of "blue Italy" suggests an imaginative association of Bradley with Elizabeth Barrett Browning's poetic heroine Aurora Leigh (1:232–35).[10] It is not difficult to imagine how glamorous her aunt must have seemed to young Edith Cooper. Carta Sturge, a university friend, remembered Bradley as "lavish, large, and one should add, glowing and stimulating."[11] William Rothenstein described her similarly as "stout, emphatic, splendid and adventurous in talk, quick in wit."[12] Bradley was a young woman in her early twenties with a modest income and no parents: she was, in short, as free as a Victorian woman could hope to be.

As Edith Cooper matured, she and her sister, Amy, explored the opportunities open to women in higher education. In the 1880s Bradley, Cooper, and Amy studied at the new Bristol University College, where Bradley renewed her acquaintance with Marshall, now wife to the college principal. Cooper took a first in philosophy (letter 90), Amy excelled at mathematics (letter 2 n. 4), and all three were mainstays of Marshall's women's debating society (letter 22).

Bristol was an exciting place to be a young woman in the 1880s. In the parlors and drawing rooms gathered women at the forefront of social reform in Britain: Margaret Tanner, the Misses Priestman, the Sturge sisters. Josephine Butler already considered them her personal "*corps d'élite*"[13] in the campaign against the Contagious Diseases Acts; but, as Judith Walkowitz has noted, these considerable women went on to lead campaigns for temperance, medical reform, the antislavery movement, the antivivisection movement, and women's suffrage.[14]

Bradley was more than an onlooker to this gathering: she was an enthusiastic participant. In September 1883 Bradley was part of the Bristol delegation to Butler's Third International Congress on the Abolition of State Regulation of Vice in The Hague (letters 66–69). She was also secretary of the Clifton Anti-Vivisection Society until 1887, and corresponded with the prominent activist Frances Power Cobbe.[15] In letter 85, Bradley writes of "a primrosey bit of cause work" collecting signatures for petitions in Sidmouth.

Cooper's life was more confined and domestic than that of her aunt. William Rothenstein described Cooper as "wan and wistful, gentler in manner than Michael but equally eminent in the quick give and take of ideas."[16] In her early letters the quick-witted girl is concealed behind the mask of dutiful daughter: Cooper reads with her parents—inexplicably nicknamed Muddie and Morin—from Wordsworth, Browning, and Arnold (see, for example, letter 69); and she helps her father with the old-fashioned hobby of pteridomania, or fern collecting, in Cornwall (letter 56).

Even at this early stage, the relationship between Bradley and Cooper was conspiratorial—based on a shared fantasy life. While studying at Newnham College, Bradley had begun a correspondence with John Ruskin, the art critic and social reformer, and subscribed to his Guild of St. George.[17] Bradley privately called Ruskin "Jack," with an intimacy that would have appalled the highly conservative Ruskin (letters 2 and 69). Cooper participated in her aunt's "Jack ardour" (letter 85) and speculated excitedly on the possibility of an impromptu meeting (letter 26).

The intimacy that Bradley and Cooper shared at this time was based also upon a common passion for aestheticism. They were devotees not only of John Ruskin but also of Algernon Charles Swinburne, Walter Pater, William Morris, and Dante Gabriel Rossetti. (See, for example, letters 2, 10 n. 6, 42, 133 n. 6, and throughout.) Bradley's letters grant Cooper entrance to a world made familiar by extensive reading: Henry Irving's production of *The Merchant of Venice;* the summer exhibitions at the Grosvenor Gallery; and on holiday in Italy in 1880, the great works of sculpture and painting. As Bradley says of the portrait of Beatrice Cenci, "Have joy in our photograph: it is marvellously faithful" (letter 15).

In many ways the bond forged between them by their delight in aestheticism is only part of their wider engagement with fields of scholarly knowledge inaccessible to earlier generations of women. Yopie Prins has noted that Michael Field's *Long Ago* (1889) was directly inspired by reading Henry Wharton's new edition of Sappho's fragments (1885),[18] and it becomes clear that Bradley and Cooper read widely on an impressively diverse range of subjects. The letters attest to the careful historical research that went into plays such as *The Father's Tragedy, William Rufus,* and *Loyalty or Love?* (all 1885), particularly by Bradley, who compiled long lists of books to be consulted. (See letter 6.) However, the poets' shared reading interests are by no means limited to research. When writing *Canute the Great,* for example, their reading included the *Paston Letters* (letter 106), the *Anglo-Saxon Chronicles,* and Charlotte M. Yonge's *Cameos from English History* (letter 109); yet the same letters also reveal plans for reading Hegel together and reading Carlyle's *Past and Present,* and they acknowledge a common affection for Browning's *The Ring and the Book* (letter 106). One of the most challenging aspects of editing these letters has been identifying the myriad of literary, biblical, and historical allusions contained within these letters, which speak to the poets' pride in their scholarly accomplishments.

The lifestyle desired and pursued by Bradley, and to a lesser degree by Cooper, was at odds with the family context within which it developed. Charles Ricketts described the Cooper household as one devoted to serious religious observance (see above), and it must have been a dour place for the aspiring young aesthetes. The nature of Emma Cooper's illness is ambiguous, but the invalid's couch was firmly at the center of family life. For Bradley, her sister was "the Sabine—the firm Spartan—the uncompromising on whom speck of vanity never fell."[19] Cooper confessed in "Works and Days" that her mother "bound and overawed me where I wanted to be free and personal."[20] Cooper's father, James, was a man of erratic temper. Cooper later wrote in her journal, "Round Michael whom he loved with passion, round me whom he loved with devotion, round Mother whom he loved with veneration he simply created a wilderness—There must be *his* love and a desert . . . no man could be received by us with comfort or dignity, every friendship was blighted as it rose to growing vigour by his hatred—yet I loved him and love him."[21] In the letters James Cooper is described as possessing a volatility whose origins are unclear. Cooper cautions Bradley in letter 90, "Also write to Paps—*as you love us*—He is dangerous" (original emphasis). This protective insularity itself probably increased Cooper's desire for the company of her worldly aunt.

There are few hints of family discontent in the earliest Bradley-Cooper letters. The nature of the household division between artistic and religious sensibilities only becomes clear in Bradley's letters to her cousin Fanny Brooks.[22] Bradley wrote, "I read my finished Isoude to my Darling to-night, and the eyes betraying perhaps a little emotion at prayer-time, I got lectured sadly for so doing . . . It is most painful to me that Sis will pursue a harassing policy. Edith has a hunted feeling, and I feel the sweetest human intercourse now granted to me, sorely checked, and broken, by unwise barriers."[23]

There are no currently identified letters between Bradley and Cooper for 1884, that most significant year in which they emerged as the successful new poet Michael Field. This gap is notable, not only because of its significance as the natal year for Field but especially because 1885 is the most prolific year for the Bradley-Cooper letters. It is impossible to know why there is this gap in the letters: it may be that the letters were separated from the rest because they map a highpoint in Michael Field's poetic career (and may reemerge); or, equally temptingly, they may reveal more about the discontent within the Cooper family and its potential sources.

Domestic tensions increased within the family in 1885. The "relation-torture,"[24] as Bradley called it, is revealed through the letters as a shell game: Katharine and Edith were partners in literature, but the niece who repeatedly turns up at Katharine's side is Amy. In April 1885 Bradley was in Sidmouth awaiting Cooper's arrival when Cooper wrote, "The Parents won't lend you the Pussy—they think ill would befall the lavender fur" (letter 73). In her place, Amy joined

Bradley. On 19 April, Bradley sent Cooper a poem, "The Stock-Dove's Lament," to which she added, "Mother must have a heart of stone if after this she Keeps you from me" (letter 87). In the next letter, it seemed Bradley had prevailed, for Cooper wrote, "*I will come,* and, heaven favouring, we will indeed be happy!" (original emphasis; letter 88). It was not to be. Bradley threatened, "*I mean to have you;* indeed I shall not come home, till they send you to fetch me. That will bring parents to their senses" (original emphasis; letter 89). While there is genuine affection between Bradley and Amy Cooper, who shares with her sister the nickname Pussie, Bradley and Cooper clearly wished to be together, and were unhappy with the Coopers' parental regulation. Echoes of this discontent can be read in Sturge Moore's unpublished study of the friendship between Bradley, Cooper, Ricketts, and Shannon.[25] Sturge Moore cites Bradley's musings on earlier days when "we discussed sex and life and adultery and the wickedness of the existence of relatives; when all things seemed possible, abolition of parents and husbands, duties and ties; when the clay of plastic life stuck to our fingers!" (fol. 2^r).

Possibly as a result of this discontent, greater intimacy of address, even sections marked "Private," began to appear in the letters in the late 1880s. These asides often refer to work in progress. Bradley wrote from Cranham in August 1887, "*Keep this,* directed and safe. Don't read to Mother—if she is in a way to scold and lecture. *I cannot bear it;* but if she is sympathetic, and can see the wonderful possibilities of the subject—speak to her of it alone" (original emphasis; letter 139).

The personal letters of the eighteenth and nineteenth centuries were not usually privileged communications, as Rebecca Earle has noted.[26] Letters were read aloud within the family circle and were collected into letter books to share with visitors. The Bradley-Cooper letters negotiate the boundaries of this private-public duality: thus, when Bradley writes to Cooper lamenting Emma's "heart of stone," it is also a direct appeal. The introduction of explicitly private sections within the letters, particularly regarding their writing, suggests that the family was no longer content to be the audience before which Bradley and Cooper performed their identities as poets. It may be that the rift in the family between religious and artistic sensibilities was now more openly acknowledged.

If it was sometimes difficult for Bradley and Cooper to be together, there is never a suggestion that Cooper's parents attempted to limit or curtail the collaboration. The most noticeable effect of their physical separation is Cooper's absence from important literary outings: Amy was Bradley's companion for her second visit to Robert Browning, and Amy accompanied her into Scotland on her first tour of the border district in 1886. This treatment seems harsh on Cooper: her vision during the writing of *The Father's Tragedy* is accepted within the family as a personal link with Lindores Castle (letter 131). Amy wrote, "It seems so impossible to think that Falkland is yours, and yet you have never seen it."[27]

The motivation behind this separation of the poets is never explicit, yet it coincides not only with their growing literary success as Michael Field but also with the period in which some critics believe that they became lovers.[28] It is not possible to identify the moment at which Bradley and Cooper became more than aunt-and-favored-niece. It may have been a gradual transition. Cooper's nickname, the Persian Puss, derives from a tendency toward nervousness. This nervousness is woven into a familial narrative that identifies Cooper in moments of particular stress as a cat up the chimney (see, for example, letters 114 and 129). As early as 1880, only Bradley could calm and soothe her. Bradley confided to Fanny, "My Persian still gives me many an anxious thought. She is doing *very little work;* still she looks strangely delicate, and too often comes to me for the peculiar sympathy she needs when the head aches are present. It is a sad and sensitive face for eighteen."[29] Their physical relationship may have developed from the intimacy of such moments.

Sally Newman has commented that personal papers seldom provide evidentiary certainty when it comes to identifying the lesbian subject.[30] Rather, the lesbian historiographer must develop new methodologies to read the silences in lesbian texts. In her reading of the correspondence of Virginia Woolf and Vita Sackville-West, Elizabeth Meese argues that, for the lesbian critic, the lesbian subject is revealed through the improper question that finds "in the space between words, the awesome passion of their engagement, even when they are (only) writing."[31] Yet is the lesbian relationship between Bradley and Cooper not also to be found in such improper questions, particularly in the silences that surround the repeated separations of Katharine and Edith, but not Katharine and Amy?

Christine White has already noted of the joint journals that several passages indicate in an unambiguous manner that Bradley and Cooper understood and experienced desire between women.[32] In the letters Bradley's woman-oriented desire is not difficult to identify. Her rapturous appreciation of the Louvre's Venus de Milo is erotically charged: "the perfect woman—perfect in and of hers[e]lf—with no thought of man, no entreaty for his love; yet with breasts so sweet one longs to drink from them, and all the lovely circles of the girl moon in Pan and Luna" (letter 9). Indeed, when a list of the paintings that most affected Bradley on her trip to Italy in 1880 is compiled—Titian's *Venus of Urbino* and *Flora;* Raphael's *Portrait of a Woman (La Fornarina)*; and Sebastiano del Piombo's *Portrait of a Young Woman;* as well as the Venuses de Milo, Italica, Capitoline, and Medici—it becomes clear that Bradley is particularly moved by the female form. Here is further evidence supporting Yopie Prins's notion that the Greek eros disseminated through Walter Pater's writing on Winckelmann to a male homosexual community was readily adaptable to a female homosexual erotics.[33] By April 1885, when Bradley sent to Cooper "The Stock Dove's Lament" (letter 87) and "Love's Sour Leisure," with the claim, "No other lover of the P's will ever mythologize on its chin so prettily" (letter 91), these have clearly become love letters.

Cooper's side of this correspondence is also intense, but is complicated by her relationship with her parents. She adopts the role of dutiful daughter without complaint; she is never intemperate in the face of the restrictions placed on her; and there is never a suggestion that she feels she should be at Bradley's side, even for the visit to Falkland. Meanwhile, with Bradley she adopted the role of the devoted wife. In 1885 she wrote, "Dearest deare, most gloriously loving, how shall I ever be a 'wiftie' worthy of you? Well, *gifts* are not always perfect and yet of some help and joy—And I have given myself to you as your spouse forever" (letter 105).

Cooper's performance of the role of the wife to Bradley's husband probably had a great deal to do with the power structure within the early partnership. While the transition to lovers probably occurred in adulthood, it is still not possible to interpret their early collaborative coupling without considering the asymmetrical nature of the early relationship. Bradley was fourteen years older than her niece, and Cooper had little concept of a life that did not include her aunt. The reproduction of subordinate roles in her letters raises questions about the extent to which Cooper was aware of performing these identities: was she merely seeking to please, or is it possible to read a more strategic, self-reflexive response to the forces vying for her affection?

While most of the letters included in this edition are from the Bodleian, the final group comes from the Pierpont Morgan Library in New York. These date from the 1890s, and they are strikingly different from the majority of letters in the Bodleian collection. The change of style and purpose illustrates the profound change in family life that followed the death of Emma Cooper from cancer in 1889. With Emma's death, the existing family affiliations—Katharine with Amy, Edith at home—were disrupted. In 1890 alone, Bradley and Cooper traveled to France and through Switzerland to Italy;[34] poor Amy was relegated to the youngest daughter's traditional role of companion to her aging father.[35] These changes are reflected in their letters, which become brief and functional, often dashed off with speed. Gone are the detailed negotiations of collaborative writing, and the pages devoted to descriptions of daily experience. In these letters Bradley and Cooper also develop a new pair of names, "Master" and "Merle." The new names may indicate a private joke based on Henry James's *Portrait of a Lady* (1881), but the letters provide no explanation.

From here on it was the joint journal, adopted in 1888 and continued until Bradley's death, that the poets used to explore their joint lives in Michael Field. It was in the journal in 1893 that Cooper described her father's unsuccessful attempt to reclaim the old family structure by demanding that Bradley leave his house.[36] It was only after the death of James Cooper (while walking in Switzerland in 1897) that there was a complete break with their earlier family life—a break that became more apparent when Amy married John Ryan in September 1899 and left to live in Ireland.

After Emma Cooper's death, the poets were practically inseparable. Together they set up their married home in Richmond, The Paragon (now an annex of the Bingham Hotel). Here they lived in aesthetic splendor in close proximity to their dear friends "the Painters," Charles Ricketts and Charles Shannon; and with their dogs, chiefly the adored Whym Chow. This pagan idyll faltered in 1906 with the death of Chow. Bradley and Cooper were devastated, leading their friend Charles Ricketts to chide them on their "excessive and dolorous lamentation."[37] They memorialized their beloved dog in the privately published *Whym Chow: Flame of Love* (1914), a volume of verse intended for circulation among their friends.

It is on the cusp of this new life that the narrative provided by the letters ends. While the last letter included in this edition dates from 1909, those dating from after 1897 offer only fragmentary glimpses of the poets' lives at Paragon and often comprise notes and short poems heralding a gift.

In the final stage of their career, both their lives and works were dominated by their conversion to Roman Catholicism in 1908. Both Bradley and Cooper seem to have found a new life and a new family in the Church as well as a new vocation as devotional poets. It soon became their only family as, with the death of Amy in January 1910, they became the last living members of the Cooper-Bradley household. It was an existence not without its struggles—conforming to the unfamiliar discipline and guilt over their pagan, probably lesbian, past was difficult—but they found valuable support from new mentors such as Father Vincent MacNabb and Father John Gray. It was not to last since, like their mothers before them, both Bradley and Cooper succumbed to cancer: Cooper in 1913 and Bradley, months later, in 1914.

After their deaths, Michael Field's work enjoyed a brief revival of interest in the 1920s before lapsing into a long period of obscurity. Nevertheless, they were remembered fondly by friends: the artist and publisher Charles Ricketts noted, "When we all come into our own, 'Michael Field' will be remembered";[38] and the playwright Gordon Bottomley wrote to William Rothenstein with this accurate prediction: "The dear Michaels? Yes, there *is* a future for their lyrical verse . . . if only someone would gather their Sappho versions [*Long Ago*], 'UTB' [*Underneath the Bough*], the poems for pictures [*Sight and Song*], and the little group of volumes with Ricketts covers issued at the end of their lives, they would return."[39]

Collaboration

When the first volume of plays by Michael Field, *Callirrhoë/Fair Rosamund,* was published in 1884, it was an immediate success. The emergence of a "New Poet" was lauded by the literary journals of the period, the *Spectator,* the *Academy,* and the *Athenaeum.*[40] The volume was so successful that it spawned a far wider popular celebrity: Bradley, holidaying in Edinburgh in 1886, described John Miller Gray's naïve speculation on the identity of Michael Field as "the wife of a school master in Clifton" (letter 122).

Literary gossip about the identity of Michael Field was rife in the literary journals, which threw out hints about the poets' gender and plurality. As early as November 1884, Bradley chided Robert Browning for teaching the *Athenaeum* to use "the feminine pronoun";[41] and in 1885, only a year after the emergence of Michael Field, J. W. Mackail of the *Academy* was referring to "Mr. Field—for so it appears simplest to call him, without inquiring too curiously into details of number or gender."[42] Although speculation had not officially uncovered their secret, it was clear to all that there was a secret to uncover.

One might perhaps expect that for Cooper—the quick, shy girl in awe of her glamorous aunt—taking up in adulthood the role of devoted wife/collaborator would mean the substitution of one form of familial repression for another. However, the Bradley-Cooper letters demonstrate that the Michael Field collaboration was a site of continual and occasionally intense negotiation. As she matured, Cooper became more assured; and, as a writer, she soon began to assert her own voice as the development of their professional collaboration demonstrates.

The first collaborative work by Katharine Bradley and Edith Cooper was the play, with included verse, entitled *Bellerophôn* (1881), published under the names Arran and Isla Leigh. Bradley had earlier published a single-authored book of verse, *The New Minnesinger* (1875), and the new play represented an extension of the pseudonym to recognize the new collaboration. The letters in this edition suggest that Bradley saw herself as the dominant partner in the Leigh collaboration—she was, after all, not only older but already a published poet. In spring 1880 she wrote to Cooper, "One fact I have discovered already [is] that the reclining statues often had *garlands* in their hands. I think I shall have to give up the orb, and substitute a chaplet in the Elgin Marbles passage" (original emphasis; letter 6). How Cooper responded to this, if she responded to this, has not survived.

Bradley's desire to be the guiding hand in the collaboration is also evident in another letter of 1880. Moved by the presence of banished pagan gods in the Pantheon, Bradley wrote to Cooper, instructing her to write a sonnet on the experience. She sets out scene and theme in the antagonism between the religions, and provides a rough semi-metrical prose outline (letter 17). Cooper complied, but even at this early stage in the collaboration, she demonstrates that she is more than merely a conduit through which Bradley's experience could flow. Cooper produced not a single sonnet but the unpublished sonnet sequence "The Pantheon at Vespers" (letter 26). These letters provide an insight into the early workings of the partnership between Bradley and Cooper, and point toward a collaborative practice that, while couched in terms that sustain the attitude of the deferential younger woman, operates through a complex process of negotiation that nevertheless proved extremely fruitful.

Throughout the 1880s Bradley and Cooper were frequently separated by the divergent pursuits of a young woman with aesthetic interests and some money of her own, and a youthful daughter dependent on her parents. Yet Cooper turned her seclusion to advantage, and the decade was a productive period for her, one in which she explored the strength of her voice.

In 1885 Cooper wrote a passionate defense of her vision of act 5, scene 1, of *The Father's Tragedy:* "To my consternation I find I have not made my vision clear. *This* is what I dreamt. In the monastery-aisle I saw the tomb—and on the tomb the figure in its marble-stillness, with the beautiful round lines of youth (cheek and chin) clear in the moonlight and the blank page of the brow glistening white . . . That was my vision—that was the truth. *You* think that I saw the body and all the peace of the beginning refers to *it* (wh: w[d] be monstrous, and no wonder you altered it.) But I feel as if I could not give up my vision—it would be giving up a heaven-sent reality. I almost weep" (original emphasis; letter 79). Cooper concludes her emotional plea for her vision, "if you won't have the *true* Vision—I shall adopt your rendering." While she couches her appeal in terms of the earlier deference, yielding to Bradley the final decision, this is nonetheless a confident assertion of the validity of her vision. Bradley herself seems to have been somewhat in awe of Cooper's visionary capacity, and on a later trip to Falkland "shuddered to think how god has spoken the truth to you" (letter 131).

In the letters it is apparent that the poets approached their writing in very different ways. Katharine Bradley had a mind that skipped rapidly from idea to idea: new plots and new characters continually suggested themselves. In Italy, Bradley thought of writing sonnets to the three Venuses (letter 9); while Cooper was in Cornwall, she mused, "I think another year there might be a St. Michael's Mount drama" (letter 48); and before *Brutus Ultor* was finished, she was already far more interested in *Canute the Great.* Cooper was of a more methodical nature, as her detailed plan for the plot of *Brutus Ultor* (see p. 140) demonstrates. In September 1885 Cooper took a strong stand against Bradley on the topic of beginning a new play, writing, "You see for a King it may do to Execute many things, but it is manifest that if a Cat is not concentrated on its prey it will come off badly, let me go on quietly with *Brutus* (as I must, if I am to do anything masterly) and I shall very soon have done it and be ready again to put heart and soul into the new subject" (letter 106). Within only a few years, Cooper had moved away from the role of adoring younger woman to confidently assert herself within the collaboration.

In his pamphlet on Michael Field, written for Mary Sturgeon's study, Charles Ricketts described the later collaborative practices of Bradley and Cooper: "Their habit of work was after long consultations and discussions to sketch out a rough scenario, and their separate work on the scenes of the play was compared, retouched and recast in progress, and overhauled at various times till finally amended and made smooth by Henry."[43] The craftsmanlike workshop suggested by Ricketts—where the rough play is retouched, recast, and overhauled—was rendered more genteel by Thomas Sturge Moore, who similarly noted that they worked in separate rooms: Cooper in the silver room near the entrance to Paragon, Bradley below stairs in an adjunct room whose walls were hung with gilded canvas.[44] Sturge Moore's emphasis on tastefully decorated separate rooms suggests an attempt to accommodate collaborative authorship to more conventional notions of (single) authorial production.

Bradley and Cooper offered a far more passionate model for their collaboration in a letter to Havelock Ellis in May 1886: "As to our work, let no man think he can put asunder what God has joined. *The Father's Tragedy,* save Emmeline's song and here and there a stray line, is indeed Edith's work: for the others, the work is perfect mosaic: we cross and interlace like a company of dancing summer flies; if one begins a character, his companion seizes and possesses it; if one conceives a scene or situation, the other corrects, completes, or murderously cuts away."[45] In the accounts by Ricketts and Sturge Moore, the collaboration proceeds in an orderly fashion within a harmonious atmosphere, but the Ellis letter wryly hints that the experience of collaboration involved a more robust, and not always pleasant, interaction. This view is supported by the journals, in which there are several intense arguments between the poets. Bradley wrote in 1891: "P. [Cooper] and I have nearly killed one another with vain and cruel reproaches over the Romuald scene. We are left with wasted eyes, reconciled hearts, and a humorous sense of the folly of alienation."[46]

Holly Laird has noted that the Ellis description of the collaboration "suggests a plurality of ways of interacting, which add up to something more than two," and "a radical free play like that of their multiple nicknames."[47] This plurality of interaction can be observed throughout the letters, which detail several different methods of collaborative practice. The structure outlined above by Ricketts may have produced *The Father's Tragedy*—but distinctly different processes were at work in the production of many of the lyrics. In the letters, poems sent to Cooper by Bradley, such as "My Deare Asleep" (published as

"A Spring Morning by the Sea" in *UTB,* 1893) and "King Apollo" (letter 74), are not significantly different in publication from the versions Bradley sent to Cooper in these letters. Mary Sturgeon writes that the volumes of Catholic poetry published by Michael Field at the end of their lives, *Poems of Adoration* (1912) and *Mystic Trees* (1913), were sole works by Cooper and Bradley, respectively, although published under the Michael Field pseudonym.[48] Another model of collaborative practice is described for "The Pantheon at Vespers" (see letter 26).

These letters indicate that the poets had no static or singular model of collaborative practice to which they worked. Rather it seems likely that, for Bradley and Cooper, the process of collaboration was a fluid one, responsive to the particular needs and circumstances surrounding each work. Michael Field's works represent the fruit of a collaboration that was subject to continual, and often passionate, negotiation, and probably differed for each text.

A Collaborative Pseudonym

In addition to providing further perspectives on the functioning of the Michael Field collaboration, these letters also suggest new ways to interpret the collaborative signature. Mary Sturgeon's explanation of the derivation of the Michael Field pseudonym is straightforward: "[It] was chosen somewhat arbitrarily, 'Michael' because they liked the name and its associations, 'Field' because it went well with 'Michael.' But it is true also that they had a great admiration for the work of William Michael Rossetti . . . and it is true, too, that 'Field' had been an old nickname of Edith. Their family indulged freely in pet names, and Edith was teased by a nurse, from her boyish appearance during a fever in Dresden, as the 'little Heinrich.' Thenceforth she became Henry for Katharine, and Katharine was Michael to her and to their intimates."[49] Sturgeon describes a partnership evenly represented in the name; the family connection is highlighted, as is the artlessness of the choice.

However, the early letters do not support all aspects of this reading. Neither nickname is commonly used, each preferring "Sim" or "Simorg" for Bradley and "Persian Puss" for Cooper. The name Michael does appear as early as 1884, but its usage suggests it is inclusive of both Bradley and Cooper, as when Bradley refers to herself as "this limb of Michael" (letter 85), or, "Of course

Michael bears the expense of all Michael's Self, if he goes to London" (letter 89). Michael did not become Bradley's favored nickname until the mid-1890s, when she began regularly signing letters as "Michael," and she became almost exclusively "Michael" in the journals.

Tracing the usage of "Field" is more difficult: Cooper preferred the name "Henry," so "Field" was never rigorously adopted, and seems to date from the mid-1890s.[50] Bradley wrote to the Rothensteins in about 1907, "Do you not know my real name? It is *Michael*—I have drawn down upon myself a power almost too terrible: the power of the balances is one I would not have sought. It is conferred on me of the Angel. However I am in Art Michael and the Dragon (chiefly Dragon, Ricketts will tell you!)—and I give you the freedom of my name. And my Fellow's *Field* (pastures of the Blessed too—but that is too long)."[51] This is a source for the association Sturgeon claims for the name Michael—the Archangel. It even goes some way toward explaining why Field should go "well with" it. By 1907 the names are firmly established, but it seems from the early letters that they derive from the pseudonym rather than producing the pseudonym. In contrast to the notion of selecting a composite name, Bradley and Cooper weave individual identities from the original collective pseudonym. Here, remarkably, the concept of the pseudonym uniting two into one shifts to allow the opposite to occur, with the same pseudonym becoming divisible into two, a reclamation of the distinct but linked subjectivities of the earlier Arran and Isla Leigh.

Conclusion

The love letters of Katharine Bradley and Edith Cooper published here represent a unique record of a premodern same-sex romance. Nevertheless, the terms by which this love affair was played out in these letters are very familiar ones. Here are all the usual tropes of the love-letter genre: not only declarations of love but also the exchange of flowers, gifts, and love poems. By insisting upon their spousal bond, Bradley and Cooper laid claim to the only relationship whose primacy was superior to a daughter's duty to her parents—a wife's duty to her husband. Yet while the love performed in these letters may have been a means of appropriating a space in which they could write, it cannot be said that the love they inscribed was no more than performance. Indeed, for the Fowl and the Pussycat—the guide and her student—this love was one that would dominate their entire lives, develop into the married idyll of Michael and Henry in their pagan Paragon on the banks of the Thames, and ultimately survive even the transition to a new faith.

Notes

1. See Treby, *Michael Field Catalogue* (hereafter referred to as *MF Catalogue*), 89–92. In all, Bradley and Cooper published during their lives one volume of poems as Arran Leigh; a play with additional poetry as Arran and Isla Leigh; eight books of verse and seventeen plays (including a masque) as Michael Field; and seven anonymous plays.

2. Field, *Works and Days,* 16. Hereafter referred to as *W&D.*

3. Laird, *Coauthored Pseudonym,* 199–202.

4. "Fairyman" and "Basilisk" were names for Charles Ricketts; Bernard Berenson was "The Doctrine." For a comprehensive list of the names invented by Bradley and Cooper, see Treby, *MF Catalogue,* 66–67.

5. Ricketts, *Michael Field,* 4.

6. Bridge, "Diary of Michael Field," fol. 62^{r}. About 1954, Ursula Bridge was commissioned to write an official biography of Michael Field. When she died in 1965, the incomplete manuscript was lodged with the Bodleian Library (MS Eng. misc. d. 983). See Treby, *MF Catalogue,* 54.

7. Sturgeon, *Michael Field,* 17.

8. Donoghue, *We Are Michael Field,* 20 and 22; Bridge, "Diary of Michael Field," MS Eng. misc. d. 983 fols. 64^{r}–66^{r} and 67^{r-v} BOD.

9. Keynes, "Obituary: Mary Paley Marshall (1850–1944)," 273.

10. E. B. Browning, *Aurora Leigh,* 11.

11. Sturge, pasted in endpapers of Sturgeon's *Michael Field.*

12. Rothenstein, introduction, ix.

13. Butler, *Personal Reminiscences,* 104.

14. Walkowitz, *Prostitution and Victorian Society,* table 1.

15. Sturgeon, 21; Mitchell, *Frances Power Cobbe,* 347.

16. Rothenstein, introduction, ix.

17. *W&D,* 143.

18. Prins, *Victorian Sappho,* 74.

19. Bradley to Fanny Brooks, [n.d.], MS Eng. lett. e. 143 fol. 56^{r} BOD.

20. "Works and Days," Add. MS 46780 fol. 13^{r} BL.

21. "Works and Days," Add. MS 26786 fols. 78^{v}–79^{r} BL.

22. The letters to Fanny Cooper, while extremely useful for understanding familial relations, fall outside the parameters of this edition. See "Editorial Method" below. These letters are held in the Bodleian Library (MS Eng. lett. d. 405).

23. Bradley, letter to Fanny Brooks, [1880], MS Eng. lett. d. 405 fols. 45^{v}–46^{r} BOD. Traditionally, Bradley's name for her sister has been interpreted as "Lis" or "Lissie." However, "L" and "S" are often indistinguishable in Bradley's handwriting (see, for instance, her writing of the word

"Sunday" in the letter pictured on p. 2.). As no other members of the family used "Lissie," it seems to me likely that the name is actually "Sis" or "Sissie." KB refers to herself as "thy own loving little Sis" in a letter to James Cooper. See KB, letter to Morin, [June 1890], MS Eng. lett. d. 400 fol. 106r BOD.

24. KB, letter to Fanny Brooks, [1884], MS Eng. lett. d. 405 fol. 104r BOD.

25. Thomas Sturge Moore, "Poets and Painters," Add. MS 61721 BL.

26. Earle, introduction, 7.

27. Amy Cooper, letter to EC, 7 Sept. [1886], MS Eng. lett. e. 31 fol. 24v BOD.

28. The "Lesbian Theory" of Bradley and Cooper was initially dismissed by Bridge, "Diary of Michael Field," fol. 217, and by Sturgeon, 74; and continues to be disputed by Ivor Treby (for example, *MF Catalogue,* 65). In 1975 Jeanette Foster included Michael Field as conjectural proto-lesbians in *Sex-Variant Women in Literature,* 14; Lillian Faderman argued in 1981 that their love should be interpreted as a Romantic Friendship (*Surpassing the Love of Men,* 210), a view contested by Christine White's "pro-sex" investigation of 1990, "'Poets and Lovers Evermore,'" 206. More recently, Emma Donoghue's biographic *We Are Michael Field* (1998) boldly asserted that Bradley and Cooper were lesbian lovers (29). For the notion that Bradley and Cooper became lovers when Cooper turned twenty-one, see Blain, "Michael Field: 'The Two-Headed Nightingale,'" 249; and Vicinus, *Intimate Friends,* 98.

29. KB, letter to Fanny Brooks, [n.d.], MS Eng. lett. d. 405 fol. 75r–v BOD.

30. Newman, "Body of Evidence," 12–13.

31. Meese, "When Virginia Looked at Vita," 90–91.

32. White, "'Poets and Lovers Evermore,'" 197–210.

33. Prins, "Greek Maenads, Victorian Spinsters," 43.

34. Treby, *MF Catalogue,* 31.

35. Flanders, *Victorian House,* 189.

36. "Works and Days," Add. MS 46781 fol. 19r–v BL.

37. Ricketts, *Some Letters,* 19.

38. Ricketts, qtd. in Delaney, *Charles Ricketts,* 276.

39. Bottomley, letter to Rothenstein, 12 Aug. 1943.

40. "A New Poet," rev. of *Callirrhoë;* Robinson, rev. of *Callirrhoë;* Marston, rev. of *Callirrhoë.*

41. *W&D,* 6.

42. Mackail, "Michael Field's New Volume," 36.

43. Ricketts, *Michael Field,* 4.

44. Sturge Moore, editor's preface, xvii–xix.

45. Sturgeon, 47.

46. Bradley, "Works and Days," Add. MS 46799 fol. 40r BL.

47. Laird, *Women Coauthors,* 87.

48. Sturgeon, 94.

49. Sturgeon, 27.

50. See Field [Cooper], letter to W. Macdonald, 9 Dec. 1895.

51. Bradley, letter to "Noli" Rothenstein, [Jan. 1907].

Chronology of the Works of Michael Field

1875 *The New Minnesinger and Other Poems* (Arran Leigh)
1881 *Bellerophôn* (Arran and Isla Leigh)
1884 *Callirrhoë/Fair Rosamund*
1885 *The Father's Tragedy/William Rufus/Loyalty or Love?*
1886 *Brutus Ultor*
1887 *Canute the Great/A Cup of Water*
1889 *Long Ago*
1890 *The Tragic Mary*
1892 *Sight and Song*
Stephania
1893 *Underneath the Bough*
A Question of Memory
Revised *Underneath the Bough*
1895 *Attila, My Attila*
1898 *The World at Auction*
1899 *Anna Ruina*
Noontide Branches
1901 *The Race of Leaves*
1903 *Julia Domna*
1905 *Borgia* (Anonymous)
1907 *Wild Honey*
1908 *Queen Mariamne* (the author of Borgia)
1911 *The Tragedy of Pardon/Dian* (the author of Borgia)
The Accuser/Tristan de Léonois/A Messiah (the author of Borgia)
1912 *Poems of Adoration*
1913 *Mystic Trees*
1914 *Whym Chow: Flame of Love*
1918 *Deirdre/A Question of Memory/Ras Byzance*
1919 *In the Name of Time*
1924 *A Selection from the Poems of Michael Field* (ed. Thomas Sturge Moore)
1930 *The Wattlefold* (ed. Emily Fortey)

Editorial Method

This edition includes 168 letters, all but a couple previously unpublished, the majority of which come from the largely neglected collection of the Bodleian Library, University of Oxford (shelfmarks MS Eng. lett. c. 148 and 149 BOD). The letters selected for this edition were those that could be identified as being written by Katharine Bradley or Edith Cooper, and whose intended recipient was the other poet.

The family preference for feline nicknames sometimes made this identification difficult, and some letters from these shelfmarks have not been included because the intended recipient was probably another family member. Similarly, misattribution has masked the extent of the correspondence, and I have included here several letters from shelfmarks associated with relatives such as Cooper's sister, Amy. Thus, letter 101, which is ambiguously addressed to "My own Precious Child," yet clearly discusses matters related to the collaboration and is signed "Thy own Spouse," is catalogued in the same shelfmark with Amy's letters, rather than with Cooper's letters.

This core correspondence has been enlarged by six Bradley-Cooper items dating from 1886, 1887, and 1888 held by the British Library in London, and sixteen letters dating from 1897 held in the Pierpont Morgan Library in New York. Not included in this edition are the few letters transcribed into the joint journals. This is because it is often difficult to differentiate the transcribed letters from the journal, and pasted-in pages can be considered either letters or diary pages written during separation from the journal itself. In either case I believe these communications are most profitably read as part of the narrative into which they have been interwoven in the journals, rather than standing as isolated and orphaned oddities at the end of this collection.

Dating the Correspondence

The letters collected here are seldom dated, often noting little more than the weekday—for example, the mocking "Sunday, 19$^{th.}$ Century" (letter 27). This is of little practical use to the editor. They were originally ordered chronologically by Cooper between 1910 and 1913; but by 1973, when negotiations began to deposit them in a library, the letters had fallen into a "muddle."[1] They were subsequently re-sorted by Henri Locard before being purchased by the Bodleian Library.[2] This edition broadly follows the chronology established by Cooper and Locard; however, where further research suggests an alternate chronology, this has been adopted. Locard's arrangement of the letters can be discerned in the folio numbers given at the bottom of the letters. The dates of significant family milestones and occasions have been cross-referenced with letters to other family members such as Fanny Brooks and Amy Cooper, and other correspondents such as Charles Ricketts and William Rothenstein, the joint journals, and the biographies of Sturgeon and Bridge. Where days are provided in the letters, conjectural dates have been provided using C. R. Cheney's *A Handbook for Students of British History* (2000). Dates that are conjectural and information obtained from postmarks (PM) appear in square brackets.

Manuscript Information

Shelfmark and folio information is provided at the bottom of each letter, along with information about previous publication of the letter. Where poems have been published, publication information is provided in a footnote.

Textual Modifications

Addresses

Where possible, the address from which the letter was sent is included at the beginning of the letter, along with the date. Conjectural addresses appear in square brackets, and where there is uncertainty an explanatory note is provided.

Spelling

Cooper's spelling is often inconsistent, and different spellings of the same word may appear in a single letter (for example, "Tintagil" and "Tintagel"). Original spelling has been retained. Where a missing word seriously impairs meaning, conjectural words are given in square brackets. Bradley in particular seems to have written her letters in great haste, which gives them spontaneity, but also leads to longer words, such as those ending with "-ing," trailing off in an indeterminate series of bumps. Where it is clear that Bradley intended such an ending, the text has been silently modified.

Capitalization

Bradley and Cooper make use of a variety of letter sizes, well beyond the capacity of printed text with its limit of two. In addition, the women have their own idiosyncratic practices: almost all of Bradley's "t's" look lowercase, even where they begin a sentence, and Cooper's "e's" occasionally look like capitals although their relative sizes vary. In deciding whether a letter should appear as capitalized or not, each incidence is judged individually, with some regard cautiously given to context and the probability of common usage. The first letter of a sentence is always capitalized. Superior letters have been retained.

Punctuation

Punctuation is reproduced faithfully from the manuscript. The only modifications are the provision of a full stop at the end of sentences that lack any indicator, the regularization of quotation marks so that they are consistently double rather than a mix of double and single, and the completion of quotation marks where only half of the set is supplied. These modifications appear silently. Incomplete ellipses frequently appear in these letters. In such cases the third period is added in square brackets.

Underlining

Underlining in the letters is indicated here by italic type, and words underlined twice have been set here in italicized small capitals.

Hyphenation

Hyphenation is often used inconsistently in the letters—for example, *to-morrow* and *tomorrow, bed-room* and *bedroom*—and is reproduced as such in the text. The exception is when words are hyphenated as a result of being carried onto a subsequent line. In this case they appear in the text in their regular form, with the hyphenation given in the textual apparatus.

Paragraphing

With the exception of opening paragraphs, indentations within the body of the letters are often slight or irregular. Editorial judgment on paragraphing is based on the suggestion of indentation within the manuscript. Occasionally, where they are writing within a confined space, as in a postcard, Bradley and Cooper use a backslash, which has been interpreted as indicating the beginning of a new paragraph.

Corrections and Alterations

Where a word is canceled or altered in the manuscript, the final reading is given in the text and the variant provided in the textual apparatus. Also included in the textual apparatus is information about the alteration such as supralineation and sublineation. Where there are significant deletions of several lines, these appear in the text as struck-through type.

Illegibility

In the very few instances where deletions render the original form indecipherable, the closest approximation is given in a footnote: for example, ~~foXXnXte~~. There are no other editorial omissions.

Abbreviations and Ampersands

Abbreviations, including the very common "wh." for "which," are reproduced in the text. Ampersands, which appear frequently in the text, have been replaced, as their use signifies little about the style of the writer. Moreover, their replacement is a standard editorial practice that improves readability. For the same reasons, the use of "& c." has been modified to "etc."

Marginalia

In concluding letters Bradley often makes recourse to the header of the first page. In a couple of instances, Cooper's conclusions are cross-written. In these cases the letter is returned to its intended sequence, and the editorial intervention is noted in square brackets, in italics: for example, *[from header fol. #]*. Marginalia are transferred where possible to the appropriate area of text and noted in the textual apparatus. Deleted marginalia appear in the textual apparatus.

Salutations and Farewells

Salutations appear in the text as they appear in the manuscripts. This means that irregularities in editorial practice reflect irregularities in the letters. Sometimes the salutation is separate from the body of the letter, and sometimes it forms part of the first line. Farewells and signatures, however, are regularized to appear indented from the left.

Notes

1. Daniel and Riette Sturge Moore, "Michael Field."
2. Clapinson and Rogers, *Summary Catalogue of Post-Medieval Western Manuscripts,* 683–84.

Abbreviations

The following abbreviations and familiar names are used by Bradley and Cooper in the letters:

A.W.F.	All-Wise-Fowl; nickname for Katharine Bradley
Bel. or Bell.	*Bellerophôn:* the first collaborative work; published under the names Arran and Isla Leigh
Brutus	*Brutus Ultor* (Michael Field)
Carloman	Working title for *In the Name of Time: A Tragedy* (Michael Field)
Cnut or Knut	Working titles for *Canute the Great,* pub. with *The Cup of Water* (Michael Field)
Edie	Edith Cooper
Et tu, Brute	Working title for *Loyalty or Love?* (Michael Field)
Hennie or Henry	Edith Cooper
Jack	John Ruskin
Katie	Katharine Bradley
Kittie Puss or Little Cat or Little Puss or Little Life	Amy Cooper; while both Amy and Edith share feline nicknames, it is possible to distinguish the cats from the kittens in specific contexts
Loyalty	*Loyalty or Love?* pub. with *The Father's Tragedy* and *William Rufus* (Michael Field)
Lucretia	Working title for *Brutus Ultor* (Michael Field)
Master	Katharine Bradley; used in 1897 letters; paired with "Merle" for Cooper
Merle	Edith Cooper; used in 1897 letters
Mick or Michael	Collectively used for Bradley and Cooper; later associated only with Bradley
Morin	James Cooper
Mud/Muddie	Emma Cooper
New Minn.	*The New Minnesinger and Other Poems* (Arran Leigh)

Persian Puss or P.P.	Edith Cooper
Pick	Amy Cooper
Sim or Simorg or Simurg	Katharine Bradley
Sis	Emma Cooper
Timmie Hors or Littel Hors	Katharine Bradley
William	*William Rufus,* pub. with *The Father's Tragedy* and *Loyalty or Love?* (Michael Field)

The following abbreviations and shortened titles are used in the notes:

Arnold	*The Works of Matthew Arnold*
AYL	Shakespeare, *As You Like It*
Bell.	Arran and Isla Leigh, *Bellerophôn*
Browning	*The Complete Works of Robert Browning*
BU	Michael Field, *Brutus Ultor*
Burns	*The Poems and Songs of Robert Burns*
Canute	Michael Field, *Canute the Great*
Call.	Michael Field, *Callirrhoë,* pub. with *Fair Rosamund*
Cup	Michael Field, *The Cup of Water,* pub. with *Canute the Great*
Cym.	Shakespeare, *Cymbeline*
DNB	*Dictionary of National Biography*
EC	Edith Emma Cooper
Fr.	French
FR	Michael Field, *Fair Rosamund,* pub. with *Callirrhoë*
FT	Michael Field, *The Father's Tragedy,* pub. with *William Rufus* and *Loyalty or Love?*
Ger.	German
Gk.	Greek
Ham.	Shakespeare, *Hamlet*
It.	Italian
Keats	*John Keats*
KB	Katharine Harris Bradley
LA	Michael Field, *Long Ago*

L.	Latin
LL	Michael Field, *Loyalty or Love?*
Lr.	Shakespeare, *King Lear*
Luc.	Shakespeare, *The Rape of Lucrece*
M&S	Ivor Treby, *Music and Silence: The Gamut of Michael Field*
Mac.	Shakespeare, *Macbeth*
MF	Michael Field
Milton	*The Works of John Milton*
MND	Shakespeare, *A Midsummer Night's Dream*
MPM	Mary Paley Marshall
MV	Shakespeare, *The Merchant of Venice*
N&CI	Hare, *Cities of Northern and Central Italy*
NT	Michael Field, *In the Name of Time*
OCD	*The Oxford Classical Dictionary*
OED	*Oxford English Dictionary,* 2nd ed.
Oth.	Shakespeare, *Othello*
Oxford DNB	*Oxford Dictionary of National Biography*
r	recto
R2	Shakespeare, *Richard II*
Rom.	Shakespeare, *Romeo and Juliet*
Ruskin	*The Works of John Ruskin*
Shakespeare	*The Works of William Shakespeare,* Globe Edition
Shelley	*The Complete Works of Percy Bysshe Shelley*
Sturgeon	Sturgeon, *Michael Field*
Swinburne	*The Complete Works of Charles Algernon Swinburne*
Tmp.	Shakespeare, *The Tempest*
UTB	Michael Field, *Underneath the Bough: A Book of Verse*
v	verso
Who's Who	*Who's Who 1897–1998*
WH	Michael Field, *Wild Honey from Various Thyme*
Wordsworth	*The Poetical Works of William Wordsworth*
W&D	*Works and Days: From the Journals of Michael Field*
WR	Michael Field, *William Rufus*
WiR	Hare, *Walks in Rome*

Love Letters of Michael Field, 1876–1909

1. Katharine Bradley, Letter to Edith Cooper

[Mon.,] 25 Dec. 1876

From Fowl to Fowlet;
From Owl to Owlet;
From Loving to Lover;
From Bard to his Brother;
From Arran Leigh
To the Voice to be;[1]
From the hand of "Own"
To the dearest Known;
From the Bird-All-Wise[2]
To the Light of his eyes;
From Friend unto Friend
After Life shall end.
Christmas 1876

MS Eng. lett. c. 418 fol. 1r BOD
Published in *M&S* (37)

1. In May 1875, KB published *New Minn.,* her (single-authored) first book of verse, under the name Arran Leigh. By Christmas 1876, fourteen-year-old EC had written her first works, "The Iwl-Dû" and "Atys and Adrastos" (both unpublished).

2. Thomas Sturge Moore explains the origin of KB's nicknames, "Sim," "Simorg," "the Fowl," "the Bird-All-Wise," and the bird-shaped signature (see letter reproduced on p. 2.) as a nickname "from Simiorg, a fabulous, Eastern bird, mentioned in *Vathek* and *Thalaba* as endowed with reason or 'all knowing'" (*W&D,* 14 n. 1). *Vathek* (1789) by William Beckford and "Thalaba the Destroyer" (1801) by Robert Southey are English attempts at Arabian tales. Beckford's simurgh is the "wonderful bird of the East" that possesses reason and the knowledge of every language (*Vathek,* 255); however, KB prefers the spelling used in Southey's epic poem, which emphasizes the simurg's role as a knowledgeable guide (8. 257–61; Southey, *Poems,* 82). This suggests that "the Simorg" represents KB's early role as mentor.

2. Katharine Bradley, Letter to Edith Cooper

[Blackheath] | [Summer 1877][1]

My Dearest,

I have written to Hales and Sumner already,[2] and must write to Cousin Fanny,[3] who is still indulging in the folly of going to the sea-side with all her

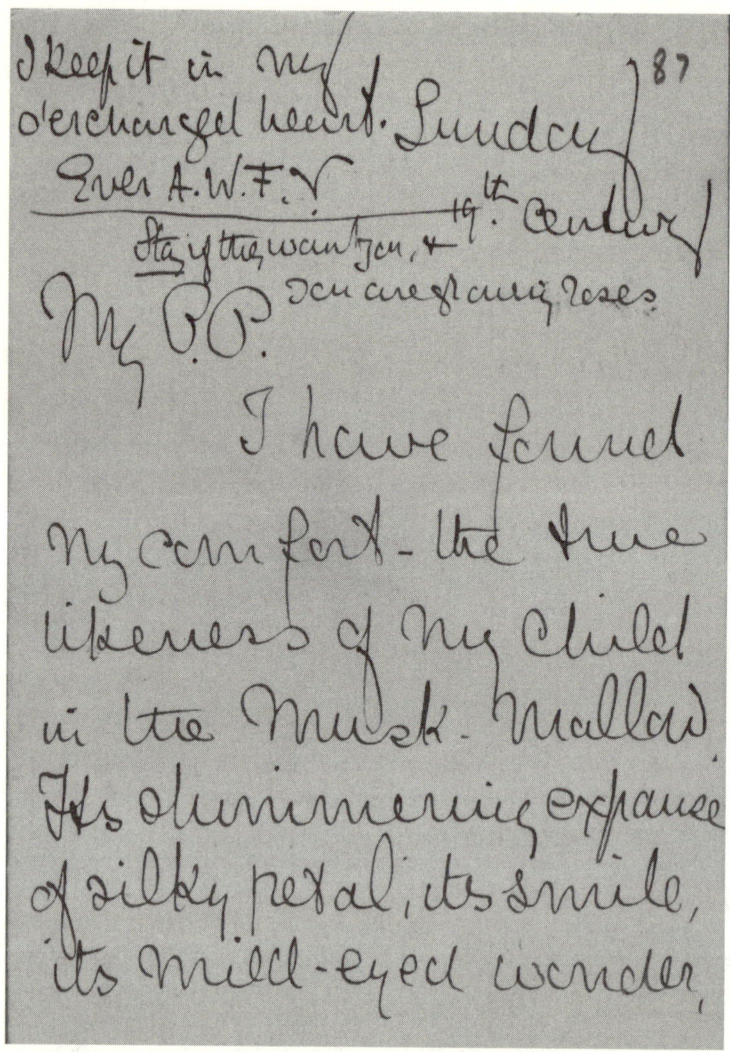

87

I keep it in my o'erchanged heart. Ever A.W.F.V. Sunday 19th Century

My P.P.

I have found my comfort – the true likeness of my child in the Musk-mallow. Its shimmering expanse of silky petal, its smile, its mild-eyed wonder,

Letter from Katharine Bradley to Edith Cooper, "I have found my comfort" [Sept. 1881]. (MS Eng. lett. c. 418, fol. 87^{r}, Bodleian Library, University of Oxford)

flock, and wants me to meet her!!. She gravely asks will Clovelly do for the chicks. I must write and make quite clear to her that there can be no mingling of the waters. Tell my darling Hobbes,[4] he need not fear. He shall have, all being well, his dear Master to himself at Clovelly. Nellie[5] is writing begging Fany to give up the mad plan. I must be most careful, or I shall give offence. If she goes, she will perhaps lose her life.

My face flushed yesterday as suddenly turning round, I beheld, at the

Grovesnor Gallery—*not* Jack,[6] and yet he might be seen at the Charing Cross station on his way home from the continent—not Jack; but Prof. Leeley.[7] Carping and not comfortable looked his spoilt visage.

I listened for his criticism of B.Jones's pictures with interest.[8] His lady companions seemed to me "Charged with folly": but his quotations from Milton and his general comments interested me.

Please, dearest, do not look for more letters. We *cannot* write. We hope to leave Paddington on Monday at twelve. Reach T'rowbridge 3-27. I don't know what will become of us after that. I fear we shall have to wait. Is that best train? Please see and write post-card faces to receive on Monday.[9] They have begged of us to stay for the "Zoo" on Monday. Of course we will not. Tell my precious Child that I have bought her present in the Burlington Arcade—it is a *wee* mosaic brooch—a little white violet on black marble back-ground. We think it looks like darling Pick[10] and hope she will always be like it. I want to buy blue china,[11] and rare tapestries, and Morris-like garments but you say I must not. God bless you, my own [*from header fol. 3*^{r}] and bring us back safely to you in our loved home. Best love to dear Morin.

Ever the same old Katie.

Best love to Mount from both of us.

MS Eng. lett. c. 418 fols. 3^{r}–5^{v} BOD

1. Dated from the Grosvenor Gallery's first summer exhibition in 1877 (Newall, *Grosvenor Gallery,* 56) which coincided with John Ruskin's return from Venice in June (Hilton, *John Ruskin,* 352). EC had already visited the exhibit, which opened in May. See EC, letter to Emma Cooper [Summer 1877], MS Eng. lett. c. 419 fols. 135–39^{r-v} BOD.

2. John Wesley Hales (1836–1914), professor of English literature; general editor of Bell's *Handbooks of English Literature, Longer English Poems,* and Milton's *Areopagitica* (*Who's Who*). KB met Hales at his ladies' classes in literary criticism at the [Birmingham and] Midland Institute, probably between 1863 and 1867. See Emma Cooper, letter to ?, Add. MS 45851 fol. 8^{r} BL. A later letter from Sumner shows he was a journalist who "noticed" *FT/WR/LL* in two newspapers (letter to KB, 23 Jun. 1885, MS Eng. lett. e. 32 fol. 147^{r-v} BOD).

3. Frances Brooks née Holinsworth (1835–98) was KB's cousin. Fanny married John Brooks, a paper merchant, and did indeed produce a "flock" of children. See family tree on p. xvi. In 1877 these ten children (George was not born until 1878) were aged between 2 and 15 years. EC called Clovelly "our sweet little Devonshire nest." See MS Eng. lett. c. 419 fol. 128$^{r/v}$ BOD.

4. Probably Amy Katharine Cooper (1863–1910), KB's younger niece. Amy attended Bristol University College with her aunt and sister in the 1880s; like the philosopher Thomas Hobbes, she excelled at mathematics (MS Eng. lett. d. 402 fol. 59^{r} BOD; Treby, *Binary Star,* 86). It is quite usual for KB and EC to use cross-gendered nicknames, and to refer to women as "he" in such instances.

5. Ellen Reith née Holinsworth (Nellie) was KB's cousin. She married an Anglican clergyman, Canon David Reith, and had two sons, Roger and George, and two daughters, Ellen and Elsie. See family tree on p. xvi. The Reiths lived in Blackheath, south of Greenwich (Add. MS 46867 fol. 181r BL), where KB would have stayed. It is probably the Reiths with whom KB plans to travel later in this letter.

6. John Ruskin. KB was an enthusiastic disciple of Ruskin and joined his Guild of St. George (*W&D,* 145), whose members called him "Master" (Ruskin, 30:3). Not only did KB avidly read Ruskin's works, passing *Fors Clavigera* around the family circle, but she privately fantasized about him, calling him "Jack" with an imaginary intimacy that would have horrified Ruskin had he known. See, for example, KB, letter to Frances Brooks [Nov. 1876], MS Eng. lett. d. 405 fol. 30v BOD. KB initiated the correspondence in summer 1875, while she was at Newnham College (Bridge, MS Eng. misc. d. 983 fol. 67r BOD). Ruskin became particularly affronted in Dec. 1877 when KB wrote that she had "lost God and found a Skye Terrier," and he peremptorily excluded her from the Guild (*W&D,* 155 and 158). Nevertheless, the correspondence continued until early 1880 (*W&D,* 167).

7. KB is confusing two noted portrait painters: Sir Peter Lely (1618–80) and Alphonse Legros (1837–1911), Slade Professor of Fine Arts at University College London from 1870 to 1892. There were several Legros portraits at the Grosvenor's inaugural exhibition (1901–11: *DNB*).

8. The 1877 exhibition featured eight new works by Edward Coley Burne-Jones (1833–98) covering almost an entire wall of the gallery. These paintings, particularly the *Days of Creation* series, caused a sensation in the art world and established him as an important artist. See Rossetti, "Grosvenor Gallery"; Newall, *Grosvenor Gallery,* 16. KB's description of the lady companions is a quotation from Job 4:16–19; Legros quotes Milton's description of the creation in *Paradise Lost* (8.243–592; Milton, 2.1:220–32).

9. Untraced.

10. Nicknames are common in the Bradley-Cooper family, and their origins are seldom explained: "Pick" is Amy Cooper; "Morin," mentioned at the end of the letter, is EC's father, James Robert Cooper (1818–97). See introduction. The "Mount" of the postscript is perhaps one of the little Brookses. "Little Mount" is mentioned in MS Eng. lett. c. 419 fol. 130v BOD.

11. Oscar Wilde's witticism linking blue china with an aesthetic lifestyle was well known by 1876, but only achieved national attention when it was caricatured by *Punch* in 1880. See Ellmann, *Oscar Wilde,* 43–44.

3. Edith Cooper, Annotated Envelope[1]

Dean Prior
The Hague—1883
Bellerophon (1881)
Callirrhoe (1884)
Madame Ristori's Lady Macbeth—July 3 1882
Irving as Shylock 1879

poem
Dean Prior
Herrick's Home
Must be 81—Aug 89 (or 87)

MS Eng. lett. d. 418 fol. 10r BOD

1. EC made notes on envelopes that appear throughout the collection recording events by putative year and subject. These notes were probably written when EC arranged the letters sometime between 1910 and her death in 1913, but the original arrangement has not survived. I have attempted to replace the notes before the letters to which they most likely refer. This envelope provides rough dates for KB's trips to Dean Prior (letters 36–38) and the Hague (letters 66–69), as well as Ristori's production of *Mac.* (letter 32) and Irving's *MV* (letter 4).

4. Katharine Bradley, Letter to Edith Cooper

[London] | [Late Mar. 1880][1]

P.P.

Front seats in the dress-circle, with good view of the whole of the stage.

Lovely Venetian scene, but a vulgar Antonio, and strutting Bassanio disenchant; and is this Portia stalking about the stage, making Cat's cradle figures with her maid Nerissa?

Do young women walk about their rooms distractedly talking of their loves,—or is it not the tender familiarities of the toilette that makes them "*open* their bosoms of their counsel sweet?"[2] I have always seen Portia in that first scene with her long hair down, Nerissa behind, learning her mistress's blushes from the mirror—the two women's hearts drawn together by the frankness that personal service provokes; no drawing-room airs, and arch looks for the audience. Then the Lady of Belmont gives her glorious self away half deprecatingly as one would give a worthless wild-flower to a friend—"would you like it?"—she is caressing, half-supplicating throughout the address, and looks-up at her lover playfully and tenderly, but the Portia Shakespeare has taught us had something in her of her great Roman namesake, that infinitude of haughtiness that makes self-abasement terrible. Shakespeare's Bassanio was simply appalled by the magnificent condescension of his lady; he could do little but blunder and blush—it was as if the heavens laid themselves at his feet; and truly a woman must be clothed with the majesty of the heavens befittingly to renounce her queendom for Love's subgection. So far disappointment, not to be redeemed by the bright haired boy Doctor who in the mercy passage has rather the air of an undergraduate reading a lesson from the grander parts of Isaiah. The words are too weighty for so slight a creature; she is occupying herself with matters too high for her. The real Portia makes that last appeal to Shylock with a noble woman's incapacity for belief in the uttermost vileness of human nature; and longing to redeem the wicked from their baseness; her manner should be full of passionate, if repressed agitation;—she hopes to the end to soften that flinty heart; and only when she gets the inexorable demand for the bond in reply—does she resume her calm legal tone, and talk officially of the pound of flesh.

And Shylock.[3] Well Persian, he is worst when he gathers the curses into his eyes, rolls their irises clean away into his brain, and leaves the eye-*balls*—a glaze of malignity—a sheet-lightning of shimmering fury—his eye brow working, with something of the intensity of his fang-like hands—and a hiss compounded of the cat's "spit" and the sibilant swearing of a snake issuing once or twice from his lips. He is fiendish in his hate, but dignified to loftiness throughout, never crouching but in irony, and in the final trial scene, leaving the room as one bowed down by calamity, a defeated hero, not the devil's slave whom the mob execrates and yells after. The audience ought to be ready to join in the yell; and isn't, so Shakespeare's lesson is missed, the nobleness of Antonio's friendship and the boundlessness of his generosity forgotten in mis-placed sympathy with a baulked fiend. That double cry of agony for ducats and daughter ought to bring the contemptuous laugh. My own belief is that Irving has not sufficient reliance on his art to dare to make himself ridiculous. I cannot see a trace of *dignity* in Shylock's character: what miser was ever dignified? When he asserts the rights of his human nature, and curses the Christian one feels with him; for the rest he is unutterably vile—worthy of Dante's lowest hell for fraud.

The moonlight scene "Sit Jessica"[4] was simply murdered—the perfect Dido lines omitted; Lorenzo declaimed the celebrated music-passage, and Jessica, by way of making a remark—observed "I am never merry when I hear sweet music."!!

Nevertheless, spite of these flaws, there is no place on earth where I am externally so happy as in a theatre, and there is no excitement possible to me—(a proposal in youth might come near it) like the excitement of the unlidding of the stage's eye. I feel I should almost like to see heaven so.

MS Eng. lett. c. 418 fols. 6^r–9^v BOD

1. The Lyceum's production of *MV* opened on 1 Nov. 1879. Modern interpretations of Shakespeare by Henry Irving (1838–1905) rejuvenated Shakespearian theater in the 1870s (Brereton, *Life of Henry Irving,* 1:272), and the 1879–80 production of *MV* was particularly successful (Bingham, *Henry Irving & Vic. Theatre,* 145). KB's comments regarding the controversy surrounding Ruskin's letter to The *Theatre* suggest this letter may have been written about Mar. 1880.

2. Hermia's words to Helena in *MND* 1.1.214–16. Michael Field's *LL* (1885) rewrites the mirror scene, inscribing a very different mistress-servant relationship between Iolanthe and her reticent Moorish maid, Azaire (1.2; *FT/WR/LL,* 236).

3. This comment suggests KB's critique of Irving was influenced by John Ruskin. In Jan. 1880 the *Theatre* published an excerpt from a Ruskin letter implying he approved of Irving's Shylock. Ruskin was offended and insisted on the publication of the entire letter, which appeared on 20 Mar. and stated that "I entirely dissent (and indignantly as well as entirely) from his [Irving's] general reading and treatment of the play" (Ruskin, 34:545). Ruskin's view had already been published in *Munera Pulveris:* "And this is the ultimate lesson . . . in which the true and uncorrupt merchant,—*kind and free, beyond every other Shakespearean conception of men*—is opposed to the corrupted merchant or usurer; the lesson being deepened by the expression of the strange hatred which the corrupted merchant bears to the pure one" (original emphasis; 17:222–23).

4. The final scene of *MV* (5.1).

5. Katharine Bradley, Letter to Edith Cooper

[London] | [Spring 1880][1]

Pretty Persian Puss, hope nothing for Bell![2] Last night the Prof. looked so pale and white with over-tire at dinner that I fore-saw it wd. be cruetly to *animals* to let him look over manuscripts that evening;[3] so, when he joined us in the drawing-room, we got into deep talks on religion instead; my fatal fascination to draw men of all creeds into earnest religious discourse, and unveiling of the inner shrines, revealing itself. I brought down Bell this morning; but the Prof. left hurriedly. I am going to leave it with him; but how much attention he will give to it I cannot say. His scholar's hints will be invaluable; but he has neither leisure of heart, nor poetry of nature enough to judge rightly of the work.

Meantime I must copy the titles of books:—old Romances and Classical, with wh. he has heaped me. He has lent me Andrew Tooke's Parthenon a perfectly blessed book, consecrated by the touch of Keats.[4] No more: despair not. Whatever Profs. Think—and we don't know yet what they do think—*our* names are written I devoutly believe in the book of this *world's immortal life.*

Let us be true to the two great tracks of Greek thought and Mediaeval Romance; the times when the head of man was at his soundest, and the heart of man was at its tenderest; and to this 19th century a goodly song shall yet be sung. Hales and I abuse Rowley[5] without remorse—as a person infatuated with facts, without recognition of their relative value.

After lunch I hope to drive to Charing Cross, deposit my box, and meet Prof. Hales in the Lycian room at the Museum, and afterwards reach Blackheath for dinner. *They* have been *most* Kind to me, let *[from header fol. 11r]* us still be brave.

Your own dear Arran
[bird symbol]

MS Eng. lett. c. 418 fols. 11r–12v BOD

1. Dated from the publication of *Bell.* in May 1881. EC dated the letter to spring 1880.

2. *Bell.* was the first of the collaborative works, and the only one published under the names Arran and Isla Leigh. The play describes Bellerophôn's treatment by the vindictive Anteia, his acquisition of Pêgasos, and the slaying of the Chimaira. The titular drama is combined with several shorter poems on the theme of classical love. The reviewers were not kind, excoriating them for lack of talent and knowledge of their subject. This possibly led them to seek a new pseudonym. See reviews of *Bell.,* by Arran and Isla Leigh: *Athenaeum* 71 (1881): 173; *Academy* 20 (1881): 196; *Graphic* 24 (1881): 198.

3. John Wesley Hales. See letter 2 n. 2. Hales's reluctant mentorship continued throughout the preparation of *Bell.* Two letters from Hales (9 May [1880] and 4 Jan. [1881], Add. MS 45851 fols. 49r–54v BL) give advice for improving the work, as well as his apologies for delay. There is a note of mock authority in KB's declaration of cruelty, as she was secretary of the Clifton Anti-Vivisection Society (Sturgeon, 21).

4. John Keats did not read Greek, deriving his mythological information from Andrew Tooke's *The Pantheon,* itself a translation of François Pomey's Latin work *Pantheum Mithicum* (Motion, *Keats,* 37). KB confuses the Roman Pantheon with the Greek Parthenon.

5. James Rowley (1834–?) was Professor of Modern History and Literature at Bristol University College from 1876 to 1905 (Carleton, *Univ. for Bristol,* 86). A letter confirms KB attended his literature classes at Bristol University College (J. Rowley, letter to KB, 21 Jul. 1905, MA2092 [unfoliated] PML).

6. Katharine Bradley, Letter to Edith Cooper

[London] | [Spring 1880][1]

Oh Persian, Persian Puss! if you only knew, if you had only been here! Last night the Professor entered the drawing room with Bell in his arms, and by and bye asked me to read some to him. I at last got through part of the 2nd Dew Maidens' Song; and then to my horror, *he* began at the very beginning "thou art so beautiful" and read very slowly, *carefully,* and without a touch of passion or pathos the 1st scene.[2] It—the torture I suffered—was like *hearing* the tooth-ache if that were possible. Anteia and Bell seemed to be meeting on "Change!!" But some of his criticisms were invaluable. For instance he showed me how the lines

—checking imperiously the wistful priest
who covets thee for heaven.

were altogether ungreek in thought, and must be altered; and objected to the "undemed" as not quite correct. To-night after lecture, we hope to have a very long turn at it, and more toothache: but doubtless good will come of the keen pain.

The Prof. could not be kinder or more helpful. He has left me with a whole pile of books—Winkelmann, Muller, Horne Tooke and others to consult,[3] and insists on my visiting the new Lycian Room at the British Museum. He thinks I ought to bathe myself a little more in the folk-lore of Lycia, and be steeped in the stories of the local divinities.

One fact I have discovered already that the reclining statues often had *garlands* in their hands. I think I shall have to give up the orb, and substitute a chaplet in the Elgin Marbles passage.[4] But as yet the Prof. cannot in the least judge of Bellerophon; for he has been thrown into gt. trouble by the death of a relation, the husband of a Cousin of theirs, and he and Mrs. Hales[5] have been greatly occupied with the poor little widow, left with one little child.

Everything in the house is curiously the same as last year. Mrs. Hales is most kind to me; and everything is done to make me entirely at home.

I have had no word from the Master.[6] If none comes, I think I shall migrate to Blackheath to-morrow afternoon. It is a lovely day. Mrs. H. and I are going to stroll out. This afternoon I am sola. I cannot say my pulse keeps time very temperately; but I feel remarkably well.

Ever, Pretty Persian
[bird symbol]

MS Eng. lett. c. 418 fols. 13r–14v BOD

1. Dated from KB's trip to London in spring 1880.

2. The Dew-maidens, Hersê and Pandrosos, cleanse the world with dew each morning. Their second chorus occurs near the end of the play (4.1.111–34; *Bell.,* 91). The play begins with Anteia declaring her love for Bellerophôn, "Thou art so beautiful / The very slaves about my house break off / Their toil, and in a wonder stare at thee;" (1.1.1–3; *Bell.,* 3). Hales's comments were taken very seriously: neither "wistful priest" nor "undemed" appears in the published text.

3. Johannes Winckelmann, *Reflections on the Painting and Sculpture of the Greeks* (1765); Friedrich Max Müller's "Essay on Comparative Mythology" (1858); John Horne Tooke's major philological work, *Epea Pteroenta* or *The Diversions of Purley* (1786), was considered outdated by the mid-1900s (*Oxford DNB*). For the visit to the British Museum, see letter 7.

4. Omitted from the published version. The nymph, Eurunomê, garlands Bellerophôn's head when he sets out to slay the Chimaira (3.4.88; *Bell.*, 74); later, Anteia imagines him reclining in triumph with garlanded head (3.6.136; *Bell.*, 85).

5. Henrietta Hales née Trafford (*Who's Who*).

6. The awaited letters from Ruskin were sent on 22–23 Mar. but were not encouraging to his "sentimental disciple," commanding her to "repent and be quiet" (*W&D*, 166–67). KB wrote at this time: "My studies of Browning have thrown light on my relationship with the Master, and the corners of my heart are hardening sufficiently to give credence to the saying of Bacon that love, *unless it be reciproque,* is rewarded by a secret contempt." See KB, letter to Frances Brooks, [Mar. 1880], MS Eng. lett. c. 418 fol. 42ᵛ BOD. Nevertheless, KB clearly desires a reconciliation.

7. Katharine Bradley, Letter to Edith Cooper

Blackheath | Fri., [Summer 1880][1]

Manäar House, Blackheath, Friday Morning
23, Carpenter Road
after Tuesday next is Cousin Fanny's address

Ah, pretty Persian puss, the baby daughters[2] have been receiving their reading lessons, and it is enough to destroy all classical remembrances, but I will strive to stuff my ears with cotton wool, and tell you all that happened to me yesterday. After lunch at one, I drove with my worldly goods to Charing Cross, deposited them at the parcels' office, and then found the dear old yellow omnibus (you remember by St. Martin's) and drove to the Museum. As the Professor had predicted, I had already "spotted" Bellerophon on his arrival just before three.—Oh Persian the Lycian Court is the very first on entrance, only we did not know we did not consider, when we were there.[3] First two immense tombs (actually dug up and brought from Zanthus about 400 BC) on one of wh. Bell is represented combating Chimaera in a quadriga; Chimaera looking like a rather discomforted boar-lion; not the "tri-parte malignity"[4] *we* know about. Then round the walls are fragments of a beautiful temple from Zanthus, of which there is a complete model and lovely torsoed figures of Nereids, that were placed between the columns of the temple. Bell. must have seen these; and there ought to be some allusion to them. They are full of rapid swift motion, a fish, or shell, or dolphin under their feet, their skirts, *not* tied-back; but wind-drifted, the loose jacket cinctured; and falling into light folds; joy—*vital* joy in the spring of every limb. The Prof. delights in them, and quoted "Sleek Panope" from Lycidas.[5] Then we had a quest for a second Bellerophon, or as an official to Hales's great delight said "Belly-ruffian," and then came upon a really valuable Lycian cast. There is no Chimaera visible *to us;* but to Pegasus with his pricked up ears, and angry head, and to Bellerophon with his set lips and intent stedfast eyes, he is clearly visible. This Bell is in no "quadriger" no fair-charioted steed, but on his own winged horse. I was obliged to confess that our Bell was much weaker, and frailer; but of course in the moment of intense struggle, even his gentle irresolute face w[d.] be firm and fired too. The Prof. and I staid and studied every point. Bell's arm is thrown straight back and in it a javelin—we thought.

After this we walked to the Elgin gallery, sat down and talked. And the Prof. presented me with a globe copy of Mallory's *Morte d'arthur,*[6] wh. with Keat's *Pantheon* I am going diligently to study. We discussed the two Isoudes,[7] and I said that it seemed to me the successful introduction of children was a great test of genius; and I spoke of the miserable little brats with whom Matthew Arnold spoils his poem. I rather think the Prof. thinks I might do something for Sir Tristram, though he did not say so.

We parted amid the old Greek tombs, and I went back to my beloved Elgins. Most sorely did I miss the Persian, *Persian* Puss; especially as I passed the vine-clad head that she loved so well. I came across another burst of Zanthus in a fresh room, and saw the celebrated Harpy tomb therefrom. The Harpies with their cruel claws are carrying away a number of unfortunate small mortals: there are images of Demeter and Proserpina (?) This too Bell. saw. Now Persian get on with your copy of Bell that I may be able to work on my return.

I now hope to go into town to the Grosvenor. Miss Smith[8] is very kind and of quiet manner; but I cannot stay here all day. Kiss a thousand times my own Amy to whom I do not write to-day because of Bell.

Ever

[bird symbol]

MS Eng. lett. c. 418 fols. 15[r]–17[v] BOD

1. Dated from the summer exhibition at the Grosvenor Gallery.

2. Ellen and Elsie Reith (b. 1876 and 1877, respectively). On another visit EC wrote to her mother, "I am sure I have talked about the children till it is enough to make them tumble over

with self-conceit; this is almost the only thing you can talk about, and a subject that is pumped out of you" (letter to Emma Cooper, [Spring 1880], MS Eng. lett. c. 419 fol. 143[r] BOD).

3. Charles Fellows acquired Lycian marbles (ca 480 BC), from Xanthos in Turkey, for the British Museum in 1842 (Smith, *Catalogue,* 1:45). Among these were three tombs: the tomb of Merehi (or Chimaera tomb), the larger Nereid Monument, and the Harpy tomb. The roof of the Chimaera tomb features relief of a charioteer, thought to be Bellerophôn, attacking the Chimaera (Smith, *Catalogue,* 2:54). The Nereid Monument is a reconstructed funerary temple with life-size marble nymphs or Nereids with "trailing garments" like those of Hersê and Pandrosos (4.1.137; *BM & Collections,* 77, 92). The winged creatures of the Harpy tomb are now believed to be heroic family members (*BM & Collections,* 69). The collection also contains tomb relief of Bellerophon, astride Pegasus, thrusting at the Chimaera (Smith, *Catalogue,* 1:350). As the Department of Greek and Roman Antiquities was extensively rearranged between 1880 and 1883 (Francis, *Treasures,* 169), the "vine-clad head" mentioned later in this letter and which is probably a garlanded statue or bust of Dionysos is untraced (Smith, *Catalogue,* 3:42–50).

4. 2.6.187 (*Bell.,* 48).

5. *Lycidas,* 97–98 (Milton, 1.1:80).

6. Sir Thomas Malory, *Morte Darthur,* Globe Ed. (1868).

7. Isolde, wife of King Mark, and Isolde of the White Hands, who Tristan married after she cured him of a poisoned arrow then deserted for his true love, the other Isoude. See Hope-Moncrieff, *R&L of Chivalry,* 103. In Sept. 1880 KB read her "finished Isoude" to EC (MS Eng. lett. d. 405 fol. 45[v]–46[r] BOD). The work is untraced, but KB and EC later published two anonymous plays based on the romance: *The Tragedy of Pardon* (1911) and *Tristan de Léonois* (1911). In his *Tristram and Iseult,* Matthew Arnold heightens the poignancy of the deserted wife by cherubic descriptions of the children (337–48; Arnold, 1:192).

8. Untraced.

8. Katharine Bradley, Letter to Edith Cooper

[1880][1]

Pretty P.

Amy Bell[2] meant no harm. She has you in the high esteem: She respects you. Poor soul—she has had no creature to teach her manners; but I am sure she means well to you. I seem to see the creature getting ready his gown,—bewildering Case with his descriptions of the patterns of archangels' dresses.[3] Oh may he have a blessed time! I can read nothing here. Every novel I try, I vomit; in the *locked* study perchance are hidden romances—Amy[4] has now packed away all our books, and is left with *her* text book and consolater the railway time-table.

[bird symbol].

MS Eng. lett. c. 418 fol. 64[r/v] BOD

1. It is hard to date this letter beyond the general observation that KB and EC met Amy Bell while attending Bristol University College about 1880.

2. Amy Bell was an orphan of the Indian Mutiny (1857–58), and one of Bristol University College's first scholarship holders. She became the first female stockbroker, but because she was unable to enter the Stock Exchange, she was required to work through a supportive firm (Carleton, *Univ. for Bristol,* 100–101). EC wrote of Bell, "She has so many race-strains in her, Dutch, Spanish, Anglo-Indian, theatrical, military, etc, etc, etc—that she is difficult to fix as a type" (Add. MS 46782 fol. 83[v] BL). As their reputation declined, the poets came to value Bell for making "the bleakness of life noble and friendship noble" (Add. MS 46789 fol. 156[v] BL).

3. The republished sermons of the Nonconformist Thomas Case (1598–1682) were quite popular. It is not clear whether the patterns of archangels' dresses are being ascribed to Case or to literary fancy. In *Mount Pisgah,* Case enthusiastically describes the angelical robes of the resurrected elect (not the archangel), which "shall more surpass it self in its freshest and liveliest colours" (2:103).

4. Probably Amy Katharine Cooper.

9. Katharine Bradley, Letter to Edith Cooper

[Genoa] | Sat., [21 Aug. 1880][1]

Hôtel Isotta[2] Saturday afternoon.
[from header fol. 22[r]] Excuse this queer note I must write as I can.
Yes, darling, a pale glassy sea, seen through masts and dark foliage from one of the palaces of the Doria! To-morrow we have an invitation, and are going to drive to an Italian Country house on the shores of the Mediterranean to see Miss Scott's friend Mrs. Budd.[3] Those who like will have opportunity of bathing in the historic Sea: I shall gaze and dream. Scott and I hope to go to High Mass at the Cathedral, then to the English service, and in the afternoon to our English hostess.

Your letter P.P. was read in the stately salon of one of the old palaces; for after A wondrous stroll through the alley-like streets of Genoa, amid fruit-stalls, dainty jewellery, high-art hand kerchiefs, and all manner of picturesqueness, I was weary, and rested in the salon of a Monsieur who was not at home when Miss Scott called at his hotel. The marble floor, the lofty decorated ceiling make one realize that one is indeed "en pleine Italie."[4] And I love my Persian's manner of writing; as the thoughts flow, write them down: and A.W.F. will clap his great wings for joy.

I will now tell you about Turin. We went first to the exhibition—but it is not the buildings, nor the big ugly palaces, nor the houses as full of windows as the beasts in Revelation of eyes,[5] and with all the lids closed!! that is of charm[.] Here, it is the women sauntering gracefully along in their black mantillas, fanning themselves contentedly; it is the pretty little schoolchildren in their dainty dress, the peasants in their peach-coloured handkerchiefs: that grand glimpse of the nude—a sailor stript to his waist and washing at the fountain! The Sa[in]ts and human guardians to match that delight my English eyes. At the exhibition it was settled that each man should seek his own and Miss Scott and I took the sculpture, wh. we discovered to be execrable. Contortions of every Kind, and Venuses—I dare not speak of them. The painting was better, much most interesting: some of the black frames suggestive to Scott. Scott and I agreed we would go through the galleries together; and the philanthropic artistic views of Miss Blythe[6] would drive us mad. After the exhibition and dinner we took a drive by the river wh. as you do *not* remember is the Po.

But I hasten to describe the regal appearance of Scott. She has a blue high-art dress with most artistic cape of the same material, her pretty gold brooch, a white lace tie, and a black-bonnet with a yellow rose. Her appearance is magnificent. She tells me she has bought a white cape for me, so I shall shine as an attendant luminary.

Oh Persian I saw such beautiful moody red handkerchiefs this morning, but the woman wanted L7. for one and Miss Scott said it was only worth L2.[7] So I was not allowed to have one. I want one to wrap my old head in and Keep it free of beasts in our night journeyings.

I am writing in a nice quiet cool salle, marble-floored; my two companions the Blythes at my side. Miss Blythe is such a good old lady, and so kind, and thoughtful for all the Rest. Her niece is very good; but Scott is the life of the whole party and by her cheeriness and racey stories revives the drooping spirits of her o'erworn travellers.

Two things I see clearly, my Persian. I can make *no* mental effort in this heat; and think of selling [the] Baretti and all my books.[8] I will try to Keep the journal; but I can *never* write in my bed-room. There my brain is on the simmer. The gloom of the salons so sternly shut from the sunlight oppresses me. The bed-room is insupportable: only in the carefully-shielded and prepared and spacious rooms is the mental life possible.

We went in Paris to Notre Dâme, and the windows are there glowing and glorious—let the Master be flung into the Seine if he dares to doubt it—only not fished up and brought into the Morgue[9]—We went there. Happily we saw nothing, but the dank-looking stretchers, and a few clothes; but we did see the photographs of those lately drowned, and they came to me in the dead watches of that night in the brain, and I cursed them, and myself for having sought them. I thought the morgue would be a place where I could study death in its calmness, forgetful of the *murdered* folk thrown into the river. *Hell* was in their faces—a record of demoniac strife! I tried instead to think of the Venus of Milo—but horror prevailed.

Yet that Venus! Oh, Persian. I never saw her till the other day—the perfect woman—perfect in and of hers[e]lf—with no thought of man, no entreaty for his love; yet with breasts so sweet one longs to drink from them, and all the lovely circles of the girl moon in Pan and Luna.[10] A lovely creature, not Cupid's Mother, not Adonis' bride; "das ewig weibliche" the eternal womanlie act is what she expresses! I am so glad to have seen her, and to descend from her to the Venuses of the Pitti and the Capitol.

I think of writing 3 sonnets one to each Venus. I shall twine your Shelley verses round your flowers and bear them faithfully to the grave.[11] They are [in need of] the slightest bit re-casting—I may add a word or two, and slightly recast: we shall see.

Now farewell, my own Darling; let me think of you as happy. With better and kinder companions the Fowl could not be. And he is going on *very* well. The Scott feeds him on tomatoes, with garlic suggestions and these cure his feverishness and qualms. The fatigue of this week has been fearful; but now I trust pleasure and rest begin. We have had a most safe and good journey hitherto, and are most grateful.

Now Miss Blythe and I are going to the post-office together. Dear love to Papa to whom I fondly hoped to write *[from header fol. 24ʳ]* of his loved Paris. He shall have a letter soon—and Am[y] and Mud.[12] Salutation and Kisses.

thy A.W.F.

MS Eng. lett. c. 418 fols. 22ʳ–25ᵛ BOD

1. Dated from KB's trip to Italy in Aug.–Sept. 1880.

2. The Grand Hôtel Isotta in the via Roma, Genoa. See Baedeker, *Italy*, 76.

3. KB met Jane Scott, "the head of the g[rea]t High Art shop in Old Bond St," at the Baker's home in Bristol (letter to Frances Brooks, MS Eng. lett. d. 405 fol. 56ʳ BOD). They were both involved in Mary Paley Marshall's women's debating society, with Scott debating the "aesthetic school" with EC (fol. 124ʳ). She had a flamboyant nature, and Mrs. Hargreaves reportedly remarked "it was an event in one's life to meet with Miss Scott" (MS Eng. lett. d. 405 fols.

124–25$^{r–v}$). As a result of this friendship, KB was invited to accompany Scott on her tour of Italy. Mrs. Budd may be the wife of William Budd, author of *Cholera and Disinfection: Asiatic Cholera in Bristol in 1866* (1883). The English hostess is untraced.

4. In the heart of Italy (Fr.).

5. Rev. 13:1.

6. Emily Blythe is briefly mentioned in KB's letter to Amy Cooper ([undated], MS Eng. lett. d. 402 fol. 1^{v} BOD).

7. L = lira.

8. Giuseppe Marc' Antonio Baretti (1719–89) was an Italian immigrant and Italian-language teacher. He wrote several books on Italian grammar and culture with prefaces by Samuel Johnson. See Bate, *Samuel Johnson,* 333–34. Whether or not KB was successful in keeping her journal is unknown (untraced).

9. Ruskin believed the modern restoration of Notre Dame had "utterly destroyed" the prominent Parisian landmark (36:291). At the end of the Place behind Notre Dame was the Paris Morgue (Hare, *Paris,* 313). The unidentified bodies displayed behind a glass screen made it cheap, popular entertainment. See, for example, Zola's *Thérèse Raquin* (76). It being high summer, KB is lucky to have experienced the morgue without bodies, as a refrigeration system was not installed until 1881 (*Thérèse Raquin,* 209n).

10. KB compares the Venus to the Girl-moon ravished by Pan in Robert Browning's *Pan and Luna* (44–48; Browning, 15:161), and to Goethe's description of the Virgin as "Woman Eternal" in *Faust* (2:5.12108–11; Goethe, trans. Arndt, 308). KB did not visit the Palazzo Pitti, although she did see the Capitol (letter 15).

11. The three proposed sonnets do not seem to have been written. The ashes of Percy Bysshe Shelley (1792–1822) lie in the New Burial Ground at Testaccio in Rome. See Hare, *WiR,* 2:397.

12. Mud or Muddie is a family name for Emma Harris Cooper née Bradley (1835–89).

10. Katharine Bradley, Letter to Edith Cooper

[Genoa] | Mon., [23 Aug. 1880][1]

Hotel Isotta, *Monday.* Supposed to be written on Sunday

My darling, my Darling, but is it really only one week since we were gathering ferns on the downs together,[2] and now here I am in the grounds of our Italian villa, the Mediterranean *dashing* at my feet—and a bluer and a grayer sea was never seen, the glorious hills cloud-capped as if I were in the Highlands, and around me vineyards olives and figs. The contrast is not so great though at tea-time for our sweet English hostess has prepared for us an English tea, and but for the delicious "pane dolce" (a sweet bread we young ones get to eat when we are faint with hunger) one might almost imagine oneself at the loved Ivythorpe tea-table. The draughts would please Mud; for we linger after tea in a room little better than a veranda and, as the stormy evening breeze comes on I begin to shiver—or to imagine the possibility—of shivering. But I must tell you my whole Sunday. Miss Scott and I went with her friend M^r. Da[w]re[3] and an old Italian artist formerly president of the academy here to the palaces Doria e La Scala (look all this up in Hare)[4] and to the churches of the Oratorio and the Annunciation.

Through influence we saw pictures that the world sees not;—the most glorious Vandykes in the world[5]—such bright human children, with no suspicion of running into cherubs—gentlemen's sons every inch, and bound for a noble life—a little Tobias, moreover (also Vandyke) fretting along with his little fish in the blithest manner, and by Leonardo da Vinci—a fiend—a woman to match the "Mona Lisa" of the Louvre[6] (we have a small photograph of this in the album) with velvet eyes and face and vitriol underneath,—oh beautiful exceedingly to see caged;—but you never can cage that spirit! The voice will never be much about a whisper; but the whole creature is venomous, her sweetness is deadly, and her kindness doom.

But here is another Vandyke a lady in all magnificence of attire, serenity and simplicity of spirit, freshness of heart and grace of form,—a perfect lady such as I have never beheld. With hands that are incarnate courtesy—and here is a mother—her little ones are brought to her for a moment;—they are quite at their ease, and perfectly unconscious and graceful; but the distance between them and their mother is immeasureable—reverence will never be taught to them, but experienced by them; they are in the courts of heaven—and that Knowledge gives a wonderful sense of behaviour. Then think of the old Fowl, very fine with his fan and his lace scarf, and his gloveless hands (no more gloves in Italy) leaning over a marble balcony and looking down on a street (Strata Nuova) consisting of nothing but palaces, with beautiful marble-entrances, and deliciously cool courtyards. The outer walls are in soft tints; the sculptures of the entrances fine, the reception rooms *superb.*

Go on writing to Florence.

God bless you all. In truest love to you each one.

Katie

MS Eng. lett. c. 418 fols. 26^r–27^v BOD

1. EC dated this letter 7 Jul., but this cannot be correct, as that was a Wednesday. The Jul. date also seems early: the first reliable PM for this trip is from Florence some seven weeks later, yet it seems unlikely KB lingered in Genoa that long. As the letter concludes by requesting EC write to Florence, the most probable date is 23 Aug. 1880.

2. For Victorian fern collecting, see letter 52 n. 10. EC and her father also collect ferns in letter 56.

3. Untraced.

4. In her travels through Italy, KB relied on the guidebooks of A. J. C. Hare, who often supplemented his tourist information with literary quotations. For instance, in *N&CI,* Hare illustrated his description of the palaces with an excerpt from Dickens's *Pictures from Italy* (*N&CI,* 1:44).

5. Sir Anthony Van Dyck (1599–1641) lived in Genoa between 1624 and 1627. During this time he painted several portraits of prominent Genovese and their children, which are now held in the Palazzo Durazzo-Pallavicini (Brown, *Van Dyck,* 85–95). The "Tobias" is *Tobia di Gian Andrea Pallavicino* (ca. 1625–27) (Barnes et al., *Van Dyck A Genova,* 264). Later in this letter, KB refers to the portrait of a magnificient lady (untraced), and to a mother with her little ones which is *The Marchesa Battina Balbi Durazzo Invrea with Her Sons Marcello and Silvestro (La Dama d'Oro)* (Barnes et al., *Van Dyck A Genova,* 70).

6. Baedeker's *Italy: A Handbook for Travellers* (1886) notes there is a "good portrait of the Lombard school attributed to Leonardo da Vinci" in the Palazzo Reale (88). KB's attitude to the *Mona Lisa* is influenced by Walter Pater's famous description of her as cruel and vampiric (*Renaissance,* 125). Compare with Michael Field's "La Gioconda" (*S&S,* 8).

11. Edith Cooper, Letter to Katharine Bradley

[Ivythorpe] | Tues., [24 Aug. 1880][1]

Tuesday.
Carissima mia,
I have been thoughtless for two days. Sunday is a mental as well as physical Sabbath—the very Lethe of Thought; and yesterday I had a violent headache; and you know that headache is a despot crushing every other power that it may reign supreme. But all the time I have constantly thought of you, watched you from my common-place bit of England—you who are miles upon miles away from my love in blue Italy—with the golden exclusiveness of the sunflower for her distant sun. It is such a pleasure to me to do any thing for you—Even to dust your mantel-board. I have just been arranging your books—a service wh. ought to inspire much reverence.—Thus to put in their places the gt. thoughts of gt. men within that universal skull—a book-case—that Pantheon of brains. May we in bound sisterhood find an honourable niche in these best—"Aux grands hommes"!!

How your letter has enriched me—given me sight of heaps of sun-dyed melons and gourds,—and sun-bronzed women, and palaces, cold as the flesh of Venuses who still live in a world that gazes at them and worships not! Your letter has made me very happy. The thought of consacrating a sonnet to Each fair manifestation of Venus delights me.[2] If you have bent before the "Eternal Womanhood" at the Louvre, this morning you will Kiss the perfect woman at Lucca, and thank God for having sent her on Earth and Jacopo della Quercia for having Kept her there.[3] I have sent a pilgrim-Kiss; may it reach you in time to be pressed by your lips on her shrine!

Yesterday we had a lecture[4]—not on the skin—but on Killomètres etc. wh. was as bad as the *tortura capilliarum* to my brains. I do not know what I should have done if Girdlestone[5] had not *presented* me with a paper of mètres etc. How funny it is that some people always *present,* never *give*! There is something of the same relation between a present and a gift as between affection and love, or produce and fruitage. A present has a stiff Kindness about it—a gift a rich abandon. A present has a sufficiency about it—a gift a super-abundance! I could never really love anyone who never *gave* me anything! Now I must practice!!

Tuesday morning again.
Oh Sim! I do not believe anyone without a pure deep heart could play Beethoven. The fingers of Saints alone could do him justice!

I have just seen a portrait of Cousin Harriet.[6] I could no longer breathe the name of Ilaria with a thought of her. Worldliness has choked the spirituallity of her face as soil the lovely curves and inlets of ancient statues. Her face is now coarse and blank—the Earth has eaten too deeply into it for any hope of restoration. Now, between us, is not a visitor like that one stamen-grown petal wh. ruins the completeness of a wild-rose?—An anomoly in the midst of the sweet normal life of home? I find it so. A guest offends my sense of proportion and perfection! How the world would execrate me if it knew my real feeling, and very righteously . . [.]

Some people do not seem to have any idea that there is an inside to anything—book, bud, human being. Their eyes are mere outsiders to any thing but the seen. This makes me Sigh in the presence of Cousin Jane. Unless you believe in an oracle, it is speechless; if you hope nothing from a human being the spirit is closed against you. So I close.

Tuesday afternoon.
Ah, I am tired! I am going to spend a little time with my *Attic Philosopher* and, I expect, quarrel with him about fame.[7]

Buon notte, my Own!!

MS Eng. lett. c. 419 fols. 8^r–9^v BOD

1. Dated from KB's trip to Italy in Aug.–Sept. 1880.

2. For sonnets to Venus, see letter 9.

3. For KB's description of the Venus de Milo as Goethe's Eternal Woman, see letter 9 n. 10. The perfect woman is the figure of Ilaria del Carretto on her tomb in Lucca Cathedral of San Martino, which was sculpted by Jacopo della Quercia (ca. 1367–1438) in 1405. KB and EC's interest stems from Ruskin's admiration of the tomb in *Modern Painters II* (4:122–23) and *Three Colours of Pre-Raphaelitism* (34:171–72).

4. EC, KB, and Amy Cooper attended the new Bristol University College in the early 1880s. It was the first higher education institution to admit women students on an equal basis with men. The college was small—two Georgian houses in Park Row, with only five lecturers and two professors; the students were tradesmen and the daughters of the town's elite. See Carleton, *Univ. for Bristol,* 100–102. "Tortura capilliarum": the twisting of the hairs (It.).

5. Reverend Robert Baker Girdlestone (1836–1923) was the Honourable Canon of Christ Church, Oxford; principal of Wycliffe Hall, Oxford; superintendent of the Translation Department of the Bible Society, 1866–76; and the author of various theological texts and pamphlets on social questions (*Who's Who*). Girdlestone was also a family friend (MS Eng. lett. d. 405 fol. 42^r BOD) who sent a copy of *Bell.* to Frederic Harrison (Add. MS 45851 fol. 59^r–60^r BL), and asked John Addington Symonds to review it (he declined). See Symonds, *Letters,* 2:675.

6. Harriet Spooner of Hertford Cottage Liphook was a relation on the Cooper side. Later in this letter, Cousin Jane may be the daughter of Jane Cooper, James's sister. See Treby, *Binary Star,* 16.

7. *An Attic Philosopher in Paris* (1853) by Emile Souvestre is a series of philosophical anecdotes written in diary form. The narrator resides in a Parisian attic and performs charitable acts for his neighbors. He is rewarded when he falls ill and those he has aided care for him. On fame, the philosopher recounts Jean-Jacques Rousseau's advice that celebrity is a misfortune because it renders one "common property" (Souvestre, *Attic Philosopher,* 112).

12. Katharine Bradley, Postcard to Edith Cooper

Florence | Thurs., [PM 26 Aug. 1880[1]]

We had a beautiful drive round the many parts of Lucca. Another p.c. to the Persian Puss.[2]

Firenze, Thursday.

I bear on my lips the marble of Ilaria's brow![3] I walked straight to the left transept, and saw her, and by and bye they *all* left me, and I kissed her on the calm forehead, the tremulously sweet lips, the sweet round chin. And I saw the breast "heaving like a low wave of the sea," the softly-folded hands; and it seemed as if I were again at Ivythorpe, looking above the Master's head.[4] I will tell you all about Pisa in a big letter. You will see the pulpit in Val d'arno. The Custode said the Master used to write there "like St. Augustine"!! Many thanks for letters.

Katie.

MS Eng. lett. c. 418 fol. 18r BOD

1. Dated from KB's trip to Italy in Aug.–Sept. 1880.

2. This suggests other untraced postcards were sent.

3. The tomb of Ilaria del Carretto. See also letter 11 n. 3. Later, KB quotes Ruskin's description of the tomb: "As a soft, low wave of summer sea, her breast rises; no more: the rippled gathering of its close mantle droops to the belt, then sweeps to her feet, straight as drifting snow" (Ruskin, 34:171).

4. Between 1879 and 1884, Ivythorpe was the Cooper family home in Stoke Bishop, an outer suburb of Bristol composed of large merchants' houses. See Jetzer et al., *Pictorial History.*

5. Ruskin (the Master) included a picture of Niccolò Pisano's pulpit in the Cathedral at Pisa in *Val D'Arno* (23: plate 22).

13. Katharine Bradley, Letter to Edith Cooper

[Florence] | Thurs., [26 Aug., 1880][1]

Thursday night.

Well, my Pretty, it is very sad, is it not? But perhaps you will be better without a cameo, and the Roman aprons are very cheap![2] So we won't fret about that. I am writing quite alone (Florence is empty)[3] in a little yellow salon, with yellow walls and I have just ordered a "limonadé pour une," so I hope I may have strength for a little talk before bed-time. I want to tell you all about that wonderful day at Pisa. There was first the walk through the covered arcades, then a swift passage through the fruit market, the blind having their poor sightless orbs held out as wares in a way that w^d. have made the Pretty shudder, and then we came upon one of the most wonderful groups of buildings in the world—the cathedral, with its magnificent bronze doors, and Galilean lamp, the Campo Sancto with its exquisite windows and frescoes by Orcagna of the last judgment etc. The Baptistery with the pulpit of Nicholas Pisano, and the leaning tower. That day we really experienced the strength of Italian sunshine: we had to *run* from one church to another, and I was concerned about our good custode's bare head. Refreshed by some wine, we went on soon after one to Lucca, and there was Ilaria, and a lovely Fra Bartolemmeo[4]—a sweet little angel harping to himself under the virgin's feet. The facade of Lucca cathedral is exquisite. Several of the pillars are in "Stones."[5] Then we had a delightful drive round the ramparts; and came on in the evening to Firenze.

I do not think I shall ever love Florence—the streets are much like Paris, only, I think, *not* so picturesque, the arno is a dark brown, not nearly so nice as the Seine, and the outside of the churches are—an acquired taste like olives.

Yesterday I had my first glimpse of the Uffizzi; and I saw, yes, dear Persian, with my own eyes the Venus de Medici.[6] Scott says the Venus de Medici courts, the Venus of the Capitol tolerates, and the Venus of Milo disdains the love of man, wh. I think well expressed. The attitude is entirely self-conscious. I cared far more for a pictured Venus by Titiano,—a woman who looked like a ripe peach in the sun, and I saw too the Fornarina, and Titian's "Flora," and the famous Leonardo da Vinci head of Medusa, of which I will get a copy to show you, when you are naughty!!

Afterwards we drove round Florence, and *then* all its beauty revealed itself. It lies in the lap of the loveliest hills—far off on a mount Fiesole!![7]

Now I am going to write to the little Cat,[8] and must have a bit of talk to Mud, so farewell my darling.

Ever your own all wise Fowl.

Kiss me yet again: and good night, my Child Good night!

MS Eng. lett. c. 418 fols. 28^{r}–29^{v} BOD

1. Dated from KB's trip to Italy in Aug.–Sept. 1880.

2. EC was not destined to get an apron as a souvenir of Rome. KB wrote to Amy Cooper, "I have seen the Roman Aprons, but they are not *applicable*. They are of coarse woollen hardstuff, with rather hard, bright embroidery." KB, letter to Amy Cooper, [Sept. 1880], MS Eng. lett. d. 402 fol. 1^{r} BOD.

3. The English in Florence moved to the mountains or the seaside for several months each year to escape the summer heat.

4. Fra Bartolommeo's *Madonna with Saints Stephen and John Baptist* hangs in the second chapel of Lucca cathedral, near the tomb of Ilaria del Carretto. Hare notes "the angel at the foot of the throne is quite exquisitely beautiful" (*N&CI*, 2:496).

5. Ruskin included a sketch of the pillars of the Lucca Cathedral in *The Stones of Venice* (9: plate 12).

6. KB and Scott may be influenced by Nathaniel Hawthorne's description of the Venus de Medici: "Her modest attitude is partly what unmakes her as the heathen goddess, and softens her into woman" (also qtd. in Hare, *N&CI*, 3:22). KB prefers Titian's *Venus of Urbino* (1538) and *Flora* (1515–17). While paintings of Venus form the basis of several poems in Michael Field's ekphrastic *Sight and Song* (1892), none seem to have originated from this trip. KB also mentions a portrait of Raphael's mistress, La Fornarina, which may be Raphael's *Lady with a Veil* or a portrait of a dark-

haired young woman (ca. 1518–19) (now attributed to Sebastiano del Piombo). See Rossi, *Uffizi & Pitti,* 192; and Scala Group, *Protagonists of It. Art,* 398. While both of the paintings are in the Uffizi, it seems likely, given KB's other preferences, that del Piombo's more erotic portrait caught her eye. Hare attributed the Uffizi's *Head of Medusa* to Leonardo da Vinci (*N&CI,* 3:25) but it is now believed to be by Carravagio, ca. 1592–1600 (Fossi, *Uffizi,* 145).

7. The direction of their trip was possibly motivated by the fact that Fiesole was the home of Walter Savage Landor.

8. Both the Cooper girls, Edith and Amy, were given a range of affectionate feline nicknames. "Little Cat" refers to Amy Cooper, and the letter is MS Eng. lett. c. 419 fols. 4[r]–5[v] BOD.

14. Katharine Bradley, Postcard to Edith Cooper

Rome | [Sat., PM 4 Sept. 1880]

First impressions of Rome.

Oh Rome, Rome, thou Mighty Race-Mother, Eve of our modern humanity, owner of all forms of life and thought precious to us, let me not see thee, thou hoary ancestress, in Parisian dress, with painted face, false hair, and eyes restless with the fluttering glances of a coquette. Let me touch thy white hair, centuries have blanched it, let me look into thy deep mystic eyes, dark with ruined hope, dim with the tears of ages, wistful with multitudinous and mingled memories, sad with sybillic solitariness. Let me touch thy wrinkled forehead—its furrows are its majesty—, let me kiss the faint flush on thy cheek, that tells me thou art not a corpse, that in thy veins still pulsate the glorious tides of thy youth. Take me to the Forum,[1] to the Capitol, to the Tiber, unclothe thyself before me, am I not thy child? Tell me thy years that I may honour thee;—hide not thy decrepitude, it will but bow me into lowlier worship.

[bird symbol]

MS Eng. lett. c. 418 fol. 19[r] BOD

1. The Roman Forum was being excavated in the 1880s. See Hare, *WiR,* 1:168–69.

15. Katharine Bradley, Letter to Edith Cooper

[Rome] | [Tues., 7 Sept. 1880][1]

Hush, Persian Puss, I have seen her—the Beatrice.[2] What is most wonderful is the paleness—for the rich Italian beauty would have been as bright as the Fornarina's[3] (next her) but for the unspeakable sorrow that has blanched the face. The few strayed locks of hair are bright chesnut, the eyes wistful and eloquent, but the trembling agony of the parted lips can be seen alone before the picture. I have never seen a mouth so tremulous—it made me think of my Pretty Persian—and the spirit convulsions to wh. her lips are subject. A *hideous* copy was near, from wh. we tried to hide ourselves. Have joy in our photograph: it is marvellously faithful. Add the blanched look from torture and tears, and all a baulked Soul in its enforced dumbness, and pain past expression at the doors of the lips, and you will have the Beatrice.

The Venus of the Capitol is a perfect woman. Most happily her garments are beside her, not on her, and the lovely form from throat to foot is unmutilated and unshrouded, the dimpled back—the real beauty of the waist is only seen in the back—made me long again and again for the attendant Scott or Blythe to turn the statue for me; and all the circling beauty of the loins Kept me in lingering adoration; but for the bosom heave Milo's Venus is to me unrivalled. The face is innocent and fair, not majestic. I went in the full blaze of noon to the Tarpeian rock!! So believe that the spirit of Rome is on me. Take an ivy-leaf from its traditional summit. My pretty pretty Persian—I saw a bust of Julian the Apostate:[4] Capital beard. His hair was Knotted under his chin and he looked very—comical *[from header fol. 30ʳ]*—did Julian the Apostate. Your own Marcus,[5] My Love, I will try to get for you!

Ever the fond old-Fowl Katie.

MS Eng. lett. c. 418 fol. 30ʳ/ᵛ BOD

1. KB's diary suggests the date is Tues., 7 Sept. 1880. See diary 16.

2. In the nineteenth century, the sensationalized story of Beatrice Cenci's rape by her monstrous father, his arranged murder, and her subsequent execution in 1599, was very popular. A portrait in the Palazzo Barberini, attributed to Guido Reni, was widely believed to be Beatrice and this association made the portrait "one of the most famous attractions of Rome" (Curran, *Shelley's Cenci,* xi). See also Baedecker, *Central Italy and Rome,* 266; Hare, *WiR,* 13th ed., 256–57. Descriptions of the portrait also appear in Percy Bysshe Shelley's preface to his play *The Cenci* (2:73)—which KB reviewed (unpub.; MS Eng. misc. 339 fol. 15ʳ⁻ᵛ BOD)—and in Nathaniel Hawthorne's *Transformation* (48). Recent scholarship suggests the portrait may be by Elisabetta Sirani, and that the subject is unlikely to be Beatrice Cenci (Pepper, *Guido Reni,* 304).

3. Raphael's *Fornarina* (with the painter's name on the armlet) in the Palazzo Barberini. See Hare, *WiR,* 1:439.

4. Julian the Apostate or Flavius Claudius Julianus (331–63), the Roman emperor who failed to reinstate paganism, was identified by EC as one of her "heroes of real life" in 1877 (MS

Eng. misc. c. 303 fol. 6r BOD). The bust is probably that in the Capitoline Museum's Hall of the Emperors, not far from the Capitoline Venus. See Hare, *WiR,* 1:126.

5. Marcus Aelius Aurelius Antoninus (121–180 AD), Roman emperor and philosopher, was also one of EC's "heroes of real life" (MS Eng. misc. c. 303 fol. 6r BOD). The museum's Hall of the Emperors featured two busts of M. Aurelius (Hare, *WiR,* 1:128), but KB is probably promising a copy of the famous statue of the emperor on horseback in the Capitoline Square. EC acknowledges receipt of the gift in letter 26.

16. Note in the hand of Katharine Bradley

[Rome] | [Tues., 7 Sept. 1880][1]

Diary

Arrived in Rome on Friday night.

Saturday morning. Sought fresh quarters, Settled in the Via Sistina.[2] Saturday afternoon went to St. Peter's.

Sunday Church of Gesu in the morning, heard the nuns of the Trinita[3] sing in the afternoon.

Monday morning, much [time] wasted in [looking for] Roman aprons, *fruitless journeys* to the post! etc. Visited however the Corsini gallery,[4] and saw all the great Ecce Homos, especially Guido's and in the afternoon, went to the Colisseum.

Tuesday. Went to the Barberini Palace (for Beatrice) afterwards to Castellani's[5] for the fine Jewel-work (none bought) and then oh joy to the Capitol, the Venus, and the Tarpeian rock. Oh joy thrice joy, and to be remembered ever.

MS Eng. lett. c. 418 fol. 39r/v BOD

1. The PM on postcard 14 indicates KB arrived in Rome on Fri., 3 Sept. 1880, which suggests that this note, probably written on Tues., can be dated to 7 Sept.

2. They stayed in a pensione in the Via Scala above the Spanish steps. See KB, letter to John Miller Gray, 21 Feb. 1887, Add. MS 45853 fol. 134r BL. Hare notes that this was the area preferred by the English (*WiR,* 1:27).

3. The Church of the Trinita dei Monti (1495) is very near the Spanish steps where they were staying. Hare notes the nuns from the adjoining Convent of the Sacred Heart were all women of rank, and were sought out as curiosities (*WiR,* 1:52–53).

4. The Palazzo Corsini's collection included the *Ecce Homos* of Guido Reni, Guercino, and Carlo Dolce (Hare, *WiR,* 2:733–34).

5. "Castellani's imitative craft" (1.3) is celebrated in the opening lines of Robert Browning's *The Ring and the Book* (Browning, 7:7). The Castellani family jewelers at 88 Via Poli were

famous, not only for their Italian archaeological jewelry, which imitated jewelry found in excavations, or for their prestigious clientele that included Nathaniel Hawthorne and the Brownings, but also for being the shop where the eponymous ring was purchased (Simpson, "Perfect Imitation," 203–4). If the jewelry was too expensive for KB in 1881, the poets would later own several pieces of custom-made jewelry designed by Charles Ricketts and made in London by Castellani's apprentice, Carlo Giuliano (Munn, *Castellani and Guiliano,* 47, 67–69).

17. Katharine Bradley, Letter to Edith Cooper

Rome | Wed., [8 Sept. 1880][1]

Rome: Wednesday morning.
[From header fol. 36^r] It is a "festa" so the Vatican is closed, moreover it is a fearfully hot day, and rest is decreed till after luncheon, when we hope to *drive to the palace of the Caesars.*[2]
My own Darling Love,

It would have made your heart ache to be in the Pantheon[3] yesterday and see the empty niches, where Athene, and all the glorious ring of Zeus once stood. If there is such a thing as dry weeping, I experienced it then. Yet they would not have liked to be there at Vespers, Aphrodite and the rest! Never have I felt the strong antagonism of the pagan and the Christian faiths so strangely. Instead of the pictured dome of St. Peter's, piled with saints, dark with judgment, or bright with victory over death, there was the plain blue sky, so dear to the happy ones of old, and the grand cupola brown and bare. Write a sonnet about it.[4] If my brain were not in *seethe* I would. Priests were chaunting and visiting the varied shrines—bearing incense to the virgin Mother—bring back Athene to her niche, and express her marvel at that, her wonder at the Crucifix, before which men are Kneeling, and at the long sepulchral wail, chastened and penitential, not frenzied, or rejoicing that ascends to heaven. Where are the filleted victims, and where the fair crowned youths? Is that dark figure on the Cross, a great Prometheus, who suffering brought good to men, while we, the great gods, lazy in the sunshine of Olympus, mingling lightly with the joys and woes of mortals, helping and strengthening them indeed, but never spilling one nectarous drop in their behalf,—our ivory limbs unscathed unworn, our brows as peaceful as the Temple Vale,[5] have lost our hold on man. My own Achilles I was strong to shelter, but would I have bowed my helmed head in the dust for him? Yet this I see: when the gods were happy, men were glad; now the Great Day stoops/bows sorrowful, and men lie sunk in shroud.

There, Persian, are the blocks: chip! Miss Blythe has in her bag the sacred flowers, that they may always be ready; and I am hoping soon to lay them where our loved ones lies.[6]

About nine, Persian, you may often feel the Fowl, passing swift into your room, so mind you always go to bed in *good* time, not to miss him: he folds both his babes in warm soft arms, he covers them with kisses, prays over them, and departs. We go to bed at nine, or before, and breakfast at eight. It is still uncertain when we leave. Miss Blythe, rightly I think, refuses to travel on Sunday; but we must at latest leave on Saturday, so post your next Sunday letter to Venice (post *on Sunday*) and then risk a post-card to Verona. I think Scott and I will very likely spend a quiet week in Venice after the rest are gone, and then home rather quickly by the Tyrol and Rhine. No hope of ober-amagau;[7] but I do not greatly lament. I begin to feel I have seen as much as I can bear. I am still very well, I can gratefully record.

Farewell *[from header fol. 36^r]* my pretty.

Ever thy own

[bird symbol]

MS Eng. lett. c. 418 fols. 36^r–37^v BOD

1. Dated from KB's trip to Italy in Aug.–Sept. 1880.

2. The Jewish quarter of Rome, also known as the Ghetto. Hare notes "everything may be obtained in the Ghetto: precious stones, lace, furniture of all kinds, rich embroidery from Algiers and Constantinople, striped silks from Spain—but all is concealed under cover" (*WiR,* 1:256).

3. Hare, like KB, dwells on the contrast between the pagan and Christian (*WiR,* 2:204–6).

4. See "The Pantheon at Vespers," letter 26.

5. The Temple Vale, or Tempe, is a valley in Thessaly near Mt. Olympus said to be so beautiful that the gods often lingered there; the poets described it as the most delightful place on Earth. See Lemprière, *Lemprière's Class. Dict.,* 613.

6. For Miss Blythe, see letter 9.

7. By 1880 the introduction of a railway line had made access to Oberammergau much easier, and the passion play was becoming well known all over Europe. See Heaton, *Oberammergau Passion Play,* 35–46.

18. Katharine Bradley, Letter to Edith Cooper

Rome | Thurs., [9 Sept. 1880][1]

Rome, Thursday afternoon.

Yes, it began with the roof, my dear little Pussie, as the post-card[2] has told you, it began with the roof, and immediately after breakfast we started for the Vatican. There we saw the great chambers of Raphael,[3] and the Transfiguration wh.—tho' very fine in colour, is all full dress and "niente." There is a picture tho' by Domenichino of great significance.[4] It is the last sacrament of St. Jerome, the old desert saint is brought in dying, by the hands of faithful followers to receive his last sacrament. He is wasted in body, dimmed, and filming in soul, the scar of death upon him. The dear old lion looks reflective. Matters too high for him are going on. But he will be guardian still, has not all been well with his Master, since his strange docility of happy discipleship began. A great church official (perhaps Pope: read Jameson, I do not remember)[5] is about to present the wafer to the dying saint, by him stands an acolyte. A fair healthful youth with lovely chesnut hair. He stands spellbound. He has never seen death before. His thought is not of the sacrament of the awaiting angels, but of this strange thing that is happening before his face. His young soul is hushed and awful; he is not terrified, the colour is bright on his cheek: he is simply feeling how difficult it is to realize in the glow of fresh life this strange transfiguration.

Of the other pictures I cared for none save the angel delivering St. Peter from prison by Raphael. The drowsiness of the guards shows that a supernatural power has drugged them; they are sunk in heavy sleep. St. Peter, just touched by the angel looks, like Mud, as if he could not trouble to be stirred, still he is obedient to the summons. In another part of the picture he is descending, wide awake, and radiant, the prison steps, with his celestial escort.

To our dismay, after a fierce walk in the sunlight, to reach the sculpture we found the gallery was closed, but Miss Blythe's Italian got us in, and we ran madly to the Belvedere. But here I am on Persian's *ground,* and the pretty Creature will p[o]ut; if I don't tell her about her dear *Copy,*[6]—for they say he is not original; so my sweet little Pick, I will let you into the secrets of the "Festa" this afternoon. Now, whenever we have lemonade (we make it to refresh ourselves with our own lemons and sugar) we meet in one of the bedrooms and call it having a festa. There are one or two curious details about these festa that may interest you. Spoons are *much* wanted for stirring. Miss Scott I think suggested hair-pins wiped, (!!!) but my gorge rose at this; ultimately we got something ivory; but yesterday evening there was another thrilling incident—Miss Blythe found a flea in or about the lemonade!!! This afternoon however a negress lady-doctor,[7] a friend of Miss Scott's who has made the fatal mistake of marrying an Italian, and is now settled in Rome, with an unprospering practice, is coming to take afternoon tea with us at four! Fancy afternoon tea in Italy!! I am in high glee at the thought, but as I do not care for too much of the foreign lady's society, I am glad that at five Miss Blythe proposes to take us a drive to the baths of Caracalla and the appian way! This is a "festa" she herself is going to give us, in celebration of a double wedding among some young friends of hers in Scotland. It was suggested that the appian way was rather a gloomy course to choose in commemoration of a bridal; but I suggested that slight change w$^{d.}$ convert it into the "appy," or as I w$^{d.}$ now put it the appia way: and then, you see, all is felicitous![8]

Our plans are formed for Venice now. All being well, we leave Rome about nine on Saturday morning,[9] hoping to reach Venice, *early* on Sunday morning. I called Miss Blythe aside this morning, and explained that if I were Kept a day and night without proper food, I should assuredly be ill, so that dear old character is going to engage Sked[10] to give us a chicken and a bottle of wine. Still I shall be thankful to see the Adriatic. We make no pause by the way.

To-night the waiter, who is skilled in the guitar is going to play to us—so the day that began with the Vatican, will end in Vanity.

Give my *best* love to dear M$^{rs.}$ Baker.[11] Is it not time that her little Phillis came. The Roman rattle is not yet bought, and I want to get something pretty for Frieda.[12] Our shopping is always being deferred. Nothing is so intolerable in the glare of sunlight; and at night we are too tired for anything, except, when we are *Very* enthusiastic the roof! But in Venice I do trust I may get something nice for my loved ones. My dearest love to Frieda. I have written one post-card to her.[13] Farewell, my darling, I shall expect many sheets for this

Ever Your *[bird symbol].*

MS Eng. lett. c. 418 fols. 31^{r}–33^{v} BOD

1. Dated from KB's trip to Italy in Aug.–Sept. 1880.

2. Untraced.

3. The Stanze della Segnatura and di Elidoro. KB's dismissal of Raphael's *Transfiguration* probably relates to the popular theory, disproved during restoration work in 1977, that pupils completed the work after Raphael's sudden death in 1520 (Scala Group, *Protagonists of It. Art,*

399). "Neinte" is nothing (It.). KB is unimpressed by some of Raphael's most famous frescoes including his *School of Athens. The Liberation of St. Peter,* mentioned later in the letter, is the last fresco attributed to Raphael, although it is believed that Giulio Romano contributed greatly (Scala Group, *Protagonists of It. Art,* 368–72).

4. Domenico Zampieri (1581–1641), *The Last Communion of St. Jerome.* St. Jerome spent four years in the desert in penitence and seclusion; his life is considered a symbol for Christian self-abasement. Michael Field included a poem on St. Jerome, based on the painting by Cosima Tura, in *S&S* (53–57).

5. Mrs. Jameson does not elucidate on the figure giving the sacrament; KB may be thinking of her reference to St. Paul who "kneeling, kisses one of [St. Jerome's] thin bony hands; the saint fixes his eager eyes on the countenance of the priest, who is about to administer the sacrament,—a noble dignified figure in a rich ecclesiastical dress;" (Jameson, *S&L Art,* 1:298). Both Jameson and KB focus their descriptions on marginal figures: Jameson on the small figure of St. Paul, KB on the acolyte; rather than on the central gold-draped figure giving the sacrament.

6. The Apollo Belvedere (ca. 130 AD) is a famous Roman copy of a Greek bronze (Daltrop, "Museo Pio-Clemente," 186).

7. Untraced.

8. The "appia way" is a pun on "happier way." The Appian Way would be gloomy for a bridal celebration, because it is lined by tombstones.

9. Sat., 11 Sept. 1880.

10. Miss Skedd was the proprietress of a pensione in the Via Scala above the Spanish steps in Rome. KB later recommended her to a friend. See Add. MS 45853 fol. 134[r] BL.

11. Hannah Baker née Hiatt (1832–99), wife of William Mills Baker. EC wrote of the Bakers, "I think we have found real friends in a delightful Church family—near neighbours, who live in a most *High Art* house, and are most refined and kindly people" (MS Eng. lett. d. 405 fol. 55[v]–56[v] BOD). Mrs. Baker seems to have been a trial. Amy wrote to EC, "Her suave manner is sometimes too much, a poly podium cannot grow in the hedge without being called 'little polypodies.' Turning to 'Mills' the other day she said 'I should never have loved you, if I had not been fond of a little bit of grit'" (MS Eng. lett. d. 402 fol. 7[r] BOD). Phillis is untraced.

12. Anna Friederika (Frieda) Girdlestone née Thoma (1839–?) was the wife of Edward Deacon Girdlestone, brother of Robert Baker Girdlestone. (See Genopro, http://familytrees.genopro.com/IainTait/Beath%20and%20Tait%20families/default.htm, accessed 9 Apr. 2007). She was a close friend of EC, who composed an acrostic for her birthday (MS Eng. lett. d. 405 fol. 64[r] BOD). The friendship cooled after James Cooper disappeared while walking in Switzerland in 1897; Frieda sent a letter warning that she had been told, through spirit writing, that he was murdered by George Globiatel (he died in a fall). See Add. MS 46788 fol. 117[v] BL.

13. Frieda's postcard is untraced.

19. Katharine Bradley, Letter to Edith Cooper

[Rome] | [Thurs., 9 Sept. 1880][1]

My dear Persian,

I have seen the fair Greek Lips with wh. you have been dowered, and the Laöcoon of course but it is Antinous to which I turn, to wh I prayed to be taken again, after the hurrying attendant led us away. I think, P.P. that the Antinous we worshipped in "art's early days"[2] at the Bath Museum[3] is a copy of the Antinous of the Capitol, the statue to which one turns gratefully from the Faun of Praxiteles—the dignity of quiet restrained manhood is such a fine rebuke to its rank sensuousness. There is all the difference between a palm-tree and a luxuriant weed. But this—the Antinous of the Vatican perhaps "the most perfect statue of the world" Hare says,[4] is even nobler than our first deity. (as compared with the Venus of the Capitol)

—"And now see
How beauty is excelled by manly grace
And wisdom that alone is truly fair."[5]

So beautiful the mouth of that bent face, small, curved, and sweet, the whole spirit and body in perfect subgection to Heavenly Law—as you read of it in Plato.[6] "For we also are His offspring."[7] Oh, and in those early days so like!! I must get a bronze of him, or a cast, and if the Master does not repent soon,[8] we will have our young Greek hero instead!!(?) Persian Puss, I must tell you about the Sistine another time.

Kind Miss Blythe has just offered to go with me—oh well, it is secret the Transformation business!!![9]

We, Miss Emily Blythe, and myself are much suffering from creatures that are running races on our arms and legs![10] That makes me think of my dear little dog of whom you never speak!! There is a cur here named. "*Arno*" Tell Puno that in a picture by Raphael of "The Last Supper," there was a cat and dog.[11]

Ever the own fond Fowl. *[bird symbol].*

Oh my Persian. Loves, and loves. I came to you at nine on swift wings, to you both!

MS Eng. lett. c. 418 fol. 38[r/v] BOD

1. Dated from KB's trip to Italy in Aug.–Sept. 1880.
2. From Thomas Hood's "The Progress of Art": "O happy time!— Art's early days! / When o'er each deed, with sweet self-praise, / Narcissus-like I hung!" (1–3; *Poetical Works,* 371).

3. As Bath Museum did not exist at this time, KB probably means the Bath Literary Institution at which many Roman artefacts unearthed with the remains of the bath complex were displayed (Borsay, *Georgian Bath*).

4. Hare, *WiR,* 2:308.

5. Eve's address to Adam in *Paradise Lost* (4.487–91; Milton, 2.1:123–24).

6. KB's understanding of Plato is influenced by Victorian Neoplatonism. The Neoplatonists saw a path for the soul to ascend toward a higher plane in the relationship between ideal Forms and their imitations in everyday life. Thus, there is a direct relationship between the appreciation of beautiful bodies and the pure vision of the Form of Beauty itself (Sheppard, *Platonism,* 10). Walter Pater appropriated Plato as a patron saint of aestheticism for his anticipation of "the modern notion that art as such has no end but its own perfection—'art for art's sake.'" See Pater, *Plato and Platonism,* 126.

7. Acts 17:28.

8. Ruskin did not repent; see letter 6 n. 6.

9. Nathaniel Hawthorne, *The Marble Faun,* published in England as *Transformation* (1860). The work was extensively used as a pseudo-guide by travelers to Rome who collected photographs (or bought packets assembled by dealers) of the works mentioned in it. See Simpson, introduction, xxxn.

10. Probably more fleas. See letter 18.

11. Tintoretto's *The Last Supper* (1592) in the S. Giorgio Maggiore in Venice displays a cat and a dog in the foreground (Hartt, *Hist. of It. Ren. Art,* 559). Puno is Punicus Niger, the family dog (MS Eng. misc. c. 303 fol. 3r BOD).

20. Katharine Bradley, Letter to Edith Cooper

Rome | Fri., [10 Sept. 1880][1]

Rome, Friday morn, before early breakfast.

My lips are now richer with the touch of the marble from Shelley's tomb! We came suddenly across the English cemetery, and of course left our carriage at once. The burial ground is full of tall cypress-trees that keep eternal incense above the dead. The fragrant air is most soothing, the place very lovely, more solemn than an English Churchyard and more sweet. The setting sun just caught the tall cypress tops. Then we came to the flat marble slab "Concordium"[2] and kneeling down I Kissed at "rich" the words from Ariel's song, how fitting for our spirit-poet.

"Nothing of him but doth change
Into something rich and strange."[3]

That is what one must feel of his immortality. He could not be one of Fra Angelico's bright-robed, tranquil-browed saints;[4] perhaps if not an inmate of our

Father's many mansioned House,[5] he has found like the swallow, a nest in its eaves and a home. I love to see the different creatures and nations for wh. God has made provision on earth, His care of them all; His delight in them all: it broadens the borders of His Heaven, and makes room for the foldless, never shepherdless souls.

There really I knelt Persian, close to the heart that had leapt at the skylark's song![6]

Then in the close adjoining cemetry we came to Keats. The words "*a Young English poet*"—and the bitter epitaph about his enemies and his desire that it should be said "His name was writ in water"—went to my heart.[7] Thought of another young English poet, dearer to me than life itself—thought of my own struggle, despised muse, unrecognised power, came dimly over me;—but listen, his despair was *not* a prophecy:—pilgrims to Rome from all Europe and America forget the yellow Tiber[8] by which they have so lately driven, by the grave of violet leaves where Adonais sleeps,[9] and one at least, through all the miles of Appian Way, could have felt no thrill like that the simple gravure of the immortal name gave to her. The flowers are there: they were withered, and I stayed not to part them—the heliotrope lay clear on Shelley's grave, and some of the other leaves I kept for Keats. These cypress spines are from Shelley's grave, and the 3 dark leaves one of wh. is for the Doctor;[10] the violet leaves are from Keats. His grave is beautifully tended; a deep low border of thick box all round, and the grave itself a violet garden. Shelley's looked unloved; the fallen spines of the cypress covering it. Most of the flowers have, I fear, been rifled: the marble is clean and bright.

A bit of old Rome comes close against his tomb—a bit of old, old wall.

Farewell, Love, I can write no more to you to-day—my last in Rome; but I record thankfully that I am still very well, and hope this last day, if possible to see the Mamertine Prisons. So I am not wholly given to idolatry!

Your own fond.

[bird symbol]

[from header fol. 34ʳ] Paste one of the violet leaves carefully *into my Keats* with such inscription as *you like.*

Dearest love to each one, Mud especially. To-day I am hoping for another letter. I have only had *one* in Rome; but Yesterday no one went to the post after English mail.

MS Eng. lett. c. 418 fols. 34^r–35^v BOD

1. Dated from KB's trip to Italy in Aug.–Sept. 1880.

2. Harmony (L.). The poet's tomb in the New Burial Ground at Testaccio is inscribed "Percy Bysshe Shelley Concordium Notus IV Aug MDCCXCII," followed by a quotation from *Tmp.* 1.2.396–401 (Hare, *WiR,* 2:397).

3. *Tmp.* 1.2.400–401.

4. KB is reflecting on the Fra Angelico paintings she saw at the Dominican Priory of San Marco in Florence. See Hood, *Fra Angelico,* 9–10. While reference is made to this visit in postcard 24, no letters have been found.

5. John 14:2. Shelley was an atheist; Cian Duffy notes the poet's reputation in the nineteenth century as "Satanic Shelley" or "lunatic angel" (*Shelley & Rev. Sublime,* 1).

6. "To a Skylark" (Shelley, 2:302–5).

7. John Keats's own epitaph reads "T*his Grave contains all that was Mortal of a YOUNG ENGLISH POET Who, on his Death Bed, in the Bitterness of his Heart, at the malicious Power of his Enemies Desired these Words to be engraven on his Tomb Stone: Here lies One Whose Name was writ in Water Feb 24th, 1821" (Hare, WiR, 2:395–97).*

8. A common Latin epithet for the Tiber, "flavus Tiber," is used by poets such as Horace, and describes the yellow-brown alluvial mud that discolors the river. See Garrison, *Horace,* 204n.

9. Shelley's *Adonais* is subtitled "An Elegy on the Death of John Keats, Author of Endymion, Hyperion, etc." (2:385).

10. Possibly Ernest Bell. See letter 62 n. 7.

21. Edith Cooper, Letter to Katharine Bradley

[Ivythorpe | Fri., [Sept. 1880][1]

Friday

My Own Dearly Loved Sim,

I cannot thank you enough for the long, interesting letter, and the gift of the green and silver leaves Athene loves. I delight in the strange, fat, fragrance, and "the berries harsh and crude" wh. "the mellowing year"—"would have Kissed into olives!"[2] Thank my foster-mother, poetic Italy, for her so gracious greeting!

I am so grieved that High Art can so degrade itself as to wear the robes of one of the worst of women. And yet all the corruption that covers itself in sage greens, and thoughtful blues, and passionate golds,[3] cannot deprive me of the firm conviction that, since, as Wordsworth sings,

"The eye it cannot choose but see."[4]

beautiful objects, noble in their forms, and pure in their colour, ought to be given it for food. In the *Attic Philosopher,* I have found two little passages wh.

convey my feeling,[5]—"All the objects wh. Surround us are . . . , in reality, So many talismans from whence good and bad influences are omitted. It is for us to choose them wisely, So as to create a healthy atmosphere for our minds." And again—"Plato has said that *the beautiful is nothing else than the visible form of the good.* If it is so, the ugly should be the visible form of evil, and by constantly beholding it, the mind insensibly deteriorates." I believe that the unhealthiness that is rank in the modern revival of Art is due to the lovelessness of its votaries. They no more love it than the last fashion in dress. Art, when loved is a noble and comely thing, but When it is followed, and not loved; it grows, like a jealous man, full of evil humours; a very Othello stiffling those who are bound to it.[6] Then, too, the devotees of High Art have forgotten Entirely the Inequality of objects of Art—the distinctions of artistic rank; and have dishonoured a blue Chinese bowl by giving to it the admiration due to an Engraving of "a picture that thinks, and whose thoughts we can divine,"[7] just as we should dishonour a carpenter by giving to him the admiration due to a poet. Would that the degrading of Art, by the affected and insincere could be stopped, and that Art might be honoured in the houses of those who live plainly and think highly!

Later—

Oh dear! I want some tea—that poetry of drink—so much! My brain is like the green chestnut rind when the bright, brown nut is gone;—there are brain-chambers, but the brain has dropped away! Cousin Jane and Paps will not come home, and the tea-pot has to be polite.

Late at night.

I must give you the sweet English "Goodnight," my loved one. I have thought of you with such a longing ache! You always sleep with me in effigy—for your portrait lies under my pillow and I kiss it.

Saturday morning.
7.30 A.M.

Good morning, my Dearest; may you have a beautiful day, giving you beauty to behold and beautiful thoughts.

I have finished Prof. Nichol's *Byron* ("English Men of Letters")—and a very unsatisfactory life it is![8] The story of Byron makes me think of the fable of Narcissus. Our English poet, like the Greek youth, only saw the reflection of himself in the Stream of life—cared only for that exaggerated reflection—and turned a deaf Ear to the Spirit of true Poetry, who dwells in silence among the heights of Earth, becoming a gracious, responsive Voice when gt. souled men lift their voices to the mountains,—true Poetry who only loves the themes and looks on the writer merely as a pen of flesh in the hand of God's inspiration. And because he remained a self-gazer he has left a self-conscious, self-centred poetry as Narcissus, his "fountain-gazing"[9] flower.

When I read Byron's *Life,* I remembered what our noble Milton wrote about the life of a worthy poet[10]—and I blessed him. And then I thought of what Wordsworth said of him—"Pure as the naked heavens."[11] We ought to love our sacred Milton!

It has just struck me that you would like to hear about St. George's Scripture schools.[12] They are to "promote such English learning and life as may abide where the wild rose grows." A scripture school is for the practice of the art of writing and for the repetition by speech or song of scriptures, ancient and modern. The instruction will differ widely from any obtainable in other schools and will consist of—

1. Reading with the practice of chant and song. 2. Writing in black letter the Elements of Prosody and Shorthand. 3. Illumination and drawing. I greatly like everything but the writing, wh. I fear would be too much what Herbert Spenser calls *ornamental* Knowledge[13]—although I am a devoted friend to most ornamental Knowledge; and deem it very important.

After breakfast.

I can hardly express my delight at your enjoyment—

"Being too happy in thy happiness!"[14]

I love your little word-painted pictures, with their rare tints (e.g. "indigo shot with sunshine") and Turneresque distances. Picture me Italy in the journal!!

You must have seen the leaning tower, vulgarised by its popularity! Goodbye, my loved wanderer! I am going to run to the post! Your letters, like a crushed rose, give me a little of the rapturous fragrance of Italy.

Your own *Isla.*[15]

I sing and sow, and on Sunday I sleep.

MS Eng. lett. c. 419 fols. 10^r–12^v BOD

1. Dated from KB's trip to Italy in Aug.–Sept. 1880.

2. EC is paraphrasing the opening lines of *Lycidas* (1–5; Milton, 1.1:77).

3. At Bristol University College, KB and EC were teased for being part of the aesthetic crowd of "people as green as their dresses" (Sturgeon, 22). The fashionable female aesthete's preferred colors were olive-greens, green-blues, reds that are almost purple, and russet purples. See Hemmingham, "Colour in Dress," 215–16. In this letter EC supports the principles of aestheticism but takes issue with its application by fashionable followers.

4. "Expostulation and Reply," 16 (Wordsworth, 4:56).

5. Souvestre, *Attic Philosopher,* 187 and 189.

6. "He stifles her" is the stage direction for Desdemona's death in *Oth.* (5.2.85).

7. Untraced.

8. John Nichols's biography concluded that Byron had a "brilliant though unequal genius" but suffered because of his unfortunate character traits (*Byron,* 216).

9. *Prometheus Unbound,* 2.4.14 (Shelley, 2:223).

10. In *Areopagitica* (14–24), John Milton praised Edmund Spenser for his understanding that virtue is not the ignorance of evil, but rather to "see and know, and yet abstain" (Milton, 4:311).

11. "Milton," 11 (Wordsworth, 3:116).

12. In the 1880s there was anxiety over the public education system's ability to teach Scripture. See Morse, "Scripture Teaching in the London Board Schools." The St. George Scripture Schools are probably a response to this anxiety. The following quotation is untraced.

13. In "Use and Beauty" (1868), Herbert Spencer described an evolutionary process by which the past was rendered ornamental through literature. Thus, the life of the medieval serfs, harsh and brutal, is romanticized into Ivanhoes and Marmions who serve "for amusement on leisure hours, and become poetical by contrast with our daily lives" (430). KB and EC met Spencer in 1890, finding him a querulous old man: "When he is wondering what the millions of the suns in the universe can mean with a religious thrill in his voice, he says in the same breath and tone, 'There is fluff coming out of that cushion'" (*W&D,* 133).

14. "Ode to a Nightingale," 6 (John Keats, 285).

15. In adopting the pseudonyms Arran and Isla Leigh, KB and EC suggested an ambiguous collaborative relationship that could have been marital or fraternal. However, by 1885 the partnership was represented as unquestionably spousal (see, for example, letter 105).

22. Edith Cooper, Letter to Katharine Bradley

[Ivythorpe] | [Sept. 1880][1]

My dearest Sim,

Thank you for your glorious gift. You have immortalized post cards, and have rivalled "the Niobe of Nations."[2] I was thunderstruck at the vast image of old Rome hiding her decrepitude. Write a few such post-cards from Venice! You know that your Pretty always appreciates your fine thoughts, and treasures them as the windfalls from your rich brain or as rose-leaves from the rose of your imagination.

Yesterday we over-walked ourselves—were greedy—and today suffer the consequences. We went with Frieda into the Leigh Woods,[3] and enjoyed their silence, and the smile of the upper sunny green, and the gentle reflective shadow of the underwood. I twined a wreath of ivy and gathered blackberry-leaves, some of them bright with crimson

"Like a splash of blood, intense, abrupt,"[4]

some gold, and some with that warm brown, founded on red, wh. is only seen in dying leaves, and clouds about the dying sun. In Rowley's[5] little garden, with a back-ground of silvery, frightened birches, are clumps of sun flowers—golden, and purpled brown—glorious to the eye. On the bridge we met the little Docter. It was a very happy afternoon!

This afternoon Flossy comes to talk; tomorrow afternoon the G's come to tea; on Saturday afternoon M.P.M. who is still not quite contented about the debate.[6] I am tired of people!

Oh, my Sim, to think you are in the "sea-girt city!" I propose *[page ends]*

MS Eng. lett. c. 419 fol. $13^{r/v}$ BOD

1. Dated from KB's trip to Italy in Aug.–Sept. 1880.

2. EC compares KB's description of Rome (postcard 14) with Byron's description in *Childe Harold's Pilgrimage,* 4.703–6 (*Complete Poetical Works,* 171).

3. Leigh Woods is on the opposite side of the Avon Gorge to the Cooper home in Sneyd Park, and would have provided a long but scenic walk across the Brunel suspension bridge. Ivor Treby suggests that the pseudonyms Arran and Isla Leigh derive from "Leigh Woods," although this is unlikely, given that Arran Leigh's *New Minn.* (1875) predates the move to Bristol (Treby, *MF Catalogue,* 29).

4. "By the Fire-side," 56 (Browning, 5:202).

5. The 1881 census gives the address of James Rowley, professor of literature at Bristol University College, as Ardmore, Leigh Woods. KB notes Rowley "has built himself a fair house on the other side of the bridge." See KB, letter to Frances Brooks, MS Eng. lett. d. 405 fol. 151^r BOD.

6. Florence (Flossie) Baker and her sister Edith attended University College. For the Baker family, see letter 18 n. 11. "The G's" are either Robert Baker Girdlestone and family, or Edward Deacon Girdlestone and his wife, Frieda (see also letter 18 n. 12). Mary Paley Marshall (1850–1944) was one of the first women students at Newnham College, and subsequently the first woman lecturer on economics at Cambridge University. KB first met MPM at Newnham in 1875 (Keynes, "Obituary," 273). She married the economist Alfred Marshall in 1877 and they moved to Bristol, where Marshall became principal of University College. Here MPM coauthored *Economics of Industry,* lectured in political economy to the mostly female day students, and started a women's debating society (Groenewegen, *Soaring Eagle,* 223–27). Her female students regarded her with awe as a personification of Newnham College and the struggle for women's education. See Marion Pease, "Reminiscences" (unpub. MS, Bristol U.), 3. EC cast her as tragically romantic: "the happy handmaiden of the broken-winged idealist" (MS Eng. lett. d. 405 fol. 56^v BOD; *W&D,* 128). Amy had recently written to KB that Carta Sturge could not participate in the forthcoming debate because she had gained a position at Manchester High School (Goodbody, *Five Daughters,* 22–28). As nobody could be found to debate KB, Marshall proposed that the motion be changed to "That classics are more important than sciences as a basis of Education" (Amy Cooper, letter to KB, [5 Sept. 1880], MS Eng. lett. c. 419 fols. 4^r–5^v BOD). For the Sturge family, see letter 31 n. 2.

23. Edith Cooper, Letter to Katharine Bradley

[Ivythorpe | Sat.–Mon., [12–14 Sept. 1880][1]

Saturday afternoon.
Rewritten.
My darling Sim,

I have been able to drop nothing into my letter-saving bank *all these days.* But do not think for that, that you are forgotten. Your portrait, like Ilaria's effigy, is being worn by Kisses pressed on it by two devoted mouths Each morning and night; that portrait also has warm rest under my pillow.

You must not tell me about photos. from Angelico[2] or I shall begin to want you back again actively, and procure some charm for drawing you from under your roof of blue Etruscan weather before the full time. All you have seen oppresses me like a gt. fortune. It has raised you in rank of being, and made me poor and fearful, though very glad. And, I Know you will not show me your coffers, but thrust in your hands and give me heaps of your fair coins. Oh Perugia!—may it give you cool breezes—wh. are southern smiles.

Later.

Uncle Cooper[3] is going to give me a M.S. of Erasmus! I shal treasure it, for I love Erasmus. The old Gentleman is very good. He brought us a beautiful field-glass, is going to send us a miscellaneous box and a portfolio for the Ruskins and Italian Art. He is completely dead to our art—a curiosity is to him Art—What grotesqueness of spirit and understanding! As bad as looking on a dwarf as humanity!

The Francia[4] has arrived and is lovely in its young simplicity! Much thanks for it. And I have also seen the beasts, for we spent the whole morning in watching……

I will tell you what we watched to-morrow. Good night, may you have sweet and beautiful dreams—the pearls of the deep night-sea!

May you kiss me as I Kiss you—my dearly loved sister-friend.

Sunday.

We have been asked to tea by Mary Paley Marshall, and tomorrow we go. She wants very much to have a talk about the debate. This is a bit of detail, at wh. my pen does not turn up its impractical nib!

Well, My Sim, we saw yesterday the polar bear in a sea bath.[5] I never saw such watery enjoyment. The springs, and dips, and floatings and rollings were endless in their variety, and actually beautiful in their grace—and you know what a Boeotian the white bear is generally. For water, that gracious, and most finely-bred of natural objects, like a graceful woman, imparts its own lithe bearing and lively ways to all that come in contact with it.

More wonderful post-cards[6]—the little Epitaphs of mighty days that will never be forgotten! My own and I shall be able to have noble talk together for a long, long time.

Sunday Evening.

You must love Rome. Think how the fibrous roots of memory reach down the dark strata of the ages, till we come to white Lucretia and Virginia "white as snowe, fallen newe;"[7] to conditor Romulus, and to remoter "pius Æneas." But more of "the Paradise, the grave, the city, and the wilderness" tomorrow. "Grim-faced night"[8] is here. Nay, she is not grim, for I see a star. I go to the window, and behold pale troops of harmonious stars on the *Golden Stairs*[9] of the milky way.

"God give you good night!"

Monday.

Yes, my dearest, you must sail down the styx of the Past to the Shadowy lands of antiquity. You must think of the glorious, simple days of Rome—not of the eighteen Centuries of her Shame. Sever yourself from Mediævalism—that incongruous building of things new and old. Enter into the fair homogeneous temple of Classicalism!

Thine, with all love, P.P.

MS Eng. lett. c. 419 fols. 6^r–7^v BOD

1. Dated from KB's trip to Italy in Aug.–Sept. 1880.

2. In postcard 24, KB notes she has seen the Fra Angelico frescos in the Dominican Priory of San Marco in Florence. Her letter regarding this is untraced.

3. Richard Spooner Cooper was a retired surgeon from Wyke Regis, Dorset. See *1881 Census.*

4. Probably F. Francia's *Madonna and Child with St. John,* which KB would have seen in the Uffizi gallery in Florence (Hare, *N&CI,* 3:24).

5. The Bristol Zoological Gardens in Clifton are not far from the Cooper family home.

6. Untraced.

7. KB and EC adapted Shakespeare's *Rape of Lucrece,* itself based on Livy's *Ab Urbe Condita,* 1.57–60 (1:197–209), for *Brutus Ultor* (1886). The description of Virginia is a quotation from Chaucer's *Romaunt of the Rose,* 1210–14. EC quotes "the Paradise . . ." from *Adonais,* 433–34 (Shelley, 2:403).

8. Given the context, it is tempting to suggest EC is quoting Robert Cumberland: "The grim night comes on" *Banishment of Cicero,* 3.2.125. As there is no evidence for EC having read this, it may be a popular phrase.

9. The stars in the Milky Way are compared to the women ascending the stairs in Edward Coley Burne-Jones's *The Golden Stairs.* This was the only Burne-Jones painting exhibited at the Grosvenor Gallery in 1880 (Newall, *Grosvenor Gallery,* 57).

24. Katharine Bradley, Postcard to Edith Cooper

Venice | [Mon., PM 13 Sept. 1880]

Home I hope by Tuesday/to-morrow fortnight, Write to Mary,[1] inclosing *letters* for me. I know of no better way. Here at least I think till *Friday.*

Venezia

Pretty Persian I have seen St. Ursula's Dream[2] in the Belle arti to-day. It is so blessed to connect Ivythorpe with all I find of most precious art in my travels, Fra Angelico's annunciation,[3] Ilaria's tomb, Beatrice, and now the Dream I have beheld with my eyes. But I have seen this morning a still lovelier St. Ursula in the Carpaccio series. Her presentation with her virgins to the Pope. Such a lovely troop of young girls—the dew of the morning upon them; fresh-eyed, eager young creatures wrapt in the joy of their mistress's consecration! They are as full of bright anticipation as we, when we started to Clovelly; but washed and clean from all sin. The face of the Pope as he looks at the fair child kneeling for his blessing expresses: "I have need to be baptised of thee, and comest thou to me?" The bridegroom kneeling by the fair creature to whom he is betrothed looks up at the Pope interested and apart. He is astonished; thinks it all a wild freak (of these Bradleys!!) but will be faithful nevertheless to the end, very much like dear Morin.

I am very well: the weather delightfully cool.

Katie.

MS Eng. lett. c. 418 fol. 20r BOD

1. Mary Louisa Hall née Brooks (1863–1921), also known as Marie; eldest daughter of Fanny and John Brooks. In 1892 she married (Alfred) Daniel Hall, the first principal of the South Eastern Agricultural College in Kent (*Oxford DNB*). KB and EC were godparents to their first son, Roger. See Add. MS 46/85 fol. 13r BL.

2. Vittore Carpaccio's *The Dream of S. Ursula* (1490) was on display in the Accademia (Hare, *WiR,* 2:60). The painting is the second in a series that depicts the life of St. Ursula. KB's preferred painting below is the third, *The Arrival of St. Ursula in Rome* (Jameson, *S&L Art,* 2:513–15).

3. Fra Angelico's *Annunciation* is a fresco in the Dominican Priory of San Marco in Florence (Hood, *Fra Angelico,* 260).

25. Katharine Bradley, Postcard to Edith Cooper

Venice | Wed., [PM 15 Sept. 1880]

Venezia, *Wednesday*

Well then, Persian, if you must know I had yesterday an immense headache, and my rage knew no bounds when we were taken to the glass works at Murano.[1] The good I got was that the burneing fiery furnace made me understand better the temptation of the 3 children. Nothing angers me like manufactures. However I had my revenge. I insisted on going to see the old Mother church of Murano,[2] with its beautiful Mosaic pavement, and solemn Madonna with the tear stained cheeks. In the afternoon we saw all of St. Marks[3] that can be Seen and,—but I won't tell you, only I have received an invitation from a gentleman[4] to call upon him this afternoon, and we are going in state in our gondola at 3. I fetch out one of my new cards and am full of joy. We took our friends to the station this morning—through the noiseless canals, past boats piled high with grapes. But I have never seen the full fruit market. Very well to-day, much better for *[from header fol. 21ʳ]* the call. Leave, we think, Friday night for Verona and Innsbruck for Sunday.

Am very happy, Katie.

MS Eng. Lett. C. 418 fol. 21ʳ BOD

1. The glass-works on the island of Murano near Venice are still visited by tourists. The three children are those thrown into a furnace by King Nebuchadnezzar for refusing to worship his golden statue (Dan. 3:1–30).

2. The Church of San Donato, also known as the Matrice or Mother Church of Murano, has a paved walk "with a green mosaic of short grass between the rude stones" (Ruskin, qtd. in Hare, *N&CI,* 2:147).

3. Hare comments, "Travellers will find it wearisome, almost impossible, to examine all the mosaics of St. Mark's" (*N&CI,* 2:30).

4. Untraced.

26. Edith Cooper, Letter to Katharine Bradley

[Ivythorpe] | [Sept. 1880][1]

The Pantheon at Vespers.[2]

Minerva[3] speaks—

I

Is this our temple? All the Forms that lent
Beauty to shapeless stone, are gone, their place
Is Empty, vain as setting without grace
Of jewels, valuless and impotent.
Where are the white limbs with dark ornament
Of wreathing ivy; where the victem crown'd
With death-devoting flow'rs[?] The lovely bound
Of happy-footed maids?—A wail is sent[,]
Such wail as wretched streams by tempests whipt
Make between mountains, to the sky above[,]
Before a form whose limbs are writhed like gaunt
Pine-boughs on Cithaeron. Convulsive-lipped
Men pale, or clasp it with terrific love.
Did our fair shapes this striken building haunt?

II

That dark form on the cross, that hangs with weight
Of agony and death, the blasted head
Caressed by thorns, whose bloody Kisses spread
Along the brow, is it some recent, gt[.]
Prometheus to suffering dedicate?
Like his of old, nailed are the hands and feet[,]
Heavy the tense flesh, and the eyes repeat
The tragic woe of Caucasus.[4] I wait
To learn this modern Titan's work for man
That thus, he hangs before our empty shrines
Intolerable; fills with groans and cries
The mighty dome's reverberating span,
And with despotic sorrow, all the signs
Of joy exiles and anguish deifies[.]

III

He died for man and lo' our shrines are bare!
Such death is claspt unto the confidence
With wh. men cincture deity; and thence

Claspless the girdle fell from us. Our care
Descended not to Earth; our lives were fair[,]
Our brows like Tempé peaceful. From on high[,]
At times we came and passed men's cities by,
And heard the Sounds of woe, saw everywhere
Death, yet we died not! If the flawless, free,
Unrivalled curvature of our grand limbs
Were marred for human sin and suffering;
If its white pride in pain's humility
Grew weak, and faint with agony that dims
Beautiful life, men still were worshipping.

IV

Thus men Embody all their misery,
And lift it up to worship and adore[.]
In a scathed form they weep and groan before
—Hideous worship! Their divinity
In Sorrowing Man's image—grim to see
As sight in Tartarus—their offrings, tears
—Gems of clear grief—and endless bitter fears,
Sepulchral chant and wail. Thus must it be,
Since Joy hath lost its godhood, and is torn
From its own mighty sanctuaries. When
His gods were happy Man was fair and gay.
—The ancient, joyous altars are forlorn;
A God of Sorrow lays his blight on men,
And sadder grows the world from day to day.

V

As lake is blue from looking unto blue
So man was beautiful, because his eyes
Were lifted up to beauty; and were wise,
Erected thus; for more and more he grew
Like to the loveliness he looked unto
In adoration. He brought lovely gifts,
—Smooth, sunny vine-coils; thyrsus-pole[5] that lifts

A piny pyramid; wheat, greenly new;
He tuned the frenzied pipe, he danced with feet
Responsive to the notes. But now he bends
Before distortion and revolting pains;
Forms, dark, uncouth, his lifted vision greets.
Wails penitential to the sky he sends:
And all his nature bears the morbid stains.

VI

This is our temple still! The cross may frown,
Like an ill-look upon our niches, bare
Of images; but every brain must there
In white thought sculpure them, and cast it down
With memory, and its stark form with crown
Of thorny rays. We are the Karyatides
Bearing Antiquity, whose power abides[.]
Built as a way to man's beginning, brown
With passing of the years. We have the age
Of mountains; and though shrouded, at our base
Men realize our greatness, vast, unseen,
And turn from the new mound—their heritage[.]
Let the black cross retain its recent place,
Our rule is here even as it hath been!

These the sonnets wh. were sent to you at Venice—my dearest—but wh. you cannot have had as they would not arrive till Saturday! If by any chance you have seen them, but [leave] this new copy unread. Remember they are but your living blocks! It is so hard to send brain-labour to you because I love you. It is sweet and bitter to bring gifts to the altar of friendship—the gift may be unworthy!

In the poor letter at Venice I thanked my dear devoted old Fowl for her glorious gift of my own Marcus.[6] It will be one of my greatest treasure. This week has been one of reformation in the rooms as a surprise to you. I quite hated you yesterday for your mysterous p.c. The gentleman could not be Jack surely![7] Oh, I do so want to know.

The announcement about your return fills me with joy.

Addio, my own old Fowl.
Your loving and purry,
Pussie.

MS Eng. lett. c. 419 fols. 14r–15v BOD

1. Dated from KB's trip to Italy in Aug.–Sept. 1880.

2. "The Pantheon at Vespers" is an unpublished sonnet sequence. It responds to KB's request of letter 17.

3. EC has changed "Athena" to "Minerva."

4. Compare "Prometheus" in letter 17.

5. A Bacchic staff surmounted by a pine cone, a tuft of ivy, or vine leaves (Smith, *G&R Biography,* 3:1129). Michael Field later adopted the thyrsos-pole as their emblem. See letterhead, MS 392/1/1 fol. 617r, University of Reading Library, Reading; and the hardcover of *W&D.*

6. For KB's promise to purchase a statue of Marcus, see letter 15.

7. It was not "Jack": John Ruskin was in northern France in the summer of 1880 studying French cathedrals (Hilton, *John Ruskin,* 411).

27. Katharine Bradley, Letter to Edith Cooper

[Ivythorpe | Sun., [1881][1]

Sunday, 19th. Century
My P.P.

I have found my comfort—the true likeness of my Child in the Musk-Mallow.[2] Its shimmering expanse of silky petal, its smile, its mild-eyed wonder, its fragility, its subdued beamy brightness as of a cloudy nature softly sunned, its shy contemplativeness, the delicacy of its rose-blanched leaves, all image to me "my pretty," all breathe of her in a way no picture could. Why yesterday I cried, and Greeked, and sewed and wrote letters, and in the evening *Kallirrhoe.*[3]

Tell the ocean that even in its creeks and inlets, its studies and attics, where its brows are somewhat furrowed with the problems of the land, it is dear to me. This earth is perplexing, and if the Infinite will penetrate it, receive the troubled currents of its rivers, its refuse, and its crumbling shores, the lonely gray will take the hues of passion, and the sand-stirred shallows flush and falter with mortal agitation. The Mother sends fondest love. None of my love will I part with, or trust to the post. I keep it in my o'ercharged heart.

Ever A.W.F. *[bird symbol].*

Stay if they want you, and you are growing roses.

MS Eng. lett. c. 418 fols. 87r–88v BOD

1. Dated from the writing of *Call.* between Nov. 1880 and Aug. 1882 (Treby, *MF Catalogue,* 29). EC's location is unknown.

2. A pressed flower remains in this letter.

3. The first of the works written under the name Michael Field, *Call.* was published in 1884. At this early stage the play's title was spelled with a "K" and had not yet acquired the umlaut over the final "e." The play received very good reviews, most notably in the *Spectator,* which called it "the ring of a new voice." See "A New Poet."

28. Katharine Bradley, Letter to Edith Cooper

[Freshwater | Tues., [Sept. 1881][1]

P.P.

It is Tuesday morning. My trunk is my writing-desk. "Hold the fort"[2] is being sung down stairs. I am vaccinated with the vulgar thing: I dare not look at Atys and Adrastus[3] or think of any thing but Colloquial English. This is a strange 2. sided life. There are the downs with their happy flowers, and the approach through the sacred shady lane (the author of In Memoriam dwelling on one side of it, and the author of Bellerophon on the other![4]) to the Undefiled: then there is the Curate[5] and the "imperfect prayers"—how my gorge rises at them—and all the influences that *des*piritualize the heart. I can hardly pray at all with such a clamour of texts and mutilated collects in my ears—I can only just look up and commend to the loving Care of Him who is the Father and Mother of humanity All the life at Ivythorpe even to the warm-beating heart of the tiny Ethiop[6]—P. I woke, I longed for you—with the longing of the mother for the babe that milks it, then of course I dreamed of you. Melancholy dreams! So mind, my dearest, to keep well, and be bright and brave. In less than a Month, Heaven smiling, we shall be on the Moors together.

I have finished Landor[7]—a sublime life;—its errors like landslips making artistic havoc. Hawthorne is in the same series, by Henry James 2/6. Please get or order it *at once,* and post on to me. I must read; the land must be "limed" that it may hereafter be fertile.

What think you of poor Baby Cecil?[8] The bells and rattle are for his heart's thrilling, poor fellow! How infinitely silly is his criticism,—sufficiently refuted by half the themes of "the Earthly Paradise." Mind you laugh at it, if questioned, and say that the popularity of Swinburne and Morris, and the delight of all true poet-lovers in Prometheus Unbound sufficiently disprove it. If any one asks what I think of it say I laugh, laugh abundantly—Winckelmann Consoles me. To use an expression of Imogen's even "the meanest garment"[9] of the Greeks is more to me than the whole body of—say the curate! Here among the seachens, baylets, downlings, and tiny orchards lives Alfred Tennysons: the true poets the Divine old man of Coniston included, amid mountains *that can grow cataracts.*[10] The Cataract-bearing hills, how I long for them! The down is the domestic mountain. It has not "sighed deep, breathed free."[11] The Isle of Wight has a sort of nature that must appear of *[from header fol. 68ʳ]* an alpine character . . . . to cocks and hens!!!

Truly said Aristotle?—Size is a *necessary* attribute of beauty.

Oh how I love thee, how I dote on thee!!

Thy Queen Titania.[12]

MS Eng. lett. c. 418 fols. 68ʳ–69ᵛ BOD

1. Dated from reviews of *Bell.* published in Aug. and Sept. 1881.

2. The American revivalists Ira Sankey (1840–1908) and Dwight Moody (1837–99), toured Britain in 1881. Their hymn "Hold the Fort" (1875) quickly became a favorite in British church circles (Kent, *Holding the Fort,* 215–18).

3. EC's juvenile play, "Atys and Adrastos" (MS Eng. poet. d. 55 BOD), was completed as early as 1874. KB may have considered adapting it.

4. Farringford, the residence of Alfred Tennyson (1809–92), is situated on the Isle of Wight. Tennyson had recently published *Ballads and Other Poems* (1880). Similarly, *Bell.* had appeared under the joint pseudonym Arran and Isla Leigh.

5. Canon David Reith (1843–1909) married KB's cousin Nellie Holinsworth. Born in Aberdeen, he rose to become canon of Rochester in 1891 (*Who's Who).* For Nellie, see also letter 2 n. 5. KB invokes William Cowper's "imperfect and defiled" prayers to vent her dissatisfaction with the household's popularized religious practices. See "Truth," 577–78 (Cowper, *Poems,* 132).

6. EC's status as Ethiope may reflect a shared sense of estrangement from the family's religious sensibility, as in *MND* 3.2.258. Alternately, it may be the result of an unknown disagreement.

7. A hagiographic biography of the poet Walter Savage Landor, by Sidney Colvin (1881). Henry James's *Hawthorne* (1879) was also part of the *English Men of Letters* series edited by John Morley.

8. A signed review by Cecil Wedmore may have appeared in a local paper. Reviews of *Bell.* were generally dismissive, attacking the author's classical "blunders" (*Academy* 20 [1881]: 196). For the Wedmore family, see letter 57 n. 4 and KB, letter to John Miller Gray, Add. MS 45853 fol. 149ʳ⁻ᵛ BL. KB defends the volume with Stopford Brooke's argument that Morris's *Earthly Paradise* (1868) is neither classically nor mythically accurate but romantic in conception (Brooke, *Four Victorian Poets,* 252–53), as is *Prometheus Unbound* (Shelley, 2:171). Like many British aesthetes, KB is consoled by Winckelmann's notion of the Hellenic Spirit as an ideal of romantic

(homosocial) male beauty from which the modern world was alienated, particularly as mediated through Pater's essay "Winckelmann." See Pater, *Renaissance* (1888).

9. *Cym.* 2.3.138–41.

10. KB recasts the Romantic turn to nature: rather than mountains passively inspiring the poetic sublime in the poet, landscape is an active force in the creation of the poet. "True poets" (including Ruskin, who lived in Coniston) are produced by the mountainous Lake District, while Tennysons are produced by landscape of a smaller scale (seachens, baylets, downlings and tiny orchards). EC later dismissed Tennyson for his "vicarage outlook" (Thomas Sturge Moore, "Poets and Painters," vol. 1, Add. MS 61721 fol. 97^r BL). Later in this letter, the cataract may be inspired by the "sounding cataract" (76) of "Lines Written a Few Miles Above Tintern Abbey" (Wordsworth, 2:261). KB concludes her argument with Aristotle's notion that beauty depends on appropriate size, neither so small as to be imperceptible nor so large as to be lost to view (Aristotle, *Poetics,* 33).

11. KB revises Robert Browning's line from *Youth and Art:* "We have not sighed deep, laughed free" (63; Browning, 6:279).

12. *MND* 4.1.50.

29. Edith Cooper, Annotated Envelope[1]

1883 about??
1882
Visit to *Brantwood* —K alone
Ruskin at Herne Hill
going to Lucca
"Loyalty or Love" while I am in Cornwall
A Birth-day Card
Humour
Malvern
Freshwater
In what year did Ruskin leave Herne Hill for Lucca in Bank Holiday week?[2]
Aug 1882?
Must be.
K at B'ham? with Fr.[3]

MS Eng. lett. c. 418 fol. $53^{r/v}$ BOD

1. Another of EC's lists, such as envelope 3, which provides rough dates for events in the correspondence.

2. Ruskin visited Lucca in Aug. 1882 (Hunt, *Wider Sea,* 386). See also letter 33.

3. For Francis Brooks, see letter 30 n. 4.

30. Katharine Bradley, Letter to Edith Cooper

[West Malvern] | [Apr. 1882][1]

To *P.P*[.]

We sigh over the common place of life, my Pretty; yet a plain, which is nothing but infinite commonplace has a serenity and completion that tumbled scenery can never give. The details fulfil, instead of disturbing the harmony; the city becomes a wreath of blue smoke; the hedgerows give gradation to the bars of bloomy tint; the rivers tracked clear to the rim of heaven lie peaceful as the Mountain tarn.

And so God who is far enough off, may see it all, and behold it, in its entirely, as still "very good."[2] This world of ours:—come and see it: we have a whole section of the globe to offer you—and learn the lesson of the great lands lying naked and open to the eye of Him with whom we have to do.

Here you can learn the very notes of the rain from the sharp little patter to the long trailing monotonous tune; and the wind on these hill tops is ¾$^{th.}$ of life.

The ear is quite filled with hearing indeed over filled; and in the midst of the blast rises a funeral bell.

Also there are cherry-blooms, lambkins, and such frail innocence as adds on horror to the sheeted gloom. One special little gust of wind is even now playing about my heart. How happy the Mother w$^{d.}$ be here.—an attendant breeze for every limb!

Young Elliot[3]—Balliol scholar with Frank[4] is or has been here. He leaves today. A *really* charming boy with soft kind eyes, and the Greek bashfulness Socrates w$^{d.}$ have praised,[5] with all this background of Scholarships—Ireland and other. Alas, Pretty, he is gone—a fair dream. Much interested in *[from header fol. 46^r]* our poems.

½ Simorg

MS Eng. lett. c. 418 fols. 46^r–47^v BOD

1. Dated from the publication of *Bell.* in 1881.

2. Gen. 1:31.

3. Sir Charles Norton Edgecumbe Eliot (1862–1931) entered Balliol College, Oxford University, in 1880. His exceptional facility with languages gained him the Hertford, Boden, Ireland, and Craven scholarships and the Houghton Syriac prize. In 1887 he became a diplomat in the East, was later commissioner to the East African Protectorate, and published extensively on African societies and on malacology (molluscs). See *Oxford DNB.*

4. Francis Brooks (1861–1936) was the eldest son of John and Fanny Brooks. He studied at Balliol College, University of Oxford, in the early 1880s, and was appointed lecturer in classics (later professor) at Bristol University College (*Who's Who*). Francis seems to have had a youthful crush on KB. See KB, letter to Frances Brooks, MS Eng. lett. d. 405 fol. 146^{r-v} BOD.

5. Plato, "Charmides," 158c. KB departs from Jowett's authoritative 1871 translation in interpreting the Greek as "bashfulness" rather than "modesty" (Plato, *Dialogues,* 1:12).

31. Katharine Bradley, Letter to Family (including Edith Cooper)

West Malvern | [Wed.,] 19 Apr. [1882][1]

W. Malvern April 19th. Evening

While the sunset is still in my eyes I will write to you my dear ones,—fresh from that majesty in heaven—my heart turns with warmer love to the dear ones on earth. What indeed have we like that thrilling splendour save the pulsing passion of our spirits.

God grant the lamp of human love be tended in us each one: seeing the desecration of the family life in the Sturges,[2] I am led to set greater store by it,—to feel the need of fostering it constantly—since only by perfect fulfilment of each human relationship, can we hope hereafter for the great Friendship. Coming in, Sis,[3] thoroughly exhausted just before a late tea—I stretched myself on our little couch—and *watching from there supine* the sun sink into purple folds of mist and hill, I thought with longing of what it wd. be to our precious invalid[4] in like manner to have drunk her fill of that rich western light. God's revelation of Himself in sunset, as far, to me, surpasses all other revelations in nature, as all the glimpses we get of His Heart and Purpose towards us in Prophet and king are surpassed by his word to us in Christ. Truly I trust you and your nestling daughter also saw the heavens opened, and won peace into your souls.

To-morrow will be given to marketing and entertaining—still marketing that involves a trudge over the hills will refresh, rather than disgust. Our souls are gradually accustoming to the wide landscape: at first we felt like the orthodox suddenly plunged into a Positivist Society.[5] We had to pull down the barns o['e]r our eyes and build greater: there was no room for us to bestow the goods wh. Nature proffered us.

You P.P. will be greatly amused to hear that young Elliot—Frank's compeer—took to us most vehemently—told Clement that he wished he had asked us to dinner—and requested that, failing that, we should be fetched to tea—his last meal. Accordingly Dot fetched us over to entertain the youth in the dying moments of his visit. He is a thoroughly charming fellow. England may well be proud of breeding such souls. He has just returned from an Italian journey and told me of the beauty of the peach-blooms on the Lido at Venice.[6] Dot and Clem told him all about Bellerophon. He was most curious to understand the mystery of the joint authorship; and came to the conclusion that when a speech by any special character was to be written we must each make a draft, then pick out the best things in each; and I suppose re-set them!!!

He is desirous to study Bell. so there P. You will have for reader "the cleverest fellow in Oxford." Please pack up a Bell. and a Minnesinger.[7] The latter I have promised Dot for *PRIVATE* consumption; the other I shall write my name in—for every copy is precious now, and lend it to Dot, who will lend it to Clem, who will lend it to his friend.

Pretty P. cease to be gray and friendless—I felt the want of you sorely at tea last night. It was pleasant to feel that our philosophic studies had fitted us to be intelligent companions to men in their higher walks: but when I thought how *you* could have discoursed on the ethics I felt a fool.

Mary Charlotte (Carta) Sturge. (From Elizabeth Sturge, *Reminiscences of My Life* [1928], reprinted with the permission of Roger Sturge)

Caroline (Dot) Sturge. (From Elizabeth Sturge, *Reminiscences of My Life* (1928), reprinted with the permission of Roger Sturge)

I am reading 1st principles,[8] and learning by heart every day a stanza of the Grecian urn.[9] I am spring-sowing. This is not the time for reaping but for turning the soil over to the sun, and dropping in the precious grain.

My little one is as good, and happy and sweet as she can be.[10] Pleasant indeed will our days be if we can hear that *[from header fol. 36ʳ]* our loved one is *prudent* and *progressing.* God love and keep you. Best love and kisses for the dear Morin. How about the wooden leg? (next page)[11]

MS Eng. lett. d. 400 fols. 36ʳ–39ᵛ BOD

1. The reference to *Bell.* suggests the date is Apr. 1881.

2. The Sturges were a prominent Bristol Quaker family. KB and EC met Mary Charlotte (Carta), Elizabeth, Helen, and Caroline (Dot) at Bristol University College and through them their brothers, Will and Clement. The Sturges' "desecration" refers to the "Militant" agnosticism of Carta and Clem (Sturge, *Reminiscences,* 152F and 124).

3. Critics have interpreted KB's name for Emma Harris Cooper as "Lis" or "Lissie" (Bridge, MS Eng. misc. d. 983 fol. 87ʳ BOD; Treby, *MF Catalogue,* 67). However, in KB's handwriting, "S" looks very like "L" (see the word "Sunday" in the letter pictured on p. 2.). Therefore, it is likely the name is "Sis" or "Sissie."

4. Emma Harris Cooper became an invalid after the birth of Amy (Sturgeon, 17).

5. The English Church of Humanity was established by Richard Congreve in 1859. Also known as Comtean positivism, it followed Auguste Comte's philosophy of humanism based on scientific process, or the belief that all doctrine must derive from empirical evidence. By the 1880s London's Chapel St. and Newton Hall were the only major societies still operating in England. Positivism never attracted many followers, but high-profile adherents such as John Stuart Mill, George Henry Lewes, and Harriet Martineau excited popular interest. See Wright, *Religion of Humanity.*

6. "The peach-blooms" may refer to the colors of sunrise or sunset. Compare with letter 35.

7. *New Minn.,* by Arran Leigh (1875).

8. EC was particularly interested in Kantian philosophy, ultimately taking first-class honors at Bristol University College. See letter 90. That this was a shared interest is clear from letters such as 81 and 82, and here KB probably means she is reading Kant from first principles.

9. "Ode on a Grecian Urn" (Keats, 288–89).

10. Probably Amy Katharine Cooper.

11. The rest of the letter remains untraced.

32. Katharine Bradley, Letter to Edith Cooper

[London] | [Thurs., 29 Jun. 1882][1]

To P.P. *beginning*

I feel as if I had seen—not Shakespeare's Lady Macbeth nor Mad. Ristori's but Lady Macbeth herself.[2] In the first scenes she is like a fiend whispering at her husband's ear, interested in him simply as her instrument, tortured by agonies of impatience when he hesitates, or trembles, or cannot understand. After the murder she stands blasted by Macbeth's doom to sleep to more;[3] he may have vulgar nightmare and vision; she takes spiritual possession of the spectral Kingdom of their common sin, and where he feels pangs of remorse, is a prey to the Vulture Memory.

In the banquet-scene after the Queenly grace and sweeping Courtsy of the—"Kind good night to all"[4]—While Macbeth still wildly raves—she stands behind him combating the inrush of frenzied thoughts—and as she utters the words "You lack the season of all natures sleep"[5]—the agonized eyes grow stiff and spectral—

In a single line all the horrors of the sleep-walking scene are re-hearsed. The suspense is overwhelming till she enters again, with those eyes,—eyes from wh. all life has been sucked—that do not stoop to seek for the spot of blood in the never to be sweetened hand—that have no part in the writhing misery of the tortured face—eyes that neither flash, nor blench, nor supplicate it seems held open by Destiny that sleep may give no moment's respite of repose to the ravished brain—on which Imagination is branding the great Murder-scene afresh.[6] She appals,—her face is more fearful comment on the 5$^{th?}$ commandment[7] than all Sinai's thunders.[8]

But I shall freeze your young blood,[9] Pretty, I desist.

I loved to see the pit and gallery enjoying its own Shakespeare, listening to the great Master—being told *the truth,* and no goody shams about Life, and Doom, and Law.

"What's done can't be undone" the moral of the play blazed out sanguine from her lips.[10] Hush, hush it would have killed you, so farewell.

Persian Cat—your hairs w^{d} have risen erect upon your head had you been there. After Saturday-night's experience I can give no better description of Madness than this—It is Memory coming to us in ghost-clothes: when the past gives up its dead, and faces us a bloody wraith. The fleeing brain beats itself to pieces against the walls of its prison-house. All this I have learnt from the face of the great actress. I don't believe she takes the fainting as real.[11] She hears that the repetition in a woman's ear w$^{d.}$ murther as it fell[12]—the swoon is expected of her—God prepares for her a murdering repetition of her crime, and holds her eyes fastened to the sight; she does not swoon then; Heaven curarizes her to suffer and Keep tranced stillness over her pain.

I suppose it was being in the Midlands, with passionate thankfulness I travelled away to the Stratford grave . . . and tell that Mother I will slay her step by step if she ever dares to talk to me of abandoning the dramatic form. It is the form the great Creator has chosen—no writter of an epostle—no lyric Singer of the beauty of His own fair works: Himself the all-comprehending audience to the great play *of* Humanity. He sees evolved before them in the spectacle of the Universe the plot of His own Creator brain. Beg the Mother not to lay the raffling too sorely to heart. I agree with her Amy had better not be here. I will do what I can. I am a good Fowl: but I cannot open the earth and swallow my relations up quick. My sympathy is dramatic; I realise the immense difficulties in this house of reform: *its godlessness you cannot comprehend.* This is to the Mud. I don't expect I shall get home till Wednesday afternoon. Meanwhile I love you each dearly. Don't think I will do anything rash. I simply write a word to Cobbe[13] to assure it that I *dare* not, having put my hand to the plough look back: but we must gravely deliberate ere we come to a decision.

I am to the Muses—You also? Be prepared for my district on Friday. I *cannot* avoid that. *Kisses to each.* Twelve o'clock. Conference this afternoon.[14]

Ever the A.W.F.

MS Eng. lett. c. 418 fols. 48r–52v BOD

1. EC confidently dated this letter to 3 Jul. 1882 (see envelope 3), but given that the annual meeting of the RSPCA in London was 29 Jun., it is probably earlier.

2. Adelaide Ristori (1822–1906) toured England in 1882 presenting her unique version of *Macbeth.* KB probably saw the play while in Birmingham visiting family. Ristori was retired but had been considered Europe's finest actress of the '50s and '60s. *Mac.* was radically reshaped to shift Lady Macbeth to the center of the action; it opened on the heath, moved to Lady Macbeth reading her husband's letter, and effectively ended with the sleep-walking scene (Bassnett, *Three Tragic Actresses,* 162). The play was reviewed well with a strong note of nostalgia for her once "great beauty and lovely voice" ("Madame Ristori at Drury-Lane," *Times,* 4 Jul. 1882).

3. *Mac.* 2.2.36.

4. *Mac.* 3.4.122.

5. *Mac.* 3.4.141. In Ristori's play this line marked the end of act 3.

6. The sleepwalking scene (5.1) was the climax of the play; Ristori reenacted the entire murder in pantomime (Carlson, *Italian Shakespeareans,* 46).

7. KB probably means the sixth commandment, "Thou shalt not murder" (Exod. 20:13).

8. Exod. 19:19.

9. *Ham.* 1.5.16.

10. *Mac.* 5.1.75.

11. Opinion was divided on whether Lady Macbeth's fainting at the end of act 2, scene 3, was genuine (Carlson, *Italian Shakespeareans,* 41). KB believes that Ristori played it as deception.

12. *Mac.* 2.3.90–91. KB uses the original form, "murther."

13. Frances Power Cobbe (1822–1904), the prominent campaigner for women's rights and founder of the Victoria Street Society for the Protection of Animals from Vivisection. KB was an admirer as early as 1875 when Cobbe was sent a copy of *New Minn.* (letter from Emma Cooper to FPC, 22 May [1875], Eng. lett. e. 15 fol. 8 BOD). In 1876, Ruskin rebuked his disciple for defending Cobbe against his public condemnation of her as a "tinkling . . . saucepan" (Ruskin 28:621–22; *W&D,* 148–49). KB's activities in the above letter probably relate to her role as secretary of the Anti-Vivisection Society in Clifton; however, her mention of a note to Cobbe may indicate that the generous friendship evident in an 1892 letter was already established (Mitchell, *Frances Power Cobbe,* 375).

14. The annual meeting of the Royal Society for the Prevention of Cruelty to Animals was held on Thursday, 29 Jun. 1882, in St. James's Hall, London. See "Prevention of Cruelty to Animals," *Times,* 1 Jul. 1882.

33. Katharine Bradley, Letter to Edith Cooper

Brantwood, Coniston | Mon., 5 Aug. 1882[1]

Bank Holiday. Gloria tibi Domine[2].

Darling,

I am comforted by 2 letters and a post-card[3] and can now tell you of the ever memorable Saturday. As our boat touched the Brantwood landing-place the first things I saw were a skipping-rope, and a little tuft of yellow poppies. We passed the lodge and the builders (for are not 7 new rooms being added to Brantwood[4]) and then stood,—and this would have been to you the most precious moment—opposite to the open front door, facing the Master's Copy of Botticelli's(?) Zipporah, and 2 long Jones figures.[5] The hall is low, the walls pale buff: I liked [it] thus at the threshold the salutation of Art. In the drawing room is "The Fair Rosamund," and the Splügen Pass[6] from wh. the blue curtain was drawn for our delight. The walls of the dining [room] are a very soft gray; the furniture and draperies a milky blue green, whilst there are rich shades of red in the turkey carpet. The Master's own window is very notable—and not I think a failure like the study paper wh. though it is a copy of a bit of a Cardinal's sleeve in an old picture—looks very much like the pattern of a large flowery dressing gown.[7] In stead of the large mirror over the mantelpiece in the dining-room is a perfectly magnificent doge of Titian, to the right of which there is a portrait of the Master's father when young, and to the left Angelica Kauffmann by Sir Joshua.[8] Of course the picture of Main interest to the person who approaches

John Ruskin, 1882, by Elliot and Fry. (The Ruskin Foundation, Ruskin Library, Lancaster University)

Brantwood in a devotional spirit is the portrait of the Master when a child.[9] A perfectly pure little human spirit he looks, receptive and *per*ceptive—his joy already in the "boo" hills for wh. he asked as background. The portraits of Pa and Ma. hang on either side. The study you have heard of from Harper[10]—it is not beautiful—nor suggestive of happy work—too crow[d]ed and scientific looking piled with Cabinets and book-Cases—except in the wondrous corner, where at a little round table the Master works by the window. We saw his seal—the motto "To-day" inscribed on the finger-tip of a solid Mass of *stalactite* and his favourite 13th. century Missal, and had a peep at his minerals. Mrs. Severn then called to her governess to show us the view from the turret-window, and the kind little Creature took us also into Mr. Ruskin's room. *There* is the lesson of Brantwood. Monastic simplicity,—the one thing needful the highest attainable art. A small iron bedstead and—eleven Turners[11] on the walls. That one glance will shame me all my life, when I desire artistic luxury. And the room itself is very small, not larger I think than the Fowl's. In the bookcase I Saw—amazement! Harriet Martineau's autobiography in 3. Vols, Hood's poems, lots of Scott of course, and, Mary[12] says, Dickens; Darwin's Origin of Species, Heroditus etc.[13] Quantities of dictionaries, and in the study side by side in old motley covers Chapman's Homer and Douglas's Virgil. The garden is rather prosaic—trim lawn in front, with a few roses on the standards, and, at the side, some blue conventional pansies such as you see in border-gardening. In the parlour at the lodge where I first saw Mrs. Severn there were vases of strictly Conservatory flowers. Behind the house there is a wood, through wh. the Master has made little paths; but the immediate surroundings of Brantwood are not, I think, as beautiful as those of Newton Leys.[14] The views of the lake—well the eye *is satisfied with seeing*. Heaven cannot be desired for its beauty by the Master of Brantwood. And every one about the homestead P. seemed so nice. The old housekeeper is a charming person, and little Violet Severn[15]—a two-years' old creature with light golden curls, a quite fitting pet for the Master in his declining years.

Mrs. Severn tried to make her receive my advances by telling her *that I knew D[earest]. papa* and I carefully explained I did *not*. You will hear with grief that Mrs. Severn herself is stout as the human imagination can stretch—bulky, globular, every outline wants altering. Her Manners are frank, Kind, and homely; on the score of refinement she would certainly *not* satisfy the Trusteds.[16] She was clad in a blue spotted morning gown, and cornelian neck-lace; and mending for her daughter a pale pink party-going dress!!! I am so happy to think the Master has a sensible Motherly woman to feed him on "real turtle soup[17] and oysters," cut his hair and beard, and nurse him through his illnesses. He leaves Herne Hill this week en route for Lucca etc. Ah My darling P. and little Kittie Puss too—how fain Wd. I have had you with me! Think much of all I tell you—it is full of significance. But what I most regoice in is that *his own people* are so full of praise of the Master—he is "infinitely precious"[18] to them quite apart from his celebrity. Many thanks to my dear. *[from header fol. 54r]* Love to the Mother, and Kittie. I will try to send *times*,[19]

Your own all loving, A.W.F.

MS Eng. lett. c. 418 fols. 54r–58v BOD

1. Brantwood, John Ruskin's home on Coniston Lake, was open to visitors thirty days a year (Ruskin, 35:xlvii), although KB's (revoked) membership in the Guild of St. George may have

provided entrance. This letter is dated from building work carried out in Aug. 1882. Bank holiday fell on 5 Aug. 1882.

2. "Glory to thee, O Lord" (L.).

3. Untraced.

4. In 1878, Ruskin experienced his first bouts of mania, which involved both mental delusions and physical weakness (Hunt, *Wider Sea,* 370–71). New rooms were added to Brantwood in Aug. 1882 to accommodate the family of Ruskin's cousin Joan Agnew Severn so that she could nurse him (386).

5. *Zipporah,* by Ruskin, is a copy from the Botticelli fresco in the Sistine Chapel (Ruskin, 37:234), and is still at Brantwood; Edward Coley Burne-Jones's *Love Leading Alcestis* depicts a scene from Chaucer (Ruskin, 19:207–8); unidentified watercolor. Burne-Jones was a particular favorite of Ruskin: his *Fair Rosamund* (noted subsequently by KB) was purchased by Ruskin's father as early as 1863 (Ruskin, 36:liii). Rosamund Clifford soon would be the subject of MF's successful early play, *FR* (1884).

6. When J. M. W. Turner's *Pass of the Splügen* became available during Ruskin's first illness, a public subscription was raised to buy it for him (Ruskin, 13:487).

7. The dining room at Brantwood features seven Gothic lancet windows designed by Ruskin (Hanson, 31); the "failed" wallpaper was copied from Marco Marziale's *Circumcision* in the National Gallery (Ruskin, 15:434n). It is, as KB notes, much like a dressing gown.

8. *The Portrait of the Doge Andrea Gritti,* now attributed to Catena, currently in the National Gallery (Dearden, *Ruskin,* 95); *Portrait of John James Ruskin* by Sir Henry Raeburn, RA (Ruskin, 35:plate 1), or possibly George Watson (Dearden, *Ruskin,* 104); it is unclear which of the two portraits of Angelica Kauffmann (1741–1807) painted by Sir Joshua Reynolds was owned by Ruskin.

9. James Northcote painted Ruskin at three and a half years old. Ruskin notes that he precociously chose the blue hills of Scotland for the background (Ruskin, 28:273 and 35:21–2). This portrait, and those of Margaret and John James Ruskin by James Northcote, RA, still hang at Brantwood.

10. Macdonald's description of Ruskin's cluttered study is quoted in Alexander Wedderburn's "A Lake-side Home: Brantwood," published in *Art Journal,* not *Harper's Magazine.* Also mentioned are Ruskin's motto, "To-day, To-day, To-day" (Ruskin, 35:390–91); the Psalter of St. Louis (Ruskin, 21:270); and the collections of minerals Ruskin put together for display in the British Museum and other institutions (Ruskin, 26:xlix).

11. Ruskin's bedroom walls were covered in paintings by J. M. W. Turner (1775–1851). Ruskin himself stated there were twenty Turners on his bedroom wall (Ruskin, 34:669), but this may be later than KB's visit. KB lists twelve Turners in letter 34. See Wilton, *Life & Work of J. M. Turner,* 350–484.

12. This may be Mary Louisa Hall; see postcard 24 n. 1.

13. Reading Martineau was forbidden by Ruskin: "not because she is an infidel, but because she is a vulgar-foolish one" (Ruskin, 29:29). He recommended Thomas Hood (15:227); Herodotus (15:226); Sir Walter Scott (35:13); and Charles Dickens (35:303). Darwin and Ruskin reportedly got on well together (25:xlvi), but Ruskin opposed the inclusion of Darwin's *Origin of Species* in the *Pall Mall Gazette*'s best hundred books (1886). His objection was not to Darwin's own work but rather that he had "collected, in the train of him, every impudent imbecility in Europe" (34:586). Ruskin owned an early edition of George Chapman's 1611 translation of

Homer and a 1553 edition of Gavin Douglas's translation of Virgil's *Aeneid* into Middle Scots (34:698).

14. In July 1867 KB and her widowed mother went to live with the Coopers in Newton Leys, Tissington, in Derbyshire. See Bridge, MS Eng. misc. d. 983 fol. 62ʳ BOD.

15. Violet is Joan and Arthur Severn's youngest daughter.

16. Alice Marion Trusted was one of the three close friends KB met during their time in Bristol (MS Eng. lett. e. 143 fol. 13ᵛ BOD). She corresponded with both KB and EC throughout the 1880s (Sturgeon, 39–40).

17. Real turtle soup, as opposed to mock turtle soup, had an iconic status as a food of the wealthy in the nineteenth century. See Pool, *What Jane Austen Ate,* 386. The quotation is untraced.

18. From Thomas Carlyle's essay on *Boswell's Life of Johnson:* "living wisdom is infinitely precious to men" (*Critical and Misc. Essays,* 272).

19. Probably train times.

34. Katharine Bradley, Annotated Envelope

Ruskin's Turners

MS Eng. lett. d. 401 fol. 43ʳ BOD

35. Katharine Bradley, Letter to Edith or Emma Cooper

[Coniston] | [Aug. 1882][1]

Skies and the mountains they light. (See the Master's Turners)[2]

—the glowing warmth of the "Heysham," the mellow sunlight of the "Tamar," the *intense* blue and passing summer cloud of the "Richmond play"—the primrose light and tender twilight shadow of "Carnarvon," the broken thunder cloud and sweet invasion of victorious light in the "Gosport," the April gleam in the "Salisbury," the feathery clouds of the "Flint," the spiritual significance of the struggling dawn in the "Constance," the golden calm of the "Coblentz," the fairyland of dawn in the "Zug," the fiery and wrathful west in the "Goldau," the stormy air of the St. Gothard,—on to the ineffable splendours, and Veiled loveliness of the Splugen,[3]—where the mountains lose their earthliness and are clad as the clouds above them, in peach-bloom and bridal gray.

Line[4]

And the toothed ridges of resisting pine
(see the Master's efforts to represent their uncountableness)[5]

Those amber *mountain* crests,—their misty bloom
And peach-like purple veiled in bridal gray.
The Splugen Pass.
As angels are to men, so are these Mountains to the Alps. This is as much a revelation as that of St. John the Divine. The mountains have yielded up their beauty, the recesses of their loveliness, and the inmost thoughts of their hearts to the painter,—as utterly as the sea will yield up its dead at the last day.[6] This is no likeness of what is beheld by travellers with mortal eyes,—it is beheld in the spirit—flushed with the bridal rose, veiled in the bridal gray—descending out of heaven from God.

Remember it is the picture of the Gray Kingdom—the Griscus[7]—gray in the blues, gray in the pinks, gray in the greens,—and the valley is the valley of the shadow of death for "the dark plain itself is only the diffused wreck of the purple mountains that rise from it, rounded like thunder clouds."

the Master

The trimmed vineyards of the plain form the central dark of the picture; the mountains are of rose, and lavender and gray: veiled gold—the hues of heaven dim in the films of the earth.—

This is for Mud, or Edie—whoever likes it. I *must* have much more time for the Turners. They are not half learnt yet,—not by *heart.* So study the legends, and be happy with our letters. God bless you all, my loved ones.

Ever the dear Fowl, *Katie*

MS Eng. lett. d. 401 fols. 44[r]–45[v] BOD

1. Dated from KB's trip to Coniston in Aug. 1882.

2. Brief descriptions for most of Ruskin's Turner collection are to be found in *Turner* (13:413–53): *Heysham and Cumberland Mountains,* 1818 (13:428); *Sunshine on the Tamar,* ca. 1813 (13:433–34), which Ruskin called "pigs in sunshine" (Wilton, *Life & Work of J. M. Turner,* 350); *Play. Richmond Bridge, Surrey,* ca. 1831 (35:254), is now titled *Richmond Hill and Bridge, Surrey* (Wilton, 397); *Caernarvon Castle, Wales,* ca. 1833 (13:440–42); *Gosport, Entrance to Portsmouth Harbour,* ca. 1829 (Lloyd, 79); *Salisbury, Wiltshire,* ca. 1828 (13:441); *Flint Castle, Northern Wales,* ca. 1834 (13:442); *Constance,* 1842 (13:454); *The Mosel Bridge at Coblenz,* painted for Ruskin in 1842 (13:454; Powell, 193–94); *Lake of Zug in the Distance* (Lloyd, *Turner,* 136); *Goldau* 1843 (13:455); possibly *The Pass of St. Gothard,* 1843 (13:456).

3. For Ruskin's particular affection for this painting, see letter 33 n. 6.

4. KB seems to be drafting verse, and it may be that the word "line" inserted here represents a rough sketching out of the shape of the stanza.

5. "[Turner's] drawing of Farnley shows what he *saw* in *one* pine;—the etching of the Valley of Chamoune shows also that he had no hope of ever representing their multitudes . . . In the Pass of the Splügen, just presented to me, the spectator must at once understand these two great and unconditional *surrenders* of his power in the Alpine presence. Upper snows, hopeless,—pines, hopeless" (Ruskin, 13:513).

6. Rev. 20:13.

7. The Grey League was a Swiss alliance of elders and nobles to maintain justice (Ruskin, 13:526). KB's subsequent description draws from Ruskin's *Turner* (13:517).

36. Katharine Bradley, Letter to Edith Cooper

Dean Prior | [Sat.,] 12 Aug. [1882][1]

Dean Prior Vicarage
Buckfastleigh
August 12th

There is in Nature a peace that passeth understanding and here—in Herrick's home, it abides.[2] There is a broad terrace walk at the top of our garden, shaded by high Scotch firs, where one can be content to rest all day, and brood on the Julia or P.P. of one's heart.[3] The way thereto is by a winding walk, with drippings of fuchsia (?) peeps of columbine, and quite a little colony of enchanter's nightshade. From our bedroom window (I have secured a table from Archie's[4] dressing room at wh. we can both write and on wh. all our books are placed, and always think of our letters as dated from hence) we overlook the graves, perhaps *his,*[5] and in front the mounting lawn up to the Scotch firs of the terrace-walk. Our house is in a hollow, and in the midst of deep airless lanes;—far away on the horizon the firm clear curves of the moors. No chance of our ever reaching them save to camp out for a day, but in every direction pleasant happy walks—the bounteous Devonshire hedgerows bringing joy to my soul. They are as cream to the spirit, rich and nourishing. We are safely removed from the Dart,[6] or any stimulating influence,—here meditation folds the "swift" wings Hamlet gave to her,[7] and contently preenes her feathers. I can understand that Herrick's burning soul must have fretted in this quiet spot: to me it is healing and blessedness.

The exquisite shape of the wide low rooms makes me long to have the P.

here to decorate the house aestheticaly. I am only just learning how important the shape of rooms is;—it impresses us like the figure of women. The light, or complexion of these rooms, is most soberly delicate; hitherto we have only thought of draperies[,] furniture and carpets, and these are simply the salient features and tresses of the chamber. The light and form are the things of most potent though unobtrusive influence on the sense. Above all things the rooms should be low. In face of the "grand old heavens"[8] a high room is an insolence. What we seek is a shelter from the storm—no ephemeral imitation of the ancient Babylonian pride.

Here I shall be dull my P.—with the honied dulness of a basking soul—I feel put out to bleach in the sun. Or—to change the metaphor—it is only motionless things that ripen,—here we lie and feel every touch of the sun's ardent pencil; we shall mellow and fertilize, we shall not be inspired—past a madrigal. For the rest I cannot think Amy will profit much by these soft airs, and we have *secretly* resolved to save up our money carefully and take a week at Dawlish[9] on our way home, if we still feel unrefreshed and have to leave here soon. The sweet blue waves broke there on golden sand, and brought home to my mind the truth of my condemnation of these northern seas as vulgar.

[from header fol. 43ʳ] Farewell. I trust the dear father came home refreshed from his bath, and that you will have a happy Sunday. Ever—O my chosen, my Delight,

Your own spouse-friend.

A.W.F.

Dear, dear Puss much love to thee.

MS Eng. lett. d. 400 fols. 43ʳ–45ᵛ BOD

1. Canon David Reith moved to a new parish at Leusden Church near Widecombe on the Moor, Devonshire, not far from Dean Prior in 1882. See Amy Cooper, letter to EC, 31 Aug. 1882, MS Eng. lett. d. 402 fols. 41ʳ–43ᵛ BOD. This suggests the trip to Dean Prior was a family visit.

2. Phil. 4:7; the poetry of discontented Devonshire exile, Robert Herrick (1591–1674) was revived in the late-Victorian period by Edmund Gosse and Algernon Charles Swinburne. See Rollin, *Robert Herrick,* 199; Gosse, "Robert Herrick," 32:177.

3. The lawn of the vicarage garden at Dean Prior slopes upward to Herrick's walk which is lined with beeches, not Scotch firs. There is no evidence that Herrick used the walk, but it may have existed in his time (Scott, *Robert Herrick,* 63); most of Herrick's love poems were addressed to Julia.

4. Probably Cousin Archie Holinsworth. See family tree on p. xvi.

5. Herrick is buried in the churchyard at Dean Prior, although the exact location is unknown (Rollin, *Robert Herrick,* xiv).

6. The stream, Dean Bourne, flows under the road between Dean Prior and the village of Dean before it reaches the river Dart (Scott, *Robert Herrick,* 62 n. 1).

7. *Ham.* 1.5.30–31.

8. Untraced.

9. KB and Amy stayed in Teignmouth, a coastal town about four kilometers south of Dawlish. See MS Eng. lett. d. 402 fol. 41[r] BOD.

37. Katharine Bradley, Letter to Edith Cooper

Dean Prior | Thurs., [31] Aug. 1882[1]

Thursday night. Aug. 30[th.]

Thou sowest not that body that shall be, but *bare grain.* The field is sown. Unseen in the furrows swells the harvest-corn of the big drama.[2] I have the characters and their attributes—clear as Banquo's line these pass before me[3]—not yet the action—or full situation. The characters are modern in their complexity—yet modern life has no flexibility—of action; its old bones are cramped;—a mythical Sicilean story, when the world was young, methinks must our drama be. Then for wit—we have had Machaion's irony—Fred's gay humour: now we have the cynic iron-cold—the jest of the scientist as he vivisects.[4] *No repetitions.* The motto for the dramatist should be "*Behold I make all things new.*"[5] Irene is the name of the Pretty. I have 8 clearly defined characters[6]—One of the heroes is a big young Shakespeare, healthy, gigantic of head and heart. On[e] of the bad characters is named Analrim!! I am beginning to feel a blood-relation to them all.

The subject is of course treachery political, conjugal,—the most diabolical form of it, the cold-blooded experimental study of pain. There are characters you will do *well*—notably Irene, Struan the young Shakespeare, and perhaps Veronica.

Pretty, even before we meet, my eyes feel their banks swoln with thought of our parting. My very kisses will be dewy with tears. I cannot let you go. The moors were not truly the moors yesterday—not like the Chagford way to Prince Town. *We* had the last 2 acts of the Dartmoor Tragedy; the scenery yesterday was mild, preliminary,—the Dart like a track of love running through a man's many-acred nature—was the one new impression. What is woman but a pleasant-fishing stream on an *[from header fol. 47[r]]* estate valuable for its timber, pasture-land etc.

"Heigh, ho the wooing o't"[7] *Farewell*[.]
My Pretty sleeps. Its little red mouth is closed.
Kisses bedew it. What then can bedew the lips but Love?
A.W.F.

*Tell Muddie, she cannot be admitted into the workshop. Only into the room where the perfect statues are *exhibted.*

My Garden.[8]

I have a garden-ground,—Oh not
To Solomon more dear
The lilied land he called his spouse[9]
Than this sweet spot my God allows
To be my comfort here;—
A pretty plot
Of musk-mallow[10] and sweet briar rose,
And yet for all my care bestows
It will not bear the Mustard-tree[11]
That brancheth to Eternity[.]

"One thing this land will ever lack"
I cried in my despair,
And weeping left the wayward soil
(An exile from my bootless toil)
Of her own self to bear.

But coming back
Through the dear fence to peer I found
The Herb of Grace, while all around
Faint fragrance filled the air.
Now of my garden boast I can
My Father is the Husbandman.

Dean Prior
Herrick's Home
August. 82.
[bird symbol]

MS Eng. lett. d. 400 fols. 47^r–48^v BOD

1. Incorrectly dated. Amy's letter to EC confirms Thursday 31 Aug. is the correct date (MS Eng. lett. d. 402 fols. 41^r–43^v BOD).

2. *LL* (1885).

3. *Mac.* 4.1.119–20.

4. Machaon is the doctor from *Call.* (1884); Alfred Durant (Fred) is a character from "Never Forgiven," an unpublished drama KB completed in Jul. 1882 (MS Eng. poet. e. 69 BOD), which Treby suggests was based on KB's love for Alfred Gerente (Treby, *MF Catalogue,* 29); the cynic of *LL* is Peter de Celano, who uses forged letters to implicate the Sicilian Margaritone in treason.

5. Rev. 21:4–5.

6. Irene became Iolanthe; Analrim became the Germanic Adheld; Struan probably became Markwald; the beautiful Sicilian noblewoman remained Veronica.

7. Robert Burn's "Duncan Gray" (Burns, 2:667; Palgrave, *Golden Treasury,* 218).

8. "My Garden" is written in the style of Herrick. It was recently published (Field, *Uncertain Rain,* 66).

9. Song of Sol. 4:12; 6:2.

10. KB sent EC a musk-mallow flower with letter 27.

11. Matt. 13:31–32.

38. Katharine Bradley, Letter to Edith Cooper

Ashburton | [Aug. 1882][1]

How daintily the Pretty does its accounts, even according to its heart's desires. It subtracts its pounds from its shilling, and the pounds remain!!! Bless it, it is growing up the unselfish and thoughtful Child I ached to see it. I was sure of my Poet, but not sure once that it would have a "religion." Dear and Blessed, might it have beheld how the ferns made a blue sheen in the radiant lanes yesterday, and walked along the beach, where years ago its Fowl gathered little shells and never dreamt of dramas—Neither does it now. It has not even thoughts—Nothing seems like anything else—the orchard's *busy* green is the only suggestive comment my brain has made to itself from the famous terrace-walk.

Ashburton

Love, Kisses

MS Eng. lett. c. 418 fols. 65^r–66^v BOD

1. The "famous terrace-walk" suggests this letter is part of the Dean Prior series of Aug. 1882.

39. Katharine Bradley, Letter to Edith Cooper

[Sept. 1882][1]

My Precious One,

A word of comfort. Hear the invocation. It belongs to Dean Proir, but could not be finished till I got here because of Pussie's illness[.]

Come, Holy Ghost![2]

Lo the poor faggots of my brain I lay
In order due
Round the stillbirth of my desire,
Burn thou there through!
At thy command
Each little stick
Shall straight grow quick
And leap—a living brand—
From crimson stem to aureate flower;
Rather than *hush,* will be
This poor dead pyre
Of soul, afire
With thee.

Or here is a thought—

the sea's lapseless obedience[3]

"O thou long-serving sea! The days of thy bondage oppress me, I am awed by thy time-worn compliance with command. As, fresh from the altars of churches, I stand by the creeping foam-ridge of thy fallen waves, or turn from the impatient devotion of an hour to the ceaseless service-s of ocean of thy tides, I am appaled by the majesty of the lapseless submission to law, the obedience that has never slacked since thy gathering waters were named of Heaven."

To morrow *the* moors, Darling,—*take comfort.* Sweet and Blessed, be patient. Last night till nine we paced the still beach in the moonlight; but the land of Grace and Brandon[4] for inspiration! Heaven keep you. Kisses—newpluckt-fruit from the garden of my Soul.

Ever, *[bird symbol].*

MS Eng. lett. c. 418 fol. 67 r/v BOD

1. Dated to Sept. 1882 largely by exclusion: it postdates the trip to Dean Prior, but in Sept. 1883 KB was overseas in The Hague. The reference to the beach and moors suggests Devon.

2. Published in *M&S* (47). The title refers to the opening phrase of an Anglican hymn, "Come, Holy Ghost, my soul inspire," which is itself a translation of a Latin hymn, "Veni Creator Spiritus" (Julian, *Dict. of Hymnology,* 245 and 1210).

3. This Herrick-like phrase was copied into a notebook by EC, but was not developed further. See MS Eng. misc. 339 fol. 61v BOD.

4. In "Never Forgiven," Grace Sweetday runs off with the aesthete Gerard Brandon. See also letter 37 n. 4.

40. Katharine Bradley, Letter to Edith Cooper

Lynmouth | Sept. [1882][1]

Lynmouth

Yes, Pretty through the old sacred walks, without the old sacred companions.[2]

Yet the sweetest September weather, and much content. Come to me, Come, A.W.F.

MS Eng. lett. c. 418 fol. 43r BOD

1. The proximity of Lynmouth to Exmoor and a common note of nostalgia suggest this letter was written at about the same time as the previous one.

2. KB may refer to their 1881 journey from Chagford on Dartmoor in South Devon to Blue Anchor and Minehead on the coast of North Devon. See MS Eng. lett. c. 419 fols. 165r–170v BOD.

41. Katharine Bradley, Annotated Envelope

1st letter from my Pretty Persian Puss
Boscastle, September 1882.

MS Eng. lett. c. 419 fol. 16r BOD

42. Edith Cooper, Letter to Katharine Bradley

[Boscastle] | [Sept. 1882][1]

Don't be sad I charge thee, by thy Pretty's lavender fur.
My darling Sim,

I have health, I have energy, I have inspiration. I drink them by throatfuls, as Thor drank from the inexhausible fountains of ocean.[2] To night thou shalt have a letter.

I kissed the one remaining cluster of bossy grapes as I laid them to rest in their basket, and I blessed you for all the fruit of your ripe love you give so bounteously to your Pretty.

The harbour draws me, and that prophetic intimation of the unseen, where the land breaks off.

All the love it is capable of the Pretty sends to you. May it attain to the stature of yours! This from Swinburne

—Love, that is blood within the veins of Time.[3]

No time for more.
Love my sweet little, longed-for Pussie.[4] Her's shall be tomorrow's letter from her old Cat.

MS Eng. lett. c. 419 fol. 17 r/v BOD

1. Dated from the envelope above. Although envelope and letter are not consecutively foliated, this seems to be the earliest of the Boscastle letters, and their separation may be a product of the letters' confused order prior to 1973. See "Dating the Correspondence."

2. Thor was tricked into drinking from a horn linked to the ocean (Guerber, *Norsemen,* 71–72).

3. *Tristram of Lyonesse,* prelude, 14 (Swinburne, 4:25).

4. Amy Cooper.

43. Katharine Bradley, Annotated Envelope

[PM Sat., 9 Sept. 1882]

2nd. letter after Tintagil

MS Eng. lett. c. 419 fol. 19r BOD

44. Edith Cooper, Letter to Katharine Bradley

Boscastle | [Sat., 9 Sept. 1882][1]

I have nothing but a low window-sill on wh. to write.

Yesterda[y]

My darling Sim,

The promise of a long letter cannot be fulfilled, for your Pretty walked at least 10 miles, and only got home from Tintagil at 7 o'clock—very tired and incapable of forming a sentence. This morning, dear little Boscastle is sun illumined and we *must* go out into the light of things.[2] The post starts a[t] 2 o'clock.

I have not yet got power to speak of what we saw yesterday. But, O Simorg, the soft lavender toes mounted the legendary height without the least trepidation and without the least assistance. To see two oceans dashing their blue thunder at your feet, to look up at the storied walls, oh, how it thrills! Tonight I will try "to speak out."[3] Now I am like Grey—with astonishment, admiration and delight. We could not make Tintagil our home. It is too cold, bleak and remote

Sketch of "Tintagil" by Edith Cooper [Sept. 1882]. (MS Eng. lett. c. 419, fol. 23^{r}, Bodleian Library, University of Oxford)

from the cheerful haunts of men.[4] And the wonderous old ruin will be more impressive in my memory from one day's inspired gaze than if I beheld it time after time. So I shall be strong and not even walk there again—if I can possibly help it.

I am looking forward to the letters wh: we must fetch. The thought of you all is the weft of my life, to wh: Nature and her loveliness is the coloured woof. I send you a bit of hare's foot clover (the symbolic Pretty) that drew its faint hoary life from the grey, crumbling ruins, that are like the quenched and abandoned pyre of Romance.

The very place where it grew may have been touched by the hand of Ysonde.[5] My other *in memoriam* is a little bit of stone from the mystic walls on wh: in golden appropriateness is a stain of lichen, wh: "reflects the sunsets of a Thousand years."[6] Love my dearest Mother, and my own little Pussie, and be blessed yourself, my darling Sim, by your devoted P.P.

The grapes quenched our thirst on the hot road from their dark skins that hold the water of Fairy-land.

MS Eng. lett. c. 419 fol. 18 [r/v] BOD

1. Dated from PM on the envelope above.

2. "The Tables Turned; An Evening Scene on the Same Subject," 15–16 (Wordsworth, 4:108).

3. "*He never spoke out.* In these four words is contained the whole history of Gray, both as a man and as a poet" (Arnold, 4:51). Arnold defends the reputation of Thomas Gray (1716–1771) by attributing his meager creative output to his depressions (Arnold, 4:65).

4. Hannah More, "Belshazzar," 138. More's *Sacred Dramas: Chiefly Intended for Young Persons* were commonly read by Victorian children as lessons on religious conformity (Ford, *Hannah More,* ix).

5. Tintagel is the setting for the court of King Mark in the romance of Tristan and Yseut (Beroul, *Romance of Tristan,* 10–11).

6. This line of blank verse may come from an unpublished poem.

45. Katharine Bradley, Annotated Envelope

[PM Mon., 11 Sept. 1882].

4th. letter.

Letter to Mud, descriptive of Minster church, and to me descriptive of Tintagil.

MS Eng. lett. c. 419 fol. 29r BOD

46. Edith Cooper, Letter to Katharine Bradley

[Boscastle | Sun., [10 Sept. 1882][1]

You and the darling Mother Shall both be fed this afternoon.
Sunday.
Darling Sim,
I am awaiting with hungry expectation the arrival of the letters.

This morning we go to the weird little church on the hill, that was robbed of its bells by the tempetuous ocean.[2] As Paps tells our hostess "—it is another blue day!" We must mind that the beauty does not tempt us too far. Yesterday we decidedly overtired ourselves.

I wonder if *Et tu, Brute*[3] is enlarging and springing up, a mustard-tree,[4] in that dear big brain. I cannot give out. I can *only take* in with Gargantuan mental mouth. Boscastle is indeed a blessed place—unlike any thing I have seen before. The mail coach has just drawn up—I hope it brings a paper traveller from Ivythorpe.

Thine own P.P.

MS Eng. lett. c. 419 fol. 22[r/v] BOD

1. Dated from PM on the envelope above. As no mail service would have operated on Sunday, it would have been posted on Monday. EC's illustrations of Tintagel and Boscastle Harbour have been catalogued with this letter, although there is no obvious reference to them in the text. See sketch on p. 70.

2. Forrabury church in Boscastle has no bells. Local superstition has it that the profanity and arrogance of the captain transporting the bells to the church caused a huge wave to sink the ship as it neared the harbor. The bells are said to chime from beneath the sea when storms are approaching "as a warning to the wicked" (Hunt, *Popular Romances,* 438–39).

3. An early title for *LL.*

4. Matt. 13:31–32. See also "My Garden," letter 37.

47. Edith Cooper, Letter to Katharine Bradley

[Boscastle] | Sun. evening, [10 Sept. 1882][1]

Swinburne's Description of Tintagel.[2]
. . . the towery way
That rose against the rising front of day,

Stair based on stair, between the rocks unhewn,
To those strange halls wherethrough the tidal Tune[3]
Rang loud or lower from soft or strengthing[4] sea,
Tower shouldering tower, to windward and to lee,
With change of floors and stories, flight on flight,
That clomb and curled up to the crowning height,
Whence men might *see wide east and west in one*
And on one sea waned moon and mounting sun.
And severed from the sea-rock's base, where stand
Some worn walls yet, they saw the broken strand,
The beachless cliff that in the sheer sea dips,
The sleepless shore inexorable to ships,
And *the straight causeway's bare gaunt spine between*
The sea-spanned walls and naked mainland[5] green.

Darling Simorg,
This is the motto of the little chapter of love I am going to write to thee, this Sunday evening. But before I turn to my remembrance of the wonderful ruins, I must demand a letter. This is no common Cerberus, whose hunger will be appeased by thin, mealy-coloured post-cards! No, no! Feed the "barking stomach"[6] of my *expectation;*—the bathos would be too great if I were to say *love.*—But indeed *that* is ravenous.

Not only my tongue, but my thought, stammers when I turn to the memory of Tintagel—The stupendous mount, the perpendicular descents, the few mystic ruins, that look like the bone of architecture dropped from between the teeth of Time! A finger-touch wears away the crumbled stone. The two remaining Arches have been cracked by the antique jaws, and the Chronian tongue has left the walls grey, with its rough loll. Tintagil is the grave of Romance—of human Romance—and Nature dare not approach it with *her* enduring Romance of ivy; She leaves it naked,—in untender awe. The yellow samphire, with golden sandal, scales the precipice, but stops short at the grim foundation of the old-hair-coloured ruin—the ruin among ruins!

Perhaps I was most impressed with the . . . "old hoar chapel, like a strait stone tomb Sheer on the sea-rocks" (Swinburne)[7] where they took Tristram to punish his sinless sin.[8] On the lower heights is the abode of warlike Man; on the highest height is the abode of the God of Chivalry. The rude altar stretches its bare adoring chest like a victim to the imminent sky. God's arch-priestly robe of blue aether almost sweeps it.

I thought of Arthur; I thought of Lancelot;—but I did not think of Tristram, Ysonde, King Mark. For their sakes I shall visit it again. (Swinburne's poem is fine, sometimes supreme, in conception; but monotonous and redundant in general execution.)

Goodnight; bless you, my dearest.

Your very own, P.P.

Love and kiss my Pussie for me. Goodnight, little one!
The rain descends.

MS Eng. lett. c. 419 fols. 27r–28v BOD

1. EC's "Sunday evening" letter carries over the impatience of her previous letter. As they are both written from Tintagel on Sunday, it seems likely they were written on the same day.

2. *Tristram of Lyonesse,* 2.42–57 (Swinburne, 4:59).

3. Swinburne: Tune] tune.

4. Swinburne: strengthing] strengthening.

5. Swinburne: mainland] mainland's.

6. Robert Herrick, "A Country Life: To his Brother, M. Tho. Herrick," 29 (Herrick, *Poetical Works,* 34). This image, which also suggests the barking, six-mouthed, female monster Scylla, also appears in *FT* 4.2.66–67 (*FT/WR/LL,* 75).

7. *Tristram of Lyonesse,* 4.53–54 (Swinburne, 4:87).

8. *Tristram of Lyonesse,* 4.230 (Swinburne, 4:93).

48. Katharine Bradley, Letter to Edith Cooper

[Ivythorpe] | [Sept. 1882][1]

P. Darling, It is wonderful how the drama grows![2] The scenes are all settled for acts I and V and I and II and nearly for act III. Ov[er] act IV I mean to spend my fondest strength. But P. I think another year there might be a St. Michael's Mount drama.[3] Hunt in guidebooks, what a solitary might live there—with seas stretching to Hispania and Colombia. Think of it, And let a little cluster of thoughts gather round it. There must be good legends, ask learn, make the graves give up their dead.

Veronica[4] is to me the figure of dominant interest—a very flower—a balsam—full of ineffable queenliness—drawing all men to her—Margarito in passionate physical worship—Celano to break in—Ah, what scenes—and the half forged plot is going on well too. I am reading *Othello*—and finding in it—oh, surely we are only half mentally awake even now. I think "Et tu, Brute" is worth keeping out of the wet for. Home darling, home on Saturday?? if you may.

He loves [bird symbol].

MS Eng. lett. d. 407 fol. 217 r/v BOD

1. Dated from references to the drafting of *LL* in Sept. 1882.
2. *LL* (1885).
3. This drama does not seem to have gone any further.
4. In *LL,* Veronica falls victim to the Iago-like Peter de Celano, and is used by him in his intrigue to implicate Margarito in treason.

49. Edith Cooper, Letter to Katharine Bradley

Boscastle | Mon., [11 Sept. 1882][1]

Ship Inn, Boscastle. (Bless the humble abode of peace!) Monday evening.

Darling Simorg,

More of Tintagel! It is not the weakness of adventure or curiosity, but the safe ardour, and huge strength of fascination that draws me to the storied place. Do not fear that I should see it too much, dwelling away from it, and looking forward to the sight of it with hunger of mind. Did I see too much of "The tree of Forgiveness?"[2] Tintagel is the birth place of Arthur and Inspiration. It is full of quickening memories—heart-holding, brain-stirring. My second visit is trebly more to me than the first. Only the chapel did I leave unvisited—there I could but sink below my former self, wh: had been lifted in the ascension of inspiration to excelling distance of thought. First we visited the largest cave, wh: the rising tide had not yet reached. It cleaves from side to side the grand foundations and mountainous bulk (moles) of Arthur's Mount, joining the two seas, wh: the Causeway divides. The further tide had gained half the cave, and we saw the bright distant waves leap up, sun-pierced, and then bow and thunder in the Straitened funereal opening. The vast Stygian Cave looks like the den of a "mighty Creature"[3]—skulls and bones of rock choke its oriface. Old Night[4] clings bat-like to the roof and clefts—the twilight walls are grey as a wolf-skin. We saw the labouring tides shake their strong white hands, like the workmen of Mont Cennis(?),[5] rejoicing that they had met in their subterranean toil.

Then we had our lunch on a rock, and actually swallowed the lamb-bread[6] sandwiches unhesitatingly—tho' it must be confessed, in my case, with shuddery pleasure.

Then the causeway invited us, with its either-hand Seas. I stood a quater-of-an-hour on this cord of stone that binds into connected existence the Twin mounts. I love it. Next we half ascended the steps, and sat there silent and apart, the samphire, the rocks, the swaying sea below us. There I thought of Tristram, and said involentarily to myself—

"Love cannot die,
Love dieth not"
"Why did we ever break love's holiest bond,
Ysonde, Ysonde?"[7]

I wonder if the thunders of this wild sea boom an excruciating concord with the tragedy of Tristram's love in Wagner's opera![8] Would I might hear it! Once in Swinburne's fine poem the sea and wind burst into agonized chorus as Ysonde recounts to Christ her shame, her sin, her impenitence, her love—in the lonely night watches.[9] Then we clomb the landward Mount, and roamed by the exalted walls, on wh: Time "feeds like a dying flame upon a brand."[10] Their appearance is inconceivably old. Decay, in them, struggles for existence with the dominant vitality of storm-wind and storm.—Decay, unmummied and unarmed! It is very terrible, and terribly piteous.

How much higher and better is it not to know that Arther *really* lived, and Tristram loved here.—It is nearly eleven o'clock; I am mightily tired, and even the coffee, to wh: you owe these long letters, refuses to work: "—And the evening is of the forth day!"[11] Goodnight, my darling. I go to kiss you all.

Your own,
Persian Pussy.

MS Eng. lett. c. 419 fols. 30[r/v], 32[r/v] BOD

1. Dated from EC's trip to Cornwall in Sept. 1882.

2. *The Tree of Forgiveness* by Edward Coley Burne-Jones was displayed at the Grosvenor Gallery's summer exhibition in 1882 (Newall, *Grosvenor Gallery,* 58).

3. Matthew Henry's Nonconformist Bible commentary contains this description of the crocodile-like leviathan of Job 41 (Henry, *An Exposition,* 24).

4. *Paradise Lost,* 1.543 (Milton, 2.1:27).

5. Italian and French workmen drilling the railway tunnel through Mont Cenis met at the center in 1871 in an heroic engineering feat considered to rival that of the Suez Canal ([Mont Cenis], *Times,* 20 Sept. 1871).

6. EC also wrote to Amy of the "thick sandwiches of bread and cold lamb" (EC, letter to Amy Cooper, Monday [11 Sept. 1882], MS Eng. lett. d. 402 fol. 49[r] BOD).

7. Untraced, possibly original.

8. The first English performance of Richard Wagner's *Tristan und Isolde* was 20 Jun. 1882 ("Wagner's Tristan and Isolde," *Times*, 22 Jun. 1882).

9. *Tristram of Lyonesse*, 5.260–73 (Swinburne, 4:101–2).

10. Probably "Laon and Cythna," 8.209–10 (Shelley, 1:362).

11. Gen. 1:19.

50. Katharine Bradley, Letter to Edith Cooper

[Ivythorpe, | Thurs., [14 Sept. 1882][1]

Thursday
Darling and most precious P.

The time is come for you to leave Boscastle, that I feel—now to the calmer, statelier pleasures of Penzance. Look lovingly, lingeringly at St. Michael's;[2]—but don't I charge you by *the Great Dreamer*[3] think of visiting it at low tide. Have a boat and go a[t] high; if it is safe and meet so to do—I know not. But better see it only from afar. One thing we don't believe in your letters. You fail to convince us that ocean could ever look with "one auspicious and one dropping eye"[4]—as you suggest. One livid closed eyelid, and the other open eye—Humbug, Pretty! These are traveller's tales. The next place you will love is the Lizard—there an exquisite womanly nature of wh. the tiniest details are worshipful. I am going after a chat with my P. to write to Symonds.[5] I shall try to make use of him. Surely when he sees such fair young women he will be the slave of both, as Girdlestone said in the days of his gallantry. What a poor cast off lover is E.D.G[.][6] now!

I am going on fast with the scaffolding of the drama.[7] The shell of the building will be up—or rather framework—*good stout* walls I warrant you—will be up, I hope, when you return, and I shall be ready for my Pretty to come in with her mural decorations, her tapestries, and wood carvings. I cannot help constructing even the political scenes, the details of wh. must be reserved till the days of our Knowledge. The times of our ignorance I am "winking at" and going on. This is *not* a bit I am going to put into Symond's letter. I have made good use of the fool. He is set on by Peter de Celano to dodge the archbishop of Salarino, whose desperate melancholy and sullenness provoke the laughter-loving rogue—He w[d.] fain see him hung up by the leg and making a long face then. Peter says *he shall.* This is Capital for a slight relief, for the fearful pressure of dramatic tragic interest but not enough: *where is the laughter of the play to spring from?* The Musselmen may be crafty and worldly wise, but I feel they can't laugh. And we cannot possibly get droll situation. Look at your grotesque rocks and ponder. This I feel as yet the only serious defect. We are almost too rich in variety of female character; Margarito, or Margaritone I cannot as yet wholly grasp. I have got at the *WORKS* of all the other characters. Tell me *freely,* do you feel you can turn from the westward-smiling seas to Sicily. If you seriously feel you must have Cornwall, doubtless I could work with you. Being inspired, I w^d. not draw you away, if you feel you will be *torn* away. *Speak:* but do not attempt any constructive work, while you are away.

Last night, after Little One was in bed, I open and carefully packed up "Miscellaneous poems" to read to Muddie the Lays;[8] and lo—I came across many of my P's dear early poems. Once more I read the invocation—"Dower me with thine own lips."[9] P. after the mighty cares and interests of the drama to go back to these early lyrics is like a gt. statesman's return to his native village. He sees the village girl who first caught his fancy—and walks by the quiet streams that made his musings musical;—he recognizes the ineffable charm of those fresh meditative days, but from the perplexities of home—politics, and absorbing interests of foreign affairs can only give to early associations the tribute of a Kindly sigh. The morning wears away; and I must write a word to "Paps."

Dear Pretty how I trust the inevitable pains are coming on to-day! Then may you be free to enjoy *quietly* the beauties of Penzance—Don't dash off wildly to Land's End at once, there's a good. My Darling—My one who has no Firster—My chiefest and too fondly-cherished;—but it's of no use Solomon-songing you—not with the Mother's right of possession, but with deep spousal spirit passions I love you. And the only Creatures I am not *[from header fol. 70b^r]* jealous of are God and Nature. Give to these Your highest, your best—and what remains to old όγη[10] the earth-mother.

γη
alias A.W.F[.]

MS Eng. lett. c. 418 fols. 70b ^r/v^, 174 ^r/v^ BOD

1. Dated from EC's trip to Cornwall in Sept. 1882.

2. St. Michael's Mount is an island accessible only by a causeway at low tide. The ruins of monastic and castle buildings crown its summit (Britton and Brayley, *Devonshire & Cornwall,* 32–33); this religious connection is probably why KB paraphrases the Holy Communion's response, "It is meet and right so to do" (*Book of Common Prayer,* 272).

3. God may be the Great Dreamer, but the phrase also suggests William Morris's "Dreamer of dreams," from *The Earthly Paradise,* 22 (Morris, *Collected Works,* 3:xv).

4. *Ham.* 1.2.8–15.

5. John Addington Symonds (1840–93) was a prominent literary figure as well as Havelock Ellis's silent collaborator on *Sexual Inversion* (1896). Robert Baker Girdlestone had sent *Bell.* to Symonds, with a request that he review it. While Symonds declined, he was interested in the idea of an aunt-niece collaboration (Symonds, *Letters,* 2:677). KB wrote to him including photographs of herself and EC, and information about *LL,* to which Symonds replied on 16 Oct. 1882, commenting that he did not think the subject very promising.

6. Edward Deacon Girdlestone (1829–92) was the author of *Vivisection: In Its Scientific, Religious and Moral Aspects* (1884), to which the Bristol and Clifton Anti-Vivisection Society printed a reply in the same year. KB is probably speaking of him metaphorically as someone with whom there has been a parting of the ways. See also letter 18 n. 12.

7. *LL* (1885); the fool referred to later in this letter is sent by Celano to spy upon the Archbishop; Salarino was later changed to Salerno; and the dialogue sketched out below appears in the play at 1.3.46–49 (*FT/WR/LL,* 243).

8. Possibly "The Lay of Love which dieth not—," which Treby identifies as one of Tristram's Lays (*MF Catalogue,* 150). The poem was included in the first edition of *UTB* (1893), which was withdrawn and decreased in the same year (Treby, *MF Catalogue,* 90). "Miscellaneous Poems" probably refers to a small group of EC's poems, including "The Lay of Love," catalogued at MS Eng. poet. d. 55 BOD.

9. A line from "To Apollo—The Conqueror," an unpublished lyric from the exercise book "The Poems of Isla for the Joy of Arran Leigh" (MS Eng. misc. e. 338 BOD).

10. Ge or Gaea, the all-nurturing Earth-mother (Smith, *G&R Biography and Mythology,* 2:195). KB signs her letter with the Greek for "Earth."

51. Katharine Bradley, Annotated Envelope

[Sept. 1882][1]

Description of the wet defile, and the accursed brambles!
9th Letter

MS Eng. lett. c. 419 fol. 38r BOD

1. The PM is 10 Sept. 1882.

52. Edith Cooper, Letter to Katharine Bradley

Boscastle | [Wed.–Thurs., 13–14 Sept. 1882][1]

Ship Inn, Boscastle.
My darling old [*bird symbol*],
The Pussie laps with purring sides the large saucer of milky paper your distant hand gives it. It yet dearly loves you, although living that life in nature, wh: al-

most de-individualizes, till one is only a "portion of that loveliness."[2] Yes. Catch Symonds with the fine live bait of *Callirrhoe*—he is a choice soul!!![3]

I am in a bitterer mood than Hamlet's. "Man delights me not, nor woman neither!"[4] O Misanthrope of Elsinore, the words are passive as your own nature—and you knew not tourists—save the company of players, and they had hearts that were touched by human things—if not by natural;—and for that grave sin your rebuke was biting. I suffer from Swiftean activity of unspeakable disgust when I pass by Tourists,[5]—their eyes as gooseberries to the Nature around them; their minds—unlike the 1st. players—incapable of human emotion and high response to ideal story—to whom Tintagel "is nothing to see"[6] but a place to be *done*. Execrable Yahoos! My heart like the snake, eats dust and descends prone onto its belly,[7] when I reflect that I am their fellow-creature. And yet that Venerable high-built ruin, wd. be but a trapping to the beauty of the wild beautiful landscape, if human love and life had not been there, and made it "the cynosure of neighbouring eyes"[8] and Nature but its ornament. Well, well, well—I must go back and take out for you the golden sights I have locked in the iron safe of my memory. In the early morning it rained. As soon as there was a pause, we started. The huge sails of the sky—the storm-cumuli—were dirtied and fouled with aerial tempest. The sea was—and continued all day—a delphinium-blue, with gt. streaks of dusky red, such as that wh: defiles the pure blue of the flower, especially on the under sides of the petals.

The first thing we did was foolish. Instead of going the orthodox way to our unseen waterfall—St. Knighton's Kieve[9] we used our private judgment and went up a narrow, lovely, Streamy, sounding, woody glen. It might have been the green tear-bottle of the weeping morning—so wet, so dank, so humid, so watery was it. It soaked my boots, it drenched the hem of my garment, it breathed into my throat. I scarcely saw the osmundas[10] and the feathered Kind of the vegetable world, that were drinking in the balmy moisture, and joyfully dripping all the length of their pinnate verdure. Then the brambles, like St. Anthony's fiends, tore my flesh with little red claws. D . . . them!!!!! We were thankful to be removed from this Vale of Tears.[11]

My feet soon got warm and dry on the high road, my dress grew less dark and heavy at the bottom, my throat cleared.

On we trudged to Trebawith Sands about 2 miles beyond Tintagel. The sand was nearly covered of the sea, but enough was left for us to behold the gt. Cornish waves become effeminate as Hannibal's soldiers at Cannae,[12] with the luxury of ease. Their mighty single onrush of blue thundering volume, was dissipated in numberless small swells. Obstruction is The creator and only-begetter of Power. When the sand was surpassed by the weakened surges, and the rocks met them with Roman obduracy, how they girt up their white wide-spreading foam, and rushed on to the firm impediment with stride of waters and stroke of waves! The prone fall of the land in this cove is quite remarkable. It seems to have tumbled forward in old exhaustion on to the soft, wind-shaken, foam-feathered bed of the sea. Requiescat in pace! Blast and billow forbid not rest. Noise is often the woof in the Garment of slumber. Under a rock we ate our humble, but satisfying, lunch—I read my letters and vainly tried to describe that cold, lucid, exquisite green of arched breakers—that green, wh: is always kinned with whiteness—snow of winter and snow of sea, edge of glacier, base of icicle.

Thursday

Then we toiled up the steep down, and gathered the autumn Squill (wh: I intended to send to the Mother, but find it has been swept away by the neat landlady) till we came to my Tintagel. We had an indescribably majestic view of land-mount—and sea-mount, causeway and towers. The mouldering donjon looked like the eyrie of Time— the grey eagle-winged old Being with the beaked scythe,—built above the amazing blue of symbolized Eternity, and holding within it the blood-bright ruby of chivalry, wh: the antique claws have snatched from Earth.

Then we ascended the ringing causeway, and stood between the two Amazonian breasts of land, rock-mailed—under the left of wh: beats the tidal heart, while round both is the iron-grey serried chain—now broken—of warlike walls. Afterwards we scrambled along the cave-pierced lower rocks, and had a parting view of the sun-illumined grandeur of the glorious scene—and then I turned my back on the dearest place in Cornwall.

Paps offered to take me on our homeward way to see St. Knighton's Kieve—"still thought, of never seen"[13]—but I had walked about 14 miles, and it would have been down right intemperance.

I am grateful for your noble, self-denying, Tantalizing, restraint with regard to our dramatic work,—wh: I ponder in my heart, but not with my brain. It is all I can do to listen to "this mighty sum of things forever speaking"[14]—this arch-Colridge of a Nature with its wondrous, interminable monologue.[15] Good bye, dearest fellow-dramatist,

Thy feline abstraction of a P.P.

MS Eng. lett. c. 419 fols. 33^{r}–37^{v} BOD

1. While the envelope's PM is 10 Sept. 1882, it seems probable from the letter's place in the Boscastle correspondence that it was written on the 13th or 14th.

2. *Adonais,* 379–80 (Shelley, 2:401).

3. John Addington Symonds, see letter 50.

4. *Ham.* 2.2.322 and 3.2.18–32.

5. Swift, *Gulliver's Travels,* 266.

6. Possibly a reference to Anthony Trollope's Lady Glencora: "What's the use of it . . . There's nothing to see, and the wind is as cold as charity" (*Can You Forgive Her?* 28).

7. Gen. 3:14.

8. *L'Allegro,* 80 (Milton, 1:37).

9. St. Knighton's Kieve is considered one of the most beautiful places in Cornwall (Hunt, *Pop. Romances,* 279). EC's tussle with the foliage is similar to Wilkie Collins's description of his attempt to reach the Kieve (Collins, *Rambles,* 155).

10. Pteridomania (fern collecting) had been extremely fashionable to the end of the 1860s, making the Coopers rather old-fashioned in maintaining their interest into the 1880s. While wealthy collectors bought exotic ferns, most enthusiasts sought their own. Cornwall's royal fern (*Osmunda regalis*) was highly prized and, by 1888, was rare in many parts of the county (Allen, *Vict. Fern Craze,* 54–56). For the Cooper family's fern collecting, see letter 56.

11. A pun on the common literary phrase, "this vale of tears," which refers to the world as a place of sorrow.

12. EC's initial impulse to write "Capua" (see "Textual Apparatus") was correct. Hannibal's soldiers were softened by spending the winter at Capua (Smith, *G&R Biography and Mythology,* 2:337); at Cannae they celebrated their greatest victory (23.44–52; Livy, *Ab Urbe Condita,* 5:347–71).

13. Untraced; possibly a paraphrase of Wilkie Collins's abortive attempt to view the Kieve. See above, n. 9.

14. "Expostulation and Reply," 25–26 (*Wordsworth,* 4:107–8).

15. Samuel Taylor Coleridge's reputation as a brilliant but unstoppable conversationalist was famously noted by William Hazlitt (*Collected Works,* 5:167).

53. Katharine Bradley, Annotated Envelope

[PM Sat., 16 Sept. 1882]

First Penzance Letter
Descriptive of St. Michael's Mount. and the Bay.

MS Eng. lett. c. 419 fol. 199^{r} BOD

54. Edith Cooper, Letter to Family (including Katharine Bradley)

[Fri., 15 Sept. 1882][1]

Mrs Mitchell,
Belle Vue,
Marazion,
Mt Penzance,
Cornwall.

Settled down at Penzance!—No, no, no, my dear Ones. Such beings as the Paps and Puss could never be happy there. I could throw the mud and bad eggs of my malediction at the place, with Carlylean energy.[2] From the distance it is fair enough—but within are narrow muddy streets, crowds of Yahoos, painted hotels—and the place is like the inside of the Phalerian Bull[3]—burning hot and airless. Not a happy memory is connected with it. This morning I was in despair. The cloudy drugget on the sky's blue floor was rolled into cumulated heaps on the horizon, and we saw the heaven in its best loveliness. But where should we find a home? Our only chance seemed to be with a froggy old maid in close rooms at Penzance. My whole soul rose up like an angry billow. Circumstances should not obstruct our joy. When we went on to the promnade far away, toy like and diminished, my eyes first rested on St. Michael's Mount. On the mainland was a streak of white—a village! My heart leapt up; I instantly proposed we should walk there (3 miles) before arranging with our froggy old maid.

Almost fainting with the atmosphere, I begin the memorable and propitious walk. The air freshened. I saw the perfect arc of the mighty bay, drawn in ochre of yellow sands by the divine Artist; and full in front the sacred Mount, in its true incomparable proportions. "Ne'er dreamed I, never saw, a sight so fair."[4] The tide was low and—Oh forgive me, sweetly-anxious friends!—I crossed with exultation.

The wet sands and sea were blooming with ripe lavender and goldened grey of seeding meadows before harvest,—the black reefs of dragging sea-weed forming an absolutely unsurpassable contrast. We walked between the waters, cut off on either hand, and roamed all over the blessed spot, whose summit is worthy of angels. It is covered with bracken and borage, the stems and leaves of wh:, with their flushed grey work in with the fleshy hue always latent in granite—and the great rocks *are* all granite. With enthusiastic courage I went up the narrow, dark, almost interminable tower stair-case, reached the very top of the castle, and laid a hand on St. Michael's Chair.[5] We were on the very point of taking humble lodgings on the very mount—the difficulty of the tide alone preventing us. We felt that here we must set up our temporary rest, and here we are—not on the Mount itself, but what is almost better, only some few hundred yards away from it—a road, and the path between the waters, alone separating us from it, in its near, yet isolated, grandeur. Our lodgings are most comfortable, and we can procure all the few necess-aries of simple life, in dear little Marazion—guarded by its "guarded Mount."[6]

The whole afternoon was wasted in the difficult—or rather slow—transit of our worldly goods from Penzance to Marazion. Tonight the Father and I took up our dear delightful mode of life, and walked—solitary and arm in arm, along a precipitous sea-wall—the full tide on one side and tamarisks on the other. We watched night shading the Mount with thick black crayon—and then the rising of the lamps in the castle. From my bed-room I see the "gt. vision." The blacksmith's shop is nearly opposite; a little sand-street quite opposite. A man with a bag-pipe played us in. Tomorrow we go probably to St. Ives. We are rather too tired for Land's End or Lizard. Last night, at the Hotel, I hardly slept at all. Now with the brevity, wh: Carlyle found to be the soul of wit in description,[7] I will try to give you yesterday.

When we left Boscastle, heartily waving to our good Mrs Forward and lingeringly looking our last, the sea was not such a Brett blue[8] as when we first saw it—the light rather streaky on it—no joyful fringe of exuberant foam. Sky:—like an agate cup—Round the edge low cumuli of the softened white of a pearl or distant snow. Country—like a mosaic pavement for the feet of the wind—the coloured fragments of field, cemented by the lines of hedge. We passed the hollow of *Slaughter Bridge* (Arthur's last battle-field) and the mussel-coloured tops of Router and Brown Willy[9]—and the granite quarry, from whose stony loins grew the Eddystone Lighthouse. I do not like Bodmin. Why?

At Bodmin there's a mad-house,[10] And that's the reason why. There is, I do not know what, of low spirits about the place. From Bodmin to Bodmin R^d.^ is very pretty—hills, round trees, beechen hedges. Our coaching-companions were quite indifferent. Journey by train:—weird, unusual sunset, a semi-circle of rays —goldened vermillion.—Then sea, trees, mines dimly seen—Nature's face in the dagerreotype(?) of Twilight. Then obliteration of minor details—the Earth one dust heap—the sky, as far as seen—like the bluish sides of a slate-quarry. Finally opaque night, torn by infrequent lights. Yahoos around us, with little ponds of saliva between their feet and rude, unbridled tongues (the very remembrance makes me shudder). Then the arch-infliction of a painted hotel. No wonder that it was only with slow, painful effort, I became worthy to look on the Sacred Mount.

Your letters are my heart's breakfast, and I cannot think how we shall get them from Penzance tomorrow. Next sheet shall have a morning-greeting. Now a good-night to all.

Their very own,

Edith, P.P. ½ J. Cooley.[11]

MS Eng. lett. c. 419 fols. 194^{r}–198^{v} BOD

1. Dated from PM on envelope above. It seems likely it was written on Fri., 15 Sept., rather than Sat., as they probably would not have traveled on a Sunday.

2. Thomas Carlyle (1795–1881), author, biographer, and historian. EC's reference to a bad temper of Carlylean energy reflects upon the furious intensity and indignation of his writings, but may also owe something to the impact of recent controversial revelations about Carlyle's domestic life by James Anthony Froude. See Broughton, "Froude-Carlyle Embroilment."

3. Phalaris burned his victims alive inside a metal bull (Smith, *G&R Biography and Mythology,* 3:235).

4. Probably a deliberate misquotation of "Composed upon Westminster Bridge": "N'er saw I, never felt, a calm so deep!" (11; Wordsworth, 3:38).

5. The projecting stone lantern of a tower built on St. Michael's Mount, Cornwall. A seat was cut from the stone in commemoration of the apparition of St. Michael appearing there, and is a dangerous climb (Hunt, *Pop. Romances,* 197).

6. "The great vision of the guarded Mount" (*Lycidas,* 161; Milton, 1:82; Palgrave, 95).

7. Shakespeare noted, "Brevity is the soul of wit" (*Ham.* 2.2.90); EC humorously suggests Thomas Carlyle was verbose even when speaking of brevity.

8. John Brett (1831–1902) was a landscape artist whose seascapes were characterized by their striking blues and greens. See *DNB 1901–1911;* "Obituary [of John Brett]," *Times,* 9 Jan. 1902.

9. Bodmin Moor has many tors, including Rough Tor (which EC names Router) and Brown Willy (Balchin, *Cornwall,* 21 and 42). KB's sonnet "Brown Willy" was published in *WH,* 183; EC's subsequent reference to the Eddystone Lighthouse may be to the new (fifth) lighthouse that had been only recently lit (1882), or to James Smeaton's more famous (fourth) lighthouse (Wryde, *British Lighthouses,* 95–102).

10. Cornwall Lunatic Asylum was in Bodmin. See "Cornwall Lunatic Asylum," *Times,* 1 Jul. 1864.

11. John Cooley was an early collaborative name, a combination of their surnames, COOper/bradLEY. Nothing was published under this pseudonym.

55. Katharine Bradley, Annotated Envelope

[Mon., PM 18 Sept. 1882]

3rd Penzance letter
Description of the tide-pools.
[written on fol. 44v under inside flap in EC's hand]
Think it will be fine.
Off to Land's End.
Flowers—Squill, Samphire.
Lady's tresses for Muddie.

MS Eng. lett. c. 419 fol. 44r/v BOD

56. Edith Cooper, Letter to Katharine Bradley

Marazion | [Mon., 18 Sept. 1882]

Marazion ("Lyonesse unswallow'd of the tides"[1])
Darling Simorg-All-Wise-Fowl,
Plumage of tamarisk will I bring you;—fit offering for your feathery omniscience. I have seen the lovely plant at every turn—responsive to the will of the sea-wind, as the billows to the influence of the moon. Its obedient grace, its heathery endurance, combined with its delicate southern green and lightsome gladness!—I love it.

I have not seen a fern in southern Cornwall.[2] The osmundas (of the north) were growing in large-fronded maturity—too old and grand, and indespensible to be dragged from the stream-edging home they made so beautiful. Paps laid a hand on one of them,—but passed on. This morning we took a long inland walk to a distant cove. Coffin-lead was the heavy sky, dreary the abandoned tin-mines,[3] mean the domesticated land with its breath sweet—as the breath of the Kine. In the meadows?—with cabbages!! Before we got to the cove, the only picture we sketched in the *Liber Studiorum*[4] of memory, was that of a white cottage, with bright thatch, hung with Virginian Creeper—setting like the sun-fuschia(?.) and passionflowers, grey—with the crown of thorns painted over with the cobalt of Paradise. To the left of the house were some windy elms, with many branches round the still pool below them.

At last we reached the rewarding Cove, and the Father was most truly the Father as he bent attentive back over the tide-pools. Indeed, indeed, but they were very fair![5] Within their salt, yet resting, water little fish—"such stuff as dreams are made of"[6]—passed by with visionary glide and disappearance; anemænies—old red, crome, apple-green, the tentacles tipped with the apple's first creeping suggestion of ripe tint,—budded or blossomed on the rocks; while wondrous exquisite, *out*-landish weeds—fair as flowers or fruit of Earth, floated or lay. How fancy-stirring are these drifted testamonies of an under-wave America, whose only Columbus is the diver, whose imperfectly-witnessed beauty we shall never see! The low diagonal rocks naturally swarthy—one leperously sea-stricken with crust of balanæ (look out this name and correct it.)

The walk home was unpleasant—a mere scramble around the cliff, and yet with this disadvantage, a race against the sure-footed never broken-winded runner—Time. We did not dine till ½ past two. And this—only the fifth dinner out of the eleven days since we left you,—will be our last, we hope. With our exertions—dinner only makes us ill, hurries us, and "causeth melancholie."[7] A light sandwich-lunch, and an encreased tea, alone suit us. We had to walk off our despondency this afternoon—gaze at the Mount and the sunset—bronzy glow about tempestuous clouds of hollow blue; walk, walk, till the distant lights of Penzance were like glow-worms on the dark bank of land. The admiration, by wh: we live, is mine here; but the love? It is all for the northward coast.

I cannot write my love with this stiff unspontaneous pen. (Sharp mew!) Tell my own Mother that I Keep Land's End for her. (We are called at six o'clock.) Let thy brain increase and bring forth fruits after its Kind (its mighty constructive Kind.)[8] Ever write to thy Pretty. Love my own other-ones for me, and thyself too. The P.P[.]—who loves you and mews for you—mews for you and loves you.

MS Eng. lett. c. 419 fols. 39r–41v BOD

1. *Tristam of Lyonesse,* 1.4 (Swinburne, 4:33).

2. For Victorian fern collecting, see letter 52 n. 10. KB also mentions fern collecting in letter 10.

3. Most of the tin and copper mines around St. Just had been abandoned by this time (Millward and Robinson, *SW Peninsula,* 120–22).

4. Book of studies (L.).

5. "Mary Hamilton" (1–2), a popular English ballad (Child, *English & Scottish Pop. Ballads,* 385).

6. *Tmp.* 4.1.156–57.

7. Robert Burton identifies diet as the first unnatural factor in the production of melancholy (1.2.2.1; Burton, *Anatomy of Melancholy,* 217). This is particularly true when diet is combined with exercise, as in EC's case (1.2.2.6; 242). Even late in the nineteenth century, knowledge of Burton's 1621 commentary was regarded as an indicator of the well-read (Jackson, introduction, xiv).

8. Gen. 1:11; *Paradise Lost,* 7.309–11 (Milton, 2.1:222).

57. Katharine Bradley, Letter to Edith Cooper

[Ivythorpe | Mon., [18 Sept. 1882][1]

Monday night.

Gallantly have I written to-night! On I went jog-trotting—a sudden turn of the road—and oh what revelation, what rapture! A new character—Veronica's first lover[2] and———but I forbear. You have excitement enough. Get the blue air into your veins, while the strong wind from Heaven blows through me,—inspire let us each of us—and in the end—what a drama—the human heart naked and unveiled.

Little do I see of my Pretty in its olive-wood, but I dare not transport her to the Mother's bed-room, lest she should not loose hold, so I peep at the Persian now and then, and say to myself, "Still quivring to the young-eyed cherubim"[3]—Only let these Celestial young buffers mind how they behave, for my jealousy is capacious from Cecil[4] upwards I am jealous of all things that look into the mild blue eyes. [page torn]

[from header fol. 175ʳ] Simorg-all wise Fowl—who is artillery-ing his stormy heart into you. Dream you like it, and lick your paws—and remember mixed metaphors are tolerated in strong emotion.

—*Ever* [*bird symbol*].

MS Eng. lett. c. 418 fol. 175ʳ BOD

1. Dated from the drafting of *LL* in Sept. 1882.

2. Andrea is the brother of the villainous Peter de Celano, who seduces Veronica and then becomes a monk after a near-fatal fever (1.1; *FT/WR/LL,* 234–35).

3. KB rewrites *MV* 5.1.62.

4. The critic Frederick Wedmore and his siblings, Cecil and Isabel, lived nearby at Stoke Druid. Cecil Wedmore later claimed it was his family who "noticed" KB and EC when they first moved to Bristol and who introduced them into Clifton society (letter to Thomas Sturge Moore, 12 Mar. 1927, MS Eng. lett. e. 31, fol. 124ʳ BOD); nevertheless, it seems they did not share the secret of Michael Field until 1886. See EC, letter to Isabel Wedmore, 6 Apr. 1886 [PM], MS Eng. lett. d. 406 fol. 27ʳ BOD.

58. Katharine Bradley, Letter to Edith Cooper

[Ivythorpe] | [Sept. 1882][1]

Darling of my Heart

Muddie says she is engaged in taking care of her body in order that You may stay[2]—so she writes not, but she begs me to say how thankful she was for your letters. She has been much better to-day,—downstairs to dinner. Little Am[y]. is away at Tintern with the Young Bakers[3] and their friends. The "little life" wanted a bright day! So we think of the daughters one at savage Land's End and one at Tintern; while the Fowl hatches and clucks. What fine big swan-eggs—what fair creatures will issue therefrom to float hereafter down the broad stream of national life.

If Amy is like St. Ives, I am like Land's End—and you, my Pretty, are like the gentle Lizard.[4] Indeed you are like a lizard. It comes out, it shines, it is friendly though shy, brilliant, timid, delicious, *lazy*. It basks in the sun; Yet it is capable of the dart of fear. We are realy getting jealous of you. You are like the wicked—You are not in trouble as other men.[5] But recollect the psalmist—I have seen the wicked spreading himself as a green bay tree. . .[6] And then, the sudden collapse. Dr. A[t]h[l]iers[7] visited us this Afternoon. He said of you "Ah, that is the daughter who does *not* go in for examinations." Well to the laundress we are the person who does not like starch;—how different is an aspect to different mortals according to their capacity and our affection. To think of defining the P. by a negation!

Imagine P. my grief at having to arrange the drawing-room this morning. I rolled the shells over on to their sides. I asked Emma[8] where "the woman" went. And I put the gray vase and the red carelessly on the piano, as if they'd had a conversation on a cliff and then gone their divers ways. (*Act* to night—where such deep waters should run) act *[from header fol. 70r]* I say. A breath of air for me before tea. Bring home some tinned sea-air for me. We expect you to return converted to Methodism by Wesley's hymns—Between 2 world's I stand and Land's end outdoor preaching.[9] Many loves and a pot of Kisses for the morn. You can have them at tea with the pilchards! The big ones are mine—

Your own loving *[bird symbol]*

MS Eng. lett. c. 418 fol. 70r/v BOD

1. Dated from EC's trip to Cornwall in Sept. 1882.

2. After the birth of Amy, Emma Harris Cooper became an invalid (Sturgeon, 17; Bridge, MS Eng. misc. d. 983 fol. 63[r] BOD).

3. Edith and Florence Baker. See also letter 22 n. 6.

4. The Lizard is associated with "barrenness and solitude" (Collins, *Rambles,* 92).

5. Job 3:17.

6. Ps. 37:35.

7. Indecipherable name: probably a lecturer at Bristol University College, because he is aware EC had not coped with the pressures of sitting her mathematics exam. See EC, letter to Frances Brooks, MS Eng. lett. 405 fol. 53[v] BOD. The professor of mathematics at the time was Dr. J. F. Main; EC later admitted he had been her first love (Add. MS 46785 fol. 105[v] BL).

8. Emma Harris Cooper.

9. KB is parodying "Stanzas from the Grande Chartreuse": "Wandering between two worlds, one dead. / The other powerless to be born" (85–86; Arnold, 1:289). The second world, Cornwall, is humorously evoked through references to its people's fervent Methodism and to its important pilchard industry (Collins, *Rambles,* 114 and 40).

59. Katharine Bradley, Annotated Envelope

[PM Wed., 20 Sept. 1882]

5th Penzance letter
Description of the Lizard.

MS Eng. lett. c. 419 fol. 48[r] BOD

60. Edith Cooper, Letter to Katharine Bradley

[Cornwall] | [Wed., 20 Sept. 1882][1]

My Cornish journey is wedded to Swinburne's *Tristram.* It is the apotheosis of the Cornish coast and seas.

"Lyonesse"

My own darling *[bird symbol],*

Over the dusk moorland, faintly enlightened by the virginal, numberless cressets of the Cornish heath, along the straight high-road, we sped to the place wh: you love. We dismounted, and were directed to the Light-house[2]—a stout, white-washed building, from wh: every noble sweep of line and romance of high-lit lamp, has vanished, and wh: stands on a low swell of mainland, without a single charm. "And did Sim love this?" moaningly whispered an interior voice. In despair, we turned along a path that filletted the brow of the cliff. Not a creature did we meet, not a voice reached our ears, except the utterly miserable wail of the sea-gulls. Dark, tide-eaten rocks began to appear—grew hopefully bolder and bolder with every encouraged step; till the thin brown rock-Lizard lay on the sea, as on a wall. Still onward, tho' we had found something worthy of All-wise love! The sea then was almost like the rippling, ennamelled, inward, blue of a shell; And those rosy whispers, wh: Dawn might have left in the ear of such a shell, found pink suggestion in the lights of the azure silvered water. At last a cove came in sight,—loveliest of Cornish scenes, lovelier than anything I have seen before. Strong be the coffee wh: would make me mad enough to try to celebrate Kynance! Those walls and pinnacles of rock, that look from the distance like gigantic cinders dropped about on the clean, sanded hearthstone of the sea-shore, how wonderful are their nearer hues—roan and myrtle-coloured, vivid here and there with mouldy green, here and there dull with bony grey! And the strange, many-coloured caves—in wh: however Colours are pre-exista[nt] rather than vitally present—fore-shadowed rather than visible! And close round the sea-polished foundations of the lustreless, yet prophetic, rocks, spreads the pavement of sand, worn so smooth by the tread of waters:—clear out of it, the rocks rise, with no dent of tide-pool, or obscurity of fringed weed. The serpentine masses are exquitely shaped and exquisitely disposed on the wheaten-coloured level of beach—while everywhere about is a sea of malachite—wonderous to behold—with "the most wild sweet waves in all the world."[3]

Everything is perfectly lovely "From floors of foam and gold to walls of serpentine."[4] And everything is so suggestive—those closed colours, wh: seem but to show the calyx of their hidden brightness—that carpet of softest pile, wh: a passing step rags and wear out, and wh: is mended and entire with one magic stretch of the large supple hands of the sea, over its worn surface. We heard the ocean blow its bellows of rock with their foamy roar.

I can no-more, dearest, for my eyelids smart with sleep, and it is late. To-morrow (if fine) we go to St. Just and see the Botellick mines.[5] Tell my little Pussie how I rejoice in her trip to the Wye and beloved Tintern. Love my darling Mother for being better, and yourself for being inspired so richly. Your thorny-claw'd-from-jealousy, yet sole,

P.P.

MS Eng. lett. c. 419 fols. 45^{r}–47^{v} BOD

1. Dated from PM on envelope 59.

2. When it was decided to replace James Smeaton's innovative Eddystone Lighthouse in the 1870s, the people of Plymouth had it removed to Plymouth Hoe where it stands today (Wryde, *British Lighthouses,* 95–102).

3. *Tristram of Lyonesse,* 8.186 (Swinburne, 4:135).

4. *Tristram of Lyonesse,* 8.203 (Swinburne, 4:136).

5. The Botallack mines were famous because tin and copper were extracted from a third of a mile below the sea (Collins, *Rambles,* 103). Botallack closed in 1871, becoming yet another derelict mining site on the peninsula (Millward and Robinson, *SW Peninsula,* 120–22).

61. Katharine Bradley, Letter to Edith Cooper

[Ivythorpe | Wed., [20 Sept. 1882][1]

Wednesday.

[T]he mild blue eyes look out toward the great Mount[2] in its veil of rain. The seven-leagued boots are not put on: the head is bent over its books, and the heart is again touched by "human things."[3] And hereafter other mild blue eyes in their disappointment will turn to the pages of John Cooley, read of the sweet wife Iolante, of the patriot Margarito, of honest Markwald and his broken heart, and be satisfied[4]—A boon, a gift!—You remember that Van dyke portrait of a knight on horseback.[5] Suddenly I came across it this morning, *It is Margarito*—the only character about whose outline I feel a little uncertain. Note the retrospective melancholy of the eyes, the chivalrous enterprise of the brow. With men of action it often seems that the tears they have no time to shed—soften with an exquisite humidity the climate of the eyes. What defiance, what Manhood in the figure. What power of cruelty, reckless passion, remor[s]e. Contrition in the face. Against the yellow pot the picture is propped up and I study.

Last night I sketched (and a good deal filled in) the trial scene.[6] Right, right every bit of it—I leave the blinding scene and Iolante's kiss to you—the Storia of Amari[7] is in 3 Vols, I find. They are going to try to get it for me secondhand. The woman-companion to my Cavalier—will I think give touches for Veronica, Carta for Azaire.[8] Mind I shall expect the ciliated heath from the Lizard. Don't break your neck though, not for that, or anything. The Pretty is a soft green sea—play and plash on the surface—through the heart of him runs the mighty cable-fibre of heart-thread, binding him to the hopes and aspirations of all the worlds—through other souls let the fishes swim and the porpoise dive:—we have the clue—the heart of the mystery—we live not in the phenomenal, but in the brain-beat of things. And so my sweet Sea Lavendar, Farewell. Thou art not a savour to me like the saints; but a *fragrance.* Some are born so. I think of you *[from header fol. 173^r]* more as scent than colour. *I* am colour glossy and dark: I exhale no blessed breath. Yet I am surely A.W.F.

MS Eng. lett. c. 418 fol. 173$^{r/v}$ BOD

1. Dated from the drafting of *LL* in Sept. 1882.

2. St. Michael's Mount. See letter 50 n. 2.

3. EC quotes her own disgust with tourists in letter 52.

4. Characters from *LL,* which was published under the name "Michael Field," and not "John Cooley."

5. Van Dyck painted several portraits of men on horseback. KB echoes Ruskin's description of Van Dyck's *Thomas de Savoie-Carignan on Horseback,* "accomplished in all ways, and tender in all thoughts" (Ruskin, 7:359), but her reference to the woman-companion suggests *Anton Giulio Brignole-Sale on Horseback,* as there are several portraits of Paola Adorno. KB saw the paintings of Brignole-Sale and his wife at the Palazzo Rosso in Genoa in 1880.

6. *LL* 5.1, in which Margaritone is condemned to burn at the stake for rebelling against his German overlords.

7. Michele Amari, *La Storia dei Musulmani in Sicilia* (1854 and 1873) (*Encyclopaedia Britannica*). It does not seem to have been translated into English.

8. Azaire, the Moorish waiting-girl whom Peter de Celano takes as his mistress, is based upon Mary Charlotte Sturge (1852–1929), known as Carta. Carta Sturge studied philosophy at Bristol University College and was joint secretary of Mary Paley Marshall's women's debating society. See letter 22. The friendship was a difficult one, with KB writing "she has a sly, secretive nature, made stranger and more reticent by Quaker upbringing" (KB, letter to Frances Brooks, MS Eng. lett. d. 405 fol. 41^v BOD). Ultimately, she moved to London where she gave lectures on philosophy.

62. Katharine Bradley, Letter to Edith Cooper

[Torquay | Sat., [23] Sept. [1882][1]

Little sea bedrooms just after halfpastseven *A.M.*

I am in my little sea bedroom and now in the tranquil morning sunlight can I write to thee. The autumn was born yesterday (Friday) it was a perfect September day, all the plague of wind gone; in the afternoon we rowed, the temperature was equable, the sea calm, in the evening as we turned inland toward the solemn bare-headed old Torrs[2] there Came as from the Holy of Holies rending the curtain of the mist,[3] the first breath of regeneration; the freshness of spring is the Natural Man—the health of autumn is of the Holy Ghost. How strange the influx of that life-sowing air amid decaying leaves and the perishing of all natural beauty!

In the spring we languish, in the summer we bask, in the autumn we breathe and live—Oh what a time we will have on the moors if this weather lasts. I hope even the darling mother drinks a little of this new wine from the Kingdom of God. Always tell me how it fares with her. I joy to hear of Kallirrhoe.[4] Don't be afraid to put in bits of your own. "So now we are no more twain; but one flesh,"[5] that the Child should bear stronger marks of resemblance to one parent than the other matters not; She is our flesh and blood. This daughter, let her be the expression of our thought and love, and all will be well.

I have not yet written a word. Bathing, or boating, or sitting on green hills I am out all day; and hold it my duty to be as amusing as I can, and cherish the for me happy superstition that as Arnold[6] expresses it a God has deigned to dwell among the abodes of mortal men. Even little Miss Westwood[7] listens most reverently to the oracle, and cannot bear interruption when Miss Bradley is talking. She says it is just as when the Doctor is talking. She is so eager to hear. That same Doctor is greatly exercising the hearts of the faithful by going off to Germany for the winter. From all I hear of him I cannot help greatly desiring to see him. Unhappily Mary[8] was wholly disenchanted when he brought her home. He talked slang the whole time and I think behaved with Culpable Carelessness by leaving Cologne where she was to meet him and compelling her to travel to Brussels alone. She did not reach there till late at night, and had the addresses of two or three hotels where he might be staying; so imagine the peril she was in. When she arrived at his hotel, he was away at the opera, and Mary did not see him that night. This combined with a slight feeling, I fancy of jealousy toward Maggie,[9] has sown bitter revolt in the subjects heart, and greatly weakened in her case his influence for good. A letter came from Maggie the other day,—one mass of slang. Fanny read it aloud; strong condemnation followed. If indeed it is "the Lord for the body and the body for the Lord"[10] how much more true is it that speech the Close-fitting inner garment of the soul should be kept Clean and pure and of bridal sanctity for Him. As flirtation desecrates true love, slang desecrates the holiness of language. People imagine they are verbally chaste if they do not swear; I believe a few oaths and fine English w$^{d.}$ not have half such debasing influence on the heart as the use of this perpetual parody on the expression of human thought. Better be an old cow with sense of the grass's fragrance, than a human creature "without form and void,"[11] reduced to Chaos again through the wilful mismingling of his elements. What a blessed gift is humour, how impossible it is to be a poet—a high one without it—for Humour defends the Shrine of sentiment as lightly and securely as Apollo his Delphic altars. It is the only safe guardian of the heart's treasures; humanity has entrusted her tears to its Keeping; it keeps virginal the privacies of the heart. The French too often for lack of it have suffered ravage of sentiment; and the German's maudlin effusiveness is hung up at the pawn brokers. The Englishman still keeps his affections with the sacrament-cup safely enchested. (*after breakfast*)

MS Eng. lett. c. 418 fols. 44r–45v BOD

1. KB's reference to the autumnal equinox suggests that this letter was written on Sat., 23 Sept. 1882, while *Call.* was undergoing final corrections (Treby, *MF Catalogue,* 29).

2. KB's description of the landscape suggests she may be in Torquay or Tor Bay. See Norway, *Highways & Byways,* 66.

3. Matt. 27:51.

4. *Call.* (1884).

5. Matt. 19:5–6, commonly used in the marriage ceremony. See *Book of Common Prayer,* 308.

6. In "The Study of Poetry," Matthew Arnold accused the public of overrating poets, particularly less talented poets, admiring them superstitiously as gods (Arnold, 6:6–8). KB interprets this as a "happy" practice with regard to herself. In paraphrasing Arnold, KB echoes the lines of Dartmoor poet Joseph Cottle: "Is there a God who deigns to dwell / With heirs of frailty here below" ("A Midnight Reflection," 9–10; Cottle, *Poems,* 71). Given KB's acquaintance with Richard Garnett, the author of Cottle's *DNB* entry, this may not be coincidence.

7. Possibly Louisa Woodward of the Church Anti-Vivisection Society, who later organized the subscription for the controversial Battersea brown dog statue memorializing the 1903 libel case (Lansbury, *Old Brown Dog,* 21). The doctor to which she refers may be Ernest Bell (1851–1933), publisher and prominent animal rights campaigner. While Bell was not literally a doctor, the fact that he completed an MA at Cambridge in 1876, and did "go off to" Germany to study, may have given rise to the nickname. KB knew Bell as president of the National Anti-Vivisection Society (*Oxford DNB*), and George Bell and Sons had published Michael Field's early works.

8. Untraced.

9. Untraced.

10. 1 Cor. 6:13.

11. Gen. 1:2.

63. Katharine Bradley, Letter to Edith Cooper

Sun., [24 Sept. 1882][1]

Sunday morning.
Oh Sweet to wake in the night, and hear the sea-gulls' cry, and better still to find our little avenue of poplar and sycamore rustling and chattering in the wind. You must turn to the old Testament to understand our feelings.[2] One may feel grateful for day, when night is done, but for air! It seemed indeed as if we must die and return to our dust.

Now our spirits are renewed. I tell my precious Amy-bird that she shall now direct our steps, and lead me wheresoever she will. One cannot escape beauty, and the dear little one will soon have to say farewell to our favourite brinks, nooks, heights, and hiding-places.

Oh P. come to me! Nature will speak to us here. She is not betouristed[3] and scared. She is like the spirits I read of in Ernest's book[4]—longing to utter so much to us—unable to win our mood. The child looks up from the mother's breast to drink her smile; we ask simply to be fed.

I believe some day I must dramatize the myth of Demetia,[5]—her seasons, her cares, and her sorrow;—why of course it is just what I should have done if they had stolen away my Pretty—sworn there should be no corn-gathering no joy of vintage for evermore. It is instantly revealed to me that I am Demetia—I could have raked that little man in the embers of immortality. And the insatiable maternity in me—the passion that needs a universe for its expression are all in her—and Simurg. P. this will have to be done; so keep this letter. I am very, very happy—awake, renewed, rejoicing. Amy is
[page missing]
[from header fol. 62^r] I declare too delicate for religion. She treated me to indigestion last Monday; so I doom her to sing a few hyms in a clear voice on the top of the downs.

Ever your own All-Wise
[bird symbol].

MS Eng. lett. d. 400 fols. 62^r–63^v BOD

1. Dated from the previous letter.
2. Ps. 104:28–29.
3. For EC's dislike of tourists, see letter 52.
4. G. E. Lessing, *Nathan the Wise* (1878), edited by Ernest Bell. In the first act, Recha is

saved from her burning house by a young Templar whom she longs to thank, but he persistently refuses to let her speak of it (1.6; Lessing, *Dramatic Works,* 257–60).

5. This dramatization does not seem to have gone any further.

64. Katharine Bradley, Letter to Edith Cooper

[Ivythorpe | Wed., [1883][1]

Wednesday.

Babes!

The Rivals[2] I read this morning in bed. That is Comedy!—Yet I have a notion there may be comedy not bright and hard like Sheridan's—not metallic Comedy—but a comedy soft, mirthful, deliciacy—a comedy of unrealized ideals, not of awkward situations. And this reflection helps me on a little way toward a definition of humour. Humour is always Concerned with ideals wit with actual absurdities. If a child bearing the Sunday dinner from the bakehouse fall, wit sees the greasy pinafore the indelicately disclosed feast *and laughs,* but Humour looks up to the child's trembling lip, and imaginative terror in the eyes.

The Balliol[3] is going to take me this morning to the reference library etc. and to-morrow, between eleven and twelve, we hope to start. How fared my pretty at Portishead? Did it kiss its hand to the ocean, and tell it how the A.W.F[.] would follow?

Blessing; write, sew, reflect, and *[from header fol. 62ʳ]* love the Fowl Always.

Ever *[bird symbol].*

MS Eng. lett. c. 418 fols. 62ʳ–63ᵛ BOD

1. EC began work on a comedy with the working title of "What's in a Name?" in autumn 1883. See MS Eng. poet. e. 70 fol. 7ʳ BOD. Like Sheridan's comedy, the play was based on confused identities: a suitor proposes by letter but neglects to include a Christian name in the address, and is accepted by his intended's aunt. It later became *A Christian Name* (unpub.).

2. *The Rivals* (1775) by Richard Brinsley Sheridan. The play continued to be performed in KB's time. See Mrs. Oliphant, *Sheridan.*

3. For Francis Brooks, see letter 30 n. 4.

65. Edith Cooper, Annotated Page

The Hague—1883

MS Eng. lett. c. 418 fol. 71r BOD

66. Katharine Bradley, Letter to Edith Cooper

The Hague | Sat., [15 Sept. 1883][1]

Hotel Paulez Saturday night (towards nine)
Ah my sweet the old fascinating Continental life—life of a people that loves leisure, and pleasant places, and worthy entourage. If you could but see this Hague—each house with a smile of its own, and such a complexion—the brick of pink, or brown rose with green or buff outer shutters; the trees received lovingly to dwell in company with the houses in lofty groups, or stately alleys, or—long lines to drop leaves into the stagnant black canals—long streaks of melancholy branding the brow of this happy-countenanced city. Nothing very old or picturesque like Antwerp—the houses frankly modern, and frankly handsome. The people—the first few hours of my experience benignant,—talking English, or being interpreted to by learned natives.

This afternoon as soon as we were refreshed we drove—the 1st. thing I saw at Hotel Paulez was Miss Estlin[2] gracious and good!!—with Miss Estlin to the little sea-side place,[3] and there I bathed, all in Dutch,—you may imagine after lady's cabin experience what this was. They gave me as it were a chemise in white flannel with no drawers: the experience though not *very safe* was delicious—"and limbs as white in their lustrous snow"[4] etc! The drive to . . . . the little sea-side place was through Magnificent alleys—nature taught civilization and behaviour; and she Can be taught exquisite Town-manners by the wise. At table d'hôte opposite to us Prof. Stuart, Mr. and Mrs Butler, and their Son Stanley also a Prof of something somewhere.[5] Mrs. Butler asked to be introduced to Miss Mary Priestman's[6] friends of whom I was once—She looks terribly ill—a woman of a great inward life, of wh. in its profoundness only the Father that seeth in Secret[7] can tell—"Surely she hath borne our griefs and carried our sorrows"[8]—an expiatory face, wonderful and sad. Prof. Stuart seems full of buoyant boy life, too frisky one wd. think for the occasion did one not Know how solemn and intense he can be. This evening we might go to a Count somebody's,[9] but are too tired. Sister Margaret's evening lace is wonderful![10] To be in her train—one of her "meinie" of itself gives distinction. Hers is a nose to command respect. The wig, if wig it be must be the native hair of an Aristocrat. All my people are marvellously good to me;—a nice little Miss Stephens next door, and little Miss Bragge—the niece—who has an inside room from mine, and who can fasten my dress, "I reckon!"[11]

Ah P. driving through the streets of London gave me my old thirst for fame: I passed the British Museum with its moony lamps—then plunged deep into the city—escaped through Liverpool St. into the quiet fields, again, and was finally found Tossing on the ocean. One lady clasped lovely bare arms above her head in a berth fronting mine, and through My sorrows of teeth etc. ministered to me of the eternal things of beauty. Holland is like land Coming to the birth, not born—It travails toward the phenomenal; it is an implication, an incidence, an essay. Once in existence it has no aspiration: it has spent itself in gigantic effort to appear. To wrest feeding-places from the barren sea, and homes for the indomititable is a worthy Toil and I can feel a fit of home-sickness forming in me. It always comes in re-action from the intoxicating deliciousness of foreign life. P.P. but I could not see you in anguish on a berth. Content you with your isle, and Europe Described thus eloquently by the Sim. Good night, my thrice-precious ones good-night. Heaven guard you!

MS Eng. lett. c. 418 fols. 81ʳ–85ʳ BOD

1. The British and Continental Federation for the Abolition of State Regulation of Vice began its third triennial Congress in The Hague on 17 Sept. 1883. KB was among the representatives from Britain. This association was an extension of the Ladies National Association (LNA) for the Repeal of the Contagious Diseases Acts formed by Josephine Butler in 1869 to spearhead a women's campaign against Britain's Contagious Diseases (CD) Acts. These acts required the registration of prostitutes, compulsory medical examinations, and possible detention in a Lock hospital for treatment. The LNA's campaign was highly successful, and the CD Acts were suspended on 20 Apr. 1883, although not repealed until 1886 (Fawcett, *Josephine Butler,* 42, 98–101). The Continental Federation extended the campaign to Europe and brought together campaigners working on similar issues. The events of this conference were reported in *The Shield,* the journal of the LNA ("International Congress," 244).

2. Mary Estlin (ca. 1820–1902) was on the executive Committee of the LNA, the Bristol Society's Committee for Women's Suffrage, and was leader of the Bristol and Clifton Anti-Slavery Society. In the 1870s she and the Priestman sisters helped form Bristol's National Union of Women Workers. See Crawford, *Women's Suffrage Movement,* 209–10.

3. Scheveningen is a fishing village that became popular with visitors to The Hague in the nineteenth century, although less fashionable than Ostend. Baedeker noted in 1884 the recent introduction of "the custom of promiscuous bathing" (*Belgium and Holland,* 240–41).

4. KB quotes from "The Song of Hêrô" (3–6): "to-night he swims fast through the golden stream, / The glittering path of the mid moonbeam; / limbs as white in their lustrous snow / As the snow-white limbs of fair Lêda's daughter" (*Bell.*, 137).

5. James Stuart (1843–1913) was a fellow of Trinity College, Cambridge University, and an active campaigner for education for women. A close friend of the Butlers, he was first treasurer of the British and Continental Federation (Jordan, *Josephine Butler,* 87–88; 165). Josephine Butler (1828–1906) was recognized at home and abroad as an influential campaigner on education and suffrage, and against prostitution, but particularly as a leader in the campaign against the CD Acts. Her husband, George Butler (1819–90) was canon of Winchester, a public examiner at Oxford University, and an activist in his own right. Arthur Stanley Butler (1854–1923) held the chair of Natural Philosophy at St. Andrew's University between 1880 and 1922. See Jordan, *Josephine Butler.* At the Congress, George Butler presented a paper and made the farewell speech (Bell, *Josephine Butler,* 172).

6. Mary Priestman (1830–1914) and her sisters, Anna Maria Priestman, Elizabeth Bright, and Margaret Tanner, were Quakers from Bristol, and prominent members of the National Society for Women's Suffrage, West of England Branch (Crawford, *Women's Suffrage Movement,* 565–66). The LNA was conceived by Butler on a visit to her intimate friends and correspondents Miss Mary and Miss Anna Maria (Jordan, *Josephine Butler,* 110). KB was probably invited to attend the Congress because of her friendship with Mary Priestman.

7. Matt. 6:3–4.

8. Is. 53:4.

9. Count van Hogendorp, secretary and treasurer of the local Federation. See picture on p. 102..

10. Margaret Tanner née Priestman (1817–1905) was president of the Western Temperance League (Tooley, "Ladies of Bristol," 453) and treasurer of the LNA (Jordan, *Josephine* Butler, 110). She was also involved with the antislavery campaign, the social science association, medical reform, peace movements, and Republicanism (Walkowitz, *Prostitution,* table 1).

11. Miss Gulielma Stephens was a delegate from the Ladies' Committee, Bridport, Dorset. Margaret Bragg was a delegate from the Plymouth branch of the LNA. See *Troisième Congrès International,* 5.

67. Katharine Bradley, Letter to Edith Cooper

[The Hague] | Wed., [19 Sept. 1883][1]

Wednesday morn. 7.45. AM

My own Love,

I must begin this letter by warning you that if you only have post-cards—or nothing, You must not rise up against me. You cannot conceive the confusion to brain and body of this Congress. Nevertheless afterward . . . . . Many thanks for the sweet bundle of Ivythorpe spices that fell into my lap, arose through my nostrils long spirit yesterday Tuesday morn. at breakfast. Ah Sweet Continue to lay a soft hand upon my throbbing head, throbbing only mentally mind, for by dint of many mineral waters, I am very well. I begin where I left off at the Mayor's reception Monday night.[2] As soon as we got into the crowded room and had bowed to host and hostess little glasses of foaming Champagne were handed round, then little patties—wicked looking little things—and tea in apparently blue *Delft* ware was being served to the fortunate. Fear not, I touched none of their evil things. I remained Very miserable—introduced at last to M[rs.] Wm Budgett's Sister![3]—didnt I grind my teeth at her—at last a nice young Dutchgirl came to me and said "Surely I was English?" To which I replied altogether, and charmed with my frank admiration for her land and respect for ther Nation, She soon received me into most loving converse, talking Very good intelligible English—though she had never been abroad. My dress she thought was quite particular—I tried to explain to her the high art position, and was relieved to find she had heard of Morris. Another—I think a Marsiein, wanted to Know if I was a Qwâke!![4]

I was glad to get away from the noisy crow[d.] where no sense was possible. Yesterday morning Miss Bragge and I who are the early riser's were faithfully at the morning prayer meeting led by M[rs.] Butler. Think of us as, I hope often there (here I have been down to order breakfast; scrabbèd eggs the waiter promises us!) One understands what is meant by a sword in the mouth, and "the sword of his lips"[5] when she speaks. She read of the casting out of evil spirits. Spirits "impurs" they were sometimes called, and said that we must do much more than over throw external institutions—we must cast out the spirit of impurity in the world. M. Humberg[6] (Miss Priestman says he is like a nicely dressed frog standing on hind legs, and he is) gave the 1[st.] discourse after preliminaries—many of the details of the Shield. His French is admirably easy, and he is dear, good, conciliatory, but entirely uncompromising. Several of the proposed resolutions of Congress were then discussed, objected to etc. etc. In one compulsory examination of the person was condemned without exception. The case of conscripts and of wet-nurses, who in Paris, according to the testimony of Mad. de Maisier(?)[7] are examined "en bloc" presented difficulties. Is the legitimate en forced inspection of feet and eyes to be objected to—This and the question as to whether the word *justice* or *morality*—or public morality should be used in the framing of one of the resolutions was debated. Then we adjourned for simple refreshments at 11. Pastor Pierson[8]—the great Dutch dominant pastor here, our staunchest friend came to the help of M. Priestman and myself as we were

Third Triennial Congress of the British and Continental Federation for the Abolition of State Regulation of Vice, The Hague, Sept. 1883. *Front row from left:* Margaret Tanner, M. de Laveleye, Josephine Butler, and Countess Precorbin. M. Humbert stands behind Margaret Tanner, and to his left is Prof. Stuart. George Butler appears behind his wife, with M. de Morsier on his right. KB and Mary Priestman are unidentifiable. (The Women's Library, London Metropolitan University)

trying to get some lunch: he spoke good English and was serviceable. That man with the long hair is a Socialist, and he will speak to-night.[9] Again to work and discussion—I really think I have confused the order of the speakers but we went at it again and were not released till towards four—including the time taken up in photographing us in the garden.[11] Don't think you will see me,—but the Tanner resplendent in the front, where she was made to go—and M[rs.] Butler—Mary Priestman and I remained obscure in the background. Finally released at four, I bought grapes and we all set off to the Zoological gardens where, in peace we sat by a pond, and watched the stork on one leg! A delicious place this garden, with the most exquisite foliage plants, and nice brilliant coloured birds I have ever seen. The moment of repose spent in it I shall long remember. Home to half past five dinner. Then a little temperance meeting, then Conference from 8 till between ten and eleven—One long speech in Dutch—toward the end a noble speech by M[rs.] Butler wh. I must try to re-produce in some moment of calm—She has all the qualities of a great actress—the controlling gesture of these delicately-gloved hands was most impressive. Hers is devotional genius:—She has all the arts of a woman of the world—but her world is the spiritual—Not a touch of affectation, or design, the grace, the infinite subtlety and "savoir-faire" of the saints of old. They are such fools modern pious people: the old pietists brought into the midst of a fearful and convicted world the might the affluence of the presence of God; and this woman *[ends]*

MS Eng. lett. c. 418 fols. 75^{r}–78^{v} BOD

1. Dated from the International Congress at The Hague, 17 to 22 Sept. 1883.

2. The *Shield* reported that the mayor of The Hague gave a "brilliant reception" on the evening of the first day of the conference, which about 300 delegates attended ("International Congress," 245). KB's description has not been preserved.

3. Mrs. William Budgett was a prominent member of the National Society for Women's Suffrage, West of England Branch (Tanner, *How the Women's Suffrage Movement Began,* 9). An early, undated letter records that EC stayed with Budgetts (EC, letter to family, n.d., MS Eng. lett. e. 31 fol. 5^{r} BOD), but the reason for KB's animosity remains untraced.

4. Possibly the woman was from Marseilles in France; the assumption that KB was a Quaker is understandable given that many women involved with social reform in Bristol were Quakers (Walkowitz, *Prostitution,* 119).

5. Is. 1:19–20.

6. Aimé Humbert, professor of jurisprudence at Neuchâtel in Switzerland (Fawcett, *Josephine Butler,* 150). At the general meeting on Tuesday, Humbert gave "an exhaustive account of the work of the Federation [in Britain], and referred to the immense influence which the recent vote of the House of Commons condemnatory of compulsory medical examination would have on the Continent" ("International Congress," 245).

7. Mme. Emilie de Morsier, the delegate from the Paris Committee of the Federation ("International Congress," 244).

8. Henri Pierson was president of the Dutch Committee for the Repeal of State Regulation of prostitution, and director of the refuges in Zetten ("International Congress," 244). He established institutions for the aid of women and girls, including a home for young girls and a Magdalene House for unmarried mothers. See Butler, *Personal Reminiscences,* 180.

9. Untraced. Public meetings were held each evening, but there is no report on the Wed. evening session. See "International Congress," 247.

10. This photograph still exists in the Josephine Butler collection of the Women's Library, London. Although untitled, the people identified in the key suggest that it is the photograph of the Third Congress in The Hague (see p. 102.). Mary Priestman and KB are indeed unrecognizable.

11. The Zoological-Botanical Gardens in The Hague had very few animals and was a place for recreation (Baedeker, *Belgium and Holland,* 238).

68. Katharine Bradley, Letter to Edith Cooper

The Hague | Sun., [23 Sept. 1883][1]

Sunday morning Hôtel Paulez La Hage (before breakfast)
My Chiefest,

This last letter must be to you:—the last letter and the first kiss for the abominable old P. Content I think you would be if you looked at the little table at wh. I am writing. There are pots—pale pure gray and blue—something like those we have—but greyer, and salt cellars of a ravishing description. There is also a gt. cluster of grapes wh. I w$^{d.}$ fain share with you for lunch. The pots Miss Priestman found the shop of—very humble. We went after dinner last night—As I retired from the Shop perfectly laden with pots—the old Dutch woman pitying my natural maladroitness re-arranged me altogether, cloak, umbrella, earthenware and sent me securely on my way—And then at half-past eight to the Count van Hogendorp's[2]—the last great reception at one of the grand aristocratic old families of Holland. Ah, P. that I tell it you even from the beginning! The young and beautiful wife had a word for each,—graceful and full of frankest charm, she was what "Jack"—"old Jack!!!" means by a lady.[3] Tea in exquisite Delft ware—no handles to the cups—was passed round. I was introduced to a Dutch gentleman—then to his wife, and then in a quiet time looked round at the brilliant Assembly, and at the room, with its Delft wall-plate, its probably family minatures, and soft tinted curtains. Afterwards in an adjoining room we gathered to hear M$^{rs.}$ Butler speak. There looked down the great ancestral Hogendorps—approvingly I should think—the stalwart humanities—*men for the torture*—not like us P. true to our convictions till the nerve is exposed, and fair-bosomed dames for whom the Valiant w$^{d.}$ gladly die.
(Resumed after breakfast and church; last committee sitting in M$^{rs.}$ Butler's drawing-room) When M$^{rs.}$ Butler rose to speak, there were round her gathered 12 people—of whom I took acount.[4] A little black Dutch lady in plainest dress, the Tanner illustrious in lace, a lady belonging to M. de Laveleye—notre cher président, in Crimson Velvet with scarlet flushes in the ribbons—elegant exceedingly—some-one I have forgotten, another black Dutch lady, an old admiral of exquisite Courtliness who has been converted at Congress, Mad. de Morsier the great Parisian worker, French, and fat, and Keen, old Fowl, Countess Schact the great German worker—suffering earnest Teutonic face, 3$^{rd.}$ black lady, M$^{rs.}$ Butler (after she sat down) and finally the Countess Precanbon—half

Spaniard half-Italian—deliciously sunned and sunny person, stout, in dove-colour, who talked softly to the people in fanning herself!! She has worked at Naples, indefatigably in Spain, and touched me more with her thrilling narratives than any other woman speaker, Yet there was her face like a soft fruit. Suffering cannot brand these delicious southern natures: it passes from them in wholesome perspiration—soupirs et angoisses—with us northerners it congeals; great ice-bergs are formed in us, and we are scourged throughout our lives by the Arctic regions of our own past agony.

While M[rs.] Butler was speaking, my eye wandered from her crucified face to a lovely little Dutch picture—light illumined above her—of a sweet young girl in white robe, Knitting by herself in the garden—the down bent face full apparently of happy love-thoughts. Infinite the relief of turning in thought from the record of sin—the sin of the world—laid on that pure woman's brow—to read the unsullied page of that fair maiden history—where the fancies one felt were purer than even the hues of the stainless cheek. So may it be among our nations ever: may we Keep for the imaginations of our young men these lovely resting-places; may they long be able to say of their betrothed, what Christ says of His Church. "Behold thou art fair, My Love, there is no spot in thee."[5]

After her address, and after last words from our sweet little frog-Secretary M. Homberg[6]—the great Count—the Hogendorp—our host—went to M[rs] Butler, and after a few sentences in French said to her, in English—"Thank, you M[rs.] Butler for the noble words you have spoken to us" etc. It was beautiful to see the gigantic heroic figure in its homage, the noble Teutonic face in its emotion!

The Dutch ladies then came to me to love and to bless me in French and in English. Truly Mary's words were a prophesy. I am to them a Dutch Madonna—their chosen, as it seems to me of all England's delegates. And it came to pass on this wise. At yesterday's prayer-meeting—or rather before, I felt I must give thanks, and having learnt from Miss Priestman that it would be meet and right so to do—I prayed in the midst of the people, and as I found from the loving gratitude of the Dutch ladies, was understood.[7] I tried to say how that gathering made clear to me the meaning of the day of Pentecost, how though we could not all understand the words of some of the prayers we had heard each man speak in the tongue in wh. he was born, through the presence of the Holy Spirit. And by and bye I prayed for the women of the Hague, when we left to begin the hard work, and especially gave thanks for these, who had adopted a tongue not their own for our sakes, and received us with such love and kindness. And the dear homely yet withal impressive and dignified ladies came to me and thanked me in a way I shall never forget. My chief sorrow is that I who have never worked received the glory. Providence must not be questioned, or it seems strange, that the living coal from the altar should be laid *on my* lips;[8] while the grand glowing hearts of my so far worthier Compatriots, should consume themselves in good works, and fervid Aspirations. My Mary Priestman—the Diana-hearted declares herself "a dumb-dog,"[9] and never prayed an audible word: however it is not for me to settle what I shall be, and the Eternal Potter has given a lip long pitcher that the thirst of men should thereat be quenched.

Of home return I can tell you little. We four hope to leave early to-morrow morn. for Amsterdam, and back to Rotterdam for the evening boat. This, Heaven favouring, reaches England *Very* early in the morn. And I might be obliged to save London Hotel expenses to do the accursed thing and come home by early train on Tuesday from London. If I can I *will telegraph* to save uncertainty and trouble. So no fears,—*Expect* a telegram. But it might happen that Miss Bragge and I lingered a day in Amsterdam . . . Anyhow the Priest-women return to-morrow night. I am *Very* well, thankful, happy. No Congress can ever be to me like this one *[from header fol. 72ʳ]* the foreign city so dear. My P. I have nothing for you, worthy of you—a photograph for Dot of the Murillo.[10] I seek a sister tile to Amy's and *cannot* get it. Woe's me, for P.! May something be suddenly revealed at Amsterdam. Dearest love to the dear guests and Mount and for Cousin Fanny's long letter: let her[11] hear this, if you like. I must no more now.

Ever, with the heart-blood

A.W.F.

Kiss for me the father, mother, Sister. Adieu.

MS Eng. lett. c. 418 fols. 72ʳ–74ᵛ, 79ʳ–80ᵛ BOD

1. Dated from the International Congress at The Hague, 17 to 22 Sept. 1883.

2. Count Van Hogendorp hosted a final reception at his house on Sat., 22 Sept. ("International Congress," 251).

3. "The woman's power is for rule, not for battle,—and her intellect is not for invention or creation, but for sweet ordering, arrangement, and decision. She sees the qualities of things, their claims, and their places. Her great function is Praise; she enters into no contest, but infallibly adjudges the crown of contest." See Ruskin, "Of Queen's Gardens," 18:121–22. For Ruskin as "Jack," see letter 2 n. 6.

4. KB notes: a Dutch lady (untraced); Margaret Tanner (letter 66 n. 10); Emile de Laveleye

of Belgium, president of the congress ("International Congress," 244); Dutch lady (untraced); M. Casembroot, admiral of the fleet (Butler, *Recollections,* 385); M. de Morsier (letter 67 n. 7); Countess Guillaume-Schack of Beuthen in Germany ("International Congress," 244); Dutch lady (untraced); Josephine Butler; and Countess de Precorbin, a Spanish activist famed for going down a mine in a basket to address miners (Butler, *Personal Reminiscences,* 185).

5. Song of Sol. 4:7.

6. Aimé Humbert, see letter 67 n. 6.

7. This probably occurred at one of Josephine Butler's informal prayer meetings. A draft held by the BOD suggests that KB's speech was not impromptu at all, but written beforehand. See MS Eng. poet. d. 75 fols. 52^{r}–66^{v} BOD.

8. Is. 6:6–7.

9. A proverbial phrase: dumb dogs that cannot bark (*OED*).

10. Dot is Caroline Sturge (letter 114 n. 5), and she desires Bartolomé Estaban Murillo's *Virgin and Child* (ca. 1655–60) which is owned by the Mauritshuis gallery in The Hague (*Bartolomé Estaban Murillo,* 11 and 168).

11. Perhaps an intentional pun on "letter."

69. Edith Cooper, Letter to Katharine Bradley

[Ivythorpe] | [Sept. 1883][1]

Blessed old Fowl,

How I wonder what it is doing in England's "sea-girt city"![2] Has it been to the quakers' meeting and experienced man's fickle Silence? Or has it only tried to reach the reality of sea and city under the grey appearance of the mist? But it is *happy.* Tomorrow I shall send you a meal—a new *Fors*[3] on women—(but I have not yet read it all; we shall read it in a circle this afternoon). On the 1st. page is a lovely little Drawing by Kate Greenaway!! of a child watching the ships on the billowing sea, sailing on as if into the golden sun in front of them. Such is the attitude of the tragedian,—hints dear old Jack—trouble and many lives in front of him—god beyond.[4] Mother and I have had a most refreshing and stimulating morning with Stopford Brooke's Lectures on Wordsworth, with the *Prelude*—with Browning's *Lost Leader* and Matthew Arnold's Memorial lines on Wordsworth.[5]

Amy and the father have been delighted with Stopford Wentworth—Father so delighted that he has given 1/ to the British and Foreign Unitarian Society!!!!

"David"[6] spoke for the first time last night:—not more delightful the first babbling words of a child, than the first utterance, harmonious and definite, of a realized character!

Mother is nice and well and yielding herself to the many—influences of Sunday.

Fanshawe[7] yesterday promised my Logic paper—*only* mine. He was pleased with my *criticism* of Mill.[8] The fresh paper was trying—I *adhered* to Mill, and said that terms are the names of things—not ideas—aducing arguments. Perchance I have involved myself in nominalism, sensationalism and no end of other monstrous "isms"—and given a dangerous mental stab to the strenuous idealism of the Fan.

Here is the mark of the paw!—The Pussie's own lavender paw extended to you. Blessings on you!

Your very own,

P.P.

David first speaks

MS Eng. lett. c. 419 fols. 1^r–3^v BOD

1. Dated from the publication of Ruskin's *Fors Clavigera: Letters to the Workmen and Labourers of Great Britain,* letter 91, Sept. 1883.

2. EC is referring to Freshford on the Isle of Wight. She repeats the phrase she used in letter 22 to describe Venice.

3. Kate Greenaway's drawing appeared on the first page of Ruskin's *Fors Clavigera,* letter 91 (Ruskin, 29:439); England was in the midst of a fad for Greenaway's work in the early 1880s, which was particularly adored by Ruskin and the emerging aesthetic movement. As well as appearing several times in *Fors Clavigera,* her work was exhibited at the Royal Academy and the Fine Arts Society (Engen, *Kate Greenaway,* 59–61).

4. In response to *Cornhill Magazine's* "Why Shakespeare Wrote Tragedy?" Ruskin wrote that what the master of tragedy had meant to be felt by the audience was "the spirit of faith in God, and hope of Futurity." See *Cornhill Magazine* 42 (1880): 153–72; Ruskin, 29:447.

5. Stopford Brooke, *Theology in the English Poets* (1874). This book was based upon the lecture series of the same title, which related religious thought to secular knowledge. Seven of these were on Wordsworth, whom Brooke regarded as a religious poet because of his view of nature as "the living Spirit of God in the outward world" (98); William Wordsworth, *The Fourteen-Book Prelude* (1850); "The Lost Leader," Browning, 4:183; "Memorial Verses, April 1850," Arnold, 1:250–52.

6. David, Duke of Rothsay, is the protagonist of *FT* (1885). The young prince is starved to death in a dungeon as a result of the machinations of his uncle.

7. Reginald Fanshawe, professor of classical languages and philosophy at Bristol University College. There seems to have been some arrangement with New College, Oxford, that enabled his secondment to Bristol. See Tilden, *Sir William Ramsay,* 85; Treby, *MF Catalogue,* 56.

8. EC is critiquing John Stuart Mill's *A System of Logic* (1843).

9. See the letter reproduced on p. 109.

Letter from Edith Cooper to Katharine Bradley, "Here is the mark of the paw" [Sept. 1883]. (MS Eng. lett. c. 419, fol. 3v, Bodleian Library, University of Oxford)

70. Edith Cooper, Annotated Page

April
To and from *Sidmouth* 1885
MS .Eng. lett. c. 418 fol. 89r BOD

71. Edith Cooper, Letter to Katharine Bradley

[Stoke Green][1] | Wed., [Apr. 1885][2]

Wednesday Evening.

Darling old Dickey-Duck,

How the Pussy loved you for your little letter! It read the warm, living words just as it was going to sleep and then had to open its heavy old lids to let the bigness of a tear out. It will be an obedient Cat and rest. Tonight it is only going to look over its lecture and then read in circle Matthew Arnold on America,[3] wh: you shall have to smile over.

This morning I was delighted in learning something more of *Amiel* in Blanche's article.[4] As soon as I have coins I shall get the book. It has a rarer charm than *Obermann* and some wonderous thoughts, that will help me in my new constructive stage—will work in with Kant.[5] One thing Amiel says wh: will comfort us, my deare and me, for last night—"If you cannot accept regret, you cannot accept *life*!"[6] And, my darling, *life* we have accepted whatever the conditions. So we will not be bitter on the old M.S.S.

They brought Mr. Grey.[7]—the Wedmores—to pry at the poor Pussy-Puss. It was as demure, tail-locked, upright, and unpurring as any ordinary Greymalkin—with a suspicious light in its eyes.

All being well you are at the "homely" abode, dearest old runaway. May you steal health and run to your real home to enjoy the rich morsel. Good night. Heaven bless thee!

P.P.

MS Eng. lett. c. 419 fol. 99$^{r/v}$ BOD

1. The Cooper family home, Stoke Green.

2. Dated from KB's trip to Sidmouth in Apr. 1885.

3. Matthew Arnold's "A Word More about America" was published in the *Nineteenth Century* in Feb. 1885.

4. Henri-Frédéric Amiel was professor of philosophy at the University of Geneva. Selections from his journal, mapping his life and unsuccessful career, were published after his death as *Fragments d'un Journal Intime* (Ward, *Amiel's Journal,* xi–xxxi). Blanche Leppington reviewed it for *Contemporary Review* in Mar. 1885, weeks ahead of its appearance in English translation (Leppington, review, 334–52). Leppington was a personal friend of KB and EC, who gave her the nickname Phillida (Add. MS 46781 fol. 13^{v} BL; KB, letter to Blanche Leppington, MS Eng. d. 120 fol. 5^{r}–7^{v} BOD).

5. Senancour's *Le Journal Intime d'Obermann* (1804) is often compared with Amiel's journal. Matthew Arnold declared that Amiel's speculative philosophy was not in the same class as

Stoke Green, Ivywell Road, Rockleaze. (Photograph by Sharon Bickle)

the untranslated Senancour (Arnold, 4:232). The "new constructive phase" refers to *BU* (1886), the plan for which was based upon Immanuel Kant's notion of the Moral Law (see synopsis on p. 140).

6. Leppington, review, 342. The bitterness associated with the "old M.S.S" may involve rejected manuscript(s). An 1885 letter from Miss Bradley to William Blackwood and Sons offers for publication a short story entitled "A Debt of Honour," but Treby suggests this is another Miss Bradley (*MF Catalogue,* 134).

7. John Miller Gray (1850–94); Scottish art and literature critic, and first curator of the Scottish National Portrait Gallery (*Oxford DNB*). In a memorial to Gray, Michael Field noted the Wedmores introduced them in 1886 (Field, "Recollections," 79), but this letter suggests he was first introduced to EC a year earlier. For Wedmores, see letter 57 n. 4. After meeting KB in Edinburgh in 1886 (letter 122), Gray became a friend, a regular correspondent (Add. MS 45853 BL), and a valued reviewer. He used his influence with the *Academy* to shepherd several poems into print (29 [1886]: 320; 30 [1886]: 309). A later review of *S&S* was less supportive and caused a rift (Add. MS 46780 fol. 62[r] BL), but nevertheless his death in 1894 was sincerely mourned.

72. Katharine Bradley, Annotated Envelope

Mother's Blessing on the proofs and a bit from the P. saying it loves the Fowl. Also it tells of "The Drops of Aganippe."

MS Eng. lett. d. 402 fol. 80[r] BOD

73. Edith Cooper, Letter to Katharine Bradley

Stoke Green | [Apr. 1885][1]

Stoke Green.

My own loving Deare,

The Parents won't lend you the Pussy—they think ill would befall the lavender fur:—and perhaps it is well that we should join when airs are milder and when we could brood together over our nest, (Brutus Ultor) which I am too tired to sit yet a while. Perhaps we could each get a week at Weston[2] if spring smiles. Bless you, how soft and warmly-feathered are your sheltering thoughts for your P! It purrs right bravely and aloud.

To comfort you here is the second proof—to the end of the 1st Act. Return with the same speed; and say good words of it or my love will fail!

I have finished my dear book of poems and got such a sweet title for it *Drops from Aganippe*[3] (the fountain of the Muses on Helicon)—with the motto:

"Begin then Sisters of the sacred well[4]

That from beneath the seat of Jove doth spring"

And they do begin—

"Thee, Apollo, in a ring" etc.[5]

Every song has a beautiful red ink heading. *Altogether it is lovely.*

Now about magazines, we cannot ask the Bakers[6] for their *Contemporary* to send it *by post.* We have had it with a promise to keep it very clean, for, as you know, Mr Baker is dreadfully particular about his magazines. The *Nineteenth Century* we could not send because we were so limited in pt. of time, as it was in requisition. The *Pall Malls* have been aridity itself; but you shall have one tomorrow.[7] When you have done with *Amiel* you shall have a vol. of *Scherer.*[8] I will learn about the little bird-book[9] tomorrow. So do not scold your Pussy-puss or it will mew all over the roofs! Carta brought the Raleigh[10] this morning—a detestible young woman, with some nice moulding in her face, but that stupid conceit that scorns the slightest display of interest in anything heavenly or Earthly. Carta goes to Clevedon. Love from the Persian's very heart to its darling Dicky-Duck.

MS Eng. lett. c. 419 fols. 66^r–67^v BOD

1. Dated from KB's trip to Sidmouth in April 1885.

2. Cooper's parents offer a poor substitution: a local trip to the seaside for an extended holiday in Devon.

3. Many of the lyrics from EC's bosom-book, "Drops from Aganippe," were published in the troubled volume *UTB* (1893), which was revised and reissued within months of publication.

4. *Lycidas,* 15–16 (Milton, 1.1:77; Palgrave, *Golden Treasury,* 91).

5. "An Invocation" appeared in the *Academy* on 27 Nov. 1886 (29:320) and in *UTB* (1893). It disappeared from the revised edition of *UTB* but was included in the U.S. edition (1898). EC noted it was originally "written for a drama on the subject of Justinia and Cyprian" (MS Eng. poet. d. 60 fol. 2^r BOD).

6. For the Baker family, see letter 18 n. 11.

7. In Apr. 1885 the *Pall Mall Gazette* was reporting Russia's impending war over Afghanistan, which was a remote and poorly understood area of the world. See Schults, *Crusader in Babylon,* 122. By Jul. 1885 the *Gazette*'s infamous "Maiden Tribute" series would make for more sensational reading.

8. Edmond Scherer was a French critic and the original editor of Amiel's *Journal Intime.* His untranslated essays on English writers, particularly Milton, were praised by Matthew Arnold (10:242).

9. Untraced.

10. For Carta Sturge, see letter 61 n. 8; "the Raleigh" is untraced.

74. Katharine Bradley, Letter to Edith Cooper

⌊Sidmouth⌋ | [Tues.,] 31 Mar. 1885

March 31st. 1885.

Ah, my Deare, I awoke at half-past five this morning, and at once took wing to the inner room where, with all its philosophies its tragedies, and deep tender heart my Schatzlein[1] was sleeping. By and bye I looked out on the sea: the sun was spreading a golden net on the water, and two tiny fishing-boats lay outside the glittering mesh; again I curled myself up in my bed, and wrote to

My Deare Asleep[2]

I did not take me to the sea,
When the winged morning wakened me
With beamy plumes; I used them right
    To bear me in an Eastern flight
Of arrowy swiftness to the bed
    Where my beloved still slumberèd.[3]
  Such peace on lip and cheek she wore
    As when the soul was monitor,
Lying half Poet and half Child

The twin divineness reconciled.[4]
And I, who scarce could breathe, to see
Her spirit in its secresy
So innocent, drew back in awe
That I should give such creature law;
Then looked/turned and saw God standing near
And to His Rule/Love resigned my deare.

But I had not said all about it, nor how its little mouth lies open—its pretty shorelines dimpled by its dreams. Then I grew pagan and invoked

King Apollo[5]

When my lady sleeping lies,
Her sweet breaths her lips unbar,
Which[6] when King Apollo spies,
With dream foot fall not to mar
The dear sleep,
Through the rosy door[7] ajar
He with golden thoughts doth creep.

Ah Pretty, Pretty! There are thousands of such songs in my heart: there is in me a mine of love—enough to make the fortune of innumerable hearts,—and it is all possessed by the P.

It is now after ten,—my Pretty is creasing its brows: it is thinking about things in themselves[8] and Tracking the secret paths of reason. Before me lies—the dazzling phenomenon the sea, fitter I think for the gaze of the mild blue eyes than foolscap and blotting paper!!

We are hoping to start in pay chaise to Salcombe Hill, and back by another hill.

Be blessed and happy. Not an anxious thought. Take 3 full days' rest before you look at "Loyalty."[9]

Love always this terrible and fiery old Fowl, who loves not as mortals but fearfully as a god.

[bird symbol]

MS Eng. lett. c. 418 fols. 107^{r}–109^{v} BOD

1. Schätzlein (Ger.) means "little treasure."

2. Published in amended form as "A Spring Morning by the Sea" in *UTB* (1893), 71–72.

3. *UTB:* slumberèd.

4. *UTB:* lines 7 and 8 removed; poem ended at line 10.

5. "King Apollo" appeared in the *Academy* on 11 Nov. 1886 (30:326), and in *UTB* (72). The subject suggests Pope's image of the sun awaking Belinda in "The Rape of the Lock": "Sol thro' white curtains shot a tim'rous ray, / And oped those eyes that must eclipse the day" (1.13–14; Pope, 72).

6. *UTB:* Which] This

7. *UTB:* door] doors

8. Kantian metaphysics distinguishes between two products of knowledge: phenomena or objects understood through the senses, and noumena or objects that have their own necessary conditions and are not affected by experience. Understanding noumena, or "things in themselves," is the primary aim of Kant's metaphysics. See Beiser, "Kant's Intellectual Development," 47.

9. *LL* (1885).

75. Katharine Bradley, Annotated Envelope

[PM Tues., 31 Mar. 1885]

April 1 1885
promises synopsis of Brutus
Summer Wind by K
[in hand of EC on verso] Too philish tomorrow[.] My duty to suck it in tonight. No Fowl-words that I can see[.]

MS Eng. lett. c. 419 fol. 57r BOD

76. Edith Cooper, Letter to Katharine Bradley

[Stoke Green] | [Wed., 1 Apr. 1885][1]

Purr, purr, purr!—
Terque quaterque beata[2]—the exam: is over and the Pussy-puss free. I send the paper to my Deare—my tender Director;—You see it was a tiresome paper—written from a general point of view and not in the least testing my particular and Special Knowledge of the Critique.[3] This is trying as I have worked out the *Analytic* to its minutest branch. Fan. will have no idea of this work.[4] All the questions, save 2 or 3, depended on original thought at the moment, wh: was

very wearing. The Exam. lasted 2 hours and a half. You see I have answered 9, and 7 were required. Fanshawe mentioning that he required them to be treated as Essays and written with regard to style. I wrote to the very end and certainly did some good work, but in the whirl I cannot remember what I said and can only trust it was well-reasoned. Davis[5] was my only rival. Suppose he is above me! He scratched indefaticably—while Fan. sighed like a furnace.[6] On the whole the Pussy-puss is not overdone,—only will require tomorrow to rest and calm itself.

You grand old creature, so you are alive: Well your P. won't let you squander your force on little dramatic morsels. If you will only be patient for 2 days (or so) the P. will send you a *complete synopsis of Brutus Ultor*[7] and the history; and all that fresh potent blood shall be given to Lucretia, who is to be a masterpiece. This I promise as I am an honourable P. The printery has stopped it seems, and Easter will intervene and then there is all *Rufus*[8] to be put thro' the press. So I can spare an evening or so from *Loyalty* and am just in the mood. In the mean time you can write *great thoughts* (I send back the *wares* with purry approval for the book) or still better some more *Drops*—I want *Drops* or better than that some songs to his Lady!![9] The *Summer Wind* is a most powerful *Drop*—why not do some *sea*-ones in your wonderful metre? You shall have stuff to work on directly, I promise if you will be patient. I will look out the Kant-thought tomorrow, I have had too much of the little old gentleman for *today*! The *Descartes* thought I think you have. I do not know where to seek it.

Be strong, my Deare; *Do not dissipate your divinity; Keep it for our great paean to the Moral Law.*[10] I can no more tonight. Thine with grateful tail, softest paws and mildest eyes,

P.P.

MS Eng. lett. c. 419 fols. 54^r^–56^v^; MS Eng. lett. d. 402 fol. 89^r^ BOD

1. Dated from the envelope above.

2. "O terque quaterque beati" (Virgil's *Aeneid,* 1.94) is literally translated as "O three and four times blessed." EC alters "beati" (male vocative plural) to "beata" (female vocative singular). See Virgil, *Aeneid,* ed. Williams, 4 (L.); Virgil, *Aeneid,* trans. West, 6 (Eng.).

3. *The Critique of Pure Reason* (1781); Kant's *Analytic,* mentioned in the next sentence, describes judgments in which the concept of the predicate is already contained within the subject. See Parsons, "Transcendental Aesthetic," 75–76.

4. "Fan." is Professor Reginald Fanshawe; see letter 69 n. 7.

5. Possibly Herbert Davies of Clifton (*1881 Census*).

6. *AYL* 2.7.148.

7. See on p. 140.

8. *WR* (1885).

9. For EC's bosom-book, see letter 73 n. 3; "A Summer Wind," or "O wind, thou hast thy kingdom in the trees," appeared in the *Academy* on 18 Sept. 1886 (30:187) and *UTB* (7–8).

10. In *BU* (1886), Brutus follows Kant's categorical imperative because he enforces the moral law in spite of the personal cost, condemning his own sons to death. See Kenny, *Western Philosophy,* 191.

77. Unknown, Examination Paper [probable appendix to letter 76]

1. Explain exactly what is meant by "critical" and "transcendental" as applied to the philosophy of Kant.

2. How far can you trace in earlier thought a critical tendency?

3. Describe carefully the distribution of the Critique of Pure Reason and the principles on which it is based.

4. How far do you think the charge of idealism is warranted by Kant's conclusions?

5. In what sense can the Ethics of Kant be called rational?

6. Point out and examine the assumptions on which the Critique of Pure and of Practical Reason appear to rest.

7. Define Kant's use of the following terms; reason, understanding, intuition, postulate, knowledge.

8. In what respects do the Ethics of Kant appear to you to fail of coherence?[1]

9. Discuss the relation between the speculative and practical reason.

10. Compare the general treatment of Ethical questions adopted by Kant and Spinoza.

MS Eng. lett. d. 402 fol. 89^{r} BOD

1. Only question not circled.

78. Edith Cooper, Letter to Katharine Bradley

[Stoke Green] | [Apr. 1885][1]

My own Deare,

May the Pussy be a little worthy of your sovereign love! The mild eyes are almost misty with delicious wonder and tremulous joy at being so richly loved. The tender morning dew-drops of song are safe in the bosom of *Aganippe.*[2] It did not think, when yesterday it sighed for a song, that two such were flying to it, from the great, triumphing wings of the A.W.F. How dear and mighty you are and how your Pussy loves you deeper than anything but Art!

Here is a proof—a good one and nearly the last. Your Pussy is purring with the great dead mouse of Kant between its little paws—not yet certain if it is a first class mouse or if that Tabby Davis[3] has caught a better. With love from the deepest well of my heart.

Thine own Pussy.

MS Eng. lett. c. 419 fol. 68$^{r/v}$ BOD

1. Dated from KB's trip to Sidmouth, Apr. 1885.

2. For *Drops from Aganippe,* see letter 73. The two songs are "My Deare Asleep" and "King Apollo."

3. EC's rival for academic honors. See letter 76. She not only received first-class honors but also discovered Davis had withdrawn (letter 90).

79. Edith Cooper, Letter to Katharine Bradley

[Stoke Green | Sat., [4 Apr. 1885][1]

My Darling Deare,

To my consternation I find I have not made my vision clear. This is what I dreamt. In the monastery-aisle I saw the tomb—and on the tomb the figure in its marble-stillness, with the beautiful round lines of youth (cheek and chin) clear in the moonlight and the blank page of the brow glistening white.[2] *Yet in spite of all this peace* and beauty the grey sprites of famine, with their poppies and corn, twist'd round the tomb and mocked the poor lean, wasted body that lay under the still satisfied effigy. I *never saw the body*—only the statue after life's fitful fever sleeping well.[3] I only felt how the body was contradicting this simulation. That was my vision—that was the truth. You think that I saw the body and all the peace of the beginning refers to it (wh: wd be monstrous, and no wonder you altered it.) But I feel as if I could not give up my vision—it would be giving up a heaven-sent reality. I almost weep.

I *saw* those sweet young lines and that white blank brow—the lie that the aspect of death gives to the quivering misery, and dark tumult of the real life that it w[d] perpetuate.

I have tried to make it clear thus;—

"Within the monast'ry
Of far Lindores I saw the straight cold tomb
And the straight marble statue (figure)—the round lines
Of slumb'ring Youth chasten'd by Death's grave stamp,
The brow a blank page of the whitest peace.
Yet all about **twirl'd* a dim company
Grey Sprites of Famine, shaking poppy-*stems***
And stalks of corn that wagg'd their lavish heads
Deriding the lean body underneath
Its effigy that still and satisfied
Lay clear against the wall."

*I must have *twirled* here—That was what they were doing—spinning round and round. Remember I testfy that which I *know*—what I have *seen.*
**I could not have *sheaves*—They held single poppies and single stalks of corn—They were too weak of substance to carry more. The way you have managed the corn and *lean* I greatly like.

If you won't have the *true* Vision—I shall adopt your rendering—altering *danced* and *sheaves* wh: are too untrue to the reality. I put out the lines about the pilgrim and penance. It seems to me it is stronger for the King only to give his vision and then Walter to break in—

"My dearest lord
And new kind master *do*"[4]

I like the rather strained simile *quite* left out. If however it is retained, your version is a great improvement. Thank you deeply for your work—but such a vision is precious and close to one and must be truthfully rendered.

I am tired and rather (teary). Perhaps I shall be more Easter-like this afternoon.
Saturday morning.

MS Eng. lett. c. 419 fol. 63[r] BOD

1. Dated from Easter Sat., 1885.

2. EC's vision is the dream of the remorseful King Robert in *FT,* who unwittingly allows the Duke of Albany to starve the King's son, David, to death in the castle of Lindores (5.1.36–50; *FT,* 100). EC's forceful argument impressed KB, and only two lines were changed in the published version of the passage that appears later in this letter: "The full serenity of cheek and chin / Cut clearer in the moonlight's marble mould" (5.1.40–41; *FT/WR/LL,* 100). See also letter 131.

3. *Mac.* 3.2.24–25.

4. *FT* 5.1.51–53 (*FT/WR/LL,* 100).

80. Katharine Bradley, Annotated Envelope

[Apr. 1885][1]

Bit about Immortality
It has parted with the last proof of "The Father's Tragedy."

MS Eng. lett. c. 419 fol. 51[r] BOD

1. This envelope is dated from its reference to Immortality, which seems to link it to the letter below.

81. Edith Cooper, Letter to Katharine Bradley

[Stoke Green] | [Easter Sat., 4 Apr. 1885][1]

Evening Greeting—happier and more Pussyian (and yet anxious as to its vision[2]). May tomorrow be radiant with glorious sunshine that the Earth may reflect that inspiring idea that rises up from the Source of God-given Reason—and is called in our speech *Immortality.*[3] Oh, my Deare, we who have felt it creative within us can lift up our hearts[4] in a way that not Even the Saints could who only possessed it. A deep Easter kiss—Soul's lips to Soul's.

Thine own P.

MS Eng. lett. c. 419 fol. 51b[r/v] BOD

1. Dated from Easter Sat., 1885. KB's poem "The Blisse of Immortalitie" takes this letter as its inspiration. See letter 93.

2. For EC's vision, see letter 79.

3. The practical necessity for immortality is defined by Kant immanently (derived through reason rather than a transcendental God) in terms of that period required for an individual to

be able to achieve the highest Good. See Fackenheim, *God Within,* 3–19; Goldmann, *Immanuel Kant,* 193–205. EC reinterprets this pursuit as synonymous with their vocation as writers.

4. EC echoes the service for Holy Communion: "Lift up your hearts." See *Book of Common Prayer,* 272.

82. Katharine Bradley, Letter to Edith Cooper

[Sidmouth] | [Easter Sun., 5 Apr. 1885][1]

Yes P. the quality in Immortality is its pricelessness; not that Thy lips will touch mine when there are no more years; but that they press soul to soul when we kiss. Duration in immortality is like extension in body,—essential, not absorbing.[2] God comes to live with us, and who can think of the old scythesman who slinks away at His entrance.

The loving old big *[bird symbol].*

~~Meanwhile, my Dearest, *I command* that you put it away from your thoughts; and that you remember the *EASTER HOLIDAYS HAVE BEGUN*. Where are the Characteristics?~~[3]

MS Eng. lett. c. 418 fol. 98$^{r/v}$ BOD

1. Dated from Easter Sun., 1885.

2. KB draws upon Cartesian physics to qualify EC's description of immortality in the preceding letter 81. Descartes argues that we comprehend bodies only through the attribute of extension (length, breadth, and depth); indeed, extension and body are distinct only in conceptual terms. Similarly, we comprehend immortality through the attribute of duration or the passing of linear time (Garber, "Descartes' Physics," 292–95).

3. Anthony, Earl of Shaftesbury, *Characteristics of Men, Manners, Opinions, Times, etc.* (1790).

83. Katharine Bradley, Annotated Envelope

[Tues.,] 7 Apr. 1885

April 7th 1885.
Amy consents to join me.
P. must remain to finish Loyalty.
[on reverse in EC's hand] [deare]st love to Marie.[1]

MS Eng. lett. c. 419 fol. 62$^{r/v}$ BOD

1. For Mary Louisa Hall, known as Marie, see letter 24 n. 1.

84. Edith Cooper, Letter to Katharine Bradley

[Stoke Green] | [Tues., 7 Apr. 1885][1]

I like the tiny hymn.[2] I am nearly mad with fright at the thought of the hat!!!

My own Deare,

The passage is right now and the Pussy-puss is calm and peaceful as an old Cat should be.

Bless you!—It was the moon light that was wanted.[3] It is *almost* settled that the Kittie-puss comes to you on Wednesday or Thursday. I am delighted, for the little thing wants to play with its tail sorely. How good and gracious you are in your heart to your Babes! The old Cat must stay at home till *Loyalty* is finished and *William* through the press—bless the big boy! You shall say nothing against him or woe to you!

I must be able to consult Freeman and Palgrave and such like.[4] How I have searched the Library through and can only find 2 books that touch on *Loyalty*—Percival's *History of Italy* and Kington's *Fredrick the Second,*[5] wh: we have consulted before. I can copy any bit from the very small account of the forged letters[6] in each and then it will not matter so much my being away from home when the *Loyalty* proofs come. But while I am writing the fore face (wanting Mazzini[7] etc) and re-constructing, I must be in loneliness and near a library. So the Pussy locks up its ardent desires to join its Deare and sends the good little kitten. I am working at the easier parts of *Loyalty* this week (It is *premonition-week*!!![8]) Next I hope to be carried thro' difficulties by inspiration. After that I shall be very glad of a complete break in work—a resting-time from the manifold of labours. This I will get at Weston or somehow with my dearest Deare, and we'll be as happy as the cowslips and thrushes. I really am going on very well, considering that all the sores in my heart have been probed afresh, and that much has been done in *many* ways. I only feel that I must have a goal of holiday—but not reach it till my work is done.

Meanwhile I promise to leave *Brutus* locked up on the straw in my brain's store-room. I have just been a trot on the Down[9] with Paps—chilled by the delicious rainy April air—with a sunny intention lurking in its gloom. While I was out, Amy Wheeler brought Herbert Baynes (the wild philosophic brother) to call.[10] His eye was at once on *The Critique.* Max Müller sent him the preface before it was printed. Then this afternoon (if the showers will let us) we go to the

Wedmores' to meet the Lewes-folk again.[11] It is wonderful to see anyone talk just in the way in wh: you have always seen Lewes talking to George Elliot in "the mind's eye."[12] "Charles," I am sure, is his father's representative in the parliament of the Present. The Bakers say that he always calls George Elliot "Mother." The tears rise in his eyes when he speaks of her, and he seems to keep for her memory a deep chivalrous passion. M$^{rs.}$ Lewes is Octavia Hill's own sister—full of the Kyrle Society[13]—a nature and face founded on the rock of philanthropy, but with the springs of living water in the large limpid eyes. We really had a delightful evening on Saturday. So you see the Pussy-Puss is "dissipating." It does not look at Philosophy—not think of Kant. It only reads Carlyle's Life and *Faust* with the Darling Mother (who rejoices in it touchingly).[14]

Yesterday we fed ourselves on the Bible, Blake and Browning—strong inspiring food! We did not forget *The* ODE. In the fields I saw the lambs rolling over each other, and one leapt into the air—high up—with Nature's quick, unconscious pathetic joy. It seemed a pulse-thrill of the great Universal Life[15] that flows through all things. Thine with heart's truth and love.

P.P.

MS Eng. lett. c. 419 fols. 58^{r}–61^{v} BOD

1. Dated from the envelope above.

2. Untraced.

3. For EC's anxiety over her vision for *FT,* see letter 79.

4. Edward A. Freeman, *The Reign of William Rufus* (1882); Francis Turner Palgrave, *The Golden Treasury* (1861).

5. Research texts for *LL* (1885): George Perceval, *The History of Italy, from the Fall of the Western Empire to the Commencement of the Wars of the French Revolution* (1825); and T. A. Kington, *History of Frederick the Second, Emperor of the Romans: from Chronicles and Documents Published within the Last Ten Years* (1862).

6. In *LL,* forged letters are at the center of Peter de Celano's plot (3.2; *FT/WR/LL,* 273–75).

7. The epigraph for *LL* was taken from Guiseppe Mazzini's "Essay on the Duties of Man Addressed to Workingmen" (*FT,* 227; Mazzini, *Duties of Man,* 54).

8. In act 2 of *LL,* the arrival of Henry VI is accompanied by portents: an owl at noon (2.1.6–7; *FT/WR/LL,* 251), and thunder during the ceremony (2.2.32; 257).

9. The Durdham and Clifton Downs. In the 1880s, Stoke Green actually overlooked the Downs. See Jones and Chown, *History of Bristol,* maps 1 and 2.

10. Amy Wheeler is untraced; Herbert Baynes seems to have been unremarkable except in his acquaintance with Professor Friedrich Max Müller, the translator of Kant's *Critique of Pure Reason* (1881). Max Müller wrote to Baynes in 1881 in appreciation of an article contributed to *Modern Thought.* See Herbert Baynes, letter to the editor, "The Late Professor Max Müller,"

Times, 6 Nov. 1900. Whether Max Müller sent the preface is unknown, although he may have circulated pages in proof to a number of people.

11. For the Wedmore family, see letter 57 n. 4. The Lewes-folk are: Charles Lee Lewes and his wife, Gertrude Lewes née Hill. Lewes was the eldest son of George Henry Lewes, longtime companion to Marian Evans (George Eliot). Gertrude Lewes was the sister of Octavia Hill (1838–1912), the influential pioneer of Housing Reform. For Lewes's relationship with Eliot, see Karl, *George Eliot,* 342–46 and 551.

12. *Ham.* 1.1.112.

13. In 1876 Octavia Hill founded the Kyrle Society, named for John Kyrle, the Man of Ross celebrated in Pope's "Epistle to Bathurst" (249–99; Pope, 252–53). The society's object was the beautification of poor housing areas by planting gardens and decorating public spaces (Bell, *Octavia Hill,* 150–53). Like KB, Hill was influenced by Ruskin, and similarly fell out with him.

14. EC and her parents are reading James Anthony Froude's *Thomas Carlyle: A History of the First Forty Years of His Life, 1795–1835* (1882) and Goethe's *Faust* (1850) (probably Anna Swanwick's translation, as they had recently become correspondents; see MS Eng. lett. e. 32 fol. 37^r–40^v BOD); and, as it is Easter, the ode referred to later in the letter is probably Wordsworth's "Intimations of Immortality from Recollections of Early Childhood" (Wordsworth, 4:279–85).

15. Kant's theory of aesthetics argues that beauty is only attained when the judment is based on a universal voice in human nature. See Schaper, "Taste, Sublimity and Genius," 376.

85. Katharine Bradley, Letter to Edith Cooper

[Sidmouth] | [Apr. 1885][1]

My P.

I did want it to be fine this morn. for Spurius Lucretius[2] had outworn me; and I wanted "the sum of things"[3] to speak to me while I rested.

The banks are really starring with primroses now: in every ditch, on every orchard slope the gentle Sisterhoods Cluster; but the apple-trees do not relax a muscle. Close-fisted old misers—one w$^{d.}$ never suspect them of such rosy wealth at heart. Branscombe is worthy of the P.—the genius of this little group of southern sea-side places Budleigh, Sidmouth, Beer, and Seaton.—A place of tinkling sheep-bells, clear rills, and Veritable pastoral peace.

As to the village, man has given it a body as it hath pleased him;—it straggles, and discontinues, and begins again, scarcely tottering toward the ocean at the end of the long recluse valley. My visit to the Vicarage with petition will long be remembered by me with pleasure.[4] The sweet dear old churchy couple, with their horror of the sin of schism, and intolerance of poachers whom they classed with common thieves—how exquisite to feel like the Lord to them, delighting in the quaint beauty of their prejudices; and by no means declaiming to them Beowulf's first speech.[5] As we were driving down Branscombe defile Amy[6] spied what she thought was a spinning-wheel, and I instantly ordered the pony to stop. We were soon gathered round a sweet peaceful 74 year old human spirit—that is not counting the pre-natal aeons. Who, we found, was not really spinning, but winding thread for lace. It is more to me than passing through a church-yard to see old age in its solitude, its penury, its impotence, still winding the threads of life. "I could not earn twopence a day" said the old creature resignedly. Still the threads must be wound; and the old hands contentedly ply their task. Husband and children seem to lie so far behind . . . like battle-fields on ground that is now tilled and peaceful. One can hardly believe those thrilling experiences have been possible to the dimming face.

The Vicar at Beer was young and high-church-music-mad, and full of anthems. I tried to be musical too,—but not beyond the point of owning the Sidmouth services "rather dreary". . .

It was Very *complex* to visit Seaton. Seven years ago, I was there in full Jack ardour[7]—but it was before my baptism and consecration,—a time of raving and externalism of which I can not help feeling slightly ashamed.

Certainly in the growth of this limb of Michael God did not make haste.

How infinitely and beyond Comparison happier it is to be Michael than not Michael. My heart is for ever giving praise. Axe-mouth is the whitest sweetest little stream-side Village touched by ocean breeze in England. It has its own Music—in the bubble of its street brook, and the cackle of its well-conditioned ducks, while its Vicarage among orchards and bossy bits of woods is a very "nesting-place for happy poets."[8] I really think I must become a Vicaress to live in one of these blessed nooks, and work the terror of schism out of my good Man's brain. The Vicar at Axmouth was not in, but I left the petition with him. This has been quite a primrosey bit of cause work P; and hitherto I have met with no rebuffs. To-morrow I must try to work in Sidmouth for one of its clergymen has given me a formidable list of names. At Seaton we saw a crane on stately leg, and coming home a yellow-hammer.

Both my young people are utterly exhausted; but *they* toiled up 3 tremendous hills. *I* went about preaching and *drove* up the hills,—except unconscionable steeeps.

P. leave Faust: set to work on Loyalty. *Command of the King.* Bless, Bless, it influx of Kisses on its head:

A.W.F[.]

MS Eng. lett. c. 418 fols. 99r–102v BOD

1. Dated from KB's trip to Sidmouth in Apr. 1885.

2. Spurius Lucretius is the father of Lucretia in *BU.*

3. *Paradise Lost,* 6.673 (Milton, 2.1:201–2).

4. This is probably a petition against animal cruelty. From the mid-1870s, petitions were one of the major campaign tools of the Societies; for example, in 1883, about six petitions were presented to Parliament for each day of its sitting (French, *Antivivisection,* 168). Anglican and Catholic clergymen were particularly supportive of the campaign. See "Vivisection," *Times,* 30 Mar. 1887. EC's request for "headings for the petitions to Hospitals" in letter 90 further supports this reading. Later in the letter, the Vicar's fear of schism probably relates to anxieties surrounding ritualism. Ritualism involved introducing Anglo-Catholic architecture, dress, and ceremony into the Broad Church. The specter of schism was raised by Lord Shaftesbury and the Bishop of Lincoln in the 1870s with the passing of the Public Worship Regulation Act (1874), which allowed for the prosecution of ritualist churchmen (A.K.H.B., "Archbishop Tait of Canterbury," 374; Bentley, *Ritualism,* 44). Although the furor over ritualism continued to the end of the century, KB regards the Vicar's concern as provincial and quaint.

5. In *WR,* Beowulf's opening speech laments the coming of the Normans (1.1.1–13; *FT/WR/LL,* 129).

6. Amy Bell or Amy Wheeler.

7. John Ruskin. See letter 2 n. 6; her baptism and consecration is KB's rebirth as Michael Field.

8. KB may be paraphrasing James Henry Leigh Hunt's *Story of Rimini:* "Places of nestling green, for poets made" (3.430; Hunt, 22).

86. Katharine Bradley, Annotated Envelope

[PM Sun., 19 Apr. 1885]

[*ripped*] [la]ys the whortle-blooms [b]etween the wings of the *Stock-dove's Lament,* thought.

MS Eng. lett. c. 419 fol. 65r BOD

87. Katharine Bradley to Edith Cooper

[Sidmouth] | [Sun., 19 Apr. 1885][1]

The Stock Dove's Lament.[2]

I sing thee with the stock-dove's throat,

Warm, crooning, superstitious note,
That on its dearie so doth dote
It falls to sorrow,
And from the fair white swans afloat
A dirge must borrow.

II

In thee I have such deep content
I can but murmur a lament;
It is as though my heart were rent
By thy perfection
And all my passion's torrent spent
In recollection.

April 13th. 1885. Sidmouth.

And see, my bonnie love, here is a branch of whortle-berry[3] for our meeting—as the almond blossom meant desertion and farewell.

Mother must have a heart of stone if after this she Keeps you from me. What is it to me to be in the woods without my Pretty swinging on the bough? It was sweet to watch the boy's pleasure picking anemones among the dried "acorn leaves," and our own dead beech-leaves. I wrote the Dove-Song a few days ago, but when you spoke of returning the French passage,[4] delayed to see if I could add a touch . . .

Coo-coo^ooo— Says the old Fowl—till his throat vibrates.

Coo Coo^oooo *[bird symbol]*.

MS Eng. lett. c. 418 fol. 90r/v BOD

1. The PM on the envelope above suggests the date (3 Apr. 1885) in the letter refers to the poem's composition rather than the letter itself.

2. Published in the first edition of *UTB,* but disappeared from revised editions. The stock dove is a typical pigeon (Campbell and Lack, *Dict. of Birds,* 462).

3. This branch has not been retained.

4. An unattributed quotation in French prefaces *LL:* "Qui ne met la poésie au-dessus de tout n'a pas le sentiment de l'histoire même, car l'histoire est le récit des efforts impuissants des hommes pour arriver à cette beauté sévère que nous trouvons dans le grand art" [He who does not place poetry above all else has no feeling for history itself, for history is the story of Man's helpless efforts to reach the severe beauty that we find in great art] (*FT/WR/LL,* 227).

88. Edith Cooper, Letter to Katharine Bradley

[Stoke Green] | [Apr. 1885][1]

My own Deare, my Stock-Dove,

Sweet, very sweet is your call to me, I love it dearly and it does not Coo in vain for me. *I will come,* and, heaven favouring, we will indeed be happy! We will talk of Lucrece and *Loyalty* and the white book[2] and feel the warm folding arms of Nature round us both. But wait a little for our dear little Pussie's sake.[3] She is getting better and parents want her to have a full week at Weston now this lovely weather is given to us. Let her have this *full* week and then *I will come. They promise that.* If we could but set her up for the Spring!

Kisses for the darling coral blossoms. My Deare and I have plucked them at Ludlow and Tintern. They seem a rosy pledge that we shall meet. I shall always keep them folded between the wings of my Stock-Dove's Lament (What a sweet voice she has!) I still send the lovely passage on the Dove's voice for the thought-book.[4]

Your Pussy was taken with melancholy yesterday when it wrote. In the evening it worked all right and happily at the prose scene between Margarito and the arch bishop[5] I think it is very nice now. You will judge. The rest I still send, I think you can work at it more felicitously and you can think about the young priest.[6] When I join you I will bring all the *Loyalty* M.S. in the rough. Send back the Scenes as soon as they are done. It will be a little rest from Spurious Lucretius.[7] I believe he has nearly killed you. The motto is not yet found.[8] The Mother came in with these words "Patriotism is God's birth-mark on His Child Man." She read them as if from Pattison—but they were her own, bless her! I have looked through Dante, Mazzini, Landor, Plato, and endless others! It seems as if no-one had written about Country.

I liked so much what you wrote about the old woman twisting the threads of life. Shan't you be glad when we reach the 5*th* Act of *William*? I am getting so tired of proofs and revises. The nervous young men in the master's absence keep sending revises over and over again (as Kegan Paul did with *Bel.*[9])[.]

"Coo, Coo" is answered by "mew, mew!" Its little heart beats for you.

Your own P.P.

MS Eng. lett. c. 419 fols. 69r–71v BOD

1. Dated from previous letter.

Emma Harris Cooper. (Courtesy of Special Collections, Bristol University)

2. *BU* (1886); *LL* (1885); the little white book is *Call./FR* (1884).

3. Amy Katharine Cooper.

4. "The Stock Dove's Lament" was transcribed into a black notebook (MS Eng. poet. f. 19 fol. 28v BOD).

5. *LL*, 3.4.

6. Andrea is the young priest who loves Veronica in *LL*.

7. A reply to KB's complaint in letter 85.

8. The final motto was selected from Mazzini. See letter 84 n. 7. Mother's words are described as if from Mark Pattison (1813–84), the rector of Lincoln College, Oxford, who was well known for his regular contributions to the *Fortnightly Review* (*DNB*). Pattison had a dry, sarcastic character and was widely rumored to be the model for Eliot's Mr. Casaubon. See Morley, "On Pattison's Memoirs," 335. EC's other potential sources are noted exiles, except for Plato, whose Socrates chose death over exile (Plato, "Crito," trans. Jowett, 1:379–83).

9. Kegan Paul published *Bell.* in 1881.

89. Katharine Bradley, Letter to Edith Cooper

[Sidmouth] | [Apr. 1885][1]

P.—It is very beautiful to see you standing up on your hind legs, pleading for the moral law![2] We will be *loyal* to that, while we love Browning. Tell Mother she is *a real scamp,*—a scoundrel of the blackest dye—to write to me so comfortably of Swanwick, and Browning—as Simeon, and seem to regard it a settled thing we were to experience that high joy—and then turn round, and turn [to] you; and say, I scarcely think it can be done.[3] Tell her to beware: her hand is on a lion's mane.

Now P. this is what we will do. We will just wait, get out Vol II[4]—see in what temper Browning replies to you (—it might be impossible to meet him) and if he is enthusiastic, we will somehow get seven days in London. Blackheath[5] I decline: it would be infra dig. But if I told Scott we w[d.] stay with her one week, and go out on the Friday Afternoon she always receives, she w[d.] do *just what I told her;* and simply trot with us to her art galleries; and leave us to go alone to the British—I should *say for study;* and not allow her to accompany us. Mother w[d.] be happy about you if you were at Kensington: and *I should not attempt any theatres* or night excitement. *But we will wait.* Meanwhile prepare for Weston Many warm clothes; for next week *I mean to have you;* indeed I shall not come home, till they send you to fetch me. That will bring parents to their senses. Of course Michael bears the expense of all Michael's Self, if he goes to London to see the Flight into Egypt—the Demetia of the British Museum,—and the old Gentleman himself![6] (I shall write to Swanwick holding out hope of June visit: *nothing* definite.)

I have got the invocation *right* in my bed this morning.

Re-read.

Now put down its moral paws: and love me, P.P. come to me: it is not natural for us to live apart.

Your own, *[bird symbol].*

An Invocation.[7]

Two of Us.

"If two of you—"[8]

"Are ye able to drink of the cup* that I shall drink
of they say unto Him: 'we are able'"[9]

Our God, though thou didst not indite
In law or psalm
The things concerning us, so we resign
Ourselves to thee,
Thou wilt accomplish in us blessedly
All thy design;
And our poor aid
Go to the glorious project thou hast made
to travail for our immortalitie.
Our best ambition Thou dost overshade
With thy great Hope;
Work out in us thy full conception's scope
Even to Calvary!
Thus it behoves
The Christ in us to suffer; we grow calm:
When God speaks by a man, the token
Is a heart broken.
We bear humanity's most bitter shame,
(King Robert[10]) Weakness, and blame;—
Yea, even that nameless land
From which the sun is banned
(Lucretia) Loathing and fearful we will penetrate:
For onslaught of Thy whelming waves we wait:
We can be killed/For thy sake Killed
All the day long, till we have quite fulfilled
What thou hast writ,—thy Word's interpreter;
And thou at last empower us, without slur
On thy dear Fame,
Unto our mortal signature
To add thy Name.

Sunday April 16. 1885.[11] Sidmouth

"Two of Us"
"If two of you"
"Are ye able to drink of the cup that I drink of?
They say unto Him: we are able."

Our God, though thou didst not indite
In law or psalm
The things concerning us, so we resign
Ourselves to thee
Thou wilt accomplish in us blessedly
All thy design,
And our poor aid
Go to the glorious project thou hast made—
To travail for our Immortalitie.
Our best ambition thou dost overshade
With thy great Hope;
Work out in us thy full conception's scope
Even to Calvary!
Thus it behoves
The Christ in us to suffer; we grow calm;
When God speaks by a man, the token
Is a heart broken.
We take humanity's most bitter shame,
Weakness, and blame,—
We cry, deserted in the olive groves)
Even that nameless land,
(Tarquin) From which the sun is banned,
Loathing and fearful we must penetrate:
Yea, alienate
From goodness, famish for thy Face obscured
In cavern of sin's seamless sepulchre,
Till all that thou dost write
We have endured,—
Thy word's interpreter;
And thou at last empower us, without slur
On thy dear Fame,
Unto our mortal signature
To add thy Name.

[bird symbol]

MS Eng. lett. c. 418 fols. 91[r]–92[v] BOD

1. Dated from the publication of *FT/WR/LL* and the first visit to Robert Browning in Jun. 1885.

2. The "moral law" usually refers to *BU* (see, for example, letter 76); however, here KB is clearly speaking of the Cooper parents' thwarting of their holiday together.

3. KB and EC were becoming more than just appreciative readers of the work of Robert Browning (1812–89). The elderly poet had initiated a correspondence in Jul. 1883, writing to thank EC for her review of *Jocoseria.* In response, EC sent a copy of *Call./FR* (Add. MS 46866 fol. 24v BL). Browning's reply was all a young poet could hope for: "It is long since I have been so thoroughly impressed by indubitable poetic *genius;* a word I consider while I write, only to repeat it—'genius'" (*W&D,* 2). By early 1885 a meeting was arranged by Anna Swanwick (MS Eng. lett. e. 32 fol. 53r BOD). Swanwick (1813–99) was highly regarded as the translator of Goethe's *Faust* (1850, 1878) and Aeschylus's *Oresteia* (1865), as well as for her soirees and her large coterie of notable friends (*Oxford DNB*). A champion of women's education, the elderly Swanwick may have viewed KB and EC as the products of all she had worked to achieve. EC described her as "very shrunk and wrinkled; but she has the graciousness of culture, and the beauty of sympathy. Her blue eyes are spontaneous and her cheeks flush with interest" (MS Eng. lett. e. 143 fol. 6r/v BOD). Browning became a supportive and enthusiastic mentor, correspondent, and friend until his death in 1889. See *W&D,* 1–43. Emma Cooper's writing '"as Simeon" refers to Luke 2:26.

4. *FT/WR/LL* was published in June 1885.

5. Blackheath, the home of Canon David Reith and his young family, would have been a difficult place to maintain one's artistic dignity. See letter 7. The Scott referred to later in this letter is Jane Scott. See letter 9.

6. This is one of the earliest recorded usages of Michael as a nickname, and KB uses it to refer to both herself and EC; the Flight into Egypt is William Holman Hunt's *The Triumph of the Innocents,* exhibited at the Fine Arts Society in Aug. 1885. KB probably read Quilter's review of the exhibition in *Contemporary Review,* as it appears mere pages from W. P. Ker's review of their own new volume of plays (Quilter, "Art," 292–93). She may have known Ruskin's 1883 prediction that it would be "the greatest religious painting of our time" (Bennett, *Artists of the PreRaph. Circle,* 91); the British Museum holds a statue of the goddess Demeter, ca. 330 BC, sitting on a throne (Francis, *Treasures of BM,* 142); "The Old" and "the old Gentleman" are nicknames for Browning.

7. An unpublished lyric also found in the black workbook (MS Eng. poet. f. 19 fol. 29r/v BOD). As the two versions are very similar, it may be that only one was sent, and an earlier draft included later.

8. Matt. 18:19–20.

9. Matt. 20:22.

10. The names that appear beside certain lines are characters: King Robert is the weak father of *FT;* Lucretia is the militant victim in *BU;* Sextus Tarquinius is her rapist.

11. This date is incorrect, as 16 Apr. 1885 was a Thurs. The poem may have been composed on Sun., 19 Apr. 1885.

90. Edith Cooper, Letter to Katharine Bradley

[Stoke Green] | [Apr. 1885][1]

Dearest and Best,

Oh, it is finished, the last proof sent, and the vastest experience of my poetic life over. It is written in blood on the tablets of my heart and long as I am a noumenon[2]—thro' the deathless years, I shall bear its marks. And here comes *William,* with his burly life, directly after that piteous end—to cary on the torch of doom even as it is in Experience.

The Greek motto[3] must be *in large type*—it is the kernel of the whole matter.

So you are forming another *Drop* for your Pussy. It will Eagerly break open its letter tomorrow to find "its pearl of morning dew."[4]

Why, the *Father's Tragedy* has made me forget to tell you that the Pussy has a 1st *Class* mouse in its paws—and Daves was not mousing at all. So it has Moral Philosophy all to itself, and Daves has his Logic. But what is the outcome of a human brain to the completed work of the holy Spirit!!

We want the headings for the petitions to Hospitals again.[5] Send without fail. Also write to Paps—*as you love us*—He is dangerous.

These mundane thoughts have slipped in and must be recorded before I forget.

About the books—we cannot send till Saturday—Then I will make up a parcel. Arnold's *Rome,* Webster, George Herbert and anything else you or Mary may desire.[6] *Use the opportunity.* I put down your name for *Diana of the Crossways* on the list of books to be brought before the committee this afternoon.[7] If it is added to the library you will have it at once—but I fear for so short a time we shall hardly know [*page ends*]

MS Eng. lett. c. 419 fols. 52r–53v BOD

1. Dated from the preparation of *FT/WR/LL.*

2. EC is a noumenon because she exists beyond other's ability to experience her, an interpretation of the human condition that suggests Descartes's "I think therefore I am." See letter 74 n. 8. This leads into the news of her academic success, and the removal from the field of her rival, Davis/es. See letters 76 and 78.

3. A quotation from Aeschylus's *Eumenides* prefaces *WR:* "Proton men euxei teide presbeuo theon / ten protomantin Gaian" (1–2) ["First among the Gods in this prayer I honour / the first prophet, Earth." See Aeschylus, *Eumenides,* 9].

4. Robert Herrick, "To Daffadils," 15–20 (Herrick, *Poetical Works,* 125; Palgrave, *Golden Treasury,* 141).

5. EC likely refers to the petition of letter 85.

6. Thomas Arnold's *History of Rome* (1845) and John Webster's *Appius and Virginia* (1654) are research for *BU;* George Herbert's poetry was recommended to KB by John Ruskin in 1878, presumably as a means of improving her own verse (*W&D,* 160); Mary may be Mary Louisa Hall. See postcard 24 n. 1.

7. George Meredith's *Diana of the Crossways* was published in Feb. 1885. It would have been a popular choice for the library committee to consider for the new Redland Library, which opened on 4 Jun. 1885. See Meller, *Leisure & Changing City,* 103–5. KB and EC established a friendly relationship with Meredith in the 1890s but had become estranged by 1899 (*W&D,* 66–110).

91. Katharine Bradley, Letter to Edith Cooper

Sidmouth | Apr. 1885

Love's Sour Leisure.[1]

"O absence what a torment wouldst thou prove
Were it not thy sour leisure gave sweet leave
To entertain the time with thoughts of love."
Shak. Sonnets.[2]

As a poem in my mind
Thy sweet lineaments are shrined.
From the memory, alas!
Sweetest, sweetest verse will pass,
And the fragments I must piece
Lest the fair tradition cease.
There is balmy air I trow
On the uplands of thy brow,
But the temples' veined mound
Is the Muses' sacred ground.
While the tresses pale are groves
That the laurelled god-head loves.[3]
There's a something in the cheek
Like a dimple still to seek
As my poet timidly

Love's incarnate kiss would flee.
But the mouth! That land to own
Long did Aphrodite moan,
Ere the virgin goddess grave
From the temptress of the wave
That most noble clime did win,
*Who, retreating to the chin
Took her boy's bow for a line
The sweet bound'ry to define,
And about the beauteous bays
Still in orbèd queenship plays.
I have all the charactry
Of thy features, and lack thee!
And by couplets to confess
What I wholly would possess
Doth but whet the appetite
Of my too long fasting sight.—
Vainly if my eyes entreat
Tears will be their daily meat.

Michael.) Sidmouth. April. 1885

*I am very, very proud of this. No other lover of the P's will ever mythologize on its chin so prettily.
Or the title may be this
His Lady's Face.
Michael chronicles in absence the lineaments of his lady's face

XXXX
Post without delay little Herbert.[4]
I cannot work without Him.
You may omit these 2 lines if you like. Give me once for all the pronounciations of Aganippe.[5] Be sure it is not Agānippe.?

Letter to the P.

No my Sweet: nothing rash. Nothing must go to Aganippe, till it has rested twelve months in your own little book. Some of the songs may only be a drop of blood from my heart—not a drop of heavenly crystal from the Muses' Spring.

I have found a beautiful motto for the little bosom-book, wh. I hope to be allowed to write in it—

> "Look, what is best, that best I wish in thee
> *This wish I have;* THEN TEN TIMES HAPPY ME."

It is perfect: it is only the great dramatists that can love. The lyrists have their "trotting burnies;"[6]—but the dramatist opens the great sluices of his nature and the land is overwhelmned. Dimly I feel it was because God "so loved the world"[7]—with such terrible dramatic clench and pain—that, individualizing Himself in Christ, His Voice could grow lyrical and low, with tones that Mary could listen to untrembling, and Peter passionately obey. The gospels indeed are the precious lyrics of God; but His dramas He is writing in the volumes of many worlds. "Search the Scriptures," P. for those lyric notes:—they are moments of the Universal; symphonies are suppressed in their simple melodies.

It is too wonderful.

K.

Calvary[8]

God when He loved the world loved *so,*
How could He show
All His great continent of Heart
And Love's content?
A man of sorrows through our midst He went;
And all His Godhead's teeming symphony
Suppressed at Calvary
To one sole part.

Good Friday. April. Sidmouth 1885.

Christ Risen

Thou, Lord, dost see
O'er Calvary
The sun full shining on the humble mound
Where thou didst suffer when
Thy Father's Will
Thou didst fulfil,

Thy passover and baptism; and then
Thou lookest round
To see thy travail among men.
Lord, art thou Satisfied? —
Or crucified
Again?

Apple-blossom

Our God in fair utilitie
To mark delight
Bestoweth
*This grace upon the apple-tree,
There is no other bud that bloweth
So rosy white

Sunday, April 19th. Sidmouth.
*such favour on the apple-tree[9]

MS Eng. lett. c. 418 fols. 110r–112v, 103r–105r BOD

1. Published in the *Academy,* 6 Nov. 1886 (30:309). It was included in *UTB* (72–74), but omitted from the revised edition.

2. Shakespeare, sonnet 39, 9–11.

3. Probably Apollo, given EC's affection for this particular god, and his association with the laurel (Smith, *G&R Biography and Mythology,* 1:230). However, KB may be referring to Artemis, Apollo's sister and female counterpart, who was also associated with the laurel (1:375) and, as the Roman Diana, was to be found in groves (1:1000).

4. A reminder of the request of letter 90.

5. For EC's bosom-book, see letter 73 n. 3. The motto quoted below is from Shakespeare's sonnet 37, 13–14.

6. Probably Robert Burns, "Bessy and Her Spinning-Wheel," 9–10 (Burns, 2:629).

7. John 3:16. KB is characterizing God as a dramatist in his creation of the life of Jesus.

8. Unpublished lyrics. Drafts also appear in MS Eng. poet. d. 56 fol. 38r BOD ("Calvary"), MS Eng. poet. e. 61, and MS Eng. poet. d. 56 fol. 38v BOD. ("Christ Risen").

9. Endnote added in pencil in EC's hand.

92. Edith Cooper, Letter to Katharine Bradley

[Stoke Green] | [Apr. 1885][1]

No, my Deare, I will *never* dedicate anything I have written to mortal man—only on the holiest shrine of my heart, to God who gave it.[2] Never, never, speak of such a thing. (Like an honourable Michael it will let me see any letters it writes?)

Ah, you have surpassed Michael himself in *Love's Sour Leisure.* It feels as if it must veil its mild astonished face—as if it could only thank you with hidden brow. (Oh, dearest Love, we cannot meet at Weston—it would kill new inspiration, *Try Clevedon*) and Oh, sweet Michael, I am inspired! Last night I shut myself up with Heaven and did nothing, for Heaven wrote out the scenes wh: are dedicated to its Moral Law. I send you the play as it was given to me last night.[3] The workman being divine, you will behold it is *very good*—Action and Passion concentrated and strong, with opportunities that demand our God to help us. (How can I go to *Loyalty*? But I *will.*) And here comes grand old Beowulf.[4] I *do* like the proof and greet it. It is such a change from the *Father's Trajedy*—sweeps in like a great blast. How blessed we have been in subjects!! It is after dinner—I have had a morning with Mother and Proofs and am afraid of head-ache if I write more. I have altered the dream-passage[5]—*well* (I think). *You* shall see the revise and settle its fate. Be blessed and beloved as I love thee.

Thy own Poet and Pussy.

Letters from the family tomorrow. Loves.

MS Eng. lett. c. 419 fol. 64^r BOD

1. Dated from previous letter.
2. The letter that this one responds to remains untraced.
3. See synopsis below.
4. KB's description of the proof of the *WR* as a "grand old Beowulf" indicates the significance to the play of this character.
5. *FT* 5.1.36–50 (100). For EC's anxiety regarding this passage, see letters 79 and 81.

Edith Cooper's synopsis of *Brutus Ultor*, [Apr. 1885]. (MS Eng. lett. c. 419, fol. 64v, Bodleian Library, University of Oxford)

Brutus Ultor "Vis et Tarquinios reges, animamque superbam Ultoris Bruti, fascesque videre receptos?"*			*Act I* The *Beauty* of the Moral Law *Act II* The *Retribution* of the Moral Law *Act III* The *Conquest* of the Moral Law *Act IV* The *Comfort* of the Moral Law *Act V* Rome—the *City of Law* proclaimed victorious by Heaven.	
Act I *Scene I.* Banqueting Hall. Sextus, Aruns, Collatinus and Brutus (the butt of the Company). They start to test their wives.	*Act II* *Scene I* Her Chamber at dawn. She sends the letter. Collatinus, Brutus Lucretius and Publius arrive. Her death. Brutus lifts the dagger and becomes his noble self.	*Act III* Scene I The Senate. Brutius, Collatinus, Lucretius, and Publius (with senators) receive the King's messengers and vote that the royal property be given to its owner.	*Act IV* *Scene I* The Judgement. *Scene II* The return home. Brutus and Publia together *The Comfort of the Moral Law.*	*Act V* *Scene I.* The Senate— Collatinus forced to give up the consulship. Poor old Lucretius elected. News brought that the Tarquins under Aruns are approaching with a great army of Etruscans. Call to arms.
Scene II. Lucretia spinning with her maids. Enter Sextus, Aruns and Collatinus. They describe their visits to the feasting wives of the Tarquins and give Collatinus the prize. Sextus is moved with passion. The Tarquins go back and husband and wife are together (a beautiful interchange of their honourable love). They part.	*Scene II.* The Forum. Brutus speaks to the people over her body. The Tarquins are banished. Brutus and Collatinus made consuls.	*Scene II* The house of the Aquilii (Brothers to Publia) The Aquilii and Titus and Tiberius meet a royal agent. They swear with dark and mystic rites to give the city to the King. Vindex behind a chest hears all—is divided between love for the youths and Brutus. In his consternation goes to Publius. →	*Scene III* The door of the Senate. Publius and Vindex wait for Brutus and break to him the conspirasy. He sends the lictors to arrest the Conspirators. The fearful first shock.	*Scene II* The battle-field. Brutus' tent. Publia has died of grief and Brutus feels that his end is already chronicled by Fate. Publius (cheery Publius) is with him. The enemy advance.
Scene III. Sextus determines to seek Lucretia.	*Scene III* Publia, Titus and Tiberius tell to each other how the Tarquins are fled. The young men mourn their companions. Brutus enters as consul—tells of the oracle and how it is fulfilled—Is called to receive messengers from the King in the Senate. A soldier brings news of Sextus' death at Gabii and describes it. *Retribution of the Moral Law.*	*Scene IV* Titus and Tiberius. To them enters Publia—The Lictors are coming. The youths are arrested before their Mother. Enter Brutus. Publia pleads for her sons and brothers. Brutus puts off her entreaties. She leaves him. His great struggle—*the Conquest of the Moral Law.*		*Scene III* The Battle. The death of Brutus. The voice calling out of the wood. *The End.*
Scene IV Lucretia's house. Sextus comes. Her clear thought contrasted with his hidden guile and passion.				
Scene V His soliloq[u]y at her chamber door.				

* "Do you wish to see now the Tarquin kings, the proud spirit of avenging Brutus and the rods of office he will retrieve?"

93. Katharine Bradley, Letter to Edith Cooper

Sidmouth | Apr. 1885

My Pretty,

A big letter was posted at East Budleigh on Saturday—a post-card on Saturday even—to the Father, a fat letter to him again Yesterday,—and a stupendous proof-bund[le] and poem to you.

All of these I trust you have now had. I have not a proof left,—*nothing.* I have to feed from *[from header fol. 106ʳ]* my own breast not my young but myself. Got a small worm of a devil well crushed inside me. Am going to send him home to hell much dissatisfied with his day's trip.

Ever A.W.F[.]

To the P.

The Blisse of Immortalitie.[1]

In Immortalitie where lies the bliss?
From death in parting we would never part,
Nor from our tears;
Methinks we do esteem his age too much
'Tis his eternal youthfulness endears.
Love, shall we triumph that our lips will touch
When there are no more yeares,
Or rather that we press Soul's heart to heart
*Whene'er we Kiss?

Easter Day. April 5th. 1885. Sidmouth

*What time we kiss

MS Eng. lett. c. 418 fol. 106r/v BOD

1. Unpublished lyric. See for comparison "An Invocation" (letter 89) and EC's Easter greeting (letter 81).

94. Katharine Bradley, Letter to Edith Cooper

[Sidmouth] | [May 1885][1]

Oh Puss, My Precious P!—

It was pained . . [.] it must be bruised . . [.] when the King crushes one of its velvet paws. But it did not mew; it only looked up at him with its large blue eyes full of tears. And that, you know, the King cannot bear.

But now its little paw is well, and he may stretch it out and even scratch with his delicate little tentacle claw any pretty revenge. We heard the wood-pigeon yesterday and I Knew it was the note Of my love to the P. It is an internal song—il y a quelque chose de sacré et de l'intim dans ce chant solitaire (ce désir que se plaint d'un note/ton, élegiaque—presque superstitieux.)[2] It tells nothing of the sun or the air—it is solitary as the song of the Highland Reaper[3]—with the forboding solitude of the heart—when the want and passion wanders desolate in the Voice that ought to have its homestead on the lips. The old Fowl has very little to say from his heart—except Co-coo°° for his mate.

You should have seen him flushing on his way to the moor.[4]

A moor is a little prayer-mat stretched for a poet's devotion.

[from header fol. 93ʳ] If no proofs come to-morrow write at once *indignantly* to the manager. Remind him he has only another month till it is out.[5] *Be cheerful: do nothing:* prepare for next week.

Your own

A.W.F[.]

MS Eng. lett. c. 418 fol. 93ʳ/ᵛ BOD

1. Dated from the publication of *FT/WR/LL* in Jun. 1885.

2. "There is something of the sacred and the intimate in this lonely song. (This desire that laments on a note, elegiac—almost superstitious)" (Fr). The irregularity of the sentence structure suggests KB is altering the original quotation, if there is one. There is a mixture of prepositions ("du sacré et de l'intime" or "de sacré et d'intime" would be usual); "se plaindre de" is to lament about something, and "note" is treated as masculine.

3. "The Solitary Reaper," 1–2 (Wordsworth, 3:77).

4. Probably Dartmoor.

5. George Bell and Sons published Michael Field's second volume of plays in June 1885.

95. Katharine Bradley, Letter to Edith Cooper

[Sidmouth] | [Jun. 1885][1]

Ah P. No more drops—no more little poems—it is starting for the cave of the Eumenides.[2] O think on what errand;—to travel to *the white Nativity of womanhood* to see and record all that passes in the lone godhead of her spirit, where never man has wandered.—The innermost modesties where love has never been told that it is naked—and in its purity looks unblushing up to God.

If indeed we can give to our Country women a Lucretia[3] that shall reveal to them *the inmost pricelessness of their own natures,*—not hold up to them merely the stainless wife—but the defilelessness of Very womanhood.... that it cannot have spot or wrinkle or any such thing and that its purity Can only be divined and approached by passion; that the cold Vestal is alien from it; that it is a revelation granted *in its fulness only to deep spousal* love.—Then, while our sisters are fighting behind the barricades for their rights, *we* shall win men back to their natural, their instinctive worship of "das ewig Weibliche,"[4] and the blundering Brutuses of this world be taught their reverence for the moral law where God would have them learn it,—*traced trembling and indelible on the tablets of a woman's heart.*

I am going first to write for my interleaved Shakespeare (Bless the Muds:[5] she never gave me anything like what that is to become) some thoughts on Shakespeare's *Lucrece.* I am struck by the divineness and purity of it, when one remembers it is the work of a young man—but, and that enlightens—of the young Creator of Desdemona—of Imogen's perfect wifehood.[6]

Is it not a stroke of consummate art to set the trembling girl astare *at* Hecuba's hoary griefs?[7]—and all the story of her heavenly shame in the blush wh. rises to her cheek as she gives her husband's letter to the homely, humbly-courtesying groom is exquisitely told.[8]

Then the meeting!

"*Both stood like old acquaintance in a trance*
Met far from home wondering each other's chance."[9]

It will be bold, but I shall ask for him to come back and write those scenes for us—*that soliloquy before Hecuba's picture;* and the lament "*when this pale swan in her watery nest* Begins the *sad dirge of her certain ending.*"[10] O P.P. that there should be such lives and our hearts not bleeding over them.

Never for an instant is Shakespeare Tarquin. He is ever with her who "still pure Doth in her poisoned closet yet endure."[11] Heaven bless him. Tears come to my eyes as I write of him entering into the nameless woe of a dishonoured woman, while all the passion of "primy youth"[12] was in his blood.

But I have just warned you away from Brutus. Don't look at Lucrece, and forget this immediately. I have just been tying up its "proofy" fragments,[13] and binding them with a strip of my turkey-red (a good colour: a *crimson* that you love) a cord of my heart's hue;—and all is well and orderly in my drawer as if the little lavender paws had wandered there.

You decide wisely and rightly to stay at home—the moral law requires it. I rejoice that the blessed Mother reads Faust with you. It must be a mouthful at a time.

—Been my first long walk to the station to-day to ask to ask for my book parcel. Not yet come. Now must *[from header fol. 94ʳ]* rest. Heaven cherish thee.

[bird symbol]

MS Eng. lett. c. 418 fols. 94ʳ–97ᵛ BOD

1. The anticipation of a book parcel containing copies of *FT/WR/LL* suggests Jun. 1885.

2. The cave of the Furies in Aeschylus's *Eumenides.*

3. *BU,* or Brutus the Revenger, is based on the story of Lucretia, whose rape by Sextus Tarquinius led to the establishment of the Republic. While the original tale comes from Livy (*Ab Urbe Condita,* 3:1.57–60), *BU*'s afterword states that *BU* is adapted directly from Shakespeare's *Rape of Lucrece* (1594) and articulates Michael Field's goal "to penetrate the mysteries of womanhood that lie, unforbidden, in its taintless depths, and, by contrast of these happy secrets with the experience vaunted by the materialist and the voluptuary to unfold 'To creatures stern sad tunes, to change their kind.'"

4. For Goethe's Woman Eternal (das ewig Weibliche), see letter 9.

5. Emma Harris Cooper.

6. In a family list of likes and dislikes, KB identified Imogen from *Cym.* as one of her favorite fictional heroines (MS Eng. misc. c. 303 fol. 4ʳ BOD).

7. *Luc.* 1443–49.

8. *Luc.* 1338–44.

9. *Luc.* 1595–96.

10. *Luc.* 1611–12.

11. *Luc.* 1658–59.

12. *Ham.* 1.3.8.

13. "Its" refers to the Persian Puss (EC) rather than to *BU.* KB is tidying away the proofs of *FT/WR/LL.*

96. Edith Cooper, Letter to Katharine Bradley

Stoke Green | [Aug. 1885][1]

Stoke Green.

Well, dear Deare, here it is! I am pleased with it in some ways, tho' it is some what slight. It has at last struck the true Keynote of the *Father's Tragedy* and has recognised the power of the *later* style.[2] It treats us with that respect wh: is the ernest of fame and also recognises true growth in our work. And won't we work on when we are together again!

Poor Cousin Minnie[3] is gone, full of love to us and saying she feels as if she were leaving home. I am very glad she has been to stay with us. Happy homes ought to offer a refuge to those who are lonely-spirited, disappointed and weary. Still, as the darling says, it will be delicious to lay our heads on each other's bosoms and be undisturbed.

Poor loves! You certainly are in the dismals. I think you must go, if well enough, straight to the Broads[4] and then on your way home take a night at Ely and see Peterborough. Lincoln you must, I fear, give up.

Tell darling Kittie I must not hear of that fearful disease of the will—hopelessness. I shall think she is a hedonist if she grows despairing at the absence of Pleasure.

At last I have seen the wonderful Norman Chapter house, and the lovely bit of Early English work in our Cathedral.[5] The Norman work is richer than any I have seen.

There is a lid of a stone coffin wh: is Saxon.[6] It represents a little naked soul held up out of the whelming power of Satan by the bottom of the cross wh: Christ holds. The divine foot is on the glaring head of the demon. Like Michael Field's book it is "less beautiful than powerful."

No, my sweet poet, don't you alter "Cut to the Brains" for any Muddie.[7] It is all right and written finally out. I rejoice to think the lovely poems are made of non-effect by recovery. The life's history will yet be written on what we thought wd. be the blank pages of death.

The dear old lady is growing quite a refined cook. She has accomplished *Fowl-Soufflé,* as Mrs Baker calls the dish:—an old fowl boned, chopped and laid with ham;—then turned out and served. She is a human soul, with a warm heart to hold it.

Poor Pussie fell down stairs yesterday with "a rumpus" (as Sarah[8] said) of rattling silver spoons and forks. A large black bruise is the only consequence. Its "eating cares"[9] of neuralgia are much better. Fondly kiss my kittie and praise her for getting better. She shall have the next long letter. The darling is very well and Paps *much* better.

A kiss (such as I give my golden-hair'd Appollo.[10])

Thy P. and Spouse.

MS Eng. lett. c. 419 fols. 100[r]–103[v] BOD

1. Dated from KB's trip to Hornsea in late Aug. 1885.

2. The *Athenaeum*'s review of *FT/WR/LL* (22 Aug. 1885) found *FT* and *WR* generally superior to *Call.*, having "a wider study of character and a more intense power of utterance" (79 [1885]: 251–52). Later, EC paraphrases this review: "The book is more powerful than beautiful."

3. Probably a Holinsworth cousin.

4. The Broads is a flat marshland area in Norfolk.

5. Between 1868 and 1888, Bristol Cathedral underwent considerable structural work to

restore the original medieval design and build two west towers (Pevsner and Metcalf, *Cathedrals of England,* 35–37), so this was probably EC's first opportunity to see inside the Cathedral.

6. "The Harrowing of Hell": a piece of Saxon stonework depicting Christ descending into Hell that was discovered after a fire in 1831 (Pevsner and Metcalf, *Cathedrals of England,* 35).

7. Unknown poem, titled from *Lr.* 4.6.197, apparently inspired by a recent illness. EC's subsequent image of the "refined cook" boning a Fowl (KB's nickname) suggests Emma's (Muds) response was a bad-tempered one. For Hannah Baker, see letter 18 n. 11.

8. Probably a servant.

9. *L'Allegro,* 135–36 (Milton, 1.1:39; also Palgrave, *Golden Treasury,* 150).

10. The Apollo Belvedere. See letter 18.

97. Katharine Bradley, Letter to Edith Cooper

[Hornsea | Sun., [23 Aug. 1885][1]

Sunday morn. in bed.

Well, Pussie, dear Elizabethan *man* I congratulate you; but what I am chiefly pleased to learn is that *I* am more vigorous than Pussie!!![2]—the male part of Michael as beseemeth our relations. This morning I am Certainly better. A grand yachting expedition is planned for Tuesday, so I am going to try—if matters Continue to improve—to arise and travel to-morrow that the dear little hedonist may follow its favourite pursuit. I shall probably rest; but there will be gleams of beauty at Runham to cheer me. I shall miss the close warm love of the Hornsea Cousins: Cousin F. has wholly won me by her tenderness, and *all* the children down to the little scapegraces are willing to wait hand and foot on the Queen, while the Balliol is entirely mine—and thinks "what happiness" it would be to read the Odyssey with C.K.[3] I put 2 pounds into an envelope, with the words, "In memory of some happy hours with Sophocles,"[4] and gave it to his mother to give him.

For Max's brooch I have written this.

On presenting Marguerite with a medallion—of Fame or Victory. . . .

"Fame for her beauty? How outstrip its ray?
What herald runs so fleet?
And Victory? Nay, Love shall win the day,
    And her dear heart defeat."

And to outstrip its ray
Were vain, light's wings are fleet;

It is a very cold day, Pussie, and I am sleepy, probably because of the Athenaeum, and the great things I must strive to do. If we go[,] the Brunel jelly —wh. I have found so supporting, will be a wonderful help to me. We ought to get into Great Yarmouth at 3.30.

Pussie, I do not think the poet should be identified with the emotion expressed;—that is not dramatic; it is one of the old gentleman's defects. But no more "an it please you" in the new volume.[6] Pure *Victorean* English—archaic in thought perhaps because our fore-fathers thought better than we, but in expression *[from header fol. 123r] never.* And we will[—]Heaven's splendour on us—go on singing "strange, sad tunes for men to change their kinds."[7]

thine.

Mick

MS Eng. lett. c. 418 fols. 123r–124v BOD

1. Dated from the *Athenaeum*'s review of *FT/WR/LL,* 22 Aug. 1885.

2. The *Athenaeum* described *FT*'s dramatic expression (EC's contribution) as rising to "almost the strength of Elizabethan men" and the composition (KB) as "powerful and essentially virile" (79 [1885]: 251).

3. The Hornsea cousins are Fanny Brooks and her eleven children (see letter 2 n. 3), including eldest son Francis, or the Balliol (see letter 30 n. 4) whose exclamation "what happiness" is a quotation from William Wordsworth's *Prelude* (2.286) (*Fourteen-Book Prelude,* 55). C.K. is Cousin Katharine. Later, Max and Marguerite are probably nicknames for Margaret Brooks, who would have been twenty years old. KB's subsequent rough verse was not developed further.

4. Sturgeon notes that KB and Francis enjoyed acting and reciting together (16).

5. KB fell ill at Hornsea, developing lumps on her arms. See KB, letter to Fanny Brooks, MS Eng. lett. d. 407 fol. 189r. Brunel, or *Prunella vulgaris,* was believed to be a cure for quinsy (*OED;* Chittenden, *Dict. of Gardening*).

6. This phrase does not appear in any of Michael Field's published plays. KB may be referring to *WR,* which has a large cast of peasant characters. The new volume is *BU.*

7. *Luc.* 1147 is also quoted in the afterword to *BU.*

98. Katharine Bradley, Postcard to Edith Cooper

[The Broads | Wed., [PM 26 Aug. 1885]

Wednesday morn.

Dearest P. The hampers are just being packed for a grand expedition to the Hickling Broad.[1] Puss, Cousin D[avid].—Alf.—Archie, and the dual—we two.[2] We may be away all night—probably shall—so I *beseech* you not to fret, if the letters are a little irregular. We shall only put up at queer little villages, where they send out letters as it occurs to them. Of course to-day is yachting. Yesterday we had our first *boating* on the Broads, after a drive of 5 miles. Would that all my dear ones had been there! To see only the narrow rim of earth between wide sky and water, to track the long soft margin of the reed-bed, to row into creeks for water-lilies, or best of all to be moored, and watch the very heave of silence's breast as she sleeps,[3] . . . . all this is for the balming of the spirit—"till every nerve has soothing." Both *wonderfully well.* Thank the precious father for his *dear letter.* Heaven shield my darling, for whom I *yearn* . . . oh more and more . . . till it is perilous.

Sim.

MS Eng. lett. c. 418 fol. 113r BOD

1. Hickling Broad is noted for its peacefulness and wild fowl (Day, *Norwich & the Broads,* 107–9).

2. Amy Katharine Cooper; Canon David Reith; Alfred and Archie Holinsworth, cousins with whom KB spent much of her childhood (Bridge, MS Eng. misc. d. 983 fol. 57r BOD); KB and her cousin Francis Brooks (the dual).

3. Compare with the preface to *Canute:* "As soon as I sailed among the Broads I discovered this shadowless, unguarded country had a secrecy and seclusion of its own. Moored close to the shrouding boundary of the reed-bed, among the water-lilies and the soft ripples, one seemed to catch the very heave of the breast of silence" (3). The subsequent quotation is from "The Guardian-Angel. A Picture at Fano" (27; Browning, 6:102).

99. Katharine Bradley, Letter to Edith Cooper

[Runham Vicarage | Fri., [28 Aug. 1885][1]

Friday morning

Sweet Wife, the hardships of early married life are beginning:[2] let us bear them together bravely, and grow all the dearer to each other for the derision of the world. There has nothing happened to us; but what is Common to all poets; let us rejoice to share their bitter herbs of adversity. Ah P. there is nothing at these times like psalms. David and his fellow-singers had the Eternal with them at all times—not only sin times—as is too much the case with Christians. There is no comfort like a past spent with the Eternal. "Remember the word unto thy servant upon which thou hast caused me to hope."[3] "Thou hast established the earth and it abideth. They continue this day according to thine ordinances . . [.]

for all are thy servants." cxix.[4] The Condition of permanence for dramatist and starry heaven is obedience to law. In subjection to Divine Law our work has been wrought, and it will abide. The time when I received the Pall-Mall could scarcely have been more inopportune. After a long day's yachting, and no food (save a cup of tea and tartine at Acle Bridge[5]) since two, we reached Runham at nearly eight;—the Sim more than half asleep. Amy had discretion to s[t]ay upstairs; and we have Kept the review a profound secret. I have torn it up to small fragments this morning that if Nellie[6] asks "Have we received any more reviews"—I may say "Yes there was one in the Pall-Mall for wh. I had no respect, and I destroyed it." I shall not mention it to the Brookses or anyone. Now with reference to it, dearie, I want to say some grave words to you.[7] Do not desert Shakespeare and the Elizabethans. Those with the sobering influence of the great Greek dramatists, whom you ought to resolve at once to study, are the only Masters for us. Every dramatic writer must be full of his Shakespeare, as every religious writer Must be full of his Bible. We Must give up the tricks, the externalities, the archaisms,—to copy these is imitation, but we must seek to study and touch life as he—Shakespeare studied and touched it, and our speech Must always be utterly different from ordinary speech; because ordinary speech is not transfigured by emotion, and the ordinary speech of an Age like ours is base with the exceeding Vulgarity of Materialism. God shall give our thought a body as it pleaseth him.

2nd Make no harsh resolve to abstain from Metaphor. Remember all our finest passages—the Athenaeum's—are in metaphor. "All the long cruel blade is still to cut." My *ruined* ears. *Is there no death in you.* etc. etc. The Murderers' speech was absolutely right, and my Harold's speech, *absolutely:* the unimmortal might have been altered, and a few of the expressions in *The Father's Tragedy.* But do not begin correcting or altering, and work freely. In *Loyalty* I was determined to avoid the cumbrousness of *Bellerophon* and make way with the action, and the Consequence was—an imperfect, not fully developed work.[8] What really saddened me was that article on Matthew Arnold in the Athenaeum.[9] "A classic to the finger tips"—"distinction and dignity of manner" but then you see P. he was not a dramatist: we have determined by Heaven's grace to give the English people plays—full of poetry and religion, and humour, and thought. They will not like this . . [.] they will Kick against the pricks,[10] but ultimately they will thankfully accept us. Ah P. I had a dream that I was going with you to receive a music-lesson from the old gentleman.[11] I very naturally objected that

You should remain to listen to me; but you w^{d}. When we arrived somehow the talk was all on the review, and *he* said he would never take in the Pall-Mall again! And also something about looking at the proofs in future.

I think by the way, we must get some one to do that. Or will the loving Mud undertake our grammar? What I am a little dreading is a sharp nasty notice in *The Times,*[12] now Parliament has done sitting. *The Times* is sent on here; but I will promise to be quite calm.

And now P. oh let me tell thee that no yachting, or beauty or *joy* in heaven or earth, can hinder me from mourning long and bitterly over our separation; It will take so long to knit us up into one piece again. And you are so far on the horizon,—you might be a tower, or a stump, or anything. Far, far away is the P. and can write no little word to its love. My heart aches for it. I will try to learn to-day when we are expected to leave. It will be nice to have some little time at home before the new journey; but if yachting expeditions are planned, I must wait. The Kind Alf leaves to-morrow—I hope he will someday Visit us. The father would love him, He will repeat the traditions of the good uncle. One great embrace.

Thine own for ever.

Sim.

MS Eng. lett. c. 418 fols. 117^{r}–121^{v} BOD

1. Dated to the Friday after Archer's review of *FT/WR/LL,* 27 Aug. 1885.

2. KB refers to William Archer's devastating review of *FT/WR/LL* in the *Pall Mall Gazette* (reprinted in the *Pall Mall Budget*). Archer took issue with the form; with the decasyllabic meter; with the metaphors and language; and concluded with the mocking declaration that Field would call a spade a "not unhorticultural implement" (Archer, "Pre-Shakespearean Playwright," 28).

3. Ps. 119:49–50.

4. Ps. 119:90–92.

5. The Bridge at Acle is an inn (Day, *Norwich & the Broads,* 108).

6. For Nellie Reith, see letter 2 n. 5; for the Brookses, see letter 2 n. 3.

7. KB urges EC to ignore Archer's criticism of their "imitations" of Shakespearean style (28), and his dislike of "affected archaisms" in *WR* (28), and reminds her that the *Athenaeum*'s reviewer (79 [1885]: 251–52) particularly commended the nobility and originality of metaphors such as "All the long cruel blade has yet to cut" (*FT* 4.6.16; *FT/WR/LL,* 97); and "Have you no death in you? Oh say your prayers; / I will keep mourning in my ruined ears" (*WR* 2.1.22–23; *FT/WR/LL,* 154). KB also reasserts the value of the Murderer's speech (3.3.), which Archer singled out as "verbose" and "circumlocutory" (28); and Harold's speech (*WR* 1.1.163–79; *FT/WR/LL,* 133–34).

8. KB echoes Robert Browning's criticism of *LL* as "not worked out enough." See EC, letter to Robert Browning, 19 Jul. 1885, Add. MS 46866 fol. 33^{r} BL. Similarly W. P. Ker, writing in

the *Contemporary Review,* found the plot of *LL* convoluted, and the characters ill-defined (Ker, review, 293).

9. Archer's review was mere pages from a laudatory review of Matthew Arnold that praised the poet as one who "adores his Shakespeare, but [who] will none of his Shakespeare's fashions." See Review of *Poems,* 229.

10. Acts 9:5 and 26:14.

11. Robert Browning.

12. No review appeared in the *Times.*

100. Katharine Bradley, Letter to Edith Cooper

Runham Vicarage | Sat., 5 Sept. [1885][1]

Runham Vicarage. Saturday, Sept 5th.
My Wife,

They are all—O priceless boon—*all* gone to market. The sun shines, and I have been round the garden, and passed the sunflowers in solitude. First I have been in one room, then another . . [.] never in the drawing-room. There is always a smell of the world there.

This little poem was given to me at Hornsea, on my sick-bed[2] in one moment's space—with a single glance at Alice Trusted's[3] sea-line, but I could not work it out there. Here, alas, there have been no deep intimacies with heaven. Some day we will clasp hands, take a yacht, and deep, deep into the reed-forests. Amy is going to spend her honeymoon here,—with the moon I suppose, for there seems no one else—but thou and I will come hither in iris-time, and "look into the mystery of things."[4] Here is the little poem.

"Thy Judgments are a great deep"[5]

"Thy judgments are a deep I will not try
By my poor eyesight dim:
When we define
We cut through some great truth; shall we incline,
To think the undulating world of brine
Closed by that solemn curve against the sky
Nay, for a sail is twinkling on the rim;
I track its flight, and know that there must be
Athwart that firm horizon-line
Soft trembling sea."

This cannot reach you till Monday. No post goes out to-morrow. Write by early post on Monday a post card to *The Lamb,* Ely.[6] We hope to leave here very early on Monday morn. [to] go to Norwich, see the cathedral, and then on to sleep at Ely. On Tuesday we shall either go on to London and return by the express leaving Paddington at 5, or, wh. is far more probable, come by way of Cambridge and Bedford, joining this same Paddington express at Didcote. Anyhow *there must be no attempt at meeting.* We cannot be home till nine, *or after.* Sing hymns and keep quiet and happy. We will do our best to return to our precious home and loved ones. Amy said yesterday she had not felt so well for years. I "have drugs inside me"[7]—and but little power this morn. My ways are peculiar as the heathen Chinee's, but I trust to Keep in travelling trim by taking precautionary measures. *[from header fol. 115ʳ]* Tell the dear Father I want a cotton-box, but a Kiss much worse. Love the Mother One.

Heaven re-unite us

Sim.

MS Eng. lett. c. 418 fols. 115ʳ–116ᵛ BOD

1. Dated from KB's visit to The Broads in 1885.
2. For KB's illness, see letter 97 n. 5.
3. KB seems to be composing a poem for her friend Alice Trusted. See letter 33 n. 16.
4. *Lr.* 5.3.16.
5. Unpublished lyric: the title comes from Ps. 36:6. See also MS Eng. lett. poet. d. 56 BOD.
6. The Lamb Hotel in Ely still stands across the street from the cathedral.
7. Possibly "Last Words of a Seventh-Rate Poet," 15 (Swinburne, 5:278).

101. Katharine Bradley, Letter to Edith Cooper

[Great Yarmouth] | [Sept. 1885][1]

Plain little room

Confound that Puss, if it has not followed us here![2]

My own Precious Child,

It is after nine o'clock tea, and we have retired here to set our correspondence in order, before a two days' yachting expedition to-morrow—whither the wind must direct.

I have written a—I trust and believe—very nice answer to Ward,[3] heartily thanking him for his criticism, owning the weakness of external imitation etc. etc. etc. His wise kind words will greatly help you. Note what he sees of the prologue. P. this Norfolk air makes me feel fulfilled of centuries of life. I must someday bring you to the keen air and the piercing sunshine; you will get painted inside and white-washed throughout ready for Hegel and the Greek.[4]

Ah now indeed a brave P. That resolve about the Greek sent a thrill of joy through me. It will make the winter a time of joy to take you by the hand and lead you up the steeps of that paradise. Keep fast hold of Brutus—and don't let me hear of any more mediaeval nonsense. Nellie[5] has asked me to go and stay with her a bit on this side Xmas, and I seriously hope to do the necessary reading at the British Museum. Not a pain shall be spared to make our Brutus a monumental work.

What you w$^{d.}$ have thought of me I knew not, but this morn. feeling I had done walking enough after a little shopping with Amy in Yarmouth, I paid a penny for a peaceful bench on the crowded beach, and was left there till an hour and a half afterwards, Cousin D[avid Reith] and A[my]. came for me, their business done, in the Carriage. There on the big bonnie sands were the people, and before them foam the fairest sea the bluest breeze the freshest: I smiled quite pleasantly at the people who desired to sell shrimps, pears, or small literature to me, and read David Copperfield[6] with an honest delight in the world as it was. It is impossible for an old historic town to be vulgar, and that Yarmouth beach was made for man. Long may he be happy there, his poet with him. I will bring the P. to these little mounds of people, and teach it to rejoice.

I have not done a scrap of Greek or Italian since I have been here; . . [.] simply become a great air-drinker. I can never cease to murmur after the P. and I love its bigger letters that make me feel as if it were walking towards me like a wherry.

I must end.

Thy own Spouse

Michael.

Embrace the parents.

P. I want to say some prayers as a penance for having neglected the soul of Emma Emery.[7] Certainly we shall receive our reward for that.

MS Eng. lett. d. 402. fols. 82^{r}–84^{v} BOD

1. Dated from A. W. Ward's letter of 17 Sept. 1885 (Add. MS 45852 fols. 75–77^{r-v} BL).
2. Possibly an actual cat.

3. Sir Adolphus William Ward (1837–1924) held the chair of history and literature at Owens College, Manchester, and was drama critic for the *Manchester Guardian* (*Oxford DNB*). KB is responding to a letter of 17 Sept. 1885, in which Ward expresses his interest in the development of a national literature, and suggests the subject matter for *Canute* (1887). See Adolphus Ward, letter to Michael Field, 17 Sept. 1885, Add. MS 45852 fols. 75–77[r–v] BL. A correspondence developed and Ward's assistance is recognized in the preface to *Canute* (4).

4. Already a good Latinist, EC was coaxed to learn Greek by KB and Browning. She does not seem to have been very successful (Sturgeon, 18).

5. For Nellie Reith, see letter 2 n. 5. Later in the letter, "Cousin D" is her husband, Canon David Reith.

6. *David Copperfield* (1850) by Charles Dickens is partially set in the town of Yarmouth (Dickens, *David Copperfield,* 28).

7. Untraced.

102. Katharine Bradley, Annotated Envelope

To Sim and Little One.
Blue Anchor[1]
Sept and Oct. *1885*
From *Puss*

MS Eng. lett. c. 419 fol. 95[r] BOD

1. Amy Cooper described the secluded seaside hamlet in Devon as "five houses and two inns . . . without a shop, or even a few bottles of *goodies* in a cottage window." See Amy Cooper, letter to EC, [1881], MS Eng. lett. d. 402 fol. 24[v] BOD.

103. Katharine Bradley, Annotated Envelope

Blue Anchor
Poor Pussie!—can not leave Brutus for *Edmund Ironsides*[1]
from Blue Anchor Sept. 1885.

MS Eng. lett. c. 419 fol. 72[r] BOD

1. Having recently visited The Broads, where *Canute* (1887) is set, KB was eager to act quickly on Ward's suggestion for a new play.

104. Katharine Bradley, Annotated Envelope

[PM Tues., 29 Sept. 1885]

Pussie has done the *wood-scene in Brutus* bless it.
Blue Anchor Oct. 1885

MS Eng. lett. c. 419 fol. 77[r] BOD

105. Edith Cooper, Letter to Katharine Bradley

[Blue Anchor, Washford] | [Oct. 1885][1]

My most beloved,
So it wants to hear what I have been doing in *Brutus.* The scene in which the woods and stream and air comfort him in the first lawless shock of agony when he recognises that he ought to judge his sons.[2] I thought that here where I feel so deeply the fresh persistent calm of Nature, that scene should be written. It is nearly done. Two more nights (when I am well) and it will be finished. I shall bring it to read to thee on our first evening. Cherish the thought for your spinning song,[3] no woman will ever be like Lucretia.

It is wise to go to town, tho' such a heavy thing that you will leave me almost as soon as I join myself to you. We have been wo fully married this year, save for that brief dear time of wh: my adored Apollo[4] is the pledge. Ah, dear, that was a spiritual gift, the one gt. gift to *me.* I "hug" it instead of you and or rather through it I am never parted from you in truth. It is very sore to me not to be with you this long sad time you have been ill.[5] Some how the bird at my heart sings to me that this new remedy will do its work. That comforts me.

Pussie could find no Squirrels to Gambol with this morning. Have you heard the curlew's note?—not like the sea-gull's distressing with the petulence and restlessness of the shoreward billows—but full of the majestic unfathomed mournfulness of the deep, far waters. Dearest deare, most gloriously loving, how shall I ever be a "wiftie" worthy of you? Well, *gifts* are not always perfect and yet of some help and joy—And I have given myself to you as your spouse forever. May we be soon fully re-united!

Thine P.P.

MS Eng. lett. c. 419 fols. 75[r]–76[v] BOD

1. Dated from envelope 104.

2. *BU* 4.2.84–101 (49).

3. There is no spinning song; however, Lucretia does encourage her women to spin. See *BU* 1.3.20–24 (6).

4. KB and EC seem to have engaged in some form of ceremony, probably involving the gift of a copy of the Apollo Belvedere. See letter 18.

5. For KB's illness, see letter 97 n. 5. The purpose of her visit may be to see her doctor, Sir Andrew Clark. See MS Eng. lett. d. 406 fol. 60^{v} BOD.

106. Edith Cooper, Letter to Katharine Bradley

[Blue Anchor] | [Oct. 1885][1]

Ah, it does not love its Pussie! Poor, poor Pussie, it mews piteously by the salt sea waves. And this is all the Pussie wants—to finish catching its rat before it goes after a mouse. You see for a King it may do to Execute many things, but it is manifest that if a Cat is not concentrated on its prey it will come off badly. Let me go on quietly with *Brutus* (as I must, if I am to do anything masterly) and I shall very soon have done it and be ready again to put heart and soul into the new subject.

What I said about Hegel was fun and due to the re-action of having been taken from the strain of philosophy into the far higher influence of Nature and Poetry. It is true I have clogged my genius this year with the dear, but rather dangerous, stuff of Pure Reason.[2]

Of course when I come home I shall do Hegel *with you.* Keep the Paston Letters[3] for me. I am *very* attracted by them. I'll read *Past and Present*[4] and in every way be your True Spouse—with the Saving clause that I must be left to dwell for a little with *Brutus* undisturbed, unless you will join me in the next few months in raising it to perfection. I am very grieved that you are still in bed, my poor Deare. And also I am a little jealous of Satan; wives don't like strange male friends.

My cold is gone and I have never felt a finer Cat—nearly as strong as when I was a northern Kitten.[5]

Prosper in Eadric,[6] cling to Brutus, and above all things love Your Puss and get well for it.

I have seen a bush hung with weasels—that may please you better than squirrels. I ever Kiss the Ring and the Book.[7]

Thy faithful P.

MS Eng. lett. c. 419 fols. 73r–74v BOD

1. Dated from Blue Anchor holiday, Sept.–Oct. 1885.
2. Immanuel Kant, *Critique of Pure Reason* (1881).
3. *The Paston Letters* (1787; repub. 1872 and 1875).
4. Thomas Carlyle, *Past and Present* (1843).
5. EC spent her childhood at Kenilworth near Coventry (Sturgeon, 14).
6. Edric Streona is an English Alderman in *Canute.*
7. Browning, *The Ring and the Book* (1869).

107. Katharine Bradley, Annotated Envelope

Oct. 1885

Blue Anchor
Pussie always mine.
the Boo.[1]
Oct. 1885.

MS Eng. lett. c. 419 fol. 88r BOD

1. Blue Anchor.

108. Edith Cooper, Letter to Katharine Bradley

Cleeve Bay | [Oct. 1885][1]

Cleeve Bay.
My darling,
I should not be in the least nervous. Many a time I shall go with my Deare to refresh her. But it would not be wise to come to the *Boo* now. The weather has broken up completely for the last week and Mrs. Henson[2] says October is their dreadful month for damp and cold.

The Darling has caught rheumatism in the legs from being on the damp ground;[3] the rooms are cold, and we shall all be delighted to return to home-comforts. I think the sea does more harm than good in such weather. We none of us are as we were at first.

It would be better to take drives on bright days with the money you would have spent. Paps proposes you should share a cab with Mother and so both take the air.

My own dearest, I am very grieved you have gone through such trials.[4] Your Pussie weeps in its heart. Yes, Pussie is coming to be your tear-bottle when your tears must flow, and your wine-cup when you are for joy. You shall always say what you really think and write it, even if it results in such sad, tho' beautiful, little poems as those that came to me this morning.[5] I am going to be your Mr Greatheart and fight your lions and Appolions, and take your hand up hill.[6] Also I shall take you to refreshing meadows where you can hear the shepherd boy and see the rosy apples overhead. But cold and dismal little *Boo* would not give your heart-delight nor bodily strength now winter is here. It is a blessed place only under Heaven's smile—then *it is blessed,* and my darling shall come. They say it is lovely in the spring. Now it is so bleak that even the sturdy Paps and his daughter can hardly force themselves on to the shore. We have taken huge walks in spite of weather and on Saturday had a glorious, keen autumn morning. But that has been our one treat in weather for a week. I am really anxious to get the Mother home. I shall come ready for the Philosophy of History[7] and Greek in the morning; holding *Brutus* back till the sacred evening. We'll get to work at once and Pussie will make you want to stay with it for a long time yet.

Is that darling Kitten on the thorns of life?[8] We can't make out her condition. Give her the fondest Kiss from her devoted old Cat. Oh, to be with you again! This wretched day we think of Stoke[9] as a haven on the shore of Paradise.

Be of good cheer and we'll twist many a bright thread with the dark one. Thine for better or for worse throughout this strange little life—always thine in the changeless realm—

Pussie.

MS Eng. lett. c. 419 fols. 89r–91v BOD

1. Dated from Blue Anchor (little Boo) holiday, Sept.–Oct. 1885.

2. Untraced. Probably the proprietress of the hotel.

3. Probably Emma Harris Cooper.

4. For KB's illness, see letter 97 n. 5.

5. Not preserved.

6. In John Bunyan's *Pilgrim's Progress* (1678), Christiana is guided by Mr. Great-heart past the Apollion or Apollyon to the shepherd boy's peaceful meadows (218–39). These are "fruitful" (237), but the apples mentioned later in the letter are not specifically noted.

7. G. W. F. Hegel, *Lectures on the Philosophy of History* (1861).

8. A coded phrase for menstrual pain. The image is probably derived from Shelley's "I fall

upon the thorns of life! I bleed!" ("Ode to the West Wind") (Shelley, 54; Palgrave, *Golden Treasury,* 388). Elsewhere Amy Cooper comments, "I would have written yesterday, but 'thorns' kept me in bed all morning and lying about the rest of the day." See Amy Cooper, letter to Michael Field, MS Eng. lett. e. 31 fol. 33ʳ BOD.

9. Stoke Green, the Cooper family home.

109. Katharine Bradley, Letter to Edith Cooper

[Stoke Green] | Mon., [Oct. 1885][1]

Keep this scribble
Monday afternoon
My Pretty Spouse,

What a more than lovely day it is. I fear for the Muddie's brain: Much rapture will make her mad. Here am I curled upon the downs, having just parted with "the Châtelaine"[2] who is about all sorts of household businesses. It is well "Boo" is given up as far as I am concerned;—for travelling just now is out of the question. A mild pink is coming over the paint; but we have *no hope.* Sarah[3] announced yesterday—did I tell you?—that it was less melankōly now, and that though the first 2 nights she had not been exactly timid, she had evidently been something, but that now we were going on well, so Merin[4] need not feel it on his conscience that he must return to cheer the maids. Little one seems certainly better and also less melankōly: yesterday afternoon *at my earnest request* she went to the Wedmore's[5] as she had been invited, and returned laden with berries, and single dahlias. While she was away Edith Baker[6] called to look after the invalid, and brought 4 nectarines, a bunch of mignonette and 2 pokers; so that we fare well on flowers and fruits. But I do not know what w[d.] have become of me but for *Cnut,*[7]—with all its wondrous dramatic capabilities. It is to me in 2 acts merely like "Fair Rosamund"—but they will be brim-full. The Catastrophe of course comes rather early but the real issue is Cnut's penitence, and expiatory pilgrimage to Rome.[8] A fine solitary figure this stranger King with the capacity for founding kingdoms, and the love of historic continuity, thwarted and undone by the crudeness of his race, and the alienation of his blood. His love of unity tempts him to consent to the murder of Edmund Ironside,[9] with whom you remember he divided his kingdom but this single act of treachery is alien to all his noble nature; and he feels he owes the English people whom he passionately loves illimitable reparation for depriving them of their native leader and sovereign. There must be a lovely scene at Ely with the monks, and peace in pilgrimage and repentance at the end. The marriage with Emma—the Old Lady of the chronicles[10]—gives opportunity for a study in the subtlest psychology.—She represents to her young husband of 22—culture—the older civilization—restitution also mingles with the feeling that makes him seek to put her on her old throne; he is subtely fascinated by her; she devotedly passionately absorbed in him.

She will freely express her feelings toward her former husband "the Unready"—as you remember she utterly re-nounced that miserable Edward (the Confessor) whm she bore to Ethelred, and only thought of Harthe Cnut—her boy by Cnut. But she is not a bit like Eleanor.—She has a much weaker, sublter nature. The re-acti[o]n from her contempt for Ethelred makes her live solely to and for her regal husband—a man wise in counsel and prompt in deed. Edmund Ironside you will have to do chiefly; history arrays a very dramatic marriage for him; and a great deal can be made of his widow's parting from her two boys—the little men who were sent to Hungary. The unity is *faith—trust—*. Bribes can be chastised till they shriek for mercy in Ethelred—Cnut once deals treachery; and he cannot be the founder of a Kingdom. To-morrow Amy is going to the library for all sorts of chronicles. Where, meanwhile is "*Cameos from English History*???"[11]—I greatly desire it.

I suppose the old AngloSaxon Chroncle[12] is desirable—Is it readable—or transla[ted]. How does one get at it? This little play, Heaven favouring me, I hope to write before Christmas,—helping you with any parts of Brutus you may indicate: I have done 2 very good little bits while you have been away; but I dare only work at that when I am at my highest. In Cnut there is opportunity for fine noble work, wh. will be a relief from raging stammering tyrants.[13] And now I do not want to come to "the Boo"—so never mourn for me.[14] But get strength for the holiest work of our lives—the real magnum opus—and for the bits of the English work I shall require of you. I thrill to write of those whose sepulchres are among us to this day.

You said you knew P. you wanted a murder. Here is a quite unhackneyed one. The Subtety of it so much greater than Becket's Altar-business and the blabbering penitent,[15]—simply a broken heart, and a great king the issue. How I love my solitary Dane in his humility and remorse I cannot tell you, nor yet how I shall hate you if you arch *[sketch of cat]* your back at him. Be a good P.

Even the dog feels the peace of this September afternoon and lies flat. Kiss Father and Mother, and spend the days by the saltsea waves. Your own fond Sim.

MS Eng. lett. c. 419 fols. 92^{r}–94^{r} BOD

1. Dated from Blue Anchor holiday, Sept.–Oct. 1885.

2. *Tristram and Iseult,* 194–95 (Arnold, 1:186).

3. Probably the servant of letter 96.

4. James Robert Cooper.

5. For Wedmore family, see letter 57 n. 4.

6. For Edith Baker, see letter 22 n. 6. The invalid is KB herself (letter 97 n. 5).

7. Early name for *Canute.*

8. This catastrophe is the murder of Edmund Ironsides by the traitor Edric Streona at the end of act 2; the play ends with Canute vowing to devote himself to England and make a pilgrimage to Rome in atonement.

9. *Canute* 3.2.164–73 (62). Ward's letter suggested Cnut's guilt as an interesting dramatic problem (Add. MS 45851 fol. 75^{r} BL). For Adolphus William Ward, see letter 101 n. 3.

10. Emma Elfgifu, widow of Ethelred the Unready (*Anglo-Saxon Chronicles,* 134 n. 1).

11. Vol. 1 of Charlotte M. Yonge's *Cameos from English History* (1868) covers the reign of Canute.

12. It seems likely KB and EC did consult *The Anglo-Saxon Chronicles,* as the lines "Merrily sang the monks of Ely, / As Canute the king passed by" (*Canute* 3.2.20–21; 89) are a direct translation from the Ely Chronicle (*Liber Eliensis,* 153).

13. *WR* reproduces the King's stammer in the text.

14. Shakespeare's sonnet 71, "No longer mourn for me when I am dead."

15. Tennyson, *Becket* (*Poetical Works,* 696–98).

110. Katharine Bradley, Annotated Envelope

Blue Anchor | [Oct. 1885]

Blue Anchor
Spousa Solis.[1]

MS Eng. lett. c. 419 fol. 96^{r} BOD

1. A folkname for the marigold; probably an incorrect Latin translation of the common name *sposa solis,* or "bride of the sun" (Chittenden, *Dict. of Gardening*).

111. Edith Cooper to Katharine Bradley

[Blue Anchor] | [Oct. 1885][1]

My dearest Deare,

I am glad you are happy—but!—and the Cat arches its back firmly—do not expect me to do *anything* but *Brutus.* It has taken me half a year to love it, and now I love, as I ever love, with simpleness and exclusion, as well as yearning rapture. Brutus is to me *all in all*—an influence that is not to be put by—my *one* aim and divine task. It is glorious to get the weight of Philosophy calmly and smilingly lifted off my brain by Nature. I feel as if spaces were being smoothed and cleared for inspiration. You won't get me to Hegel just yet. Too must philosophy has clogged my wings this year. Muddie sitting by a reedbed! It is a sight to make the sylphs and naiads dance and sing. Paps has been to the moors[2] and I have seen Eden-like orchards.

Mother will only let me send this scrap. So little Kittie must wait till to-morrow. Kiss her and give her a stroke from the paw-paw.

Yesterday afternoon gather crimson leaves and *damask* late honeysuckle-buds.—The Sunset a glow of bright-coloured vapour.

Dearest love, my Own husband. I send you this blue flower[3]—I, your spousa, and so make you a brilliant complement.

MS Eng. lett. c. 419 fol. 97[r/v] BOD

1. Dated from the Blue Anchor holiday, Sept.–Oct. 1885.
2. Exmoor.
3. Not retained.

112. Edith Cooper, Annotated Envelope

Blue Anchor | Fri., 2 Oct. 1885

ca. Oct 2
Blue Anchor 1885

MS Eng. lett. c. 419 fol. 85[r] BOD

113. Katharine Bradley, Annotated Envelope

[PM Fri., 2 Oct. 1885]

Blue Anchor Oct. 1885.
P. has inconceivable revelations in Brutus.
Oct. Blue anchor 1885

MS Eng. lett. c. 419 fol. 84r BOD

114. Edith Cooper, Letter to Katharine Bradley

[Blue Anchor] | [Fri., 2 Oct. 1885][1]

My darling,
I have written a very pretty letter to Mr Ernest and sent Holt's blotted letter.[2] I only just saved it from the destructive fingers of the Muds. The reviews are meagre but less hostile than I had imagined.[3] How the Bell is at your feet—I mean the female altho' the gentleman is in the Same humble position.[4]

I wish you would mend, my darling. True, the little doctor[5] Said it would cease once before and it did. So I fix my hopes on her words. I have so thought of you to day, for we walked to *Road*water on the mineral line and then getting tired, *rode* to Washford in the shaky old-fashioned carriages and got out to go down a *road* I went along with my deare to Cleeve Abbey. I stood under the gate-house and looked in the stream where we saw so many darting fish. They were all gone, but memories of you took their place. The weather is very cold, stormy and dull. We are getting tired of it.

I have finished the scene in *Brutus* and it has taken a gt. deal out of me, so that tho' I am "cram full" of conception I must rest a little (This is *private*) I am entering imaginative realms more absorbing and heart-filling than *The Father's Tragedy*. I am wholly given up to Brutus. Do you know, dearest, I think I must not read the scene to you till this new inspiration is spent. I lose intensity and centralization of faculty if I spend it by the Emotional strain of giving it aloud to another. You have no idea what is working in me. I know for *Brutus*' sake you will let me be silent a little. Then I will read to you and tell you all about *Brutus* and you shall tell me all about *Knut.*[6] I love the thought of that drama DEEPLY—but I must not hear about it till I have done the god's will with this gt. inspiration. You will know, dear love, and forgive me—especially as I love *Knut* and have taken it to my heart distantly already. I am very tired. Oh dear! That our poor fleshly parts are so inadequate! I am going for a blow;[7] and a little sunlight will fully refresh me if it will but Come.

Kiss my darling little Kitten. Yes, I shall be frightened to death with the meeting; Pussie will have to be dragged by its tail down the chimney.[8] Deep love to my own Deare,

From the Spouse and Persian Puss.

MS Eng. lett. c. 419 fols. 81r–83v BOD

1. Dated from PM on the envelope above.

2. For Ernest Bell, see letter 62 n. 7. Henry Holt published the American edition of *Call./FR.*

3. Reviews of *FT/WR/LL* in the *Spectator* ("New Plays," 1885, 58:910–12), the *Academy* (Mackail, "Michael Field's New Volume," Jul.–Dec. 1885, 28:36–37), and the *Athenaeum* (Jul.–Dec. 1885, 79:251–52) mingled guarded praise with sharp (but only rarely brutal) criticism.

4. Amy Bell (letter 8 n. 2) and Ernest Bell were not related, in spite of their common surname.

5. Dr. Caroline Sturge (1861–1922), or Dot, was one of the Bristol Sturges (letter 31 n. 2). She entered the London School of Medicine for Women in 1882 and often gave up her time to tend friends. Caroline set up practice as a midwife in 1897, became a consultant for the Elizabeth Garrett Anderson Hospital, and retired to a cottage near Bristol in 1909 (Sturge, *Reminiscences,* 142–46).

6. *Canute* (1887).

7. EC probably means she is going out for some fresh air, however, both poets were also fond of cigarettes (Treby, *M&S,* 18).

8. A family saying that describes EC's nervous disposition. See, for example, Amy Cooper's letter to EC: "I think you would be up the chimney for good if you ever came here" (7 Sept. [1886], MS Eng. lett. e. 31 fol. 24r BOD).

115. Katharine Bradley, Letter to Edith Cooper

[Stoke Green] | [Oct. 1885][1]

Ah Mick,[2] my beauty, haven't I just been thankful you were away safely. It must have no tears in its mild blue eyes, and indeed it would not, if it knew how wholly happy I am. Yesterday I suffered; from dread of the examinaton[3] and getting used to new conditions; but I comforted myself with Dante "En la sua voluntade est nostra pace"[4]—my soul returned to her rest, a radiance as from Heaven illumined me; and once more I feel quite close to me the Divine Spirit.

I summoned P. all the spirits of my ancestors to my aid,—the gentle and blessed women who have taken so meekly the bodily cross, and seemed to smile victoriously on me. I would not have been without this experience. And I feel that knowing infirmity and sickness will but bind me closer to the humanity I love so well—the poet should know all things—the strange agonies of mortality—the rebellion and submission of the flesh, the discomforts of the earthly tenement that the heavenly may be desired.

And the Doctor[5] positively assures me that my work will not be *interferred with in the least;* nor, she thinks, with help, my walking power.

So just think, Pussie, what fine times we can have. Do not for *the world* think of returning one minute before the time. We should have no welcome for you; but by Wednesday we hope to have a bonnie one. My little Doctor has been just tenderness and goodness itself to me,—so patient, yet frank, honest and open.

And P. there must be times when I shall not seem thoroughly myself—that I cannot help . . [.] she says such cases are accompanied with hysteria—and you must not turn hard against me, but be tender, and let our tears mingle, till the light shines out! But never try the *unsympathetic* cure. Because it w$^{d.}$ break my heart. The ever bounteously fond, and most cheery.

K.

MS Eng. lett. c. 419 fols. 86^{r}–87^{v} BOD

1. For KB's illness, see letter 97 n. 5.
2. Michael or Mick has been generally considered by critics to refer specifically to KB, but this suggests an early shared usage.
3. A physical examination, most likely conducted by her doctor, Sir Andrew Clark. See letter 105 n. 5.
4. From Dante's *Paradiso:* "And in His will we find our peace" (3.85; 318).
5. For Dr. Caroline Sturge, see letter 114 n. 5.

116. Katharine Bradley, Annotated Envelope

[PM Sat., 3 Oct. 1885]

They will be good to me and help me.
Oct. 1885.

MS Eng. lett. c. 419 fol. 80^{r} BOD

117. Edith Cooper, Letter to Katharine Bradley

Cleeve Bay | [Sat., 3 Oct. 1885][1]

Cleeve Bay.

My darling Joy,

How thankful I am that you have been so brave and that the worst is known. It is a relief to me, for I was beginning to vaguely fear worse things. Of course the old Pussie wept with the Shock of Knowledge, but as I stood on the open moors I felt how blessed it was that nothing was hidden. Yes, my most Deare, we shall have beautiful times together and when you are sad and changed, your old grey Pussie will purr you back into comfort and never make its tail stiff. These illnesses are sent to make us love one another more fully, and we shall be sweeter and better for nursing and cherishing the darling Sim who has always been mighty and boundless in love to us. And, Oh, it is so heart-easing,—it makes me thank God—that your work—our dramas—will not in the least suffer, but will grow in strength wh: has nothing to do with your feebleness. Long live *Knut* and *Lucretia*! It leapt to my heart with joy that you were not going to London yet. I long for us to be together—reading, making dramas and loving each other with many loves. I am looking forward to Wednesday with eagerness, tho I have been very happy at the *Boo.* The darling has not been quite so well this week. Pussie, in spite of "indig."[2] is fresher and far less tired.

What a nest we will make our little home, warm and soft for our own! That you should feel Dante's loveliest line is all I could hope for you as support and highest strength. All the rest you want your pussie will do for you,

Ever and always *your* Pussie.

MS Eng. lett. c. 419 fol. 78^r–79^v BOD

1. Dated from PM on the envelope above.
2. Possibly indigestion.

118. Katharine Bradley, Letter to Edith Cooper

[Stoke Green] | Sun., 4 Oct. 1885[1]

Against the day of my burial.[2]

"And one of them shall not fall on the ground without your Father."[3]

Not even a sparrow falleth to the ground,
Father, without thee,
I will not doubt thee;
Choose thou for me a grassy mound
Where I may lie
With leaves about me.

In heaven—ah there
It is too brave;
I need to die,
And for the couch of my mortality
the close and cloudy comfort of a grave.

Sunday Oct 4th. 1885.

This is for the P. The motto for to-day is "Say as you think, and speak it from your souls,"[4]—so ever I,—and it rains and looks so nice and green grassward;—nevertheless I will stay with the P. if it would rather—K.

MS Eng. lett. d. 407 fol. 221r/v BOD

1. Dated from previous letter.
2. Unpublished lyric.
3. Matt. 10:29.
4. Probably a motto of KB's own devising.

119. Katharine Bradley, Letter to Edith Cooper

[Stoke Green] | [Oct. 1885][1]

Darling Wife,

Such a nice letter from Ellis this morning with wonderful Socialistic papers.[2] He has been reading the book again, and found *The Father's Tragedy* as splendid as ever—Rufus he likes better.

An acquaintance of his, from careful examination of internal evidence, is confident that the book is written by a man and a woman[3]—Ellis has another theory—I believe that of single female authorship; but he does not say.

Sweet Love—You are to me As an angel,—fresh from the bosom of God. Yet ever Know that if the great Lord Love him self should ever come to you—to him I will freely give you.

Heaven cherish you.

Sim.

MS Eng. lett. c. 418 fol. 122$^{r/v}$ BOD

1. Dated from Ellis's letter. See H. H. Ellis, letter to Michael Field, 1 Oct. 1885, MS Eng. lett. e. 32 fols. 106^{r}–109^{v} BOD.

2. Henry Havelock Ellis (1859–1939), writer and sexologist. KB and EC had seen Ellis at the National Gallery, KB describing his face as "the meeting place of culture and democracy" (MS Eng. lett. e. 31 fol. 20^{r} BOD), and EC liking his "sensitive, gentle lips, and eyes of gentlest purity—in manner shy and quiet—with a thin, sensitive voice, and a quiet, direct way of speaking" (fols. 14^{v}, 15^{r}). During the early 1890s Ellis, his sister Louie, and KB became close friends, sharing an appreciation for theater, wine, and poetry. See Add. MS 46779 fol. 3^{v} BL. In this early letter Ellis writes that he wishes to send them papers on the Fellowship of the New Life and "The Woman Question" (MS Eng. lett. e. 32 fol. 106^{r}–109^{r} BOD). Bridge notes that KB attended meetings of the Fellowship of the New Life at Merstham, but whether this pre-dates the meeting with Havelock Ellis is unclear. See Bridge, MS Eng. misc. d. 983 fol. 135^{r} BOD.

3. Ellis confides George Moore's view that Michael Field is a male-female collaborative partnership (MS Eng. lett. e. 32 fol. 108^{r-v} BOD).

120. Edith Cooper, Postcard to Katharine Bradley

[Stoke Green] | [Fri.,] 25 Dec. 1885

"A light-winged toy of feathered Cupid"[1]

It can but live a single day,
And then its message fades away.
A Kiss on either wing it bears:
Take each;—and if it die who cares?.

My "flying soul"[2] is with you.

Xmas. 1885.

P.P.

MS Eng. lett. c. 419 fol. 98^{r} BOD

1. Unpublished lyric. The original source for this quotation seems to be William Hazlitt's review of *Shelley's Posthumous Poems,* in which he describes the "Ode to Naples" as having "made of light-winged 'toys of feathered Cupid,' the flaming ministers of Wrath and Justice" (Hazlitt, *Collected Works,* 10:267).

2. Alexander Pope, "Eloisa to Abelard," 325 (Pope, *Poetical Works,* 111).

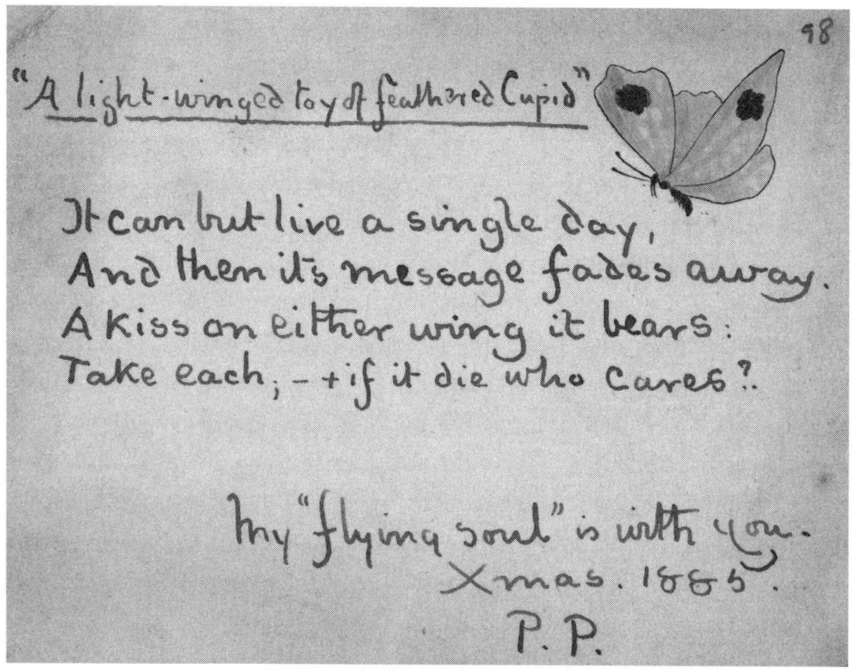

Postcard from Edith Cooper to Katharine Bradley, "A light-winged toy of feathered Cupid," Christmas 1885. (MS Eng. lett. c. 419, fol. 98[r], Bodleian Library, University of Oxford)

121. Katharine Bradley, Annotated Envelope

M[r.] Gray discovers Michael.

Add. MS 45853 fol. 110[r] BL.

122. Katharine Bradley, Letter to Edith Cooper

[Edinburgh] | [Aug. 1886][1]

What has given the brightness and charm to our week in Edinburgh has been that the M[r.] Gray who reviewed Brutus in *The Academy*[2] got our rooms for us, and has since proved our Most devoted and valorous knight. We believed he knew all about Michael—because, when rowing was discussed—he asked me if I had ever rowed up to Godstow where it was rumoured Fair Rosamund was buried.[3] Where I ejaculated like an old crone—and when the word was repeated professed I had heard she was buried there, but had never been to Oxford! On Sunday night we went to Gray's rooms—most exquisite from an aesthetics, literary, and art point of view. He has a first edition of Browning's Pauline, and he has also *The Germ,* besides the most interesting etchings and prints.[4] On Sundy morning he took us to S. Giles's,[5] and yesterday afternoon the Queen's Drive round Arthur's Seat. To-day I have given wholly to Miriam;[6] but yesterday suddenly while we were driving (it was after a discussion of the sale of poets' works) he said "I suppose there is no doubt that Michael Field is the wife of a school master in Clifton." I said no (meaning Michael Field was not that) and receiving coat one of scarlet on my cheeks. This was just as we were getting into the carriage after visiting a horrid old Inn in "a close" of the High Street,—I mean visiting it because it was condemned, not for something to drink—and when I found the wretch facing me I received coats 2, 3 and 4 of vermeil on my cheeks—so that my green bonnet must have blanched in the glow—and thought of ending all by a leap and away—so intolerable it was to feel those remorseless painters at their scene-painting on my face. He too perceiving lava grew frightened. Amy said I was convicted of lying, when we got home, and I had had a sharp thought that my words might be misinterpreted so I wrote to Gray confessing all.[7] When he called to-day though our Daniell friends[8] were at lunch, I thought by his "heightened" manner that note and brought him news, and this afternoon he has had it all out with Amy. "A thunder clap" it has been to him—though what more he can to to serve us I know not.

Private. We do not think of going to dear Nellie[9] till Saturday—our sightseeing has been interrupted through our Miriams illness, and we hope to leave her pretty bright, if we delay a day or so. I alas! after practical [ends]
~~her on every point, we cannot trust any verdict of his. Her illness and the operation have been kept entirely secret from her mother who is in very delicate health, so please do not mention it [to] any~~

Add. MS 45853 fols. 111^{r}–113^{v} BL.

1. Dated from letter to John Miller Gray, 24 Aug. 1886, Add. MS 45853 fols. 116^{r}–117^{v} BL.

2. John Miller Gray lauded Michael Field as "a true descendant of our old dramatists" in his review of *BU* (Gray, review, 320). EC had previously met Gray at the Wedmores' house in Bristol, and he soon became a beloved friend as well as a generous reviewer. See letter 71 n. 7.

3. Rosamund Clifford, mistress of Henry II, was buried before the High Altar of Godstow Nunnery. The Isis River, site of the island where the nunnery's remains are located, was a popular place to punt (Williams, *Oxfordshire,* 68–71). Rosamund was the subject of Michael Field's *FR* (1884), one of their most popular plays.

4. Robert Browning, *Pauline, A Fragment of a Confession* (1833). *The Germ* was the short-lived literary magazine of the Pre-Raphaelite Brotherhood (Dobbs, *Dante Gabriel Rossetti,* 61–67).

5. The restoration and remodelling of St. Giles's church had only recently been completed, in 1883 (Masson, *Edinburgh,* 46–61).

6. Miriam Daniell was an active member of the Bristol Socialist Society (Waters, *British Socialists,* 86). KB may have met Miriam through the Fellowship of the New Life (letter 119 n. 2, Add. MS 46777 fol. 67[r] BL) or at Bristol University College. In 1894 EC noted the death of Miriam after leaving her husband for a young American socialist (Add. MS 46782 fol. 42[r] BL). A letter from KB to the unnamed gentleman acknowledges Miriam's death in childbirth, and rebukes him for the assumption that as "modern women" they were sympathetic to the lovers. See KB, letter to Sir, MS Eng. lett. d. 120 fols. 81[r]–82[v] BOD.

7. In this letter KB begs Grey to "do your utmost to conceal the dual authorship, and in fact will treat me as chivalrously as you would the Pretender, were he in hiding" (Add. MS 45853 fols. 114[r]–115[v] BL).

8. Most likely the family of Miriam. See above, n. 6. As the spelling is different, it seems unlikely KB is referring to Henry Daniel, publisher of *Noontide Branches* (1899).

9. Nellie and David Reith (letter 2 n. 5) were holidaying at the Parsonage in Wemyss Bay, Inverness, on the western coast of Scotland (MS Eng. lett. c. 109 fol. 104[v] BOD). Reith was born in Aberdeen, although he spent most of his life in England (*Who's Who*).

123. Katharine Bradley, Letter to Edith Cooper

[Wemyss Bay] | Thurs., [2 Sept. 1886][1]

Thursday night nigh 9 oclock.

I have been standing quite alone on our little beach, and feeling how excellent it was to be there—the parson[2] away and only the dear Lay God with me. How wonderful to feel the soft matting of sea-weed under me, yet at noon I seemed in the heart of inland beauty. That moon making a faint track on the waters to me will grow strong and ripe for Melrose[3]—Nature's candle held to antiquity. It is low tide and the large jelly-fish glitter—that is like P. when the Infinite has deserted her, and she lies a poor pulp on the sand. To recognise that the river of life is Tidal, it gives us to drink, and anew suffers us to thirst. What joy like its influx. Come and give spring-tide to my poet. Another thought.—The instant we come in contact with the universal God is with us—Sorrow is universal—and death—how about sin—Is that too one of the meeting points with Him? I mean—when we die we do not of course reach the universality of death, so with sin, it is when we come in contact with it as a force in the world, not when we *commit* sin—that its part and lot in God May be realised. But I am like the old lady puzzled, and Cousin David can't help me.

P. I cannot tell you how I joy to learn Dorothy Wordsworth loved Coleridge.[4] She is the only English woman I rank as a poet,—a divine Creature for whom William Could not have altogether sufficed. What other woman has ever had her heart right Toward Nature, has ever felt of one blood with the forests, the little hills, and the mountain breezes. Think on that dreamy Samuel, and how life must have gone aMaying with him,[5] when Dorothy felt his genius.

Tired! Good night. How happy no trouble of Maid and boy comes between me and my poet. We are rich in books—*Diana*[6] and Burns. That old Gentleman[7]—Why did he not come to Scotland. Oh but I would have been bitter to him,—I w$^{d.}$ have brought to bear on him all my man-torturing machines.

Again—Heaven bless thee! Good night.

Friday Morning.

Calm, coming sunshine, and peace. This from little Gray[8] (see other envelope) I have just directed proofs to *the Academy,* and stated I should like the poems to appear in *different* numbers.

They read well in print. Please keep tenderly the bit of rare heather. On my return I shall fasten it in my Canterbury Burns, and I am going to write for one of the beautiful photographs as well—that it may be a true Michael Book—full of associations. Is it not nice to think of the Nephew high on the hills thinking of his great poet, and plucking a flower for him?[9] I am waiting for 10 oclock post to come in to sit long on the shore.

Farewell, my own love.

Simiurg *[bird symbol].*

[annotated on fol. 138^{v} by EC]

Scotland. 1886

Sept 6 on

K and A in Melrose

Abbotsford

Cousin David

Gray

MS Eng. lett. c. 418 fols. 135^{r}–138^{v} BOD

1. Dated from John Miller Gray's letter of 2 Sept. 1886.
2. Canon David Reith. See letters 2 n. 5 and 122 n. 9.
3. Melrose Abbey (Whyte, *Exploring Scotland's Historic Landscapes,* 77–78).

4. Samuel Taylor Coleridge's description of Dorothy as "a most exquisite young woman" was well known (Gittings and Manton, *Dorothy Wordsworth,* 64–66).

5. The chorus of Robert Herrick's "Corinna's Going a Maying" (Herrick, *Poetical Works,* 67).

6. George Meredith, *Diana of the Crossways* (1885).

7. "The old Gentleman" is usually Robert Browning, but KB seems to be thinking of the Scot, John Ruskin. For the source of their dispute, see letter 32 n. 13.

8. John Miller Gray, letter to KB, 2 Sept. 1886, Add. MS 45853 fol. 5 BL. The proofs refer to seven of Michael Field's poems that Gray arranged to appear in the *Academy* between Sept. and Nov. 1886: "The Summer Wind" (18 Sept.); "The Sands of Death" (9 Oct.); "Love's Sour Leisure" (6 Nov.); "King Apollo" and "Love and Death" (13 Nov.); and "An Invocation" (27 Nov.) See the *Academy* 30 (1886): 187, 240, 309, 326, 363. The heather mentioned later in the letter was sent by Gray for good luck (Add. MS 45853 fol. 5 BL).

9. Gray had written to KB describing a delightful day in the hills (Add. MS 45853 fol. 5 BL). For KB, Gray becomes a metaphoric nephew of Robert Burns.

124. Katharine Bradley, Letter to Edith Cooper

[Wemyss Bay] | [Sept. 1886][1]

Almund (kissing Cara) or it may be Hubert

I love her far beyond all kissing's pace,
Faster than thought;—the very breath I *warm*
Has not so close an access to my heart.[2]

Darling, be happy:

"Be blest and beloved as I love thee."[3] Tell the Mother Nellie sisterly thinks with Jeremy Taylor fasting is not for "weary travellers"[4] and I have everything I desire. It is tired—having helped to write to Ellis, Scott[,] Bakers[5]—Love dear parent. We are looking forward to receiving dear Pap's letter.

Thine own
Sim

[corner ripped] Here is what I wrote to her last evening—It may suggest a line for Almund—

"And then no more of thee and me."
"Ah sweet, sweet face
I dote upon,
and love beyond all Kissing's pace,
I were content

In my strait monument
    To be
And think upon thee in thy starry place,
    All tether gone,—
Even the tie
    That made us one.

MS Eng. lett. c. 418 fol. 172[r/v] BOD

1. Dated from KB's trip to Scotland in Sept. 1886.

2. In *Cup,* Almund says, "I love you far beyond all kissing's pace, / Faster than thought, with every breath I draw" (2.2.103–4; *Canute/Cup,* 146). The poem that extends this idea written below does not appear anywhere else.

3. *Erechtheus: A Tragedy,* 1131 (Swinburne, 7:399).

4. Jeremy Taylor's "Rules for Christian Fasting" prohibit the imposition of fasting on the sick, the elderly, pregnant women, the poor, little children, and wearied travelers (4.5.14; Taylor, *Holy Living,* 203). Edmund Gosse noted that *Holy Living* "is to be found in most households where books of any gravity of composition are admitted." See Gosse, *Jeremy Taylor,* 69. For Nellie Reith, see letter 2 n. 5.

5. For Havelock Ellis, see letter 119 n. 2; for Jane Scott, see letter 9 n. 3; for the Baker family, see letter 18 n. 11.

125. Katharine Bradley, Letter to Edith Cooper

[Wemyss Bay] | Sun., [5 Sept. 1886][1]

Yet a word with my darling before church. Brodick[2] is henceforth Michael's watering place. Where he has mountains to climb, pine woods to rest in, a smooth sand beach, and the deep to penetrate. I speak advisedly: from the pier one looks down into the the atmosphere of Burne Jones's *Mermaid.*[3] That is absolutely true. We saw the cool green bottom, the Clouds of purple sea-weed—the little white shells bright on the sand. We all drove to the head of Glen Rosa (in Arran) and then walked along a broad Valley with pine woods on one side, and a widely-curving, bracken haunted stream in the midst. A slatternly stream, with here and there sandy beaches, of curious Quakerly Colour—pale grays and brown, winding thoughtfully along, extremely loveable and odd—But I always feel as if Nature flung her arm round me when a stream comes to walk with me through the hills. By and bye the rest went on and Elsie[4]—whose Godmother I ought to have been—sat with me by the water. We watched the golden wrinkles in the stream.

In the afternoon we lay on the smooth sands, watching the play of artists' or other wise men's children, and the joy of bathers in the limpid bay. To me the mountains of Arran are more than all my memories of the Alps—I love to see the draughtsmanship of God. It is fine pencillng in the sky I care for,—not so much the strength of the hills, as earth's thoughts in exaltation,—earth lifting herself up, an audacious searcher into divine mysteries. No wonder our old driver said—"those who have been well about the world say there is no place more bonnie."

Puss, write to-morrow Monday morning—by *half-past nine* post. Then we shall have a letter before we leave early on Tuesday. Do this. On Tuesday write post office Melrose—

We will unfold more or our plan. Father I hope to write to to-morrow. Mortal haste—Immortal love. Simurg.

[bird symbol].

MS Eng. lett. c. 418 fols. 127^r–129^r BOD

1. Dated from KB's trip to Scotland in Sept. 1886.
2. Brodick Bay is situated on the Isle of Arran (Magnusson, *Treasures of Scotland,* 11). From Wemyss Bay, Arran is a short boat trip across the Firth of Clyde.
3. Edward Coley Burne-Jones, *The Depths of the Sea* (1886). See Wood, *Burne-Jones,* 96.
4. Nine-year-old Elsie was the youngest daughter of KB's cousins Nellie and David Reith (*1881 Census*).

126. Edith Cooper, Letter to Katharine Bradley

[Stoke Green] | Sun., [5 Sept. 1886][1]

Sunday morning.

Ah, my love, my poet, such a scene for you when you return! I have wrought in a frenzy—the very fumes of Delphos.[2] And I once thought the Southampton Scene[3] would be such a dull, old dolt of an affair! I have been bold as a lion in treatment. The tales of Norway and its rugged scenes—the reading of Catullus' *Atys,*[4] the most unique and overwhelming poem that Rome has given to the world, have set my horses of Apollo Gallopping at full Speed for a short, but precious, time. I see your joy, my own, own

Pussie.

Friday night

Good night, good night, my own loves. To think I may be kissing you lips to lips in the little home this time next week—Oh, dear bliss! The Sturges[5] have been happy,—and we, ah, we have been happy with those cards from the lovely country. Many rowan berries for my birds.

Saturday night.

I wonder if the pulse of the lightning will thrill the sky tonight as last night. It was wonderfully fair.

Kisses, my joys, kisses

[from header fol. 49^r] You invoked the blessing!

MS Eng. lett. c. 419 fol. 49^r/v BOD

1. Dated from KB's trip to Scotland in Sept. 1886.

2. EC is comparing herself with the Delphic oracle. See EC's vision during the writing of *FT* in letter 79, and KB's reception of it as a truth in letter 131.

3. In the Southampton scene (1.4), Canute is proclaimed King of the North, while London gives allegiance to Edmund Ironsides. Canute declares his desire to embrace Christianity and his new country, and his repugnance for his barbarian origins is manifest in his audience with the prophetess, Gunnhild. Edric assures him his love for Emma, the widow of King Ethelred, is requited (*Canute/Cup*, 33–46).

4. In Catullus's poem 63, the goddess Cybele sends a lion to attack her fugitive devotee Attis/Atys in order to reclaim his fidelity (Catullus, *Catullus*, 129–39).

5. For the Sturge family, see letter 31 n. 2; the postcards are untraced.

127. Edith Cooper, Postcard to Katharine Bradley

[Stoke Green] | PM Mon., 6 Sept. 1886

God speed you, darlings—may you have joy with Nature and Antiquity, and bring some comfort to that poor little soul whom, I feel, I shall never see again.[1] Parents are "doing nicely" and, Puss, filled with the Cold air, is as full of dream and vision, and ardour for the young Dane.[2] Alas! I forgot my town dears. I see about it this morn. Forgive a mouser's giddy pate. The Old Pussy.

MS Eng. lett. c. 419 fol. 104^r BOD

1. Miriam Daniell. See letter 122 n. 6.

2. King Canute of *Canute* (1887). See previous letter.

128. Katharine Bradley, Letter to Edith Cooper

[Wemyss Bay] | Mon., [6 Sept. 1886][1]

Monday morning.
My Darling,

My Dahlia, there is no news in the whole world as heaven-opening as this that the King, the divine one, is with you.[2] Did he come to me I would none of him. Let him be with my love. That is the meaning of Hinton:[3] women Can give joy to women. They can rejoice to see the bridegroom with the bride, and depart uncaressed. To give the lover to the beloved—ah ultimate gift and greatness of the heart! It is possible—it shall be sung.[4]

It was *last night* I felt a great warming of the heart towards thee. Going out into the garden of the soul I found thousands of fresh flowers out there, all wide and fragrant for the love of my Dahlia. I prayed so for my darling her soul might be *restored*. Last night at psalms I thought of her—"wait thou the Lord's leisure."[5] It must be her motto. They are taking up stair covers, and the brawl of departure begins. I must not write more. To-morrow, and Wednesday; (but post on Wednesday pretty early) *direct letters to Melrose post-office*. Do this! Is it not sweet of the Puss to forward you a view of Falkland.[6] You must have it framed. The inscription is a triumph. I have for my P. *nothing*—nor for any one. Now and then it opens its lips in a Kiss-like song; *but* of material substance it has nothing.

Yet that Dash[7]—where we hope to spend the night to-morrow,—but I cannot think that can come to pass. We think of giving up the Yarrow;—little Gray has given us every direction, but to see it on a Coach—and the swan might not be there.[8] Let Heaven direct me there with P. walking hand in hand. How happy it is to-day writing out its scene in red and black! I have *quite forgotten*—how I ended the last scene in Canute—I Know it was temporary not eternal; and must all be done again.

We shall feel leaving Scotland sorely. It is "a dear, dear land"[9] with whom I should like to have permanent relation through Amy's Edinburgh name.[10] That week was indeed without rival.

Do not write more. Go back to Catullus, and Comfort the Mother. Thine to the innermost little heart crease.

Simurg.

MS Eng. lett. c. 418 fols. 130r–132r BOD

1. Dated from KB's trip to Scotland in Sept. 1886.

2. King Canute of *Canute* (1887).

3. KB is probably referring to the moral philosophy of James Hinton (1822–75). She may have been introduced to Hinton's works by Havelock Ellis, who wrote the introduction to *The Law-breaker and the Coming of the Law* (1884). Hinton's views on marriage seem to have been uniformly bleak. See White, *Nineteenth-Century Writings,* 275.

4. In act 3 of *Canute,* Edith, wife of the traitor who killed Edmund, is driven mad by the death of her son and attempts to drown herself. She meets Elgiva (Edmund's widow), they find comfort in each other's arms, and she takes Edith back to her cell to devote her life to God (thus giving the lover to the beloved) (3.3.127–32; *Canute/Cup,* 98). David Moriarty has read this scene as explicitly lesbian ("Michael Field," 124).

5. Ps. 62:5.

6. Falkland Palace in Fife is the site for the murder of David, Duke of Rothsay, in *FT.* The picture is untraced.

7. It is about eighty miles from Weymss Bay to Melrose, and Yarrow would represent a detour of several miles.

8. The swan that William Wordsworth did not see in "Yarrow Unvisited, 1803" (43–48; Wordsworth, 3:84; Palgrave, *Golden Treasury,* 352). For John Miller Gray, see letters 71 n. 7 and 122.

9. *R2* 2.1.57. This refers to England in Shakespeare's play rather than Scotland (362).

10. A pun on "Pick" (Amy Cooper's nickname) and "Pict" (the ancient inhabitants of Scotland).

129. Katharine Bradley, Letter to Edith Cooper

Falkland | Tues., [Sept. 1886][1]

Bruce Arms
Falkland! (opposite the palace)
Tuesday night *8' oclock etc.* My pulse cannot keep time.

I could carouse wi['] the ghosts.[2] Look on your photograph.[3] Our living eyes look on that picture. Revolt mingles with the strong excitement. It is like jolting in an omnibus through the streets of Jerusalem. Three miles from Falkland Road to the town through heavy, solemn country—occasional wood, fine range of hills (perhaps the Perthshire Highlands in the background)—but P. I shall be glad when it is over—To track such a past is unendurable—one must only meet with it in the realms of imagination where all things are possible—there will be moonlight on the towers to-night; there are lights flickering in the lower windows. Never must the P. come here. It w[d.] never return to me from the chimney.[4] I feel depersonalizing: wild, reeling laughter is my safety. To think of that strict arrest of youth so close, so close, those days of gnawing hunger and pent thirst. Do not think of it: but leave me to read the new Father's Tragedy,[5] Heaven favouring me, on our return. I am thankful it is not with us. It would be like reading of the dead with the Corpse to turn to.

They say many visitors have been here this summer! (Why?) The palace is, as you must see, dark as if built by the destinies—simple and terrible even now. And to-morrow—O my Greatest my poet—to-morrow we hope to see Lindores.[6] It must be long before another letter reaches you. We cannot see the palace till 10, and must toil faithfully as pilgrims, if we are to reach Melrose to-morrow evening. We crossed the Firth of Forth for your sake. This visit is our present to you. Heaven give thee such and such thing, but Heaven cannot give thee *[from header fol. 26^{r}] more of itself than in the Father's Tragedy.*

[bird symbol] Simurg.

MS Eng. lett. e. 31 fols. 26^{r}–27^{v} BOD

1. Dated from KB's trip to Scotland in Sept. 1886.

2. John Todhunter, *Helena in Troas,* 13–14. Todhunter's recently published one-act play had been performed in 1886 (*Oxford DNB*). KB and EC knew "Toddy" (*W&D,* 183) as part of the London literary circle in the 1890s and described him in 1906 as one of their "hoar contemporaries" (*W&D,* 249).

3. A photograph of Falkland Palace; see previous letter. Falkland is special to EC because of her vision during the writing of *FT.* See letter 79. Amy Cooper wrote, "It seems so impossible to think that Falkland is yours, and yet you have never seen it" (MS Eng. lett. e. 31 fol. 24^{v} BOD). Later in the letter, KB describes the visit as a gift to EC.

4. For EC as a cat up the chimney, see also letter 114 n. 8.

5. KB and EC redrafted several of their works after publication, eagerly following the advice of critics, friends, and literary acquaintances. The most notable case was *UTB,* reissued within twelve months of its release.

6. Lindores Abbey is much farther north than the other abbeys mentioned. In the nineteenth century it was derelict (Coulton, *Scottish Abbeys,* 80).

130. Edith Cooper, Letter to Katharine Bradley

[Stoke Green] | [Sept. 1886][1]

My loves and great joys,

To write this last letter nearly makes me leap; I want you, want you. Yet I nearly hated you this morning when I thought of you as where I ought to be, where it would thrill me to the depths to be. You rogues, we guessed enviously.[2]

My dear Husband, I have a scene to lay at each foot—the Southampton and the Olney[3]—3 large scenes, written in prophetic fury—I have never in all my life done so much work at the same time: night and morning, and dawn and Evening I have been at my Muse's business,[4] never getting overtired. I do not think the stream is yet dry—and shall recast the 1st Scene, if I find I am not deceived. But it must soon stop, and then—Oh, to have my darlings to feed on, and to listen, and purr, and rub sides against them! I must not meet you so late at night, they think. But the door will be full of joy. As Catullus beautifully says to his returning friend *Quid me laetius est, beatiusve*?[5] Glad, and blessed indeed I shall be to kiss my Poney[6] and Kitten. Oh *come.*

MS Eng. lett. c. 419 fol. 50[r/v] BOD

1. Dated from KB's trip to Scotland in Sept. 1886.
2. EC is referring to the trip to Falkland. See letter 129.
3. *Canute* 1.4 and 2.2.
4. EC substitutes "Muse" for "Father" in Luke 2:49.
5. Catullus, "A Welcome Home to His Friend," 9.11. The literal translation is "What is gladder or happier than I?"; but translators often interpose a gendered subject: "What man is gladder or happier than I?" (*Catullus,* 41).
6. "Poney" or "Littel Hors" is a nickname for KB.

131. Katharine Bradley, Letter to Edith Cooper

Melrose | [Sept. 1886][1]

Melrose 2 o'clock and after. Looking on Abbey Window.
With the strong excitement of Melrose and Dryburgh upon me, my Dahlia, I cannot write of Falkland and Lindores,[2] but I cut out from little black book 2 pages,—poor scraps, but what I wrote verily there—After seeing the palace, in driving rain we were trotted off to Lindores.

We have brought you ivy-leaves from his cell[3]—a narrow chink, giving air and light enough for torture—and *quite low to the ground.*

I did not think we should really see that. I have never seen Amy so excited. O P. the tears did not come till we were driving away and passed a great ripening wheatfield. I almost shuddered to think how god has spoken the truth to you. As Ruskin says "Imagination is the truth-telling faculty."[4]

The gardener at my request gave me sweet-peas, and these with the ivy-leaves and oats from Lindores I hope to fasten in my little black book and write down in my own and, the Canon's room all I want to tell my Dahlia about her own Country.

Abbotsford is full of the most intoxicating interest—blindingly, overwhelmingly full; and Dryburgh a very garden of antiquity. One ought to live there the whole of a cloudless summer day. We sat among the maps, below the starry window of the refectory joying in the barberry berries that drooped over the high chapel wall. There are soft pink hues in the stone,[5] and the mellow autumn berries mixed with these exquisitely. I shall always associate the barberry with Dryburgh as the wild roses with *Glastonbury.*[6]

And this word, darling, brings me to *the* joy, the gift, to think of the Olney scene too, at wh. I should have stuck dead. The whole of Canute is yours. I do not wish to lay finger on him more. I should grieve to think we were coming home, did I not fear you might be tempted to over-work. Don't do that, dearest. I swear I will not keep you from your work, or unbottle a single flask of Fife wine on Saturday if you still seethe. When this fit of work is over: and I have had the glorious rehearsal[7]—let us put Canute away, and wait till P. finishes the last scene, when Heaven next visits her.

My very soul is an inn: all sorts of guests thronging in and pushing out. I am a quiet woman, and like best one orderly set of lodgers.

Ah that I came back feeling I had the male of *The Water Maiden*[8] for my subject, and winter toil—I wait and seek Heaven's purpose. As for parents I simply dote on them: but tell them, I cannot write. Excitement, and fatigue, mingle with the drowsing influences of fresh air; but I Know I shall "awake, and remember and understand."[9]

Do not imagine we shall enter 2 fiery comets from the north: give us but a boiled fish and a fire, and gradually our chafed spirits will revive.

P. Melrose gives me the most shuddering dread of a florid style.[10] Oh—may we be ever Norman,—at most early English—decorated and damned—never.

Such ruins by moonlight are for the tourist; and it does not much matter that the hotel is close to them—unholy walls!

To reach Dryburgh one has to cross the Tweed, and walk a quarter of a mile through bowery ways like a true pilgrim. Here all the air is polluted with hotel breezes.

But I will end with Abbotsford, and the blessed spirit, who there gathered round him all his spirit loved.[11]

Dearest love and Kisses to each one, parents and puss. God give us meeting.

Simurg

MS Eng. lett. c. 418 fols. 139ʳ–142ᵛ BOD

1. Dated from KB's trip to Scotland in Sept. 1886.

2. Melrose and Dryburgh are ruined abbeys on the English-Scots border (Whyte, *Exploring Scotland's Historic Landscapes,* 85–86); Falkland and Lindores are sites associated with *FT.* See letter 129. KB's subsequent reference to the black book is probably the black notebook, MS Eng. poet. f. 19 BOD.

3. It is unlikely KB saw the cell of David, Duke of Rothsay: he starved to death in the Great Tower at Falkland in 1402; the old castle was completely replaced in 1500 (Magnusson, *Treasures of Scotland,* 133). In *FT,* David is incarcerated in an underground dungeon.

4. In *Modern Painters,* John Ruskin wrote that the imagination's "true force lies in its marvellous insight and foresight,—that it is, instead of a false and deceptive faculty, exactly the most accurate and truth-telling faculty which the human mind possesses" (Ruskin, 4:44).

5. Pink sandstone ruins are usually associated with Melrose Abbey rather than Dryburgh. See Whyte, *Exploring Scotland's Historic Landscape,* 77–78.

6. In the nineteenth century there was renewed popular and archaeological interest in Glastonbury, although it remained in private hands until 1907. See Carley, *Glastonbury Abbey.*

7. Possibly a private reading between friends. Emma Donoghue notes that a theater manager wanted to put on *WR* but the production never eventuated (Donoghue, *We are Michael Field,* 41). The only known production of a Michael Field play was the Independent Theatre's performance of *A Question of Memory* in 1893. See Macdonald, "Disillusioned Bards," 18–29.

8. An unfinished MS of a play entitled *The Water Maiden* is held by the BOD (MS Eng. misc. c. 653). It may have been inspired by Burne-Jones's *The Depths of the Sea.* See letter 125.

9. "Evelyn Hope," 55 (Browning, 5:176).

10. The ruins of Melrose Abbey are Gothic (Whyte, *Exploring Scotland's Historic Landscape,* 77–78).

11. The blessed spirit of Abbotsford is Sir Walter Scott.

132. Katharine Bradley, Letter to Edith Cooper

[Scotland] | Thurs., [16 Sept. 1886][1]

Thursday even.

O Persian it was just standing by his bed—feeling the solemnity of that incarnation—miracle of miracles—God revealed in that humble cottage.[2]

One does not feel the mystery even at Stratford so great—Here it is in very truth—"He Took upon Him the form of a servant."[3]

Then too his handwriting, how heroic! The "Scots whom Bruce hath often led"[4] is there,—the eloquent hand of a free man, full of majesty and flowing curve.

Two Bibles given by her lover to Highland Mary—2 streaks of hair, caught in the blank fore-page of one of them. Pussie Verily shall one day have a tiny

Vellum book in which it shall write Blake-wise[5] its own poems, and it shall have Simurg's girl, golden hair caught in it tenderly, Burns's way.

the auld brig o'Doon.

A poet's stream—not brawling,— a mirror for the trees.
My darling's own name of *Michael* is written in the lowly birth place.

Bitterly the grief presses—he is *[from header fol. 133ʳ]* a poet—by his lyrics. He has sung out the very heart of his country. "And I would have given thee also such and such things."[6] Then, Lord God—song—gift—song, song!

Simurg.

MS Eng. lett. c. 418 fols. 133ʳ–134ᵛ BOD

1. Dated from KB's trip to Scotland in Sept. 1886.

2. Robert Burns's cottage in Alloway.

3. Phil. 2:5–7.

4. Robert Burns, "Robert Bruce's March to Bannockburn," 1–2 (Burns, 2:707).

5. The poet William Blake inherited a notebook from his favorite brother, Robert, who died in 1787. Between 1790 and 1818, Blake used the notebook extensively, even turning it over and writing back to front. See Bentley, *Stranger from Paradise,* 63.

6. An understandably loose quotation of "I wad hae gi'en them off my hurdies / For ae blink o' the bonie burdies" ("Tam O'Shanter," 157–58; Burns, 2:562).

133. Katharine Bradley, Letter to Edith Cooper

[London] | [Wed., 23 Mar. 1887][1]

This letter is for P's eye alone.
She can give of it as many bits as she likes. I am now going to write to father.
Dear love to parents.
This letter darling you are to read carefully yourself; and only give "Paps" bits. The orphan letter[2] will amuse you. Does not it seem madness not to stay for the Annual and Cardinal Manning.[3]

Your own love
Sim.

Pussie, when it was not babbling of Pussie to the old gentleman, it was babbling of Puss.[4] But really it can only shake its head for joy to think of what he was, of his warm, fondling tender manner, and watchful, loving eyes. "I want to strip you of all these things he exclaimed"—but a wonder as to what wᵈ· become of the "heap[in]g hair" kept me from unbonnetting.[5] We discussed Mʳ· Gray and "the golden brows" of the Francia; and then I told him all about a cup of water[6] and *Pussie*—what Puss w^d. make of it, and how he was to like it. And he said "I'll look to like if looking liking move!"[7] Get the right quotation. In the midst of the talk, when my hand was ungloved for tea, he caught it vehemently saying "And you do the lyrics."

Truly, Love, I w^d. fain put back the clock of time 30 years and be loved by Robert Browning in his glorious Manhood. He always thinks of you when he loves you—not I am sure of any pleasant sensations to himself:—he seems full of regoicing in one's spirit. I told him all about the Sapphics[8]—and of how we meant no more harm than George Herbert when he took a text from Holy Writ, and wrote a hymn thereon, and I especially warned him the metres were of the plainest. "All that I can do with my poor scholarship shall be done" he said, with evident *deep interest in the project;*—his only fear being of the post—but Miss Browning added "Register"![9] So, all being well, as soon as we get home you and I—(*no-one else*) will look over our Sapphics and get them in order to despatch at once. Look in my year books for copies, and if some are wanting, get home copies written out, for we Must have duplicates. I doubt whether the old gentleman can do much for them: but I feel as if I must write one or two to him I love him so. When he brought Elsie's letter[10] I told him I should be jealous if the lady to whom I was bearing it was not much younger than I, and he said—attacking me in his sudden way "Oh you have plenty or quite enough letters from me." When I added "No: Michael had; I had only received two he rejoined "Well, you have only to write to me and say you are in town to receive a note saying "Come to-morrow." And yet P. it went to my heart to feel somehow the remoteness of age about him. The whole of the mighty intellect is there, but it seems as if one had to climb a high tower to it.[11] And the dear old gentleman was sleepy and tired. I rather grieve to think of Kensington[12] he will be too much harassed. He is so glad to hear we are working;—Puss, we will have fine times with him in Paradise.

Tell, Mother, the more I think of her conduct to Sir Andrew,[13] the worse it seems. He has taken no notice, and not yet given us an appointment

Add. MS 46866 fols. 247^r–246^v BL [abridged version published in *W&D,* 18–19]

1. Dated from Robert Browning's letter of 22 Mar. 1887 confirming an invitation for KB and Amy to visit him the next day. See Robert Browning, letter to KB, 21 Mar. 1887, Add. MS 46866 fol. 80^r BL.

2. Untraced.

Robert Browning, 1888. (National Portrait Gallery, London)

3. The annual meeting of the Victoria Street and International Society for the Total Abolition of Vivisection was held on 29 Mar. 1887. Frances Power Cobbe was one of the speakers, as was Henry Edward Manning (1808–92), Cardinal Archbishop of Westminster (*Times,* 30 Mar. 1887). Manning was in his seventies and no longer attended many public events, so this would have been a rare opportunity to see the controversial vice president of the society (McClelland, *Cardinal Manning,* 209).

4. KB and EC first visited Robert Browning in May 1885. This visit occurred on 22 Mar. 1887 with Amy coming in place of Edith. Two disparate reasons were given: KB pleaded problems with the new volume (Add. MS 46866 fols. 77^{r}–78^{v} BL); Amy told Sarianna Browning that it was parental possessiveness of Edith (Add. MS 46866 fol. 236^{v} BL). The proliferation of feline nicknames here results in confusion: KB may mean she (it) "babbled" of EC to Browning; or of both her nieces; or Amy may be the "it" that did the babbling.

5. Amy's letter to EC notes that a high wind had made their hair unpresentable. See Amy Cooper, letter to EC, 23 Mar. 1887, Add. MS 46866 fol. 240^{r} BOD.

6. They discuss John Miller Gray (letter 71 n. 7); F. Francia's *Madonna and Child with St. John,* which KB would have seen in the Uffizi in 1880 (see EC's receipt of photo, letter 23); and *Cup* (pub. Oct. 1887), a play based on Dante Gabriel Rossetti's note about a king who falls in love with a young girl who gives him a cup of spring water. As the king must marry another, his hunting companion marries her, but every year she meets with the king at the spring with a cup of water. He dies after her daughter gives him water (Rossetti, *Works,* 615). In Field, the girl (Cara) dies from sorrow when her son, fathered by the king, dies.

7. *Rom.* 1.3.97 (716).

8. *LA* (1889) is a book of lyrics extending Sappho's fragments. Browning provided detailed suggestions on rhyme and Greek translation for *LA* and heartily praised the final manuscript (Add. MS 46866 fol. 91r BL).

9. Sarianna Browning, the poet's sister, suggests they should send the MS by registered mail.

10. Little Elsie Reith gave KB and Amy two pence to buy violets for the elderly poet. Browning was touched by the child's gesture, and immediately wrote a note of appreciation (Add. MS 46866 fol. 238r BL).

11. EC described the remoteness they perceived in the seventy-five-year-old Browning: "He is always the poet with us; it seems impossible that he goes behind a shell of worldly behaviour and commonplace talk, when he faces society, yet it is so. In his own room, in his study, he is Rabbi Ben Ezra, with his inspired, calm, triumphant old age" (*W&D,* 23).

12. Browning moved to 29 De Vere Gardens, Kensington, in June 1887 as his house at 19 Warwick Crescent suffered from "faulty construction" (Ryals, *Life of Robert Browning,* 234).

13. Sir Andrew Clark, KB's own physician. See letter 105 n. 5. The first symptoms of the uterine cancer that would kill Emma Cooper in 1889 were probably emerging at this time.

134. Katharine Bradley, Copy of Letter to Robert Browning to Edith Cooper

[Blackheath] | [Mar. 1887][1]

Christchurch Vicarage Blackheath.

Dear Mr. Browning,

Elsie[2] could read your letter herself. When she had read it the little creature came and clasped me tight. She has a fearless little soul full of love. It is only when I come to your house that I feel to be a poet means to behave divinely to people to

"disdain not one's own thirst to slake
At the poorest love was ever offered."[3]

I feel now quite dumb, and unable to say even to Edith almost what it was to me to be with you and your Sister at Warwick Crescent last night,—like Dante unable to record what the blest spirits said

"Ne la corte del Cielo ond' io rivegno,
Si trouvan molte gioie care e belle
Tanto che non si possan trar del regno"[4]
Affectionately yours
Katharine H. Bradley.

I will write to-morrow, darling—Nellie[5] is here, killing me with talk. It would be desecration to speak of yesterday now.

Add. MS 46866 fols. 84^{r}–85^{v} BL

1. Dated from the visit to Browning in Mar. 1887.
2. For Elsie Reith's gift to Browning, see previous letter.
3. "Christmas Eve," 512–13 (Browning, 5:69).
4. "In the court of Heaven, whence I have returned, / Are many gems so precious and beautiful / That they may not be taken out of the kingdom" *Paradiso* 10.70–72; Dante, *Divine Comedy,* 3:110–11).
5. For Nellie Reith, see letter 2 n. 5.

135. Katharine Bradley, Letter to Edith Cooper

[London] | Fri., [1887][1]

Friday,
Ah, my own Love, it is such a sweet summer morning; and we are going to see the Thames[2] in his courting days—when he was romantic and dreamy—before the cares of the great city came upon him. Will you be the invisible fourth of our little company?

You see from Hales's note[3] how yr. poet is loved . . . I think I shall try on Monday, or Wednesday to get to see him. On Tuesday at 2, all being well, we are at Queen's Square on the "blue pot"[4] expedition. I do not at all think we shall go to the Academy. I pray that the visions of beauty I have beheld may *stay* with me;—and it is grief to know that some at least must fade;—I will not taint their purity by the sight of a mass of coarse, false art, such as I Know awaits me in the academy. I cannot, love, describe the minerals rightly, without going to see them again, and I can't do that.[5] And Amy told you I think of the glorious Vision of winged creatures that threw a flood of light over the gray-brownness of the fish Museum, as I was firmly insisting, in spite of Amy's weariness on the inspection of the "Linka. Linka. Para-doxus"[6]—there were brazilian moths;—

winged creatures of surpassing beauty—of range of colour from pearly Violet and bridal gray to the deepest dusk greens and velvets. The shells were wonderful; but these were more marvellous still.

Your Göthe[7] is here all right, looking very clear and keen, and not in any way lovable. Mud's "Approach"[8] is also here—We may have seen Miss Jay[9] yesterday for there were lots of people at work at Turner drawings,—indeed the whole set of *working* rooms was crowded with artists. We shall, without fail, get home some time next week, my Pet;—but I cannot clearly say *when.* You are having a Very happy time with Mud, and doing many good works for the grateful fowl. But what are you giving away to Mud? I am indignant to think of your distributing My Goods and Chattels. It is a sweet little song you give me[10]—Does it come out of anything, or live by itself. I can get no reading but a bit of "Fors"[11] and Dante,—but I have enough to think about for many months. Kiss the All-Wise, and ever in love, cling to and desire him.

[bird symbol drawn as two long, thin leaves with two flowers underneath]

MS Eng. lett. c. 418 fols. 147[r/v], 148[r/v] BOD

1. The absence of datable events makes it difficult to fix a time for this letter. Annotations on the letter, possibly by EC, read "Summer (after 1885)" and "1888." I have dated it to about the time of KB's visit to Browning because she is involved in reading Dante at the time of this letter and in the previous letter. As mention is made of Emma Cooper, it must be before her death in 1889.

2. They are coming from Oxford, the source of the river Thames.

3. For John Wesley Hales, see letter 2 n. 2 and letters 5–7. Hales's note is untraced.

4. KB articulates some of the primary tenets of an aesthetic lifestyle: the desire for blue china, as in letter 2 n. 11; and a dislike for the conservative Royal Academy of Arts (Hamilton, *Aesthetic Movement*, 23). The pot is a gift for EC; see letter 137.

5. KB and Amy may have visited the Royal Aquarium, opposite Westminster Abbey, which featured various displays in addition to tanks of exotic sea creatures. It also included art galleries, reading rooms, a skating rink, and an orchestra. By the 1890s it was no longer respectable, and the building was demolished in 1906. See Weinreb and Hibbert, *London Encyclopaedia,* 662.

6. Possibly the Australian platypus, *Ornithorhynchus paradoxus.* Linka Linka may indicate that the animal was viewed as an evolutionary curiosity or missing link.

7. Possibly a portrait of the German poet.

8. Emma Harris Cooper (Mud) had a particular fondness for Turner's *Approach to Venice,* 1844. When she was dying she requested her copy of the picture be brought to her (Add. MS 46778 fol. 37[r] BL).

9. Untraced.

10. Untraced.

11. Ruskin's *Fors Clavigera.*

136. Edith Cooper, Annotated Envelope

To Sim
Birdlip—Coldswold. July—1887.
From P. The virtues of *Canute.*

MS Eng. lett. c. 419 fol. 105[r] BOD

137. Edith Cooper, Letter to Katharine Bradley

[Stoke Green] | Thurs.-Fri., [Jul. 1887][1]

Thursday Evening Twilight.
My own love,
Somehow I cannot help coming, with tears in my eyes, from looking on my little pot,[2] (wh: holds the letter, the inscription, and the dried flowerets)—coming to tell you how dear you are, and how precious your illness makes you.[3] I used to receive so entirely in our love-bond, and now I can give a little; and it makes our mighty-sweet tie holier and more beautiful to me.

Yes, always think that you are dearer, more truly between the angels' wings of my Holy of Holies, in my heart's building of love, than when you were wholly strong.

Friday morning

And my little Horse is lying looking at the view from under the beech-columns, for it is too hot and bright for the shadowless Common-land. Ah, there will be no leisure for thee tomorrow morn. I send another Grand proof,[4] just including the opening of the love-scene. I am struck deeply with the breadth, that epic quality, in the lines—and the great level of workmanship in *Canute.* I have never so liked a drama in proof, never felt so much that the work of our hands was established. In the proofs send there is a great deal to do; the style is generally so fine, that inequalities here and there cannot be borne. I have stated on slips of paper all I think about needed corrections, amplifications etc. Now you must work, little, pale horse![5]—really labour. If you can, return the proof to me on Sat. afternoon, and I will copy all corrections into the clean copy, on Sunday, and send to B. and T.[6] by Monday. But if you want time, do not scruple to take it, for Time and Space must bow like slaves to our "Mighty work."[7] I send

Gunhild in revise;[8] how perfect it reads now, thanks to thee, lonely Birdlipian reviser! Work directly after breakfast at the table, and then take proof and revise "out into the light of things"—"let Nature be your teacher."[9] I am sure the great view and beaches will teach you to think well of the Spirit's work accomplished in *Canute.*

B. and T. have acknowledged the *Cup,* and the Scene of Canute, and also promised carefully to insert the new passage. Had you not better send to me the passage on the Lord's Prayer,[10] that that too may find its place—where Ethelnoth approaches Canute. You did not send me that lovely passage, and I think you better, as I can make B. and T. understand more clearly than you can.

I am going on very well, only tired with the dragging pain, and quite weary with long sitting up to proofs. I missed a letter very much this morning. We had a p.card from Freda, on her way, and "wouling" for Edward!![11] It is dinner-time, and I must stop; but I shall try to write a sheet of chat by and bye. Is it dining on a leveret?[12]

Just before tea.

We have been waiting all afternoon for the great Scott to come and read *Thou m[ay] Janet;*[13] but she came not—only dear Rosa, who did not seem to get on with Miss Jane.[14] Tomorrow we are going to take Jane to see Mrs Oldland's[15] Aloes in long-promised bloom; that will supply the element of excitement wh: she seems to need and require rather urgently. You do not seem to have broken her in at all adequately. She wants to talk all day, and cannot be got to sit down to her book or Kerchief.

The Dr Will[16] call yesterday-morning went off admirably. He is a nice, reliable person, just a little less brilliant than Clem. but full of excellent talk. His wife Julia is indeed in the "sere and yellow leaf;"[17] She is surely advanced in to the vale of years much further than Muddie, though she wears hat and plumes and juvenile flowered gown. I give up to morrow morning as lost, for Parnell is coming, and at twelve o'clock sweet Millicent Wedmore has asked to come and say *goodbye.*[18] I severely refused any earlier hour than twelve; but Parnell comes as soon as the dew is dry.

Mother, like a barbarian, refuses to ask her to dine, but will give her sunstroke rather than bread. It has been very hot today; but every now and then latterly I have felt that little touch of consecrating chilliness that means the approach of the noble Autumn. Then my darling will grow better. The stable smell continues; Father tonight is going to see How,[19] and every effort is to be made to stop the nuisance. Some folks say we cannot get redress, because horse manure is not unhealthy. But we shall try.

Will Sturge examined our Etruscan pot, and declares that it is genuine old work. That is a pleasing announcement.

Mother tries with Jane, but is wonderfully sturdy. The old friends are going a trot on to the downs, this Evening. I wonder you got on so well with Jane; she soon reduces me to mild inanity, she cares so little to listen, and her talk is of unknown people. Still I am industriously good to her.

Schopen:[20] advances; I have nearly done him for the first time, and have read a quarter of Ribot's French exposition. A great twofold love for Sat. and Sunday. Kisses, O my love,

Thy wife and P.

MS Eng. lett. c. 419 fols. 106^{r}–109^{v} BOD

1. Dated from previous annotated envelope.

2. The pot is a gift from KB. See letter 135. This interest in collecting pots probably explains their renewed friendship with Will Sturge, who was a collector of Etruscan vases (Sturge, *Reminiscences,* 95). See also letter 140.

3. KB fell ill in Oct. 1885. See letters 97 n. 5, 100, and 108.

4. *Canute/Cup* was published in Oct. 1887 (Treby, *MF Catalogue,* 31).

5. Given KB's illness and her common nickname of Little Hors, this may be a joke based on Rev. 6:8.

6. Probably publishers from George Bell and Sons, who were responsible for the new volume of plays.

7. *Paradise Regain'd,* 1.183–87 (Milton, 2.2:183).

8. The Scandinavian prophetess in *Canute.*

9. "The Tables Turned: An Evening Scene on the Same Subject," 15–16 (Wordsworth, 4:57).

10. *Canute* 3.4.45–54 (*Canute/Cup,* 49–50).

11. Frieda and Edward Girdlestone. See letter 18 n. 12. Possibly "woulding": an expression of ineffectual desire (*OED*); The postcard is untraced.

12. A leveret is a small animal without much meat (*OED*); EC may be asking if KB is lacking intellectual nourishment.

13. For Jane Scott, see letter 9 n. 3; the opening line of "May Janet" (Swinburne, 2:43).

14. Miss Rosa Baker is an elderly member of the Baker family. See Bridge, MS Eng. misc. d. 983 fol. 240. For Baker family, see letters 18 n. 11 and 22 n. 6. Miss Jane may be the cousin Jane mentioned in letter 11.

15. Untraced.

16. Dr. William Allen Sturge (1850–1919) was the elder brother of Carta and Dot. See Sturge, *Reminiscences,* 93–100; for Sturge family, see letter 31 n. 2. Later in the letter, Clement Young Sturge (1860–1911), with his noted sense of humor and accomplished mimicry, proves more entertaining than his sober, accomplished brother. See Sturge, *Reminiscences,* 119–23.

17. Julia Sturge née Sherriff (1846–1926) was Will Sturge's second wife. They married in July 1886. She was head of the Nursing Institute at Nice. See Sturge, *Reminiscences,* 93–100. In spite of EC's attribution of great age (*Mac.* 5.3.23; 807), Julia Sturge was the same age as KB.

18. Millicent Wedmore was the only child of Frederick Wedmore. For Wedmore family, see letter 57 n. 4. Parnell is untraced. It is possibly a nickname for a friend who shared the radical opinions of Charles Stewart Parnell (1846–91).

19. Probably a neighbourhood dispute.

20. Arthur Schopenhauer (1788–1860) believed that the highest point of human achievement was represented by art and aesthetic experience, and was particularly interested in the role of the individual in a world of suffering. Given EC's vocation, and her family's susceptibility to fatal cancers, EC would have found much to agree with in this work. See Janaway, introduction, 1–3; EC also refers to Théodule Ribot, *La Philosophie de Schopenhauer* (1885).

138. Edith Cooper, Annotated Envelope

The Potter's Wheel for the Persian Pussie.
August 8th. 1887.
Birdlip

MS Eng. lett. c. 418 fol. 143r BOD

139. Katharine Bradley, Letter to Edith Cooper

[Birdlip] | [Mon.,] 8 Aug. 1887

Private

Beginning. P. we should have walked together down the a beech path to Cranham, and heard the cattle-bell tinkle as we drew near to the sacred little spot. Again we saw the group of rustling aspens, the dark stacks of firewood;—the dove-cote, the little chill brook pottering among the stones,—the bright fragments of burnt earth, and orange and rose lights am[o]ng the stored up flower-pots in the yard—finally the old potter himself faithful to his wheel.—Creative—fashioning—reminding all men that nature must be pliant in the hands of art. P. I crossed the plank and got am[o]ng the great burdock-leaves, where I could hear the rustling of the stream. And there among the sturdy growths, I felt it was given to Michael to write "The Potter's Wheel"[1]—As "The Cup of Water" gets down to the well-springs of the heart—so "The Potter's Wheel" should touch the primal *Creative instincts of man*—the laying of his *hands to the clay*—his plastic power—the discipline of art—the fellowship it opens with God. The very heart of Michael ought to be in it and it should be full of the deep emotions behind labour and thought. A love-story there must be in it—but it must tell of the *artist's* passions and desires—deeper holier than the lover's—untouched by time. The story has not been given to me yet, but a fierce, gypsy girl came to me—begging from the woods—and I somehow felt that she—the potter (he must be young) and a miner; with sweet country-woman bringing balm to the scarred young hearts and their furnace-trials contained the elements of tragedy. Above—innumerable beech-leaves;—the wood ever present to "comfort and retrieve."[2]

Think P. the first great influence on man [is] His labour—especially when it is creative—think what the spinning-wheel was to the Greeks[3]—and the Potters Wheel has never been adequately touched. S. Paul only fumbled[4]—One cannot know *beginnings,* until one has entered into its mystery. *Keep this,* directed and safe. Don't read to Mother—if she is in a *[from header fol. 146r]* way to scold and lecture. *I cannot bear it;* but if she is sympathetic, and can see the wonderful possibilities of the subject—speak to her of it alone. "Open-gaze"[5] at it P. Dutch-picture the little scene on the brain. *Do not hack or wear yourself.* Yield not to vanity, and refuse *to go out in the Sun.* Love him the Young potter-*poet—and idealist.* There shall be no stooping to peasants' ways or language. Genius shall—of Heaven's favour—fashion the speech—also. Great strong English like the burdock-leaves.

Simurg.

August 8th. 1887

MS Eng. lett. c. 418 fol. 146r/v BOD

1. There is no surviving play based on this plot, but the sonnet "Life Plastic" was published in *WH* (1908).

2. In *FT,* King Robert promises "comfort and release" (4.5.166; *FT/WR/LL,* 88), although the king's intention is indeed to comfort and retrieve. KB suggests a role for the beech-wood similar to the feminized Earth in *WR,* benign rather than vengeful.

3. In death each soul must choose a new pattern from the spinning wheel in the lap of the goddess Necessity and be reincarnated, or respun, according to that pattern. See Plato, *Republic* 10.616–17, trans. Waterfield, 373–75.

4. Rom. 9:20–21.

5. "Open-gaze" may be an early version of the visual aesthetics articulated in the preface of *S&S* (1892): "The aim of this little volume is, as far as may be, to translate into verse what the lines and colours of certain chosen pictures sing in themselves; to express not so much what these pic-

tures are to the poet, but rather what poetry they objectively incarnate. Such an attempt demands patient, continuous sight as pure as the gazer can refine it of theory, fancies, or his mere subjective enjoyment" (*S&S,* v). For the relation of MF's "pure" gaze to the importance of sight in Matthew Arnold and John Ruskin, see Fraser, "Visual Field," 555–56.

140. Katharine Bradley, Letter to Edith Cooper

Birdlip | [Mon.,] 8 Aug. 1887

August 8th 1887. *Birdlip.*
We have seen the potter's wheel—the brown clay—taken in its aimless lumpdom, moulded, hollowed, turned, *touched*—the hand inexorable tender, the artist's throughout:—beholding I shuddered at predestination! Yet not the clay, but the potter has cause to complain; 7 long years Must he toil, ere with a thumb-pat he can curve a spout. Humble dairy-bowls we may be, and yet have Much to be grateful for: we are the fruit of skilled labour, over us Creative Art has lingered, curiously wrought by the Master Craftsman. Let us give thanks that we are severed from Ohaplessness,[1] that distinction has been given to us, that we are dimpled by the Divine finger-marks. Would you had been there! The spinning-wheel teaches of life, the potter's wheel of destiny—of how gratitude can grow up under the very shadow of doom. We all bear the art-mark enough: we should have been coffin-mould but for certain unearned selection—now see—we have a brim, we are bowls and goblets. Gloria tibi, Domine.[2]

At the sage green—and sunken blue and bonnie brown pots we stared, till at last the good old Devonshire woman cried "I give you 6 or 7 minutes more to decide." After that she signified she wd. probably bundle us out. I availed myself of the respite to get a pretty *cracked* piece for Persian cat—dull sage and blue. Amy's pretty little pig—your gift—and from us each a charming little bit for dear Nellie. Do you approve the home return on Monday?

My dress—I meant to scold you. *[bird symbol].*
Write Et Tu[3] at once. Miserable

MS Eng. lett. c. 418 fols. 144r–145v BOD

1. *Haplessness* is a rare word for "ill-starred fortune," or "unluckiness" (*OED*). It may be that the use of the prefix "O" is meant to provide emphasis.

2. Glory to thee O God (L.).

3. You also (L.).

141. Katharine Bradley, Annotated Envelope

Reigate | [Mar.] 1888

I have to give up the Cone!

MS Eng. lett. c. 418 fol. 151ᵛ BOD

142. Katharine Bradley, Letter to Edith Cooper

[Blackberry Lodge], Reigate | [Mar.] 1888[1]

Hush, My Love—the Heath is claret-dusk with the ling, and there are 6 noble fir-mounds, and at the foot of one (pace Mr. Sladen's uncle[2] peering at me from his Mansion) I pricked out in cones L H. for *Littel Horse;* but be not offended for, by and bye—I tried to write in the runnels of the silver sand P.P.—and so our royal poets' hunting-field is found[3]—where the wind incarnates in the pines. For P.—I began to fear this was a too-much be-cawed country—the rooks in their lofty elms convey a sense of parsonic solemnity to the groves—and I wanted a bit of earth where we might "sigh deep laugh free."[4] There is a real heath-path—as at Dartmoor leading up to the Mill,[5] and all the lines of the landscape are gracious, rippling, and free.

Here is a bit of ling, and I am going to smuggle in a tiny Cone.

Oh he is for the Country this Littel—the air, and the out-door life!

Tell dear little one Pussie was in the light this morning; and is getting quite a Reigate cat,[6] though they still have to watch the doors—the little teeth—*[from header fol. 149ʳ]* I hope you closed them tight on Helgar's han*d*![7] My Dear, dear! Take the hug as read—

the Littel

MS Eng. lett. c. 418 fols. 149ʳ–150ᵛ BOD

1. Dated from the family's move to Surrey in 1888.

2. Untraced.

3. KB is probably referring to *TM,* although at this time they would have been deeply into writing *LA.*

4. *Youth and Art,* 63 (Browning, 6:279). KB also used this quotation in letter 28.

5. The Mill is the ruined building on the bank of the West Dart where tin miners once worked. See Hemery, *High Dartmoor,* 415.

6. The family moved to Blackberry Lodge in Reigate in 1888 (Sturgeon, 31). In this case, KB may mean a real cat.

7. Untraced. Possibly a nickname.

143. Katharine Bradley, Annotated Envelope

Browning—1888

Add. MS 46866 fol. 248[r] BL

144. Katharine Bradley, Letter to Edith Cooper

[London] | [May 1888][1]

Private

Now darling I *must* pour out all in my heart about Browning—so hug me—and keep this to read to Muddie. He was more golden sweet than ever—and "no worse that you are here"—said the old Blessed. I verily believe it is one of the joys of his life to have any part of Michael with. His warm hand was upon my shoulder, or heart, caressing me constantly, and he kissed my brows at parting. He said—as he took me up to his study—"I hope you are satisfied with your success. I have found the admiration of the best judges—I care for no other—equal to my own." When I said we had got into great trouble over *The Cup*—he said "they have *stupidly, stupidly* misunderstood it."[2] He asked about the Sapphics;[3] and I said *you* had been writing some—"a bridal song, and I am jealous—it is better than mine"—but the old evidently thought that was my kind way of putting things*!!!* and believes *I* am the well-spring of the lyrics!!!!! Again he said "But are you writing any other tragedy. So I had to confess *Queen Mary*.[4]—I alluded to Swinburne; but he said "Your way of writing would be different from *his long screeds.*"

At the last when he begged us to write and tell him of our fortunes—I said "But M[r.] Browning you are the person to comfort with your doctrine *of failure —he did not at* all seem inclined to preach it and said—"But I hope *you* will succeed." You will rejoice to hear that he looked and seemed far brighter and younger than last time, is very well. Sir A. Clarke[6] says Browning is so scandalously well. When I asked him if he were writing any more poems for us—he said—Oh I shall die in harness, I could not help entreating "Oh, but not yet." "No, no, not yet"—he added cheerily to stop my pain.

It was just like going to see M[r.] Shakespere him self at New Place. The Littel *[from header fol. 259[r]]* Must now eat. He has had no dinner for 2 days, and feels accordingly. *The Littel*

Your Love

Thy littel Hors!

[from footer fol. 260^r] He was very pleased with your messages.

Add. MS 46866 fols. 259^r–260^v BL.

1. Dated from the *Athenaeum's* review of *Cup.*

2. Browning was delighted with *Cup,* writing to them of its "subtle truth" and beautiful expression (Add. MS 46866 fol. 108^v BL). Oscar Wilde also reviewed *Cup* favorably (*Woman's World,* Feb. 1888, 275–79). However, most reviewers found the play's endorsement of an extramarital liaison "unnatural" coming from an author now known to be female. See *Spectator* 16 (1887): 1538. KB noted that the *Atheneum's* review was "full of quite curious spite" (Add. MS 46777 fol. 7^r BL).

3. *LA* (1889) includes two bridal songs: "No other girl—O bridegroom, thou art right—" (*LA,* 67–68) and "Dear Bridegroom, it is spring" (*LA,* 80).

4. *TM,* a play based upon the life of Mary, Queen of Scots, was published in 1890; Swinburne had already treated the subject in his trilogy: *Chastelard* (1865), *Bothwell* (1874), and *Mary Stuart* (1881).

5. Browning's "La Saisiaz" notes, "Only grant a second life, I acquiesce / In this present life as failure" (258–59; Browning, 14:185).

6. KB's own doctor, Sir Andrew Clark. See letter 105 n. 5.

145. Katharine Bradley, Letter to Edith Cooper

[London] | Sun., [1889][1]

Sunday afternoon

sola, sola, sola![2]

Dearest,

Only conceive of it—A temperance sermon this morning from Stopford[3]—told the Hors to abstain from eating another oat—on my return Amy[4] found too ill to come to dinner! Alone, alone I ate my fowl—my cream, my sweets. All alone and curled up I studied this afternoon My Shakespere Sonnets (Introduction) and Selections from Swinburne—where I read of My Helen of Troy—Mary the Queen.[5]

But my heart is dark with grave-thoughts and the dripping rain—and the last time I was here—when I returned with the living Mud to Kiss[6]—Oh wan, sweet face—though loved so fondly—loved it now seems not enough!

Come, Pussie, if you are well, and the day not hopeless; if I find you not—I shall come home by the 11.1. train reaching Redhill 12.12. I go on loving Puss, as fast as the wheat grows in Spring. I never stop one minute. This morning in the Cup of Coldwater Chapel[7]—I thought—how, it may be, as the night falls on the busy peoples of Paradise—quiet souls may creep away—and standing on the threshold of our Father's house, think in the porch-shadow—of the welcome to be one day there. Let us make a tryst of meeting in spirits thus, Big Boo.[8] Little Hors will have to think about his sins, and the nice virtues thy've grown into, besides, doubtless, being Much bothered with Apostles; but, when the stars come out, and you Know they do: they are not on the floor, but all right in the sky above the porch—*then* he will think of the τεκνον[9] or Child to whom—wherever God may put him—the whole current of his being sets. Is it not serious?—five oclock, and no summons from poor Amy. She is just as kind and trusting as ever—and very fair—my lady of the golden eye-lids!!!

Give my love to Morin—and tell him I thought of My two, at my solitary dinnertime.

A kiss for you each one

Your own Simmy.

Boo—travel with *Mary* Warren[10]—I shall be in time to meet you; but if I were a minute after ten, go straight into the 1st. class general waiting-room Charing Cross.

K.

MS Eng. lett. c. 418 fols. 152r–153v BOD

1. Dated from the death of Emma Cooper in Aug. 1889.

2. "Alone, alone, alone!" (It.) Shakespeare's clowns use the cry to attract attention: for example, *MV* 5.1.39.

3. Stopford Brooke (1832–1916) seceded from the Anglican church to preach liberal theology and to write poetry and literary criticism. See Standley, *Stopford Brooke,* 23–26. His sermons at Bedford Chapel in Bloomsbury were often on literary or socialist themes, and drew a secular crowd from across London. See Jacks, *Life & Letters of Stopford Brooke,* 2:450.

4. Probably Amy Bell. See letter 8 n. 2.

5. KB was probably reading R. H. Stoddard's edition of *Selections from the Poetical Works of A. C. Swinburne* (1884). Mary Stuart was often depicted in nineteenth-century plays as so beguiling that men would risk all for her. See Taft, "Tragic Mary," 266–67. KB's use of the possessive in claiming Mary as "my Helen of Troy," recalls Swinburne's Rosamond, who identifies herself with a female archetype that stretches from Helen to Guenevere: "The face caught always in the story's face" (255–56; Swinburne, *Rosamond: A Play,* 7:212). In reply to Swinburne, MF's Mary reads Helen as neither femme fatale nor archetype, but as a misread queen, the "clay" and "live creature" being entirely distinct (*TM* 5.3.16–50; 215–16).

6. Emma Harris Cooper died of cancer on 20 Aug. 1889. While the death was devastat-

ing, it was also liberating. EC later confessed, "She did not understand my need of freedom, she bound and overawed me where I wanted to be free and personal. Such an influence is a crime against me" (Add. MS 46780 fol. 13[r] BL).

7. Brooke's Bedford Chapel.

8. A rare nickname.

9. Child (Gk.).

10. Mary Isabel Warren née Brodie. She married [Sir Thomas] Herbert Warren in 1886, shortly after he became president of Magdalen College, Oxford (*DNB 1922–1930*). Mary Sturgeon drew upon Herbert Warren's undergraduate recollections of the poets in her biography (Sturgeon, 22).

146. Katharine Bradley, Letter Card to Edith Cooper

[En route to Canterbury] | PM Sat., 8 Oct. 1892

Dearest and Best, We pause at the respected town of Chatham—ah no—we go on—My Sweet I trust by this time is at Durdans,[1] curled up on its lonely little hearth. Oh Henry, οπαις[2]—*ME*—me thou burnest. I *have* a fearful accès to Henry. I feel quite lonely and unprotected without the little boy. Dearest, I am now going to read of these other 2.—whom mysterius Fate means to make our partners—in other words I am going to push into the black bag for Mary's letter.[3]

Hennie [do] not do Carloman[4]—Hennie write of Lady Seaton's[5] just 2 years ago—the thick fog, the bewildering worldliness, then the luminous face—Soul striking against soul.

I think of writing of carrying in the roses—that first bridal-gift to you—without jealousy only with joy. My dear Henry, it, is quite dark. If Amy is not there, I will never go to the Cold Water cure!

Thy own *[from header]* Love, *Litel*

MS Eng. lett. c. 418 fol. 154[r], BOD

1. In Mar. 1890 the family moved to Durdans, Wray Park Road, in Reigate, Surrey. Charles Ricketts described Durdans as "a typical, comfortable English home" modified by Morris curtains and wallpapers and photos of Italian paintings. See Ricketts, *Michael Field,* 1.

2. Inexperienced boy (Gr.). After 1891 the name "Henry" eclipsed "Persian Puss" as EC's principal nickname. It derives from EC's stay in the Dresden fever hospital in Aug. 1891 for scarlet fever: a German nurse developed "a terrible, fleshly love" for EC, kissing her passionately, and naming her "little Heinrich" when her hair was cut boyishly short (*W&D,* 62–63). KB anglicised this to Henry (Sturgeon, 27).

Bernard Berenson, 1887. (Berenson Archive, reproduced by permission of the President and Fellows of Harvard College)

3. Untraced. These two are Bernard Berenson (1865–1959) and Mary Costelloe née Smith, later Berenson (1864–1945). Berenson had a profound influence on the Michael Field relationship. They met the young art historian in Paris in Jun. 1890 and attended his talks at the Louvre (Add. MS 46778 fol. 134$^{r/v}$ BL). Meeting again in Aug. 1890 (Add. MS 46778 fols. 102^{v}–103^{r} BL) and Feb. 1891, Berenson flirted with EC, playfully comparing himself to the faun of *Call.* (Add. MS 46779 fol. 19^{v} BL). By 1892 a triangle had developed: EC was in love with Bernard; Bernard with the married Mary Costelloe; Mary was initiating divorce proceedings to marry Bernard. See Samuels, *Bernard Berenson,* 1:140–43. In this letter KB and EC have returned from a tortuous stay in Paris with Berenson and Costelloe, after which EC wrote: "From that moment my life can be expressed in two words—infatuation and wounds" (Add. MS 46780 fol. 112^{r} BL). For further discussion of the Berenson-Field relationship, see Vicinus, "Sister Souls."

4. "Carloman" is a play based on the son of Charles Martel, who renounced his family and position to become a monk. It was published posthumously as *NT* in 1918. Adolphus William Ward sent them the idea for the play (Add. MS 46785 fol. 12^{r} BL). For Ward, see letter 101 n. 3.

5. On 14 Aug. 1890 KB and EC attended an "At Home" held for the American novelist Louise Chandler Mouton (1835–1908) by Lady Seton, where they first saw the "luminous" face of young Bernard Berenson. His conversation revitalized the gathering for them. EC wrote that he "glowed, with eyes that hide their light and then scintillate like an aspiring rush of flame, at the name of Timoteo Vite" (Add. MS 46778 fol. 103^{r} BL).

147. Katharine Bradley, Letter Card to Edith Cooper

Canterbury | [Sun.,] 9 Oct. 1892

The Silent Pool[1]—Canterbury October 9th. My Sweet,

It is just the day for Ethelbert,[2] Virginia creeper, and Cathedral courts—I pace and pace. In church I was thinking of Becket and his dramatist[3]—then I nearly laughed to think of P. writing—"thou burnest us"[4]—While the historic fowl lingered in his pew.

There is a service to-morrow in wh. "the old buffs"[5]—some flags, are going to be laid finally to rest in the church. I think at the thought—*I go.* (I am writing in my bedroom with a fire, and on a writing-table I have forced them to supply me with!! Amy is visiting Elsie[6]—we are to meet in Cathedral for even. service. Oh my Big-hearted One—Oh my Large Loving Boy—Good night!

Michael

MS Eng. lett. c. 418 fol. 155r BOD

1. The Silent Pool, or Sherbourne Pond, was made famous in Martin Tupper's *Stephan Langton, or The Days of King John. A Romance of the Silent Pool* (1858). See also "The Silent Pool at Albury," *Times,* 20 Aug. 1902.

2. KB may be planning a play about St. Ethelbert, the first British king to convert to Christianity (Baring-Gould, *Lives of the Saints,* 2:406–9). No play was published.

3. *Becket,* by Alfred, Lord Tennyson. EC called the play "twaddle." See EC, letter to Fanny Brooks, MS Eng. lett. e. 143 fol. 79r BOD. Tennyson died on 6 Oct. 1892, and KB would attend the funeral in Westminster Abbey on 12 Oct. (Add. MS 46780 fol. 140r BL).

4. Possibly from an early draft of "Carloman."

5. The Old Buffs are the third East Kent Regiment, and St. Michael's Chapel in Canterbury Cathedral is known as the Buff's Chapel. See Woodman, *Architectural History* 176. On 7 Aug. 1886, the *Times* noted the presentation to the regiment of a new flag by Prince Albert Victor of Wales. See "Presentation of Colours," 7 Aug. 1886. This service probably involved placing new colors in the regiment's spiritual home, where they still hang.

6. Amy Cooper; for Elsie Reith, see letters 125, 133, 134.

148. Edith Cooper, Annotated Envelope

A Letter and a Letter-Card sent from My Love at Watford
Feb. 1893
(*Carloman* grows—Act II done)

MS Eng. lett. c. 418 fol. 156r BOD

149. Katharine Bradley, Letter Card to Edith Cooper

[Euston Station, London] | [PM Wed., 18 Jan. 1893]

Euston.[1] Very comfortable—after tea.

This is to give my Love, my Euston love.—It makes me fierce to think of Gabè[2] enjoying thee to the core. Amy and I have been grieving over poor Isabel's abortive visit.[3]—But it comes of seeking happiness under impossible environment. For poor little Bell[4] exception had to be made—but why I demand should we all suffer *horribly* for 3 days—in friendships name. Apply the ethics of the Modern to friendship. Henry—every one of whose *long, slim* little locks I love—awake to-morrow to be loved—awake, awake!—I have the pressure of the Mystic ring[5] on my finger, and there is another on my dear Love's Capable hand. Hennie, my man, write Carloman.[6] It is deliciously mild. Cheer up Hennie, for I am getting stronger every day. We will yet do something for the men and women among whom we live and breathe, God helping us the *[from header fol. 157r]* dear Lamb (Female)

Friday night—c/o Miss Seawell[7]

14G· Port-man. Mansions.

Baker St. W.

Do look in my case or box If Isabel's letter could be found.

MS Eng. lett. c. 418 fol. 157r/v BOD

1. Written en route to Watford. David Reith became Vicar of St. Andrew's Church in Watford in 1892 (*Who's Who).*

2. "Gabè" may be short for "Gabriel Meadow" or "Gabriel Maine," the pseudonyms proposed for Berenson and Mary Costelloe for their catalogue of artwork of Hampton Court. See Add. MS 46779 fol. 58r BL. The more accurate form would be "Gabé."

3. Marian Isabelle Wedmore (1857–96): Isabel or Bella was an early Bristol friend. See letter 57 n. 4. By 1895 KB noted Isabel's "wild passion" for EC, and described the "wolfish leanness on her face as if mad harass had thinned it . . . she treads on the quick of her own soul whenever she speaks" (Add. MS 46783 fol. 11r BL). KB was asked to edit Isabel Wedmore's papers when she died in 1896, but the MS "Beads" was returned to her brother, Cecil, in April 1923 (Cecil Wedmore, letter to Thomas Sturge Moore, 4 Apr. 1923, MS Eng. lett. e. 31, fol. 122r BOD). Wedmore cryptically noted that death had "removed the cause" for its remaining unpublished (letter to Thomas Sturge Moore, 22 Apr. 1922, MS Eng. lett. e. 31, fol. 112v BOD).

4. Amy Bell. See letter 8 n. 2.

5. There are no further details on this mutual gift, however, rings were exchanged in 1897 and 1899 (Add. MS 46786 fol. 96v–97r BL; Add. MS 46788 fol. 6v BL).

6. EC did throw herself into writing *NT,* with KB noting on her return that two acts had been completed (Add. MS 46781 fol. 5r BL).

7. Mary Seawell (MS Eng. lett. d. 402 fol. 180r BOD).

150. Katharine Bradley, Letter to Edith Cooper

[Canterbury] | Fri., [20 Jan. 1893][1]

Friday morn.
My Love,

I am pierced with joy. It is inconceivable Act II. finished? Forbid it, little gods—I feel an old woman "Spectatorial" of these Vast things. Henry, plunge me in Carloman—let him come forth wild and free—having found in the darkness the truth—that God is not in it, nor in what it stands for—not in the convent, but in the world, waiting to be made flesh in men. Henceforth Carloman recognises and receives the God in himself—but he is mad to go forth—He tells this out simply and genuinely to the Prior and the brethren—in a glorious, heretical, rhythmic speech.[2] The brethren gather round him with burning hearts. He draws men to leave the convent, as S. Dominic drew them to leave their homes. Damiani alone keeps his brain in the strait path . . [.] To calm the tumult he sends Carloman to work with Rachis:—hence use your scenario to end.[3] It is admirable.

But let the beginning be good. You will find bits of studies for a conversation between Marcomir and Campulus.[4] Campulus is the full cheery Monk the Littel would have been, bless him, if he had been in the clorister, with a great sense of the harvests, and the pleasure of labour, and *health*.

I cannot get Carloman into a sufficiently horrible and despairing state. Yet with regard to everything but his secret, and indeed because of his secret he would be most unhappy like an artist who at last has Vision of his picture—and everything is taken away from him[5]—Dear Littel cannot continue—Archie[6] is feeding him with *the Thing* and telling him about Billy's bill, and how the French are always slanging the English etc. etc.

My Pet—the man yesterday spoke of Grace.[7] He was a shy, quiet soul, like Carloman but less "éxalté." No one understood him—the Chairman frowned. I noticed through the replies of his humility—what sarcasm lurked. I think humble people are sarcastic—they have taken their own right place, and accepted the true limits of things—and they laugh a little bitterly at those who play antics. P. Congratulate me—I have been asked to go to Egypt with the very Rev[d.] and his wife.[8] Fancy that, Hedda,[9] dear! Everybody is very kind. I engage Briggs[10] to take me a great walk in a park. But I shall not be allowed to think of Henry! I shall hear about wars and rumours of wars[11] and late and early communion! My pretty Love, at once tell Father, *next Thursday* we shall be engaged for ...... Ghosts.[12] We are afraid Nellie Chizzola[13] may Choose that day.—It will be all right if Father Knows that day is pre-engaged.

My Pretty, I hope to come back to-morrow afternoon by train leaving 4.20.

Give my dear love to Morin—tell him we were in 4 omnibuses, 3 trains, and one cab yesterday—that we began with an abbey and ended with a chapter and yet I hope to return without having taken the veil—a pure lay woman. I must now go out—Oh my Pretty, my Love, Henry, My Boy!

My dearest stop!

—You shall not go on, or work late. *Do no work* to-morrow. I charge you. Do let me have a little plump boy.

—No states—or bad nights. Look at the photographs.

Your own fond love

Littel Lambie

MS Eng. lett. c. 418 fols. 158$^{r/v}$, 159$^{r/v}$, 160$^{r/v}$, 161$^{r/v}$ BOD

1. Dated from the production of *Ghosts,* 26 Jan. 1893.

2. *NT* 3.202–17 (47).

3. In the final act, the dying Carloman is imprisoned, but makes his peace before death and receives the blessing of St. Boniface.

4. Campulus the cheery monk does not exist in the final play. The opening scene is between Carloman and St. Boniface.

5. In act 5 Carloman repudiates his vows and returns to his palace to find his son dead, his wife a harlot, and his brother in a pact with the Pope. He is imprisoned and dies declaring, "There is no secret hid in life—illusion, / That is the great discovery" (5.205–6; *NT,* 91).

6. Probably Archie Holinsworth. See postcard 98 n. 2. The thing and Billy's bill are untraced.

7. Possibly an Anti-Vivisection Society meeting, as in letter 133.

8. A postcard of camels in the PML collection reads, "This is Bistra, Lion" (MA 2092 unfoliated PML). While Bistra is in Algeria, this postcard probably dates from the same trip, and suggests the parents of Lucy (Lion) Fitzpatrick issued this invitation. Lucy Fitzpatrick (1869–1957) was a close friend of Alys Russell née Pearsall Smith (Mary Berenson's sister). She was nicknamed "Lion" for her black hair, and later married Robert Phillimore. See Russell, *Selected Letters,* 44 n. 1.

9. Henrik Ibsen published *Hedda Gabler* in 1890, and EC listed Edmund Gosse's English translation in their "Books read—1891." See Add. MS 46779 fol. 163^{v} BL. KB's use of "Hedda" here may be an adaptation of the more common nickname "Hennie," or it may be that KB is making an elliptical comment on the resemblance between General Gabler and the imperious and intractable widower James Cooper. Family tensions were building in the house and would erupt in late Feb., with Cooper demanding that KB leave. Faced with losing his daughter as well, Cooper did not enforce the eviction. See Add. MS 46781 fol. 19$^{r–v}$ BL.

10. Untraced. Possibly the coachman.

11. Matt. 24:7. British-occupied Egypt was politically unstable throughout the period. There

had been a massacre of European nationals during Arabi Pasha's insurrection of 1882. See "The Situation in Egypt," *Times,* 21 Feb. 1895. This may be why the Fitzgeralds ultimately chose Algeria.

12. KB attended a private production of Henrik Ibsen's *Ghosts* at the Athenaeum theater on 26 Jan. 1893 (Add. MS 46781 fol. 3[v] BL). Doubtless, the success of this performance by J. T. Grein's independent theater had an impact on the poets' expectations when Grein offered to produce *A Question of Memory.* The play, presented on 27 Aug. 1893, was a humiliating experience for the women. See Add. MS 45852 BL, and Macdonald, "Disillusioned Bards."

13. EC sent Nellie Chizzola a letter on 12 Jan. 1892 in commiseration for the death of her husband (Add. MS 46780 fol. 12[v] BL).

151. Katharine Bradley, Letter to Edith Cooper

[Durdans] | [Fri.] 1 Jan. 1897

Thank God for Babes![1] New Year's Day 1897.
With apologies to Michael Field

MA2092 fol. [14[r]],[2] PML

1. Queen Elinor's speech from *FR* begins "Thank God for boys!" (3.1.129) (*Call./FR* 151).

2. As the letters from PML are uncatalogued and unfoliated, I have provided a provisional numbering.

152. Edith Cooper, Annotated Page

Master's[1] beloved Letters from Hastings in February 1897.[2]

MA2092 [1[r]], PML

1. A nickname for KB. See letter 153 n. 3.

2. KB is in Hastings with Amy Bell. See Add. MS 46786 fol. 15[r] BL. For Amy Bell, see letter 8 n. 2.

153. Katharine Bradley, Letter to Edith Cooper

[London] | [Mon., 22 Feb. 1897][1]

Private
University Club for Ladies,[2] 47 Maddox St. W.
Feb 1897.
My Merle,[3]

This is my first letter! I am terribly self conscious—I quiver . . . I want My Merle!

Let me tell you the character of our club is Changing. There are ladies here who drink beer for lunch.

Being half-drunk with *good* claret, I naturally resent this!

Listen, Merle. I have secured a good, central dress circle—(a return the liars say!) and behold I go in my singleness, to Court.[4]

Like Solomon,—I feel like a little child, I know not how to go out, or how to go in[5]—I do not stay to inquire whether this has anything to do with the claret.

In any case I have had a long talk with Ricketts clerk[6] on asylums for the aged. We agree all men should retire at 60 to give the young a chance. They should be provided plentifully with Tobacco.[7] Merle, my Merle! I drink to thee in the black cup.

Thou—o my Love! *Michael.*

[from header (24^r)] No fear if I am not home till ten; if I saw the Mauds[8] and they asked me to tea—par example.

MA2092 [24^r–25^v], PML

1. Dated from PM on the envelope embossed UC [26^v]. Petals were sent with this letter; their marks remain visible on the paper.

2. KB was made a special member of the Ladies' University Club in Dec. 1891. See Add. MS 46779 fol. 146^r BL. EC described the club as "a modest, refined little London home for us—Morris papers and furniture, excellent magazines, writing cabinet, dressing-room, lunch-room, pleasant housekeeper" (fol. 146^r).

3. In the small collection of PML letters, KB and EC develop a new pair of names: Master (as in letter 156) and Merle. The *OED* notes that "merle" is a poetic name for the blackbird, but the Master-Merle combination may indicate a private joke regarding Henry James's sinister Madame Merle in *The Portrait of a Lady* (1881).

4. The Court Theatre presented a series of matinee performances of *Mariana* in Feb. 1897. This "gloomy and tragic story of passion and feminine caprice" was inspired by Ibsen, and written by the Spanish playwright Echegaray, with Elizabeth Robins taking the lead role. It traced the tragic story of a woman in love with the son of the man who seduced and betrayed her mother. See "Court Theatre," *Times,* 23 Feb. 1897.

5. I Kings 3:7.

6. KB and EC met Charles Ricketts and Charles Shannon in 1892 (Sturgeon, 37). A close relationship developed between the two couples both privately and professionally. Michael Field contributed to their magazine, the *Dial,* and the Vale Press published several Michael Field volumes with Ricketts providing illustrations. Ricketts's clerk, Charles John Holmes (1868–1936) had been working as a bookkeeper at Ballantyne Press when Ricketts offered him the job of managing the Vale Press (Legge, *Affectionate Cousins,* 97). Delaney credits Holmes with the financial solvency of the Vale Press (*Charles Ricketts,* 106). In 1893 Holmes founded the Studio, which introduced the work of Aubrey Beardsley, and in 1904 he was elected Slade Professor of Fine Arts

at Oxford. He was later knighted for his work as Director of the National Portrait Gallery and the National Gallery (*Oxford DNB*). EC described Holmes as "a good, good-tempered creature with a native gift of fun" (Add. MS 46787 fol. 127ʳ BL).

7. Tobacco was, after all, the original Bradley family business (Sturgeon, 14).

8. There is a single reference to a visit by Mary Maud in the journal for 1896, but whether this is a nickname or an actual name is unknown. See Add. MS 46785 fol. 99ʳ BL.

154. Katharine Bradley, Postcard to Edith Cooper

[Hastings] | [Wed.,] 24 Feb. 1897

Feb 24, 1897

Past *3* Bridges—but there are none between me and my Boy. Every one has the influenza and there is an east wind. The one topic of conversation is the murder.[1] But there are 4 angels round my bed—one in each corner—and one an elderly, male angel—not too strong!! He wears spectacles; if he turned Restive, I could dash these inward.

The sky is lightsome and pleasant.

Eastbourne Here I have seen a sea-mew with Henry!

Here are the downs that have made me mo[o]dy even as little waves—

θαλαΤΤα![2]

O Henry.

MA2092 [13ʳ], PML

1. On Thurs., 11 Feb. 1897, Miss Elizabeth Camp was found murdered in a railway compartment when her train arrived at Waterloo Station ("Murder in a Railway Carriage," *Times,* 13 Feb. 1897). "The Railway Murder" was reported in detail over the next week, exciting a high level of interest and public debate on the safety of railway travel (*Times,* 19 Feb. 1897; Blomfield Jackson, letter to the editor, 16 Feb. 1897).

2. The sea (Gk.).

155. Katharine Bradley, Letter to Edith Cooper

[Hastings] | [Feb. 1897][1]

My Merle,

Good-night! I am wild and lonely in my little back-bedroom. All genial stars settle round my Merle! I lie inland looking towards the Boy! Nighty, nighty! Heaven be with 'oo.

Morning
—The birds do not sing here "hey, ding-a-ding-ding."[2]—The salt has got into their little throats—a bird must sing inland.
—At my lonely breakfast I look forth on the ravening sea. Alas! The pier, just opposite, a big bone sticking in the monster's throat.

Grey rawness and wind; but all my flesh rises up to welcome the Infinite,—the 24 hours' cure is being wrought in me, and home, on Heaven's wings to l[ove] to-morrow.

I was nuda-nudissima[3] when the maid brought thy jewel-letter to my door.

—This is the first of my letters for which a casket of infinite price[4] must be bought—Amy's bell rings—I *rush* forth to post this. I *must* have a minute alone by the sea.

By this time thou hast received —

Hennie! My All-one
Michael.

MA2092 [21r/v, 22r/v], PML

1. Dated from KB's trip to Hastings in Feb. 1897.
2. *AYL* 5.7.21–22.
3. Bare, uncovered or destitute (L. or It.).
4. *MV* 3.2.193–95.

156. Katharine Bradley, Letter to Edith Cooper

[Hastings] | [Feb. 1897][1]

Darling,

We have been having great fun in Chairs, being wheeled about: but it is cold, and I have no more peace. Don't attempt to meet me to-morrow my own Love.—I am so much better, and Stronger—but all will be undone—if you don't keep well.

Remember there is no br*a*ndy in our room now.—But have a *little* with good hot water, if cold.

—I can write or feel no more poetry now I am anxious.

Hennie, my Boy! You will make me swear never to leave you—And then I shall have no more letters—and I love my *[from header (3r)]* letters.

Thy own dearly lvg
Timmie Hors[2]—

Thy Master.
Hennie!

MA2092 [3r/v], PML

1. Dated from KB's trip to Hastings in Feb. 1897.
2. A variation on KB's nickname "Littel Hors."

157. Katharine Bradley, Letter Card to Edith Cooper

[Hastings] | [PM Thurs., 25 Feb. 1897]

Dearest, All this outer leaf I shall spend in anger and rage! I have just received thy 2 post-cards. Sleepless and cold, sleepless *because* cold. Tell Amy to lie still and hot, and think she is a pie baking in the oven! You *must be kept warm:* it is dangerous for you to be cold. I am very grim—and shall send a wire.—I want to return, finding thee well.

Bless oo! My own love! *Simurg.*

MA2092 [2r], PML

158. Katharine Bradley, Annotated Envelope

[Hastings] | [PM Thurs., 25 Feb. 1897]

From M.F.
K. Had *no ink*!!

MA2092 [5r/v], PML

159. Katharine Bradley, Letter to Edith Cooper

[Hastings] | [Feb. 1897][1]

5, White Rock *Hastings*
Precious,

Thy dear second letter is just come!—I ordered Campion[2] posted on Wednesday *evening,* to greet thee this morning. This I hammered into "the Child of the Hour"[3]—I said—but no matter—thou hast these wave-riding ships, some on the crest, some in the trough! We love them together.

Hennie, I did clasp the teeth of my little-band this morning; and tried to tie a bow. Alas, it resembled, when complete a white, shaggy peony, drooping with heavy rain!

But when, by invitation, I went *in* to say Good-morning to Amy, *she admire[d]* it—So, Darling, has his reward.

Merle, your letters are *so* wonderful, they strike me silent. But my silence is the silence of the big sea, and a Kingdom in itself . . . Alack, I have no more gifts for Hennie—I like him to receive something every four hours[4]—but I give him in perpetual sacrament and Real Presence myself:—Believe in the real presence—oh verily!

Now we go out—a shopping! I fancy—No Battle—only Health—Good to love oo' Hennie, good to love oo' with. Hennie! My dearest! Farewell for a m[onth].
Michael.

MA2092 [16$^{r/v}$, 17$^{r/v}$], PML

1. Dated from KB's trip to Hastings in Feb. 1897.

2. *Fifty Songs by Thomas Campion* (1896). EC noted in "Works and Days" (24 Feb.) that the book came from Ricketts, and is decorated with "a flotilla of little ships on wave-lines with wave-crests here and there" (Add. MS 46786 fol. 14^{v} BL).

3. Richard Hengist Horne's poem "The Great Peace-maker: A Submarine Dialogue" depicts a dialogue between the sea and the spirit of man, which is personified in the recently invented telegraph. The telegraph is described as "the Child of the Hour," 293 (Horne, *Great Peace-Maker,* 32).

4. In Feb. 1897 KB wrote in "Works and Days": "Before noon I send by post roses to my Love. It is my purest pleasure. To choose them, to direct them, to spend on them—to impoverish for their sake? And to dream the imagined opening. Besides, they are what my love is like—a synonym for the universal equivalent, Eros, equivalent to Aphrodite. And they just smell sweet and the secret of their passion is smothered away in the heart of the beloved" (Add. MS 46786 fol. 15^{v} BL).

160. Katharine Bradley, Letter to Edith Cooper

Fri., [26 Feb. 1897][1]

Friday—*the Day*[2]
Merle,

This is to welcome to-day with thee.

In bed—, I kissed thee, printing my kisses on the lips of God. He will surely give them thee again.

The Master thine

MA2092 [11r], PML

1. Dated from KB's trip to Hastings in Feb. 1897.
2. Possibly her last day away from EC.

161. Katharine Bradley, Letter to Edith Cooper

[London] | [Wed., 17 Mar. 1897][1]

University Club for Ladies, 47, Maddox Street, W.
Now will I sing to My Beloved a song of My Beloved touching his hats.—He must have a fair Tuscan black against the face and trimmed with one of these *super-hu[man]* ribbons.

—I made my self base for thy sake, and put on the *Tam o'f Shanter*!—Very charmi[n]g also in colour, and canvas.

I have toiled for thee, nothing but thee since I came—Save a solitary pair of small shoes, necessary against Senlis.[2]

High in the dress-circle am I and bow to sit!

The jugged hare[3]—turns in the jug at sound of my name!

Blessings on the 4th. Act. and the—Carpet-beating and the shadows!!

The Master.

MA2092 [18r/v, 19r/v], PML

1. Dated from the PM on the envelope embossed UC [7v].
2. In May 1897 KB and EC traveled to Senlis in France to research the setting for *AR* (Add. MS 46786 fol. 62r BL). The new play was based on the life of Anne, the widow of the French King Henri I, who fell in love with Raoul in the forests of Senlis.
3. Jugged hare was a common farm dish: Isabella Beeton recommends frying the hare, then placing it in a tightly covered jar in a stewpot of water and boiling until tender (Beeton, *Book of Household Management,* 521). In listing her base attributes, KB seems to be saying that even the lowly jugged hare recognizes her.

162. Katharine Bradley, Calendar for Edith Cooper

1898

Bonne Année
1898 Henry . . . Sweet joy I call thee!

MS Eng. lett. c. 418 fol. 162r BOD

163. Katharine Bradley, Annotated Envelope[1]

For Field's Michael April 1899. *Old Ivories*

MA2092 [27^{r}], PML

1. This envelope with its black border is probably a remnant from the period of mourning following the death of James Robert Cooper in 1897.

164. Katharine Bradley, Draft of Poem Sent to Edith Cooper

Durdans | [Fri.] 21 Apr. 1899.

Old Ivories.

A window full of ancient things, and while,
Lured by their solemn tints—I crossed the street[1]
A face was there that in its tranquil style,
Almost obscure, at once remote and sweet[2]
Moved me by pleasure of similitude—
For, flanked by golden ivories[3] that face,
Her face[4] looked forth in even and subdued
Deep power, while all the shining, all the grace
Came from the passage[5] of Time over her,
Sorrow with time; there was no age, no spring;
On those smooth brows no promise was astir,
No hope outlived: herself a perfect thing,
She stood by that time-burnished reliquy
Simple as Aphrodite by the sea.

Field's Michael
Friday, April 21st 1899. Durdans![6]

MA2092 [unfoliated], PML, Published in *Wild Honey* (1908).

1. *WH:* street] street,
2. *WH:* sweet] sweet,
3. *WH:* ivories] ivories,
4. *WH:* face] face,
5. *WH:* passage] passing,
6. This poem was composed shortly before the household at Durdans was disbanded.

165. Katharine Bradley, Annotated Envelope

Important
Hennie!
Sweet, Sweet, Sweet, how sweet!

MA2092 [15$^{r/v}$], PML

166. Katharine Bradley, Letter to Edith Cooper

Paragon | [Mon.,] 19 Jun., 1899

Henry!
Paragon, Richmond Surrey.[1]
June 19$^{th.}$ 1899
A hundred pounds for my heart's joy,—and begone dull care.[2]
Michael.

MA2092 [4$^{r/v}$], PML

1. After Amy's engagement to John Ryan, Professor of Mechanics and Engineering at Bristol University College, KB and EC began looking for a new place to live. Ricketts and Shannon (letter 153 n. 6) found The Paragon, their "married home," on the banks of the Thames at Richmond (Sturgeon, 51; Add. MS 46788 fol. 74^{r} BL). Here, the two couples, the Poets and the Painters, met weekly to discuss art and literature, and to gossip. See Ricketts, *Letters,* 6–7. The Paragon is now The Bingham Hotel, Richmond.

2. EC wrote (20 June 1899), "I came home to find a strange letter that had not come through the post laid on the study table for me—£100 from my dear Love tenderly given, at sacrifice to herself, that the weight of my heavy expenses might be lightened. I had wings—clean, sweeping joy. Our little home wd. not have a corner's weight of debt in it—Beloved!" (Add. MS 46788 fol. 76^{v} BL).

167. Edith Cooper, Postcard with Note to Katharine Bradley

[Fri.,] 25 Dec. 1903

This stork hath left her lonely river[1]
To bless the Manor roof forever;
Hath left her willow and her reeds

To make a nest where kindness heeds;
With pillared feathers white to raise
A flag-staff of continual praise
For love she fondles with her love,
And peace that she sustains above.
Christmas 1903

MS Eng. lett. d. 407 fol. 207r BOD

1. Unpublished lyric. With this lyric is a picture of a stork (fol. 205r).

168. Katharine Bradley, Annotated Newspaper Cutting

[Mar. 1909][1]

Mr. Henry Le Strige Bramber Amice[2]
"eating and drinking"
scale of eating 60 sandwiches an hour. without ceasing!
Don't keep this[.] It is a moment's ornament.

MA2092 [8r], PML

1. This cutting is dated from the Retreat at the Convent of the Assumption, Mar. 1909.

2. This odd fancy corresponds with a note on the back of the "Order of the Day" for the Retreat at the Convent of the Assumption, Kensington Square:

Henry Le Strige Bramber Amice
Melcom Moffat Pertinax Linnet
Talla, Munierie, Mellinhail, Avalon,
Yulier, Merle, Ermenonville, Lapper (MA 2092 unfoliated)

KB and EC attended this retreat on 29 Mar. 1909, shortly after their conversion to Roman Catholicism in 1908. EC notes in the journal that they quarreled cruelly, but made up and went "tear-drenched to our pallet-beds" (Add. MS 46799 fol. 65r BL). It may be that this loving nonsense is KB's attempt to defuse the tension between herself and EC, and EC and her confessor, "Goss," whom Treby identifies as Edward Fitzgibbon (42).

"Mr. Henry LeStrige." Annotated newspaper cutting, ca. March 1909, MA2092. (The Pierpont Morgan Library, New York)

Textual Apparatus

Letter 2	line 2	[1st] to *supralinear addition*
	line 9	lose] lo~~o~~se
	line 23	black *supralinear addition*
Letter 3	line 5	July 3 1882 *supralinear addition*
Letter 4	line 8	? *supralinear addition*
	lines 12–13	deprecatingly] deprecating-ly
	line 14	worthless] worth-less
	line 17	namesake] name-sake
	line 21	befittingly] befitting-ly
	line 24	undergraduate] under-graduate
	line 27	uttermost] utter-most
	line 34	shimmering] ~~irradiating~~ ~
	line 36	once or twice *supralinear addition*
	line 37	never] ~~not~~ ~
	line 49	perfect] per-fect
Letter 5	line 12	consecrated] con-secrated
Letter 6	line 9	the wistful priest *supralinear addition*
	line 16	Winkelmann] Win~~c~~kelmann
	line 16	Tooke and] ~ ~~o~~and
	line 22	chaplet] ~ ~~i~~
Letter 7	line 4	receiving] re-ceiving
	line 16	beautiful] beaut~~y~~iful
	line 31	arm] ~~hand~~ *supralinear addition*
Letter 8	line 5	with his] ~ ~ ~~dress~~
Letter 9	line 15	that] ~ ~~wa~~
	line 24	fountain!] ~ ~~wa~~
	line 50	so] ~ ~~fiercely~~
Letter 10	line 2	only] on~~e~~ly
	line 22	photograph] photograph~~y~~
	line 32	immeasureable] "*e*" *supralinear addition*
Letter 11	line 3	is] ~ ~~as~~
	line 5	headache] head-ache

	line 11	Thus *supralinear addition*
	line 20	[2nd] at] ~ ~~&~~
	line 27	There] ~~The is~~ ~
	line 38	coarse] co~~u~~arse
	line 40	ruins] ~ ~~to~~
	line 40	in the midst] ~ ~ ~ ~~of the midst~~
	line 50	Ah] A~~O~~h
Letter 12	line 8	head] ~~brow~~ *supralinear addition*
Letter 13	line 3	[1st] the] t~~w~~he
	line 13	Pisano] Pis~~s~~ano
	line 15	one] one~~e~~
Letter 14	line 12	that *supralinear addition*
Letter 15	line 14	the] ~ ~~lovely~~
	line 21	beard *supralinear addition*
Letter 17	line 27	bows *supralinear addition*
Letter 18	line 7	desert] ~ ~~dese~~
	line 11	discipleship] disciple-ship
	line 14	spellbound] spell-bound
	line 16	before] ~~on~~ *addition in red ink*
	line 20	guards] ~ ~~is~~
	line 34	(!!!) *supralinear addition*
	line 36	or about *supralinear addition*
	line 38	practice,] ~ ~~to~~
	line 48	now] ~~N~~ ~
	line 48	Rome *supralinear addition*
	line 49	morning] morn-ing
	line 50	that] ~ ~~to~~
Letter 19	line 2	been] ~ ~~ord~~
	line 8	sensuousness] sensuous-ness
	line 16	and] ~ ~~obe~~
Letter 20	line 4	keep] ~~make~~ *supralinear addition*
	line 14	mansioned] man-sioned
	line 27	by] and *overwritten*
	line 31	lay] lay~~ed~~
	line 36	cypress] ~ ~~falling th~~
	line 38	Rome] ~~roam~~ *supralinear addition*

Letter 21	line 9	thoughtful] thought-ful
	line 9	cannot] can-not
	line 18	constantly] constant-ly
	line 22	[1st] it] ~~she~~ *supralinear addition*
	line 22	[2nd] it] ~~she~~ *supralinear addition*
	line 23	humours;] ~; ~~and~~
	line 27	divine,"] ~,' ~~if~~
	line 38	effigy] eff~~a~~igy
	line 43	beautiful] beau-tiful
	line 49	becoming] be-coming
	line 51	merely] ~~only~~ *supralinear addition*
	line 54	When] ~~I~~When
	line 54	I remembered] ~ ~~was~~ ~
	line 54	wrote] ~~S~~wrote
	line 56	Wordsworth] Words-worth
	line 57	love] ~ ~~of~~
	line 61	repetition] ~ ~~of~~
	lines 61–62	modern] ~~modr~~ ~
	line 66	everything] every-thing
	line 74	! *supralinear addition*
	line 75	post] post~~e~~
Letter 22	line 9	Frieda] Fr~~e~~ieda
	line 9	and enjoyed] ~~e~~and ~
	line 11	underwood] under-wood
	line 11	ivy] ~ ~~and~~
Letter 23	line 17	Gentleman] Gentle-man
	line 20	understanding] understand-ing
	line 20	bad as] ~ a~~i~~s
	line 30	wh.] ~. ~~by~~
	line 35	Boeotian] Boetian *added in purple ink*
	line 39	together] to-gether
	line 44	pius] piu~~is~~s
Letter 26	line 32	death] ~ ~~hath~~
	line 49	Sorrowing] ~~P~~ ~
	line 59	blue] ~~bliss~~ *supralinear addition*
	line 62	Erected] ~ ~~thus~~

	line 70	greets] greet *supralinear addition*
	line 79	Antiquity] ~~a~~Antiquity
	line 95	as] ~~for~~ ~
	line 98	your] ~~my~~ ~
Letter 28	line 21	What] ~~How~~ *supralinear addition*
	line 22	infinitely] in-finitely
	lines 30	old man of] ~ ~ ~~of Man of~~ ~ *supralinear addition*
	line 35	? *supralinear addition*
Letter 30	line 22	bashfulness] bash-fulness
Letter 31	line 6	us *supralinear addition*
	line 8	fostering] foster-ing
	line 23	wh.] ~~with wh.~~ *supralinear addition*
Letter 32	line 1	P.P.] ~~B~~ ~
	line 4	husband's] hus-band's
	lines 5–6	After the murder] ~~Macbeth's~~ ~ *supralinear addition*
	line 6	Macbeth's] ~~his~~ ~ *supralinear addition*
	line 8	common *supralinear addition*
	line 10	Queenly] ~~G~~Queenly
	line 16	those] ~ ~~corpsed~~
	line 17	do not] ~~never~~ *supralinear addition*
	line 19	that neither flash, nor blench, nor supplicate it seems *supralinear addition*
	line 21	branding] ~ ~~with torture irons afresh~~
	line 22	$5^{th?}$] ~~1~~$5^{th?}$
	line 30	have *supralinear addition*
	line 36	of *supralinear addition*
	line 38	curarizes] curari~~r~~zes
	line 43	Singer] ~~s~~Singer
	line 48	open] ~ ~~up~~
	line 52	anything] any-thing
	line 55	Be] ~~P~~Be
Letter 33	line 4	Brantwood] Brant-wood
	line 9	(?) *supralinear addition*
	line 17	mantelpiece] mantel-piece

	line 35	bookcase] book-case
	line 52	and I carefully explained I did *not. supralinear addition.*
Letter 35	line 2	sunlight] sun-light
	lines 3–4	primrose] prim-rose
	line 6	feathery] ~~Rainbow~~ *supralinear addition*
	line 6	clouds] clouds~~lets~~
	line 10	mountains] ~ ~~put~~
	line 10	earthliness] ~ ~~and put on glistering apparel.~~
	line 15	crests,— *supralinear addition*
	line 29	the Master *sublinear addition*
Letter 36	line 9	bedroom] bed-room
	line 10	room *supralinear addition*
	line 26	furniture *supralinear addition*
	line 38	unrefreshed] un-refreshed
Letter 37	line 19	feel] fill *overwritten*
	line 21	to] ~ ~~Holy Str~~
	line 44	lack" *supralinear addition*
	line 46	soil *supralinear addition*
	line 50	I found *supralinear addition*
Letter 38	line 5	beheld] ~~so~~beheld
	line 8	orchard's] or-chard's
Letter 39	line 3	because] be-cause
	line 23	ceaseless] cease-less
	line 23	-s of ocean *supralinear addition*
	line 23	appaled] appal~~l~~ed
	line 24	lapseless] lapse-less
Letter 42	line 1	Don't] ~~Dot~~ ~
	line 6	remaining] remain-ing
	line 8	bounteously] bounteous-ly
Letter 44	line 6	sentence.] senten~~s~~ce~~,~~.
	line 6	This] ~~t~~Th~~e~~is
	lines 22–23	abandoned] ~~forsak~~ ~
	line 27	stain] ~~star~~ ~
Letter 46	line 9	springing] spring-ing
Letter 47	line 3	rising] ~~towery~~ ~

	line 5	Tune] T~~t~~une
	line 28	crumbled] c~~h~~rumbled
	line 30	loll] ~~ton~~ ~
	line 31	enduring] ~~immutable~~ *supralinear addition*
	line 32	naked] ~~a bare~~ ~
	line 32	—in] ~~—with~~ ~ *supralinear addition*
	line 38	highest] ~~heighest~~ ~
Letter 48	line 2	and I and II *supralinear addition*
	line 4	guidebooks] guide-books
	lines 6–7	There . . . dead *marginalia*
	line 14	Home] ~ ~~all~~
Letter 49	line 7	? *supralinear addition*
	line 9	Only] On~~s~~ly
	line 11	distance] ~~his~~ ~
	line 13	Mount] M~~m~~ount
	line 15	up *supralinear addition*
	line 16	Stygian *supralinear addition*
	line 17	Night] N~~n~~ight
	line 20	subterranean] sub-terranean
	line 22	unhesitatingly] un-hesitatingly
	line 22	must] ~~much~~ *supralinear addition*
	line 27	sea] ~~e~~sea
	line 36	to Christ *supralinear addition*
	line 39	existence] existence~~,~~
	lines 39–40	dominant] domin-ant
Letter 50	line 17	Pretty] ~~p~~Pretty
	line 23	Salarino] ~~Celano~~ *supralinear addition*
	line 23	provoke] ~~be~~ ~
	line 26	tragic] ~~in~~tragic
Letter 52	line 5	de-individualizes] de-indiv-idualizes
	line 9	tourists] tour~~e~~ists
	line 11	sin] ~~fault~~ *supralinear addition*
	line 11	rebuke] re-buke
	line 12	pass] pa~~u~~ss
	line 18	landscape] land-scape
	line 19	neighbouring] neighbour-ing

	line 20	golden sights] ~~memories~~ *supralinear addition*
	line 25	especially] specially *supralinear addition*
	line 27	our] ~ ~~s~~
	line 27	Kieve] K~~e~~ieve
	line 29	of] ~~to~~ *supralinear addition*
	line 29	weeping] weep-ing
	line 30	garment] gar-ment
	line 32	drinking] ~ ~~it~~
	line 35	Tears] ~~t~~Tears
	line 39	behold] ~~see~~ *supralinear addition*
	line 40	Cornish] ~~c~~Cornish
	line 40	Cannae] ~~Cap~~ ~
	lines 41–42	dissipated] dis-sipated
	line 46	remarkable] remark-able
	line 48	rest] re~~S~~st
	line 58	eyrie] ~~eyrie~~ *supralinear addition*
	line 59	built] ~~build~~ *supralinear addition*
	line 60	claws] ~ ~~f~~
	line 64	while *supralinear addition*
	line 64	both] ~~wh:~~ *supralinear addition*
	line 64	warlike *supralinear addition*
	line 74	Nature] ~~n~~Nature
	line 74	monologue] mono-logue
Letter 54	line 12	the sky's] ~~Heaven's~~ *supralinear addition*
	line 13	and] ~~t~~ ~
	line 13	heaven] ~~sky~~ *supralinear addition*
	line 16	promnade] prom-nade
	line 21	freshened] ~~began to~~ ~
	line 21	in] ~~with the~~ *supralinear addition*
	line 23	true] ~ ~~e~~
	line 26	wet *supralinear addition*
	line 28	forming] ~~s~~ ~
	line 28	absolutely] ~~ol~~ ~
	line 28	unsurpassable] unsurpass~~ed~~able *"able" supralinear addition*
	line 28	contrast.] ~ ~~and~~

	line 28	We] ~~w~~We
	line 28	walked] ~~passed~~ *supralinear addition*
	line 30	borage,] ~, ~~whose~~
	lines 31–32	granite] ~, ~~the flowers of wh: ear-drops cut form the lapis lazuli, sapphire of the sky—hang in lovely ob[?] of ornament~~
	line 33	reached] ~~and~~ ~
	line 38	path] ~~way~~ ~
	lines 39–40	comfortable] com-fortable
	line 43	the] ~ ~~dear~~
	line 44	mode] m~~a~~ode
	line 44	and] ~ ~~han~~
	lines 53–54	lingeringly] linger~~l~~ingly
	line 59	*Bridge*] ~~*b*~~*Bridge*
	line 65	sunset] sun-set
	line 66	goldened] ~ ~~w~~
	line 66	Then] ~~Twilight~~ ~ *supralinear addition*
	line 67	face] ~ ~~seen~~
	line 67	dagerreotype] dagerotype *"r" supralinear addition*
	line 71	hotel] hot~~a~~el
Letter 56	line 8	(of the north) *supralinear addition*
	line 17	passionflowers] passion-flowers
	line 18	were] ~~were~~ ~
	line 22	resting] ~~restlin~~ ~
	line 24	apple-green,] ~, ~~and~~
	line 29	rocks] ~ ~~are~~
	line 29	swarthy—] ~— ~~but~~
	line 29	leperously] ~ ~~with~~
	line 31	was *supralinear addition*
	line 35	causeth] ~~caut~~ ~
	line 37	despondency] ~~e~~despondency
	line 38	glow] ~~lights~~ *supralinear addition*
Letter 58	line 4	been *supralinear addition*
	line 27	converted] con-verted
Letter 60	lines 5–6	cressets] cre~~e~~ssets
	line 9	low] ~~low~~ ~

	line 15	on *supralinear addition*
	line 16	then *supralinear addition*
	line 16	like] ~ ~~molten~~
	line 16	inward, *supralinear addition*
	line 17	And] ~~a~~And
	line 17	wh: *supralinear addition*
	line 18	such *supralinear addition*
	line 18	water] ~~Sea~~ *supralinear addition*
	line 19	scenes] ~~sights~~ ~
	line 22	like] ~ ~~cindered~~
	line 22	gigantic *supralinear addition*
	line 22	sanded] ~ *indecipherable deletion*
	lines 22–23	hearth-stone *supralinear addition*
	line 23	-shore *supralinear addition*
	line 24	mouldy] mould~~e~~y
	line 25	however Colours] ~ ~~the spirit of e~~ ~
	line 25	are] ~~is~~ *supralinear addition*
	line 29	the rocks] ~~they~~ *supralinear addition*
	line 30	exquisitely *supralinear addition*
	line 35	closed] ~ ~~clo~~
	line 37	magic] ~~mage~~ ~
	line 38	worn *supralinear addition*
	line 39	ocean] ~~sea~~ *supralinear addition*
Letter 62	line 2	morning] morn-ing
	line 12	the] ~ ~~our~~
	line 29	and] ~ ~~going on~~
	line 30	might be] ~~was~~ *supralinear addition*
	line 32	night.] ~. ~~Of cour~~
	line 32	combined] com-bined
	line 37	speech *supralinear addition*
	line 39	language] lang~~r~~uage
	line 41	such] ~~the be~~ *supralinear addition*
Letter 63	line 4	understand] under-stand
	line 7	renewed] re-newed
	line 8	our] ~~to~~ ~
	line 11	betouristed] be-touristed

	line 13	unable] ~~the~~ ~
	line 16	[1st] her] ~~are~~ *supralinear addition*
	line 24	doom] ~~de~~ ~
	line 24	her *supralinear addition.*
Letter 66	line 7	leaves] ~ ~~eve~~
	line 17	etc! *supralinear addition*
	line 26	how] ~~a~~how
	line 27	somebody's] some-body's
	line 28	! *supralinear addition*
	line 30	hair] ~~t~~hair
	line 32	from] ~ ~~a~~
	line 38	sorrows] s~~t~~orrows
Letter 67	line 14	none] no~~t~~ne
	line 27	[1st] the] ~ ~~sw~~
	line 28	read] ~~retu~~ ~
	line 33	Shield] ~~s~~Shield
	line 34	uncompromising] uncom-promising
	line 36	of the person *supralinear addition*
	line 37	wet-nurses] wet-~~nour~~ nurses
Letter 68	line 12	reception] recep-tion
	line 14	beautiful] ~~charming~~ *supralinear addition*
	line 16	Delft] ~~d~~Delft
	line 28	président,] prés~~i~~dent,
	line 39	wholesome] whole-some
	line 51	His] ~~h~~His
	line 54	her,] ~, ~~going~~
	line 69	work,] ~, ~~of lu~~
	line 79	the] ~ ~~lips~~
	line 85	So no fears,—*Expect* a telegram *supralinear addition*
Letter 69	line 5	meal *supralinear line*
	line 6	circle] ci~~l~~rcle
	line 8	sailing] s~~l~~ailing
	line 11	stimulating] ~ ~~;~~
	line 11	Stopford] ~~Sp~~ ~
	line 14	Wentworth] Went-worth

	line 15	delighted] de-lighted
	line 26	mental *supralinear addition*
	line 32	*David first speaks upside down*
Letter 71	line 4	then] then~~n~~
	line 13	my] m~~a~~y
	line 18	runaway] run-away
Letter 73	line 7	for] ~~o~~for
	line 11	my] ~~my~~ ~
	line 17	beautiful] beau-tiful
Letter 74	line 19	secresy] ~ ~~With passion?—ho!~~ *on verso in red ink*
	line 25	shorelines] shore-lines
	line 25	its] ~~his~~ *supralinear addition*
Letter 76	line 2	beata] beat~~ur~~a
	line 6	[*2nd*] the] ~~n~~the
	line 13	indefaticably] in-defaticably
	line 17	morsels] mor~~e~~sels
	line 18	*complete*] *com-plete*
	line 18	*complete . . . Ultor underlined in red ink*
	lines 19 20	masterpiece] master-piece
	line 20	honourable] honour-able
	line 26	have *supralinear addition*
Letter 77	line 3	tendency] ten-dency
Letter 78	line 5	to *supralinear addition*
Letter 79	line 5	blank] ~~blanl~~ ~
	line 7	corn,] ~ ~~mock~~
	line 9	fitful] ~ ~~fear~~
	lines 9–10	simulation] sim-ulation
	line 10	[*2nd*] that] ~ ~~a~~
	line 14	[*1st*] the] ~~that~~
	line 20	(figure) *sublinear addition*
	line 20	lines] ~ ~~of Youth~~ *sublinear addition*
	line 21	Of] ~~Chasten'd b~~ ~
	line 23	*twirl'd*] ~~th~~ ~ *underlined in red ink*
	line 24	*stems underlined in red ink*
	line 26	lean] ~~poor~~ *supralinear addition*
	lines 29–33	*I . . . like. *red ink*

	line 40	is *supralinear addition*
	right margin	-cendental S[xxxx] *written across edge of page*
	right margin	~~homogenous with the Category (wh: constitutes its unity) because it is general and founded o[n] a rule *a priori*~~
Letter 81	line 3	idea] ide~~e~~a
Letter 82	line 3	extension] ex-tension
	line 8	~~remember~~] ~ ~~b~~
	line 9	~~?~~ *supralinear addition*
Letter 84	line 9	through] through~~t~~
	line 17	re-constructing] re-con-structing
	line 18	Deare] ~~d~~Deare
	line 22	somehow] some-how
	line 24	considering] con-sidering
	line 27	in] ~~is~~ *supralinear addition*
	line 38	chivalrous] ~~chil~~ ~
	line 39	a] ~ ~~soa~~
	line 40	limpid] ~~lim~~ ~
	lines 44–45	inspiring] in-spiring
	line 45	Ode] ~~Old~~ ~
	line 45	I] ~~on~~I
Letter 85	line 4	every] ~ ~~or~~
	line 14	their] ~~her~~ *supralinear addition*
Letter 87	line 18	? *supralinear addition*
Letter 88	line 5	a] a~~t~~
	line 7	full *supralinear addition*
	line 18	rough] rough~~t~~
	lines 19–20	Lucretius] ~~S~~Lucretius
	line 21	in] ~~o~~in
	line 27	keep] ~ ~~seen~~
Letter 89	line 17	indeed] in-deed
	line 50	bear] ~~take~~ *supralinear addition*
	lines 55–56	For . . . Killed *supralinear addition*
	line 86	Weakness, and blame,—] ~~We cry~~ ~, ~ ~,— ~~deserted in the olive groves;~~ *supralinear addition*
	line 90	must] ~~will~~ *sublinear addition*

	line 90	penetrate:] ~, *overwritten*
Letter 90	line 6	Experience] Ex-perience
	line 8	you] you~~r~~
	line 9	tomorrow] tomorrow-~~morning~~
	line 10	*Tragedy*] ~~Tradge~~ ~
	line 12	a] ~~the~~ ~ *supralinear addition*
	line 15	*as . . . us underlined in red ink*
	line 20	*Use . . . opportunity underlined in red ink*
	line 21	committee] com-mittee
Letter 91	line 2	thou prove *supralinear addition*
	line 3	leave *supralinear addition*
	line 15	ground.] ~./~~Where amid the azure rills/Aganippe drops distils~~/
	line 41	other *supralinear addition*
	line 41	ever] ~ ~~ev~~
	line 57	in thee *supralinear addition*
	line 61	overwhelmned] over-whelmned
	line 71	*so supralinear addition*
	line 75	went; *supralinear addition*
Letter 92	line 1	*No underlined in red ink*
	line 1	*never underlined in red ink*
	line 8	*Try Clevedon supralinear addition*
	line 13	How . . .*will supralinear addition; red ink*
	line 14	*Trajedy*] *Tradedy overwritten*
Synopsis row 1 column 2 line 5 the]~ ~~n~~		
Letter 93	line 6	not] ~ ~~myself but~~
	line 17	touch *supralinear addition*
Letter 94	line 6	claw] ~~paw~~ *supralinear addition*
	line 8	intim] intim~~ite~~
	lines 8–9	(ce désir . . . superstitieux.) *supralinear addition*
Letter 95	lines 2–3	*the . . . womanhood underlined in red ink*
	line 3	godhead] god-head
	line 5	unblushing] un-blushing
	line 6	reveal] re-veal
	line 7	*the . . . natures underlined in red ink*
	line 11	*in . . . spousal underlined in red ink*

	line 12	behind] be-hind
	lines 15–16	*traced . . . heart underlined in red ink*
	line 16	*indelible*] *~~e~~indelible*
	line 18	write] ~ ~~a Lucretia~~ *[only words on 95^{v}]*
	line 20	divineness] divine-ness
	line 23	*at underlined in red ink*
	line 25	husband's] hus~~t~~band's
	line 26	exquisitely] ex-quisitely
	lines 28–29	*'Both . . . chance.' underlined in red ink*
	line 28	*in a trance supralinear addition*
	lines 31–32	"*when . . .* Begins the *sad . . . ending." underlined in red ink*
	line 35	pure] ~~t~~pure
Letter 96	line 3	Keynote] Key-note
	line 6	together] to-gether
	line 10	delicious] de-licious
	line 11	undisturbed] un-disturbed
	line 15	Tell] Tell~~,~~
	line 15	Kittie] Kittie~~,~~
	line 16	hedonist] hed-onist
	line 18	Norman] Nor-man
	line 22	whelming] ~~whemln~~ ~
	line 30	*Fowl-Soufflé underlined in red ink*
	line 31	with] ~~with~~ ~
	line 34	consequence] con-sequence
Letter 97	line 3	!!! *supralinear addition*
	line 9	tenderness] ten-derness
	lines 21–22	And . . . fleet; *variation added at the bottom of the page*
	line 23	because] be-cause
	line 25	supporting] sup-porting
	line 30	fore-fathers] fore-~~th~~fathers
Letter 98	lines 6–7	Yesterday] Yester-day
Letter 99	line 2	beginning] be-ginning
	line 14	food] ~ ~~safe~~
	line 19	reviews] re-views

	line 25	religious] re-ligious
	line 26	copy] ~~imitate~~ *supralinear addition*
	line 27	—Shakespeare *supralinear addition*
	line 32	*2nd supralinear addition*
	line 57	anything] any-thing
Letter 100	line 11	honeymoon] honey-moon
	line 11	here] ~~there~~ *supralinear addition*
	line 20	sky *supralinear addition*
	line 30	Bedford] Bed-ford
	line 30	Paddington] Padding-ton
	line 33	yesterday] yes-terday
Letter 101	lines 4–5	correspondence] corres-pondence
Letter 105	line 17	distressing *supralinear addition*
	line 18	restlessness] restless-ness
	line 18	unfathomed] unfathom-ed
Letter 106	line 3	Execute] Ex-ecute
	line 4	concentrated] concen-trated
	line 5	if] ~~I~~if
Letter 108	line 4	refresh] re-fresh
	lines 8–9	home-comforts] home-com-forts
	line 22	give *supralinear addition*
	line 22	nor] or *supralinear addition*
	line 25	themselves] them-selves
Letter 109	line 14	with] ~ ~~sunflowe~~
	line 16	and] ~~2~~and
	lines 24–25	with . . . kingdom *supralinear addition*
	line 26	he owes] ~~t~~~ ~~k~~~
	line 27	illimitable] ~~endless~~ *supralinear addition*
	line 29	Old] O~~o~~ld
	line 32	her *supralinear addition*
	line 33	[*1st*] old] ~~1~~old
	line 40	deed] ~~bed~~ *supralinear addition*
	line 47	??? *supralinear addition*
	line 51	indicate] in-dicate
Letter 111	line 4	simpleness] ~~swift~~ ~
	line 5	*one*] ~~own~~ ~

	line 9	clogged] ~ ~~by~~
	line 9	reedbed] reed-bed
Letter 113	line 3	anchor *supralinear addition*
Letter 114	line 5	humble] hum-ble
	line 10	along *supralinear addition*
	line 15	conception] con-ception
	line 16	imaginative] imag-inative
	line 19	centralization] central-ization
	line 25	! *supralinear addition*
	line 27	sunlight] sun-light
Letter 115	line 5	returned] re-turned
	line 9	without] with-out
	line 17	returning] re-turning
Letter 122	line 3	believed] be-lieved
	lines 10–11	On Sundy] ~~Yest~~ ~ ~
	line 17	after] ~ ~~receiving~~
	line 23	convicted] ~ ~~to~~
Letter 123	line 9	is] ~~it~~ *supralinear addition*
	line 36	Nephew] ~ ~~o~~
Letter 124	line 1	or it may be Hubert *supralinear addition*
	line 17	pace, *supralinear addition*
	line 19	my] ~~a~~my
	line 21	place, *supralinear addition*
Letter 126	line 3	Southampton] South-ampton
	line 14	for] ~~o~~for
Letter 127	line 3	as *supralinear addition*
	line 4	my] ~~t~~my
Letter 128	line 6	bridegroom] bride-groom
	line 17	inscription] in-scription
	line 25	in Canute *supralinear addition*
	line 27	feel *supralinear addition*
	line 27	leaving] leav~~e~~ing
Letter 129	line 9	To track *supralinear addition*
Letter 130	line 8	at my] a~~b~~t ~~w~~m~~r~~y
Letter 131	line 1	Looking] ~ ~~tow~~
	line 5	we] we~~re~~

	line 9	O] O~~t~~
	line 10	almost] ~~always~~ *supralinear addition*
	line 23	too] ~~two~~ ~
	line 28	and] ~ ~~pa~~
	line 40	be] ~ ~~ves~~
	line 43	a quarter of] ~~half~~ *supralinear addition*
Letter 132	line 4	One] ~~When~~ *supralinear addition*
	line 4	Stratford] Strat-ford
Letter 133	line 25	scholarship] scholar-ship
	line 34	plenty] ~ ~~of~~
	line 34	or quite enough *supralinear addition*
	line 38	remoteness] re-moteness
Letter 135	line 4	invisible] in-visible
	line 5	company] com-pany
	line 12	minerals] minrals *overwritten*
	line 16	"Linka. Linka. *supralinear addition*
	line 16	brazilian] ~~A~~brazilian
	line 26	grateful] grate-ful
	line 27	distributing] dis-tributing
Letter 137	line 8	angels'] angel~~'s~~s'
	line 17	drama] ~~work~~ *sublinear addition*
	line 20	needed *supralinear addition*
	lines 22–23	on Sunday, *supralinear addition*
	line 30	of] ~~from~~ *supralinear addition*
	line 34	clearly] c~~e~~learly
	line 36	morning] morn-ing
	line 41	read] ~~see~~ *supralinear addition*
	lines 56–57	sunstroke] sun-stroke
	line 59	Then] T~~Th~~en
	line 63	examined] ~ ~~of~~
	line 65	tries] tr~~r~~ies
	line 65	are going] ~ ~ ~~are going~~
Letter 139	line 2	*Beginning left margin*
	line 2	beech] beech-~~wood~~
	line 3	we] ~ ~~stooped~~
	line 4	group] ~~Use charxxates~~ ~ *left margin*

	line 4	firewood;—] ~~u~~firewood;— ~~the colours and brick~~ [indecipherable deletion]
	line 5	the dove-cote] dove-cote *supralinear addition*
	line 5	stones] ~ ~~withxxxety us any as it were the ?? industry of the villiage and the idleness of the sturdy slopes~~
	line 6	earth, and]~, ~ ~~store pots~~
	line 8	nature] ~ ~~was~~
	line 30	wonderful] won-derful
	lines 33–37	be . . .1887 *left margin*
Letter 140	line 3	inexorable] in-exorable
	line 3	tender *supralinear addition*
	line 4	predestination] pre-destination
	line 8	Master] ~~Divine~~ *supralinear addition*
Letter 142	line 4	tried] ~~wr~~ ~
	line 7	convey] ~~transfer~~ *supralinear addition*
Letter 144	line 10	misunderstood] misunder-stood
	line 21	so *supralinear addition*
	line 23	harness] haness *supralinear addition*
	line 28	Your] ~~W~~Your
Letter 145	line 19	in] ~~of~~ *supralinear addition*
	line 28	dinnertime] dinner-time
Letter 146	line 1	respected] re-spected
	line 3	οπαις] οπαις~~α~~
	line 8	Seaton's] ~~Chatham's~~ *supralinear addition*
	line 11	carrying] carry-ing
Letter 147	line 9	Amy] ~~E~~Amy
	line 10	service] ser-vice
Letter 149	line 2	Love] love *overwritten*
	line 4	environment] environ-ment
	line 6	of the] ~ fr *overwritten*
Letter 150	line 31	Fancy] ~~think of~~ *supralinear addition*
	line 34	! *supralinear addition*
	line 38	leaving *supralinear addition*
Letter 153	line 16	retire] re-tire
Letter 154	line 3	conversation] con-versation

Letter 156	line 4	will *supralinear addition*
	line 6	our] ~~your~~ *supralinear addition*
Letter 157	line 3	oven!] ~ ! [indecipherable deletion]
Letter 160	line 2	Merle] Me ~
Letter 161	line 5	! *supralinear addition*
	line 10	hare] ~~hair~~ ~

Bibliography

Works by Katharine Bradley and Edith Cooper

Manuscript and Archival Sources

The only catalogue of Michael Field manuscripts is Ivor Treby's *The Michael Field Catalogue: A Book of Lists* (1998). To this, Treby added "significant addenda" in *Uncertain Rain,* 236–37.

Bodleian Library, University of Oxford

Bradley, Katharine. Letter book. MS Eng. lett. d. 120.

———. Letters to Edith Cooper 1876–ca. 1898. MS Eng. lett. c. 418.

———. Letters to James and Emma Cooper. MS Eng. lett. d. 400.

———. Letters to James and Emma Cooper. MS Eng. lett. d. 401.

———. "Year book 1883 and 1884." MS Eng. poet. e. 61.

Bradley, Katharine, and Edith Cooper. Letters to Amy Cooper. MS Eng. lett. d. 402.

———. Letters to Emma Cooper and Frances Brooks. MS Eng. lett. e. 143.

———. Letters to Frances Brooks. MS Eng. lett. d. 405.

———. "Songs of Sundry Nature." MS Eng. poet. d. 60 fol. 2.

———. Survey of family likes and dislikes. 12 Jan. 1878. MS Eng. misc. c. 303 fols. 4–6.

Bradley, Katharine, Edith Cooper, and Amy Cooper. Letters to various recipients. MS Eng. lett. e. 31.

Cooley, J. "Never Forgiven." 21 Jul. 1882. MS Eng. poet. d. 73.

Cooper, Edith. Letters to Katharine Bradley and family members. 1875–87. MS Eng. lett. c. 419.

Field, Michael. Letters to Michael Field. MS Eng. lett. d. 407.

British Library, London

Bradley, Katharine, and Edith Cooper. Letters regarding *A Question of Memory.* Add. MS 45852.

———. Letters to John Miller Gray. Vols. 1–2. Add. MS 45853–54.

———. Letters to Robert Browning. Add. MS 46866.

———. Letters to various recipients. Add. MS 45851.

———. Letters to various recipients. Add. MS 45867.

———. *"Michael Field" and Fin-de-Siècle Culture and Society.* Marlborough: Adam Matthews Publications, 2003. [Microfilm of BL collection.]

———. "Works and Days." 30 vols. 1868–1914. Add. MS 46776–46804B.

Houghton Library, Harvard University

Bradley, Katharine, and Edith Cooper. Letters to William and "Noli" Rothenstein. Papers of William Rothenstein. BMS ENG 1148(486).

Pierpont Morgan Library, New York

Bradley, Katharine, and Edith Cooper. Letters to Edith Cooper/Katharine Bradley. Uncatalogued. MA 2092.

St. Andrew's University, Edinburgh

Field (Edith Cooper). Letter to W. Macdonald. 9 Dec. 1895. MS PR4699. F5, unfoliated.

Facsimiles

Reading University, Reading

Bradley, Katharine. Letter to Elkin Matthews. 27 Jan. [1893]. MS 392/1/1 fol. 617.
Cooper, Edith. Letter to Dr. Todhunter. 9 May 1894. MS 202.1.1 fol. 592.

Published Works

Anon. *Borgia: A Period Play.* London: A. H. Bullen, 1905.
Anon. [By the Author of Borgia]. *The Accuser/Tristan de Léonois/A Messiah.* London: Sidgwick and Jackson, 1911.
———. *Queen Mariamne.* London: Sidgwick and Jackson, 1908.
———. *The Tragedy of Pardon/Dian.* London: Sidgwick and Jackson, 1911.
Field, Michael. *Anna Ruina.* London: David Nutt, 1899.
———. *Attila, My Attila! A Play.* London: Elkin Mathews, 1896.
———. *Brutus Ultor.* London: George Bell and Sons, 1886.
———. *Callirrhoë/Fair Rosamund.* London: George Bell and Sons, 1884.
———. *Callirrhoë/Fair Rosamund.* New York: Holt, 1884.
———. *Canute the Great/The Cup of Water.* London: George Bell and Sons, 1887.
———. *Dedicated: An Early Work of Michael Field.* London: George Bell, 1914.
———. *The Father's Tragedy/William Rufus/Loyalty or Love?* London: George Bell, 1885.
———. "An Invocation." *Academy* 30 (Jul.–Dec. 1886): 363.
———. *Julia Domna.* London: Ballantyne Press, 1903.
———. "King Apollo." *Academy* 30 (Jul.–Dec. 1886): 326.
———. *Long Ago.* 1889; Portland: Thomas B. Mosher, 1897.
———. "Love and Death." *Academy* 30 (Jul.–Dec. 1886): 326.
———. "Love's Sour Leisure." *Academy* 30 (Jul.–Dec. 1886): 309.
———. *Music and Silence: The Gamut of Michael Field.* Ed. Ivor Treby. N.p.: De Blackland, 2002.

———. *Mystic Trees.* London: Eveleigh Nash, 1913.
———. *Noontide Branches.* Oxford: Henry Daniels, 1899.
———. *Poems of Adoration.* London: Sands and Co., 1912.
———. *A Question of Memory.* London: Mathews and Lane, 1893.
———. *The Race of Leaves.* London: Ballantyne Press, 1901.
———. "Recollections by Michael Field." In *John Miller Gray: Memoir and Remains.* 2 vols. Edinburgh: David Douglas, 1895.
———. "The Sands of Death." *Academy* 30 (Jul.–Dec. 1886): 240.
———. *A Shorter Shîrazâd: 101 Poems of Michael Field.* Ed. Ivor Treby. N.p.: De Blackland, 1999.
———. *Sight and Song.* London: Mathews and Lane, 1892.
———. *Stephania: A Trialogue.* London: Mathews and Lane, 1892.
———. "The Summer Wind." *Academy* 30 (Jul.–Dec. 1886): 187.
———. *The Tragic Mary.* London: George Bell and Sons, 1890.
———. *Uncertain Rain: Sundry Spells of Michael Field.* Ed. Ivor Treby. N.p.: De Blackland, 2002.
———. *Underneath the Bough: A Book of Verses by Michael Field.* London: George Bell, 1893.
———. *Whym Chow: Flame of Love.* Hammersmith: Eragny Press, 1914.
———. *Wild Honey from Various Thyme.* London: T. Fisher Unwin, 1908.
———. *Works and Days: From the Journals of Michael Field.* Ed. T. and D. C. Sturge Moore. London: John Murray, 1933.
———. *The World at Auction.* London: Ballantyne Press, 1898.
Leigh, Arran. *The New Minnesinger and Other Poems.* London: Longmans, Green and Co., 1875.
Leigh, Arran, and Isla. *Bellerophôn.* London: Kegan Paul and Co., 1881.

Works Cited

Manuscript and Archival Sources

Bodleian Library, University of Oxford

Bridge, Ursula. "The Diary of Michael Field: A Biographical Study of a Forgotten Poet." MS Eng. misc. d. 983.
Swanwick, Anna, Havelock Ellis, J. A. Symonds, et al. Letters to Katharine Bradley and Edith Cooper. MS Eng. lett. e. 32.

Bristol University Library, Bristol

Pease, Marion. "Some Reminiscences of University College, Bristol." Unpublished pamphlet. 2 Feb. 1942.

Sturge, M. Carta. Notations written on inside covers of Mary Sturgeon's *Michael Field* (1922). Dated Sept. 1922.

Tanner, Sarah Jane. "Essay on Michael Field." 1922. MS 95.

British Library, London

Moore, Thomas Sturge. "Poets and Painters: The Friendship between Michael Field, Miss Bradley and Miss Cooper (The Poets) and Ricketts and Shannon (The Painters). Selections from their letters and journals." Ed. Ursula Bridge. Vol. 1 of 3. Add. MS 61721.

Houghton Library, Harvard University

Bottomley, Gordon. Letter to William Rothenstein. 12 Aug. 1943. Papers of William Rothenstein. BMS ENG 1148(153) fol. 46.

Private Manuscripts

Moore, Daniel, and Riette Sturge Moore. Letter to Dr. Richard Hunt. 30 June 1974. Held by Leonie Sturge-Moore.

———. "Michael Field." N.d. Held by Leonie Sturge-Moore.

Women's Library, London

"Troisième Congrès International, La Hague 17–22 Septembre 1883."

Secondary Sources

1881 Census of England and Wales. Salt Lake City: Corporation of the President of the Church of Jesus Christ of Latter Day Saints, ca. 1990. [Microfiche.]

Aeschylus. *The Eumenides.* Trans. Hugh Lloyd-Jones. London: Prentice-Hall, 1970.

A.K.H.B. "Archbishop Tait of Canterbury." *Longman's Magazine* 18, no. 106 (Aug. 1891): 362–74.

Allen, David Elliston. *The Victorian Fern Craze: A History of Pteridomania.* London: Hutchinson, 1969.

Amari, Michele. *Storia dei Musulmani di Sicilia.* 2nd ed. 1880; Catania: R. Prampolini, 1933–39.

Amiel, Henri-Frédéric. *Amiel's Journal: The Journal Intime of Henri-Frédéric Amiel.* Trans. Mrs. Humphry Ward. 2nd ed. 1885; London: Macmillan, 1909.

The Anglo-Saxon Chronicles. Trans. and ed. Michael Swanton. London: Phoenix, 2000.

Archer, William. "A Pre-Shakespearean Playwright." Rev. of *Canute; Cup of Water,* by Michael Field. *Pall Mall Budget* 33 (27 Aug. 1885): 28.

Aristotle. *The Poetics of Aristotle.* Trans. S. H. Butcher. London: Macmillan, 1936.

Arnold, Matthew. "A Word More about America." In *Philistinism in England and*

America, ed. R. H. Super. Ann Arbor: Univ. of Michigan Press, 1974: 194–217. Vol. 10 of *The Complete Prose Works of Matthew Arnold.* 11 vols. 1960–74.

———. *The Works of Matthew Arnold.* 15 vols. London: Macmillan, 1903.

Arnold, Thomas. *History of Rome.* Vol. 1. London: B. Fellowes, 1845.

Baedeker, Karl. *Baedeker's Belgium and Holland.* Leipsic: Karl Baedeker, 1884.

———. *Central Italy and Rome.* Leipsic: Karl Baedecker, 1909.

———. *Italy: A Handbook for Travellers.* Leipsic: Karl Baedeker, 1886.

Balchin, W. G. V. *Cornwall.* London: Hodder and Stoughton, 1954.

Baring-Gould, Rev. Sabine. *The Lives of the Saints.* 16 vols. Edinburgh: John Grant, 1914.

Barnes, Susan, Piero Boccardo, Clario Di Fabio, and Laura Tagliaferro. *Van Dyck A Genova: Grande Pittura e Collezionismo.* Milano: Electra, 1997.

Bartolomé Estaban Murillo, 1617–1682. London: Weidenfeld and Nicolson, 1982.

Bassnett, Susan. *Three Tragic Actresses: Siddons, Rachel, Ristori.* New York: Cambridge Univ. Press, 1996.

Bate, W. Jackson. *Samuel Johnson.* New York: Harcourt Brace Jovanovich, 1977.

Beckford, William. *Vathek.* 1786; Delmar, NY: Scholar's Facsimiles and Reprints, 1972.

Beeton, Isabella. *The Book of Household Management.* London: S. O. Beeton, 1861.

Beiser, Frederick C. "Kant's Intellectual Development: 1746–1781." In *The Cambridge Companion to Kant,* ed. Paul Guyer, 26–61. Cambridge: Cambridge Univ. Press, 1992.

Bell, E. Moberly. *Josephine Butler: Flame of Fire.* London: Constable, 1965.

———. *Octavia Hill: A Biography.* London: Constable, 1942. Rev. of *Bellerophôn,* by Arran and Isla Leigh. *Academy* 20 (Jul.–Dec. 1881): 196.

Rev. of *Bellerophôn,* by Arran and Isla Leigh. *Athenaeum* 71 (Jul.–Dec. 1881): 173.

Rev. of *Bellerophôn,* by Arran and Isla Leigh. *Graphic* 24 (Jul.–Dec. 1881): 198.

Bennett, Mary. *Artists of the Pre-Raphaelite Circle.* London: National Museums and Galleries on Merseyside, 1988.

Bentley, G. E., Jr. *The Stranger from Paradise: A Biography of William Blake.* New Haven, CT: Yale Univ. Press, 2001.

Bentley, James. *Ritualism and Politics in Victorian Britain: The Attempt to Legislate for Belief.* Oxford: Oxford Univ. Press, 1978.

Beroul. *The Romance of Tristan.* Trans. Allan S. Fedick. Ca. 1180–1200; Harmondsworth, UK: Penguin, 1970.

Bingham, Madeleine. *Henry Irving and the Victorian Theatre.* London: George Allen and Unwin, 1978.

Blain, Virginia. "'Michael Field, the Two-headed Nightingale': Lesbian Text as Palimpsest." *Women's History Review* 5.2 (1996): 239–57.

The Book of Common Prayer and Administration of the Sacraments and Other Rites and Ceremonies of the Church According to the use of the Church of England. Oxford: Oxford Univ. Press, n.d.

Rev. of *Borgia: A Period Play. Academy* 68 (1905: Jan.–Jun.): 657–58.

Borsay, Peter. *The Image of Georgian Bath, 1700–2000* Oxford: Oxford Univ. Press, 2000.

Brereton, Austin. *The Life of Henry Irving.* Vol. 1. London: Longmans, Green and Co., 1908.

The British Museum and Its Collections. London: British Museum Publications, 1982.

Britton, John, and Edward W. Brayley. *Devonshire and Cornwall Illustrated.* London, 1832.

Brooke, Stopford. *Four Victorian Poets.* 1903; New York: Russell and Russell, 1964.

———. *Theology in the English Poets.* London: Henry S. King, 1874.

Broughton, Trev Lynn. "The Froude-Carlyle Embroilment: Married Life as a Literary Problem." *Victorian Studies* 38, no. 4 (Summer 1995): 551–86.

Brown, Christopher. *Van Dyck.* Oxford: Phaidon, 1982.

Browning, Elizabeth Barrett. *Aurora Leigh.* 1864; Oxford: Oxford Univ. Press, 1993.

Browning, Robert. *The Complete Works of Robert Browning.* Ed. Roma A. King Jr. et al. 16 vols. Athens: Ohio Univ. Press, 1969–98.

Budd, William. *Cholera and Disinfection: Asiatic Cholera in Bristol in 1866.* Bristol: Hemmons, 1883.

Bunyan, John. *The Pilgrim's Progress from This World to That Which Is to Come.* Ed. James Blanton Wharey. 1678; Oxford: Clarendon Press, 1960.

Burns, Robert. *The Poems and Songs of Robert Burns.* Ed. James Kinsley. 3 vols. Oxford: Clarendon Press, 1968.

Burton, Richard. *The Anatomy of Melancholy.* Vol. 1. 1621; London: J. M. Dent, 1932.

Butler, Josephine. *Personal Reminiscences of a Great Crusade.* 1898; Westport, CT: Hyperion Press, 1976.

———. *Recollections of George Butler.* Bristol: Arrowsmith, 1892.

Byron, George Gordon, Lord. *The Complete Poetical Works.* Ed. Jerome K. McGann. Vol. 4. Oxford: Clarendon Press, 1986.

Campbell, Bruce, and Elizabeth Lack, eds. *A Dictionary of Birds.* Calton: T. and A. D. Poyser, 1985.

Campion, Thomas. *Fifty Songs by Thomas Campion.* London: Ballantyne Press, 1896.

Rev. of *Canute; Cup of Water. Spectator* 16 (1887): 1538.

Carleton, Don. *A University for Bristol.* Bristol: Univ. of Bristol Press, 1984.

Carley, James. *Glastonbury Abbey: The Holy House at the Head of the Moors Adventurous.* Woodbridge, UK: Boydell, 1988.

Carlson, Marvin. *The Italian Shakespeareans.* Washington, DC: Folger, 1985.

Carlyle, Thomas. *Critical and Miscellaneous Essays.* Vol. 2. London: Chapman and Hall, 1887.

———. *Past and Present.* London: Chapman and Hall, 1843.Case, Thomas. *Mount Pisgah.* London: Thomas Milbourne, 1670. [Microfilm.]

Catullus, Gaius Valerius. *Catullus.* Ed. G. P. Goold. London: Duckworth, 1983.

Chaucer, Geoffrey. *The Romaunt of the Rose.* Ed. Charles Dahlberg. Norman: Univ. of Oklahoma Press, 1999.

Cheney, C. R., ed. *A Handbook for Students of British History.* Cambridge: Cambridge Univ. Press, 2000.

Child, Francis James, ed. *The English and Scottish Popular Ballads.* Vol. 3. New York: Cooper Square, 1962.

Chittenden, Fred J., ed. *Dictionary of Gardening.* 2nd ed. 5 vols. Oxford: Clarendon Press, 1951.

Clapinson, Mary, and T. D. Rogers. *Summary Catalogue of Post-Medieval Western Manuscripts in the Bodleian Library Oxford.* Vol. 1. Oxford: Clarendon Press, 1991.

Collins, Wilkie. *Rambles beyond Railways; or Notes in Cornwall Taken A-foot.* 1851; London: Westaway, 1948.

Colvin, Sidney. *Landor.* London: Macmillan, 1881.

"Cornwall Lunatic Asylum." *Times,* 1 Jul. 1864, 11F.

Cottle, Joseph. *Poems; Malvern Hills; An Expositulatory Epistle to Lord Byron; Dartmoor and Other Poems.* 1823; New York: Garland, 1978.

Coulton, G. G. *Scottish Abbeys and Social Life.* Cambridge: Cambridge Univ. Press, 1933.

"Court Theatre." *Times,* 23 Feb. 1897, 8A.

Cowper, William. *The Poems of William Cowper.* Ed. J. C. Bailey. London: Methuen, 1905.

Crawford, Elizabeth. *The Women's Suffrage Movement: A Reference Guide, 1866–1928.* London: UCL Press, 1999.

Cumberland, Robert. *The Banishment of Cicero.* London: J. Walter, 1761.

Curran, Stuart. *Shelley's Cenci: Scorpions Ringed with Fire.* Princeton, NJ: Princeton Univ. Press, 1970.

Daltrop, Georg. "The Museo Pio-Clemente." In *The Vatican: Spirit and Art of Christian Rome,* ed. John P. O'Neill and John Dailey, 176–89. New York: Harry N. Abrams, 1975.

Dante Alighieri. *The Divine Comedy: A New Verse Translation.* Trans. C. H. Sisson. Manchester: Carcanet, 1980.

Day, J. Wentworth. *Norwich and the Broads.* London: B. T. Batsford, 1953.

Dearden, Jane S. *Ruskin, Bembridge and Brantwood.* Keele: Ryburn, 1994.

Delaney, J. G. Paul. *Charles Ricketts: A Biography.* Oxford: Clarendon Press, 1990.

Dickens, Charles. *The Personal History of David Copperfield.* 1849–50; London: Oxford Univ. Press, 1948.

Dictionary of National Biography. Ed. Sir Leslie Stephens and Sir Sidney Lee. 22 vols. London: Oxford Univ. Press, 1959–60.

Dobbs, Brian and Judy. *Dante Gabriel Rossetti: An Alien Victorian.* London: Macdonald-James, 1977.

Donoghue, Emma. *We Are Michael Field.* Bath: Absolute, 1998.

Duffy, Cian. *Shelley and the Revolutionary Sublime.* Cambridge: Cambridge UP, 2005.

Earle, Rebecca. Introduction to *Epistolary Selves: Letters and Letter-Writers,* 1–14. Aldershot, UK: Ashgate, 1999.

Ellmann, Richard. *Oscar Wilde.* London: Penguin, 1988.

Engen, Rodney. *Kate Greenaway: A Biography.* London: Macdonald, 1981.

Rev. of *The Father's Tragedy; William Rufus; Loyalty or Love?* by Michael Field. *Athenaeum* 79 (Jul.–Dec. 1885): 251–52.

Fackenheim, Emil L. *God Within: Kant, Schelling, and Historicity.* Ed. John Burbidge. Toronto: Univ. of Toronto Press, 1996.

Faderman, Lillian. *Surpassing the Love of Men: Romantic Friendship and Love between Women from the Renaissance to the Present.* New York: William Morrow, 1981.

Fawcett, Millicent. *Josephine Butler.* London: Assoc. for Moral and Social Hygiene, 1927.

Flanders, Judith. *The Victorian House: Domestic Life from Childbirth to Deathbed.* London: Harper Perennial, 2004.

Ford, Charles Howard. *Hannah More: A Critical Biography.* New York: Peter Lang, 1996.

Fossi, Gloria. *The Uffizi.* Firenze: Giunti Gruppo Editori, 1999.

Foster, Jeanette Howard. *Sex Variant Women in Literature.* Baltimore: Diana Press, 1975.

Francis, Frank. *Treasures of the British Museum.* London: Thames and Hudson, 1971.

Fraser, Hilary. "A Visual Field: Michael Field and the Gaze." *Victorian Literature and Culture* 34 (2006): 553–71.

Freeman, Edward A. *The Reign of William Rufus.* 2 vols. Oxford: Clarendon Press, 1882.

French, Richard D. *Antivivisection and Medical Science in Victorian Society.* Princeton, NJ: Princeton Univ. Press, 1975.

Froude, James Anthony. *Thomas Carlyle: A History of the First Forty Years of His Life, 1795–1835.* 2 vols. London: Longmans, 1882.

Garber, Daniel. "Descartes' Physics." In *The Cambridge Companion to Descartes,* ed. John Cottingham, 236–57. Cambridge: Cambridge Univ. Press, 1992.

Garrison, Daniel H. *Horace: Epodes and Odes.* Norman: Univ. of Oklahoma Press, 1991.

GenoPro. "The Beath and Tait Family Tree with Connected Families." http://familytrees.genopro.com/IainTait/Beath%20and%20Tait%20families/default.htm. Accessed 9 Apr. 2007.

Girdlestone, Edward Deacon. *Vivisection: In Its Scientific, Religious and Moral Aspects.* Clifton: J. Baker & Son, 1884.

Gittings, Robert, and Jo Manton. *Dorothy Wordsworth.* Oxford: Clarendon Press, 1985.

Goethe, Johann Wolfgang von. *Faust.* Trans. Anna Swanwick. London: Henry G. Bohn, 1850.

———. *Faust: A Tragedy.* Trans. Walter Arndt. 1808/1832; New York: W. W. Norton, 1976.

Goldmann, Lucien. *Immanuel Kant.* Trans. Robert Black. London: NLB, 1971.

Goodbody, Margaret. *Five Daughters in Search of Learning: The Sturge Family, 1820–1944.* Bristol: Top Copy, 1986.

Gosse, Edmund W. *Jeremy Taylor.* London: Macmillan, 1904———. "Robert Herrick." *Cornhill Magazine* 32 (1875): 176–91.

Gray, John Miller. Rev. of *Brutus Ultor,* by Michael Field. *Academy* 29 (Jan.–Jul. 1886): 320.

Gray, Robert. *Cardinal Manning: A Biography.* London: Weidenfeld and Nicolson, 1985.

Groenewegen, Peter. *A Soaring Eagle: Alfred Marshall, 1842–1924.* Aldershot, UK: Edward Elgar, 1995.

Guerber, H. A. *The Norsemen.* New York: Avenel, 1986.

Hamilton, Walter. *The Aesthetic Movement in England.* 1882; New York: Garland, 1986.

Hanson, Bruce. *Brantwood: John Ruskin's Home, 1872–1900.* Coniston, UK: Brantwood Trust, n.d.

Hare, A. J. C. *Cities of Northern and Central Italy.* 3 vols. London: Daldy, Ibister and Co., 1876.

———. *Paris.* London: George Allen, n.d.

———. *Walks in Rome.* 2 vols. New York: Routledge, n.d.

———. *Walks in Rome.* 13th ed. London: Kegan Paul, 1913.

Hartt, Frederick. *A History of Italian Renaissance Art.* London: Thames and Hudson, 1970.

Hawthorne, Nathaniel. *Transformation, or The Romance of Monte Beni.* 1860; London: Smith, Elder and Co., 1883.

Hazlitt, William. *The Collected Works of William Hazlitt.* Ed. A. R. Waller and Arnold Glover. 13 vols. London: J. M. Dent, 1902.

Heaton, Vernon. *The Oberammergau Passion Play.* 3rd ed. London: Hale, 1983.

Hegel, G. W. F. *Lectures on the Philosophy of History.* Trans. J. Sibree. London: George Bell and Sons, 1861.

Hemery, Eric. *High Dartmoor: Land and People.* London: Robert Hale, 1983.

Hemmingham, Lucy. "Colour in Dress." In *The Late Victorians: Art, Design and Society 1852–1910,* ed. Bernard Denvir, 214–16. London: Longman, 1986.

Henry, Matthew. *An Exposition of the Five Poetical Books of the Old Testament.* London: T. Darrack, 1710. [Microfilm.]

Herrick, Robert. *Poetical Works of Robert Herrick.* Oxford: Clarendon Press, 1915.

Hilton, Tim. *John Ruskin: The Later Years.* New Haven, CT: Yale Univ. Press, 2000.

The Holy Bible. Cambridge: Cambridge Univ. Press, n.d.

Hood, Thomas. *The Poetical Works of Thomas Hood.* Ed. William Michael Rossetti. London: E. Moxon and Son, n.d.

Hood, William. *Fra Angelico at San Marco.* New Haven, CT: Yale Univ. Press, 1993.

Hope-Moncrieff, A. R. *Romance and Legend of Chivalry.* London: Bracken, 1985.

Horne, Richard Hengist. *The Great Peace-Maker: A Submarine Dialogue.* London, 1872.

Hudson, Derek. *Martin Tupper: His Rise and Fall.* London: Constable, 1949.

Hunt, John Dixon. *The Wider Sea.* London: Dent, 1981.

Hunt, Leigh. *The Poetical Works of Leigh Hunt.* Ed. H. S. Milford. London: Oxford Univ. Press, 1923.

Hunt, Robert. *Popular Romances of the West of England.* 1865; New York: Benjamin Blom, 1968.

Ibsen, Henrik. *Three Plays: The Pillars of the Community, The Wild Duck, Hedda Gabler.* Trans. Una Ellis-Fermor. 1890; Harmondsworth, UK: Penguin, 1950.

"International Congress at The Hague." *Shield* 469 (6 Oct. 1883): 244–51.

Jacks, Lawrence Pearsall. *The Life and Letters of Stopford Brooke.* Vol 2. London: John Murray, 1917.

Jackson, Blomfield. Letter to the editor. *Times,* 16 Feb. 1897, 12F.

Jackson, Holbrook. Introduction to *The Anatomy of Melancholy,* by Richard Burton, 1:vii–xvii. London: J. M. Dent, 1932.

James, Henry. *Hawthorne.* London: Macmillan, 1881.

———. *The Portrait of a Lady.* 1881; London: Penguin, 1986.

Jameson, Mrs. Anna. *Sacred and Legendary Art.* 10th ed. 2 vols. 1848; London: Longmans, Green and Co., 1888.

Janaway, Christopher. Introduction to *The Cambridge Companion to Schopenhauer,* 1–17. Cambridge: Cambridge Univ. Press, 1999.

Jetzer, Penny, Diana Bourne, Elizabeth Floyd, et al. *A Pictorial History of Stoke Bishop and Sneyd Park.* Bristol: Stoke Bishop and Sneyd Park Local History Group, 1998.

Jones, F. C., and W. G. Chown. *A History of Bristol and Its Suburbs.* Bristol: Reece Winstone, 1977.

Julian, John, ed. *A Dictionary of Hymnology.* London: John Murray, 1915.

Kant, Immanuel. *Critique of Pure Reason.* Trans. Friedrich Max Müller. London: Macmillan, 1881.

Karl, Frederick. *George Eliot, Voice of a Century.* New York: Norton, 1995.

Keats, John. *John Keats.* Ed. Elizabeth Cook. Oxford: Oxford Univ. Press, 1990.

Kenny, Anthony. *The Oxford History of Western Philosophy.* Oxford: Oxford Univ. Press, 1994.

Kent, John. *Holding the Fort: Studies in Victorian Revivalism.* London: Epworth, 1978.

Ker, W. P. Rev. of *The Father's Tragedy; William Rufus; Loyalty or Love?* by Michael Field. *Contemporary Review* 48 (Jul.–Dec. 1885): 292–93.

Keynes, John Maynard. "Obituary: Mary Paley Marshall." *Economic Journal* 54, no. 214 (Jun.–Sept. 1944): 268–86.

Khayyám, Omar. *The Rubáiyát of Omar Khayyám; Six Plays of Calderon.* Trans. Edward Fitzgerald. 1859; London: J. M. Dent, 1928.

Kington, T. A. *History of Frederick the Second, Emperor of the Romans: From Chronicles and Documents Published within the Last Ten Years.* Cambridge: Macmillan, 1862.

Laird, Holly. "The Coauthored Pseudonym: Two Women Named Michael Field." In *The Faces of Anonymity: Anonymous and Pseudonymous Publication from the Sixteenth to the Twentieth Century,* ed. Robert J. Griffin, 193–209. New York: Palgrave Macmillan, 2003.

———. *Women Coauthors.* Urbana: Univ. of Illinois Press, 2000.

Lansbury, Coral. *The Old Brown Dog: Women, Workers and Vivisection in Edwardian England.* Madison: Univ. of Wisconsin Press, 1985.

Legge, Sylvia. *Affectionate Cousins: T. Sturge Moore and Maria Appia.* Oxford: Oxford Univ. Press, 1980.

Lemprière, J. *Lemprière's Classical Dictionary.* 3rd ed. London: Routledge and Kegan Paul, 1984.

Leppington, Blanche. Rev. of *Amiel's Journal* by Henri-Frédéric Amiel. *Contemporary Review* 47 (Jan.–Jun. 1885): 334–52.

Lessing, G. E. *The Dramatic Works of G. E. Lessing.* Ed. Ernest Bell. London: George Bell and Sons, 1878.

Liber Eliensis. Ed. E. O. Blake. London: Royal Historical Society, 1962.

Livy. *Ab Urbe Condita.* Trans. B. O. Foster. Vols. 1, 3, and 5. London: William Heinemann, 1957–61.

Lloyd, Michael, ed. *Turner.* London: Thames and Hudson, 1996.

McClelland, Vincent Alan. *Cardinal Manning: His Public Life and Influence, 1865–1892.* London: Oxford Univ. Press, 1962.

Macdonald, Jan. "'Disillusioned Bards and Despised Bohemians': Michael Field's *A Question of Memory* at the Independent Theatre Society." *Theatre Notebook* 31, no. 2 (1977): 18–29.

Mackail, J. W. "Michael Field's New Volume." Rev. of *The Father's Tragedy, William Rufus, Loyalty or Love?* by Michael Field. *Academy* 28 (Jul.–Dec. 1885): 36–37.

Magnusson, Magnus. *Treasures of Scotland.* London: Weidenfeld and Nicolson, 1981.

Malory, Sir Thomas. *Morte Darthur: Sir Thomas Malory's Book of King Arthur and of His Noble Knights of the Round Table. The original edition of Caxton.* Introduction by Sir Edward Strachey. London: Macmillan and Co., 1868.

Marston, P. B. Rev. of *Callirrhoë; Fair Rosamund,* by Michael Field. *Athenaeum* 77 (Jul.–Dec. 1884): 24–25.

Masson, Rosaline. *Edinburgh.* London: Adam and Charles Black, 1912.

Mazzini, Joseph. *The Duties of Man and Other Essays.* 1844; London: J. M. Dent and Sons, 1907.

Meese, Elizabeth. "When Virginia Looked at Vita, What Did She See; or, Lesbian: Feminist: Woman—What's the Differ(e/a)nce?" In *Lesbian Subjects: A Feminist Studies Reader,* ed. Martha Vicinus, 85–101. Bloomington: Indiana Univ. Press, 1996.

Meller, H. E. *Leisure and the Changing City, 1870–1914.* London: Routledge and Kegan Paul, 1976.

Meredith, George. *Diana of the Crossways.* 1885; London: Virago, 1980.

"Michael Field." *Spectator* 58 (1885): 810–811.

Millward, Roy, and Adrian Robinson. *The South West Peninsula.* London: Macmillan, 1971.

Milton, John. *The Works of John Milton.* Ed. Frank Patterson. 18 vols. New York: Columbia Univ. Press, 1931–38.

Mitchell, Sally. *Frances Power Cobbe: Victorian Feminist, Journalist, Reformer.* Charlottesville: Univ. of Virginia Press, 2004.

[Mont Cenis]. *Times,* 20 Sept. 1871, 7B–C.

Moore, Thomas Sturge. Editor's preface. *Works and Days: From the Journals of Michael Field,* ed. T. and D. C. Sturge Moore, xv–xxi. London: John Murray, 1933.

More, Hannah. *Sacred Dramas: Chiefly Intended for Young Persons.* 6th ed. London: T. Caddell, 1789. [Microfilm.]

Moriarty, David. "'Michael Field' (Edith Cooper and Katherine Bradley) and Their Male Critics." In *Nineteenth Century Women Writers of the English Speaking World,* ed. Rhoda B. Nathan, 121–42. New York: Greenwood, 1986.

Morley, John. "On Pattison's Memoirs." In *Nineteenth Century Essays.* Chicago: Univ. of Chicago Press, 1970.

Morris, William. *The Collected Works of William Morris.* Vol. 3. New York: Russell and Russell, 1966.

Morse, Thomas D. C. "Scripture Teaching in the London Board Schools." *Times,* 18 Jul. 1881, 10F.

Motion, Andrew. *Keats.* London: Faber and Faber, 1997.

Munn, Geoffrey C. *Castellani and Giuliano: Revivalist Jewellers of the Nineteenth Century.* London: Trefoil Books, 1984.

"Murder in a Railway Carriage." *Times,* 13 Feb. 1897, 12C.

Newall, Christopher. *The Grosvenor Gallery Exhibitions.* Cambridge: Cambridge Univ. Press, 1995.

Newman, Sally. "Body of Evidence: Aileen Palmer's Textual Lives." *Hecate* 26.1 (2000): 10–38.

"New Plays." Rev. of *The Father's Tragedy; William Rufus; Loyalty or Love?* by Michael Field. *Spectator* 58 (1885): 910–12.

"A New Poet." Rev. of *Callirrhoë; Fair Rosamund,* by Michael Field. *Spectator* 57 (1884): 680–82.

Nicols, John. *Byron.* London: Macmillan, 1880.

Norway, Arthur. *Highways and Byways in Devon and Cornwall.* London: Macmillan, 1923.

"Obituary [of John Brett]." *Times,* 9 Jan. 1902, 4B.

Oliphant, Margaret. *Sheridan.* English Men of Letters Series. London: Macmillan, 1883.

The Oxford Classical Dictionary. Ed. M. Cary, J. D. Dennison, J. Wight Duff, et al. Oxford: Clarendon Press, 1949.

Oxford Dictionary of National Biography. Ed. H. C. G. Matthew and Brian Harrison. 60 vols. Oxford: Oxford Univ. Press, 2004.

Oxford English Dictionary. Ed. J. A. Simpson and E. S. C. Weiner. 2nd edition. 20 vols. Oxford: Clarendon Press, 1989.

Palgrave, Francis Turner. *The Golden Treasury.* 1861; London: Penguin, 1991.

Parsons, Charles. “The Transcendental Aesthetic.” In *The Cambridge Companion to Kant,* ed. Paul Guyer, 62–100. Cambridge: Cambridge Univ. Press, 1992.

The Paston Letters and Papers of the Fifteenth Century. Ed. Norman Davis. Vol. 1. Oxford: Clarendon Press, 1971.

Pater, Walter. *Plato and Platonism: A Series of Lectures.* 1893; London: Macmillan, 1910.

———. *Studies in the History of the Renaissance.* 1888; London: Macmillan, 1910.

Pepper, D. Stephen. *Guido Reni.* Oxford: Phaidon, 1984.

Perceval, George. *The History of Italy, from the Fall of the Western Empire to the Commencement of the Wars of the French Revolution.* London: G. B. Whittaker, 1825.

Pevsner Nikolaus, and Priscilla Metcalf. *The Cathedrals of England: Southern England.* Harmondsworth, UK: Viking, 1985.

Plato. “Charmides.” In *The Dialogues of Plato,* trans. Benjamin Jowett, 1:1–35. Oxford: Clarendon Press, 1953.

———. *The Republic of Plato.* Trans. Robin Waterfield. Oxford: Oxford Univ. Press, 1993.

Rev. of *Poems,* by Matthew Arnold. *Athenaeum* 79 (Jul.–Dec. 1885): 229–30.

Pool, Daniel. *What Jane Austen Ate and Charles Dickens Knew.* New York: Simon and Schuster, 1993.

Pope, Alexander. *The Poetical Works of Alexander Pope.* Ed. Adolphus William Ward. Globe Edition. 1869; London: Macmillan and Co., 1961.

Prins, Yopie. “Greek Maenads, Victorian Spinsters.” In *Victorian Sexual Dissidence,* ed. Richard Dellamora, 43–81. Chicago: Univ. of Chicago Press, 1999.

Quilter, Harry. “Art.” *Contemporary Review* 48 (Jul.–Dec. 1885): 295–300.

“The Railway Murder.” *Times,* 19 Feb. 1897, 11F.

Ribot, Théodule. *La Philosophie de Schopenhauer.* Paris: Alcan, 1885.

Ricketts, Charles. *Michael Field.* Ed. Paul Delaney. Edinburgh: Tragara Press, 1976.

———. *Some Letters from Charles Ricketts and Charles Shannon to Michael Field (1894–1902).* Edinburgh: Tragara Press, 1979.

Robinson, A. Mary F. Rev. of *Callirrhoë; Fair Rosamund,* by Michael Field. *Academy* 25 (Jan.–Jul. 1884): 395–96.

Roden, Frederick. *Same-Sex Desire in Victorian Religious Culture.* New York: Palgrave, 2002.

Rollin, Roger B. *Robert Herrick.* New York: Twayne, 1992.

Rossetti, D. G. *The Works of Dante Gabriel Rossetti.* Ed. W. M. Rossetti. London: Ellis, 1911.

Rossetti, William Michael. “The Grosvenor Gallery.” *Academy* 11 (Jan.–Jun. 1877): 396–97.

Rossi, Filippo. *The Uffizi and Pitti.* London: Thames and Hudson, 1966.

Rothenstein, William. Introduction to *Works and Days: From the Journals of Michael Field,* ed. T. and D. C. Sturge Moore, ix–xiv. London: John Murray, 1933.

Ruskin, John. *The Works of John Ruskin.* Ed. E. T. Cook and Alexander Wedderburn. 39 vols. London: George Allen, 1903–12.

Russell, Bertrand. *Selected Letters of Bertrand Russell: The Private Years, 1884–1914.* Ed. Nicholas Griffin. London: Routledge, 2002.

Ryals, Clyde de L. *The Life of Robert Browning: A Critical Biography.* Oxford: Blackwell, 1993.

Samuels, Ernest. *Bernard Berenson: The Making of a Connoisseur.* Vol. 1. Cambridge: Belknap, 1979.

Sankey, Ira. *Sacred Songs and Solos.* London: Morgan and Scott, 1875.

Scala Group. *The Protagonists of Italian Art.* Florence: Scala, 2001.

Schaper, Eva. "Taste, Sublimity, and Genius: The Aesthetics of Nature and Art." In *The Cambridge Companion to Kant,* ed. Paul Guyer, 367–93. Cambridge: Cambridge Univ. Press, 1992.

Schults, Raymond. *Crusader in Babylon: W. T. Stead and the Pall Mall Gazette.* Lincoln: Univ. of Nebraska Press, 1972.

Scott, George Walton. *Robert Herrick, 1591–1674.* London: Sidgwick and Jackson, 1974.

Senancour, Etienne Pivert de. *Le Journal Intime d'Obermann.* 1804; Paris: Livre de Poche, 1984.

Shaftesbury, Anthony, Earl of. *Characteristics of Men, Manners, Opinions, Times, Etc.* 1790; Cambridge: Cambridge Univ. Press, 1999.

Shakespeare, William. *The Works of William Shakespeare.* Ed. William George Clark and William Aldis Wright. Globe Edition. Cambridge: Macmillan, 1864.

Shelley, Percy Bysshe. *The Complete Works of Percy Bysshe Shelley.* Ed. Roger Ingpen and Walter E. Peck. 10 vols. London: Ernest Benn, 1965.

Sheppard, Anne. "Plato and the Neoplatonists." In *Platonism and the English Imagination,* ed. Anna Baldwin and Sarah Hutton, 3–18. Cambridge: Cambridge Univ. Press, 1994.

"The Silent Pool at Albury." *Times,* 20 Aug. 1902, 2D.

Sheridan, Richard Brinsley. *The Rivals; The Duenna; A Trip to Scarborough; The School for Scandal; The Critic.* Ed. Michael Cordner. Oxford: Oxford Univ. Press, 1998.

Simpson, Claude M. Introduction to *The Marble Faun: or, The Romance of Monte Beni,* by Nathaniel Hawthorne, xix–xliv. Columbus: Ohio State Univ. Press, 1968. Vol. 4 of *The Centenary Edition of the Works of Nathaniel Hawthorne.* 23 vols. 1962–1994.

Simpson, Elizabeth. "'A Perfect Imitation of the Ancient Work'—Ancient Jewelry and Castellani Adaptations." In *Castellani and Italian Archaeological Jewelry,* ed. Susan Weber Soros and Stefanie Walker, 201–28. New Haven, CT: Yale Univ. Press, 2004.

"The Situation in Egypt." *Times,* 21 Feb. 1895, 15A.

Smith, W., ed. *A Dictionary of Greek and Roman Biography and Mythology.* 3 vols. London: J. Murray, 1873.

Southey, Robert. *The Poems of Robert Southey.* Ed. Maurice H. Fitzgerald. London: Henry Froude, 1909.

Souvestre, Émile. *An Attic Philosopher in Paris.* Trans. John Herron Lepper. 1853; London: Cassell, 1929.

Spencer, Herbert. "Use and Beauty." In *Essays: Scientific, Political and Speculative,* 1:429–33. London: Williams and Norgate, 1868.

Standley, Fred. *Stopford Brooke.* New York: Twayne, 1972.

Sturge, Elizabeth. *Reminiscences of My Life.* Bristol: J. W. Arrowsmith, 1928.

Sturgeon, Mary. *Michael Field.* London: George G. Harrap, 1922.

Swift, Jonathan. *Gulliver's Travels.* Ed. Herbert Davis. Oxford: Basil Blackwell, 1965.

Swinburne, Algernon Charles. *The Complete Works of Algernon Charles Swinburne.* Ed. Edmund Gosse and Thomas James Wise. 20 vols. 1925; New York: Russell and Russell, 1968.

———. *Selections from the Poetical Works of A. C. Swinburne.* Ed. R. H. Stoddard. New York: Thomas Y. Crowell, 1884.

Symonds, J. A. *The Letters of John Addington Symonds, 1869–1884.* Ed. Herbert M. Schueller and Robert L. Peters. Vol. 2. Detroit: Wayne State Univ. Press, 1968.

Taft, Vicki L. "*The Tragic Mary:* A Case Study in Michael Field's Understanding of Sexual Politics." *Nineteenth Century Contexts* 23, no. 2 (2001): 265–95.

Tanner, Sarah. *How the Women's Suffrage Movement Began in Bristol Fifty Years Ago.* Bristol: Carlyle, 1918.

Taylor, Jeremy. *Holy Living.* Ed. P. G. Stanwood. Oxford: Clarendon Press, 1989. Vol. 1 of *Holy Living and Holy Dying.* 2 vols. 1989.

Tennyson, Alfred Lord. *Poetical Works Including the Plays.* London: Oxford Univ. Press, 1959.

Tilden, William. *Sir William Ramsay.* London: Macmillan, 1918.

Todhunter, John. *Helena in Troas.* London: Kegan Paul, Trench and Co., 1886. [Literature Online: Chadwyck-Healey LION].

Tooley, Sarah A. "Ladies of Bristol and Clifton." *The Woman at Home* (Nov. 1936): 442–54.

Treby, Ivor. *The Michael Field Catalogue: A Book of Lists.* N.p.: De Blackland, 1998.

———. *Binary Star: Leaves from the Journal and Letters of Michael Field, 1846–1914.* N.p.: De Blackland, 2006.

Trollope, Anthony. *Can You Forgive Her?* Vol. 2. London: Oxford Univ. Press, 1953.

Tupper, Martin. *Stephan Langton, or The Days of King John: A Romance of the Silent Pool.* 22nd ed. 1858; Guildford: Biddles, 1923.

Vicinus, Martha. *Intimate Friends: Women Who Loved Women, 1778–1928.* Chicago: Univ. of Chicago Press, 2004.

———. "'Sister Souls': Bernard Berenson and Michael Field (Katharine Bradley and Edith Cooper)." *Nineteenth-Century Literature* 60, no. 3 (2006): 326–54.

Virgil. *The Aeneid of Virgil.* Ed. R. D. Williams. London: Macmillan, 1972.

———. *Virgil: The Aeneid.* Trans. David West. London: Penguin, 1990.

———. *Aeneid.* Trans. Gavin Douglas. 4 vols. 1513; Edinburgh: Printed for the Society by W. Blackwood, 1957–64.

"Vivisection." *Times,* 30 Mar. 1887, 9F.

Walkowitz, Judith. *Prostitution and Victorian Society.* Cambridge: Cambridge Univ. Press, 1980.

Ward, Mary (Mrs. Humphry). Introduction to *Amiel's Journal,* by Henri-Frédéric Amiel, vii–xliii. 1885; London: Macmillan, 1909.

Waters, Chris. *British Socialists and the Politics of Popular Culture.* Stanford: Stanford Univ. Press, 1990.

Wedderburn, Alexander. "A Lake-side Home: Brantwood." 2 parts. *Art Journal* (Nov. 1881): 321–24; (Dec. 1881): 353–57.

Weinreb, Ben, and Christopher Hibbert. *The London Encyclopaedia.* London: Macmillan, 1983.

White, Christine, ed. *Nineteenth-Century Writings on Homosexuality: A Sourcebook.* London: Routledge, 1999.

———. "'Poets and Lovers Evermore': Interpreting Female Love in the Poetry and Journals of Michael Field." *Textual Practice* 4.2 (1990): 197–212.

Who's Who 1897–1998. CD-ROM. London: A & C Black; Oxford Univ. Press, 1998.

"Why Shakespeare Wrote Tragedy?" *Cornhill Magazine* 42 (1880): 153–72.

Whyte, Ian and Kathleen. *Exploring Scotland's Historic Landscapes.* Edinburgh: John Donald, 1987.

Wilde, Oscar. Rev. of *Canute the Great; The Cup of Water,* by Michael Field. *Woman's World,* Feb. 1888, 275–79.

Williams, Ethel Carleton. *Companion to Oxfordshire.* London: Methuen, 1943.

Wilton, Andrew. *The Life and Work of J. M. Turner.* London: Academy Editions, 1979.

Winckelmann, Johannes. *Reflections on the Painting and Sculpture of the Greeks.* 1765; London: Routledge, 1999.

Wood, Christopher. *Burne-Jones: The Life and Works of Edward Coley Burne-Jones (1833–1898).* London: Weidenfeld and Nicolson, 1998.

Woodman, Francis. *Architectural History of Canterbury Cathedral.* London: Routledge and Kegan Paul, 1981.

Wordsworth, William. *The Fourteen-Book Prelude.* Ed. W. J. B. Owen. 1850; Ithaca: Cornell Univ. Press, 1985.

———. *The Poetical Works of William Wordsworth.* Ed. E. de Selincourt and Helen Darbishire. 2nd ed. 5 vols. Oxford: Clarendon Press, 1952.

Wryde, J. Saxby. *British Lighthouses: Their History and Romance.* London: Fisher Unwin, 1913.

Wright, T. R. *The Religion of Humanity.* Cambridge: Cambridge Univ. Press, 1986.

Yonge, Charlotte M. *Cameos from English History.* London: Macmillan, 1868.

Zola, Émile. *Thérèse Raquin.* Trans. Andrew Rothwell. 1867; Oxford: Oxford Univ. Press, 1992.

Index

Note: Michael Field's works are included alphabetically within the index. Abbreviations for MF's works are listed on pages xlii–xliii. Abbreviations for names include MF (Michael Field), KB (Katharine Bradley), and EC (Edith Cooper). Italicized page numbers indicate illustrations and figures. Bold page numbers indicate biographical information.

Recent Books in the Victorian Literature and Culture Series

Linda Dowling
The Vulgarization of Art: The Victorians and Aesthetic Democracy

Tricia Lootens
Lost Saints: Silence, Gender, and Victorian Literary Canonization

Matthew Arnold
The Letters of Matthew Arnold, vols. 1–6
Edited by Cecil Y. Lang

Edward FitzGerald
Edward FitzGerald, Rubáiyát of Omar Khayyám: *A Critical Edition*
Edited by Christopher Decker

Christina Rossetti
The Letters of Christina Rossetti, vols. 1–4
Edited by Antony H. Harrison

Barbara Leah Harman
The Feminine Political Novel in Victorian England

John Ruskin
The Genius of John Ruskin: Selections from His Writings
Edited by John D. Rosenberg

Antony H. Harrison
Victorian Poets and the Politics of Culture: Discourse and Ideology

Judith Stoddart
Ruskin's Culture Wars: Fors Clavigera and the Crisis of Victorian Liberalism

Linda K. Hughes and Michael Lund
Victorian Publishing and Mrs. Gaskell's Work

Linda H. Peterson
Traditions of Victorian Women's Autobiography: The Poetics and Politics of Life Writing

Gail Turley Houston
Royalties: The Queen and Victorian Writers

Laura C. Berry
The Child, the State, and the Victorian Novel

Barbara J. Black
On Exhibit: Victorians and Their Museums

Annette R. Federico
Idol of Suburbia: Marie Corelli and Late-Victorian Literary Culture

Talia Schaffer
The Forgotten Female Aesthetes: Literary Culture in Late-Victorian England

Julia F. Saville
A Queer Chivalry: The Homoerotic Asceticism of Gerard Manley Hopkins

Victor Shea and William Whitla, Editors
Essays and Reviews: The 1860 Text and Its Reading

Marlene Tromp
The Private Rod: Marital Violence, Sensation, and the Law in Victorian Britain

Dorice Williams Elliott
The Angel out of the House: Philanthropy and Gender in Nineteenth-Century England

Richard Maxwell, Editor
The Victorian Illustrated Book

Vineta Colby
Vernon Lee: A Literary Biography

E. Warwick Slinn
Victorian Poetry as Cultural Critique: The Politics of Performative Language

Simon Joyce
Capital Offenses: Geographies of Class and Crime in Victorian London

Caroline Levine
The Serious Pleasures of Suspense: Victorian Realism and Narrative Doubts

Emily Davies
Emily Davies: Collected Letters, 1861–1875
Edited by Ann B. Murphy and Deirdre Raftery

Joseph Bizup

Manufacturing Culture: Vindications of Early Victorian Industry

Lynn M. Voskuil

Acting Naturally: Victorian Theatricality and Authenticity

Sally Mitchell

Frances Power Cobbe: Victorian Feminist, Journalist, Reformer

Constance W. Hassett

Christina Rossetti: The Patience of Style

Brenda Assael

The Circus and Victorian Society

Judith Wilt

Behind Her Times: Transition England in the Novels of Mary Arnold Ward

Daniel Hack

The Material Interests of the Victorian Novel

Frankie Morris

Artist of Wonderland: The Life, Political Cartoons, and Illustrations of Tenniel

William R. McKelvy

The English Cult of Literature: Devoted Readers, 1774–1880

Linda M. Austin

Nostalgia in Transition, 1780–1917

James Buzard, Joseph W. Childers, and Eileen Gillooly, Editors

Victorian Prism: Refractions of the Crystal Palace

Michael Field

The Fowl and the Pussycat: Love Letters of Michael Field, 1876–1909

Edited by Sharon Bickle